Meal Prep And Nutrition

4 Books in 1:

Meal Prep Cookbook

Emotional Eating

Autophagy

Intermittent Fasting

By

Alan Dieter

Meal Prep Cookbook for Beginners

Useful Weekly Plans.
Simple, Healthy Keto Recipes
Ready-To-Go Meals for Kids and Busy Family

Easy Cooking Steps to Save Time, Money, Lose
Weight and Feel Better

By

Alan Dieter

Table of Contents

6

9

Introduction

There is a wealth of information to get you started. We will discuss how to perform meal prep and better understand you are setting your unique methods using these suggestions. As you begin your nutritional journey, it's vital to understand better the healthy eating pyramid is simply an elaborate grocery list.

The food pyramid is a triangular diagram introduced initially in Sweden in 1974. The *Food Guide Pyramid* was developed in 1992 by the United States Department of Agriculture (USDA) to display food groups according to their values. The plan was updated to *My Plate* in 2011. The guidelines are divided into four categories comprised of these food items:

- Vegetables are 40%
- Grains are 30%
- Fruits are 10%
- Proteins are 20%

Know What Your Body Is Craving

To maintain a healthier body, you need to take care of its needs and know what it's craving. These are a few suggestions to consider:

Soda: You may have a calcium deficiency if all you want is the delicious taste of soda pop. Try eating, kale, broccoli, sesame seeds, mustard greens, or legumes to help remove the urge.

Sugary Foods: Several things can trigger the desire for sugar, but typically phosphorous, and tryptophan are the culprits. Have some chicken, beef, lamb, liver, cheese, cauliflower, or broccoli.

Chocolate: The carbon, magnesium, and chromium levels are beckoning a portion of spinach, nuts, and seeds, or some broccoli and cheese.

Salty Foods: It is possible that you may have a chloride deficiency. Enjoy a few olives, celery, tomatoes, or add some sea salt to your diet.

Cheese: You may be lacking the essential fatty acids deficiency. Help remedy the craving with some walnuts, ground flaxseeds, chia seeds, sesame seeds, flax oil, legumes, broccoli, kale, or mustard greens.

Fatty or Oily Foods: The levels of calcium and chloride need repair with a serving of spinach, broccoli, cheese, or fish.

You will have an array of meal plans to choose from consisting of simple preps, Keto diet preps, and kid-friendly preparation lists.

Chapter 1: Meal Prep Principles

Save a Ton of Effort and Time: All it takes is a few tasty recipes and a little bit of your valuable time. In most of the cases, these recipes are geared towards a fast lifestyle and will be ready with just a few simple steps. After some time and practice, you will know which ones will be your favorites.

Use Your Freezer: Purchase meat when it's on sale and buy it in bulk. Freeze it for later. Assemble your meals in zipper-type bags and defrost when you want a quick and easy meal.

Mix & Match: If you have a busy lifestyle, purchase veggies and fruits pre-chopped and peeled and create an omelet or a stir-fry dinner. Use divided containers and prep into them.

Use Batch Cooking: Use a big pot on the stovetop or a slow cooker to prepare a batch of soup, chili, curry, or other delicious meals. By using sheet pan meals and dump dinners, you can save a ton of time and have a variety of meals.

By using these suggestions and the additional ones provided in your new cookbook, you will derive so many more benefits, including eating healthier, dropping a few unwanted pounds, and saving money since you will eliminate wasted food. It all comes down to your organization and multitasking skills. It can begin by choosing one strategy each week to improve your meal prepping skills.

Meal Prep – Storage & Reheating

Don't store hot food in the fridge: Keep your refrigerator set at an adequate temperature (below 40° Fahrenheit). If your refrigerator is warmer than this, it promotes the growth of bacteria. Any drastic temperature changes will cause condensation to form on the food items. You need to let your prepared food cool down in the open air - before putting it in a container and closing the lid. The increased moisture levels can open the door to bacteria growth.

Label the Containers: There are some other things you have to consider when freezing your meals. You should always label your container with the date that you put it in the freezer. You also need to double-check that your bottles, jars, or bags are each sealed tightly. If your containers aren't air-tight, your food will become freezer burnt and need to be trashed.

Meat Cooking – Internal Temps

- **Poultry** - should reach a minimum of 165° Fahrenheit.
- **Whole cuts of lamb, pork, and beef** - a minimum of 145° Fahrenheit.
- **Ground veal, pork, lamb, and beef** - a minimum of 160° Fahrenheit.

Correct Refrigerator Organization

Since you are taking the incentive to understand meal prep better, you also have to consider the proper storage of your valuable products. You have several compartments in the refrigerator to store your prepared foods. You must understand which foods store best in each location.

- *Lower Shelves*: This is generally the coldest section of the refrigerator, making it an ideal space for dairy, eggs, and raw meat. Your unit may have individual drawers for these items to ensure a consistent temperature.

- *Top Shelves*: Once you have prepared your meals or smoothies, it's recommended to place them on the upper shelves since these are items used most often. They also have the most consistent temperature settings.

- **Sealed Drawers:** Fruits and veggies should get stored in this space while avoiding the mixing of meat, fruits, and vegetables. Storing these foods together can create a risk of cross-contamination.

- **Doors:** Many refrigerators have a door to access frequently retrieved food items - available as pullout drawers without opening the main door. Non-perishable items such as drinks, some condiments, water, and other items that don't quickly spoil could be placed here.

- **Top:** Don't place bread or baked products on top of the refrigerator. The heat from the fridge could cause it to spoil more quickly.

Equip the Kitchen

A Good Set of Scales: Portion control is essential for baking bread. You want a scale that will accommodate your needs. Consider these options:

- ***Seek a Conversion Button:*** You need to know how to convert measurements into grams since not all recipes have them listed. The grams keep the system in complete harmony.
- ***Removable Plate:*** Keep the germs off of the scale by removing the plate. Be sure it will come off to eliminate the bacterial buildup.
- ***The Tare Function:*** When you set a bowl on the scale, the feature will allow you to reset the weight back to zero (0).

Accurate Measuring Tools: A measuring cup and spoon system that shows both the Metric and US standards of weight is essential, so there is no confusion during food prep.

Sifter: Purchase a good sifter for under $10, and you will be ensured a more accurate measurement for your baking needs.

Immersion or Regular Blender & Food Processor: These are useful in many stages of meal preparation at the restaurant level as well as in your kitchen.

Buy a Spiralizer or a Sharp Knife & Paring Knife: You can prepare zoodles, which are noodles cut from zucchini easily.

Preparation – Useful Items

An unglazed terra cotta tile at the bottom of a clean oven or a baking stone might be a good investment if you are planning on doing a lot of baking at home. You can also purchase an upgraded stand mixer with a dough hook. It's a good idea to have a few different sized loaf pans.

You should also invest in several mixing bowls to use.

A bench knife, better known as a dough scraper, can be used to clean surfaces, divide the dough, and to pre-shape the loaves of bread. Some even use it to dice veggies and apples.

- **Sheet Pans/Rimmed Baking Sheets:** (2) 12x18-inch pans.
- **Skillets:** Choose from a cast-iron skillet or a 10-12-inch nonstick skillet with a lid.
- **4-Quart Saucepan:** Prepare veggies using this type of pan, for example.
- **8-quart covered stockpot:** Prepare your favorite stews and soups.

- *Meat Thermometer:* To ensure proper cooking.
- *Garlic Press or Spice mill:* These two utensils add additional flavor to your food and reduce the temptation of using a shaker of salt.
- *Vegetable Steamer:* This is essential because it will make the preparation of healthy vegetables much simpler without the use of oil or butter.
- *Cutting Boards:* Purchase individual boards for produce and meat/fish/poultry. You can also purchase plastic cutting 'boards' which are easily cleaned

These are a few additional items that will assist you with the baking process:

- Measuring cups for liquid and dry ingredients
- Measuring spoons
- Rolling pin
- Medium to large-sized saucepan
- Rubber spatula
- Wire cooling rack
- Bread cutting board
- Electric mixer
- Plastic wrap – damp tea towel

Parchment paper will be used for most of the recipes. The baking pans are lined with the paper, and the baked goods do not stick. For most baking needs, you can omit the oils if you choose the paper instead. However, some recipes use paper and oils.

Purchase or Prepare the Containers You Want to Use

These are some guidelines for those:

- Mason Jars – Pint or quart-sized
- Ziploc-type freezer bags
- Rubbermaid Stackable - Glad Containers
- Freezer Safe
- Microwavable
- BPA Free
- Reusable
- Stackable

Popsicle Molds or Push-Up Pop for Smoothies

You can purchase ice-pop clear pouches for <u>one-time</u> use or use a <u>mold</u> to reuse many times. Save money by using freezer bags to avoid using freezer space with a quart-sized freezer-safe Mason jar.

Chapter 2: Multitasking Skills UsingTime Organization

Meal prep might seem a bit challenging at first, but remember—you don't need to prep all of your meals at one time. You can begin with the meats one evening, and veggies the next; it's all up to you!

- *Time Selection:* Choose a time to do your meal prep, so you do not have any interruptions

- *Take Advantage of Your Crockpot & Slow Cooker:* You will find the crockpot a must if you have a busy lifestyle. These are just a couple of ways you can benefit from its use:

- *Get Ahead of the Meal:* Preparing food with a slow cooker can put you ahead of the game. You can prepare the cooker the night before if you have a busy day planned. All it takes is a few minutes of preparation. Just add all of the fixings into the pot and place it in the fridge—overnight. The next morning, transfer to the counter to become room temperature. Turn it on as you head out of the house.

- ***Take A Physical Inventory of the Pantry and Other Food Storage Areas:***
  Purchase your food items in bulk to save money. Therefore, you are saving money while on the ketogenic diet is vital. Purchasing your items in bulk can make a severe impact. Shop around and explore your areas for stores such as Walmart, Costco, or Sam's Club. These stores generally have bargain prices. Check your area for local farms that raise their animals on pasture feeding or a local market for fresh produce. After you find a good deal, stock up and purchase pantry items such as seasonings and flour. You can freeze many things and save a bundle of cash.

- ***Choose the Menu Plan:*** Gather your favorite recipes or try some new ones.

- ***Decide How to Prep:*** Do you want to prepare all of the chicken, pork, or other meal selections one night and the veggies the next night? Or: Do you want to cook each meal individually but in bulk? No worries, either way, since each of the recipes has instructions for individual prep tips as well.

Consider These Additional Tips

- Chop your veggies in advance. Make veggie packs to use for tacos, pasta, and stir-fries. You can also use them for snacks.

- Prep starches in advance, including rice and quinoa on a Sunday, and use them for the week.

- Prepare and freeze plenty of healthy fruits and yogurt into a delicious smoothie for the entire week. Enjoy one for breakfast or any time you have the craving.

- Purchase foods in bulk to be used for taco meats, breakfast burritos, fajita fillings, soups, egg muffins, and so much more.

- As you prep, include lean proteins for the weekends in a container for a quick grab 'n' go snack or luncheon for a weekend journey.

- See where your recipe ingredients overlap for different meals. For example, onions and peppers are often used.

- Prepare and freeze the freshly prepared chicken in different marinades so you can have a quick and healthy meal option.

- Consider freezing your meals even if it is just one portion, for those emergencies when nothing else will do!

- Prepare a batch of breakfast options ahead of time. Think about some of the recipes included in your new cookbook, such as overnight oatmeal in a jar if you are on-the-go.

- Prepare batches of dressings and sauces ahead of time, so you always have a delicious option to spice up your meals.

Guidelines for Dairy – Meats & Veggies

- ***Choose fresh meats and dairy when possible:*** Try to find meat and dairy that has an expiration date for as far in the future as possible. These choices will tend to remain fresh and last longer. This also applies to the "sell by" dates. The further in the future, either of these dates is, the surer you can bet that the food is going to last the week.

- ***Purchase Whole – Not Chopped Meats & Veggies:*** You can save big by chopping or slicing your own meats and vegetables. You will pay for the person that is doing the cutting for your convenience.

- ***How to Freeze & Reheat Your Meats:*** For meals that are scheduled to be eaten at least three days after cooking, freezing is a great option. Freezing food is safe and convenient, but it doesn't work for every type of meal. You can also freeze the ingredients for a slow cooker meal, and then dump out the container into the slow cooker and leave it there. This saves a lot of time and means you can pre-prep meals up to 1-2 months in advance.

The last food safety consideration you need to make with regards to meal prepping is how you reheat food. Most people opt to microwave their meals for warming, but you can use any other conventional heating source in your kitchen as well. The reason people love the microwave for heating their meal prep meals is that it's quick and convenient.

However, you have to be careful with microwaving because over-cooking can cause food to taste bad. To combat this, cook your food in one-minute intervals and check on it between each minute. You can also help your food cook more evenly and quickly but keeping your meat cut into small pieces when you cook it. You should never put food directly from the freezer into the microwave. Let your frozen food thaw first.

Food reheating and prep safety will become second nature over time. Meal prep can be overwhelming and require a lot of thought and patience, but it becomes a lot easier once you get used to it. Many of the mistakes are easy to avoid.

However, mistakes do happen, and as such, it's best to cook for short periods rather than longer ones, so you have less of a risk of making a mistake and needing to scrap everything you have prepared for that substantial period of time. While it is a lot and seems complicated, meal prepping is the best way to set yourself up for success.

Chapter 3: Simple Meal Prep

Week 1

Day 1

Breakfast: Avocado & Egg Breakfast

Yields Provided: 4

Ingredients for Prep:

- Brown rice (.5 cup)
- Large eggs (6)
- Olive oil (2 tbsp.)
- Minced garlic (2 cloves)
- Chopped kale (4 cups)
- Freshly grated parmesan (.25 cup)
- Sliced avocado (1)

Method of Prep:

1. Prepare a pot of boiling water (1 cup) and prepare the rice of choice according to the directions provided.

2. Arrange the eggs in another pan with 1-inch of cold water. Once it's boiling, let it simmer for one minute. Cover and transfer the pan from the burner to rest for 8 to 10 minutes. Use a colander to drain the eggs and peel.

3. Use the medium heat setting to warm the oil. Toss in the pepper flakes and garlic. Sauté for one to two minutes. Fold in the kale, stirring until wilted (5-6 min.)

4. Shake in the parmesan.

Tips for Meal Prep:

1. Let the fixings cool thoroughly.

2. Use a divided container to store the eggs, rice, kale, and avocado.

Lunch: Beef Soup

Yields Provided: 4

Ingredients for Prep:

- Ground beef sirloin (1 lb.)
- Olive oil (1 tbsp.)
- Low-sodium beef stock (32 oz.)
- Whole wheat flour (.33 cup)
- Yellow onion (1)
- Mixed celery & carrots (1 lb.)

Method of Prep:

1. Prepare a soup pot using the oil (med-high heat setting) until it's hot.

2. Add the beef and flour. Simmer for about 5 minutes.

3. Chop and toss in the celery, carrots, and onions. Pour in the stock and stir. Lower the heat setting to medium.

4. Continue cooking the soup for about 15 minutes.

Tips for Meal Prep:

1. Cool thoroughly before ladling into four mugs or other storage containers.
2. Securely close the tops if using a plastic container.
3. Freeze for longer storage. Date the package and use it within several months.

Dinner: Mediterranean Whitefish

Yields Provided: 4

Ingredients for Prep:

- Raw white fish fillets - cod, tilapia, sole, etc. (4 - 4 oz.)
- Olive oil (4 tsp.)
- Mediterranean spice mix or chopped fresh oregano
- Optional: Fresh lemon (as desired)

Mediterranean Spice Mix:

- Dried onion flakes (4 tsp.)
- Dried oregano (1 tsp.)
- Crushed dried parsley (4 tbsp.)
- Ground thyme (1 tsp.)
- Crushed dried basil (2 tsp.)
- Garlic powder (1 tsp.)
- Sea salt (1 tsp.)
- Ground black pepper (.25 tsp.)

Method of Prep:

1. Warm the oven broiler to high.

2. Drizzle the fish with oil. Season using the Mediterranean spice mix.

3. Broil the fish until it's opaque and flakes easily when tested with a fork (3-5 min.).

Tips for Meal Prep:

1. Arrange the cooked fish in a shallow pan or baking sheet and pop into the freezer for quick freezing.

2. Wrap the fish in a moisture-resistant paper or freezer bag. It will store well for up to one month.

3. To thaw, just pop the bag into a pot of boiling water for about five minutes.

4. Spritz to your liking using fresh lemon juice before serving.

Snack: Avocado Hummus Snack Jars

Yields Provided: 4 jars

Ingredients for Prep:

- Chickpeas (1 can)

- Tahini (.5 cup)

- Avocado (1)

- Garlic (2 cloves)

- Lemon juice (1 tbsp.)

- Salt (.5 tsp.)

- Water (.25 cup)

- *Optional Fixings:*

- Sliced sun-dried tomatoes or antipasto
- Celery, carrot, or cucumber sticks
- Assorted chips, crackers, etc.
- Suggested: Vitamix
- Also needed: 4 salad mason jars/other containers

Method of Prep:

1. Rinse and drain the chickpeas. Mince the cloves and dice the avocado.
2. Combine all of the fixings (omit the optional fixings).
3. Remove the lid and stir as needed until fully mixed (5 min.)
4. Scoop the mixture into the jars and top with the desired toppings.

Tips for Meal Prep:

1. Store in the fridge for a quick and healthy snack.
2. Enjoy within the first two or three days for the best results.

Day 2

Breakfast: Broccoli Cheddar Egg Muffins

Yields Provided: 6

Ingredients for Prep:

- Whole eggs (8)
- Egg whites (4)
- Optional: Dijon mustard (.5 tbsp.)
- Broccoli (2 cups **)
- Shredded cheddar cheese (.75 cups)
- Pepper and salt (as desired)
- Diced green onions (2)

Method of Prep:

1. Set the oven at 350° Fahrenheit.
2. Prepare six muffin tins with paper liners or cooking spray.
3. Whisk all of the eggs, salt, pepper, and mustard. Blend in the green onions, broccoli, and cheese.
4. Divide the batter into the tins and bake for 12-14 minutes.
5. Use either fresh and steamed or defrosted and frozen broccoli.

Tips for Meal Prep:

1. Transfer the muffins to the countertop to cool.
2. Store in the fridge to use for a quick breakfast.
3. Serve when they are puffy and thoroughly cooked.

Lunch: Apples with Almonds & Figs Salad

Yields Provided: 6

Ingredients for Prep:

- Dried figs (6)
- Large red apples (2)
- Celery (2 ribs)
- Fat-free lemon yogurt (.5 cup)
- Slivered almonds (2 tbsp.)
- Carrots (2)

Method of Prep:

1. Chop the figs and celery. Peel and grate the carrots. Core and dice the apples.
2. Mix the fixings, beginning with the celery, apples, and figs.
3. Prep the carrots and almonds and store them in individual dishes if desired.

Tips for Meal Prep:

1. Store the fixings in the fridge using either individual salad dishes or in one large bowl. Be sure the salad is covered.
2. Stir and blend in the yogurt when it's mealtime.
3. Garnish with the carrots and almonds.

Dinner: Pork Chops with Creamy Sauce

Yields Provided: 4

Ingredients for Prep:

- Black pepper and salt (.5 tsp. each)
- Onion powder (.5 tsp.)
- Center-cut pork loin chops (4 - Approx. 4 oz. each)
- Non-fat Half & Half (.33 cup)
- Fat-free chicken stock (.33 cup)
- Dijon mustard (1.5 tbsp.)
- Dried thyme (A pinch)

Method of Prep:

1. Shake the salt, pepper, and onion powder over the chops.
2. Using the med-high heat setting on the stovetop, prepare a large skillet with cooking spray.
3. After the pan is heated, arrange the chops in it and fry for three to four minutes per side. The internal temperature should reach a minimum temperature on a meat thermometer of 145° Fahrenheit.

Tips for Meal Prep:

1. At this point, place the prepared chops in a container with a lid to cool.
2. Measure and add the chicken stock into the pan and deglaze the browned bits. Stir in the mustard and Half & Half.
3. Lower the temperature setting to medium and continue cooking for about 7 minutes. When the sauce has thickened, add the thyme.
4. Set the sauce aside to cool. Freeze if you won't be using the sauce

within one day.

5. Wrap the chops well and store them in the fridge until time to eat. Serve with the sauce and your favorite side dish.

Snack: Bacon Cheddar Cheese Crisps

Yields Provided: 3

Ingredients for Prep:

- Cooked bacon (3 strips)
- Shredded cheddar cheese (1 cup)

Method of Prep:

1. Set the oven ahead of time to 350° Fahrenheit.

2. Prepare a baking tin with a sheet of parchment paper.

3. Pour about one tablespoon of the cheese onto the tray for each serving. Break the bacon to bits and add to the piles of cheese.

4. Bake for 5 to 8 minutes and let cool.

Tips for Meal Prep:

1. Blot the grease away with a paper towel.

2. Fully cool and store in a container in the refrigerator until the desired time to serve.

Day 3

Breakfast: Gluten-Free Roasted Grapes & Greek Yogurt Parfait

Yields Provided: 4

Ingredients for Prep:

- Seedless grapes (1.5 lb./4 cups)
- 2% plain Greek yogurt (2 cups
- Olive oil (1 tbsp.)
- Honey (4 tsp.)
- Chopped walnuts (.5 cup)

Method of Prep:

1. Warm the oven to reach 450° Fahrenheit and place the pan inside.
2. Discard the stems from the grapes and rinse them. Wipe using a towel and toss into a mixing container.
3. Wipe with a towel and put it in a bowl. Spritz with oil and toss to coat and bake for 20 to 23 minutes. They will look slightly shriveled. Stir about halfway through the cooking process.
4. Take the pan from the oven. Cool for five minutes.
5. Meanwhile, assemble the parfaits by adding the yogurt to the glass.
6. Once the grapes are cooled, garnish the yogurt with a teaspoon of honey, two tablespoons of the walnuts, and a portion of the grapes.

Tips for Meal Prep:

1. Prepare each of the four servings into individual dishes.

2. Keep the parfait in the refrigerator for up to three days.

Lunch: Tomato & Olive Salad

Yields Provided: 10

Ingredients for Prep:

- Cucumbers (5)
- Red or purple onion (half of 1)
- Green olives (2.25 oz. can/jar)
- Black olives (5 oz. can or jar)
- Tomatoes (5 large)
- Crumbled feta cheese (4 oz.)
- Red wine vinegar (.25 cup)

Method of Prep:

1. Chop the olives, cucumbers, and tomatoes. Crumble the feta.

2. Combine all of the fixings except the vinegar.

Tips for Meal Prep:

1. Store the dressing and salad fixings in individual containers.

2. Pop it into the fridge until it's time to eat.

3. Drizzle the dressing on top of the salad and serve.

Dinner: Chicken & Asparagus Pan Dinner

Yields Provided: 8
Ingredients for Prep:

- Chicken breasts (4 lbs.)
- Avocado oil (1 tbsp.)
- Trimmed asparagus (1 lb.)
- Sun-dried tomatoes -(4)
- Thick-cut bacon (4 slices)
- Salt (1 tsp.)
- Pepper (.25 tsp.)
- Provolone cheese (8 slices)
- Also Needed: 1 baking pan

Method of Prep:

1. Slice the chicken into 8 thin pieces. Chop the bacon and tomatoes into one-inch pieces.
2. Heat the oven to reach 400° Fahrenheit.
3. Add oil to the baking pan with the chicken and asparagus. Top it off with the tomatoes, bacon, pepper, and salt.
4. Bake until the chicken reaches 160° Fahrenheit internally - or about 25 minutes.
5. Toss in the asparagus and cheese.
6. Garnish with the bacon and tomatoes. Bake another three to four minutes until the cheese has melted.

Tips for Meal Prep:

1. Simply prepare the chicken and store it in the fridge for several days.

2. Place it into plastic bins or freezer bags until ready to use.

3. Prepare the asparagus when ready to eat and combine with the cheese. Garnish and serve.

Snack: Bacon Knots

Yields Provided: 4

Ingredients for Prep:

- Raw bacon (16 slices)
- Shredded parmesan (.25 cup)
- Minced garlic (4 cloves)
- Minced parsley (1 tbsp.)
- Pepper & Salt (to your liking)

Method of Prep:

1. Straighten one slice of bacon. Tie it into a knot.

2. Take another slice, and tie another knot around the first one. Continue until done.

3. Place the chain on a parchment-lined baking tin.

4. Warm up the oven to reach 400° Fahrenheit.

5. Sprinkle the bacon with the garlic and bake for 15 minutes.

Tips for Meal Prep:

1. When crispy, remove from the pan and chill in the refrigerator until mealtime.

2. When it's time to serve, heat the oven to 400° Fahrenheit. Sprinkle using the parsley and cheese.

3. Bake for one or two minutes until hot. Break apart and serve.

Day 4

Breakfast: Spinach Muffins

Yields Provided: 6
Ingredients for Prep:

- Nonfat milk (.5 cup)
- Eggs (6)
- Crumbled low-fat cheese (1 cup)
- Spinach (4 oz.)
- Chopped roasted red pepper (.5 cups)
- Chopped prosciutto (2 oz.)

Method of Prep:

1. Set the oven temperature at 350° Fahrenheit.
2. Combine the eggs, milk, spinach, cheese, prosciutto, and red peppers. Whisk well.
3. Lightly spritz a muffin tray with a cooking oil spray.
4. Dump the batter into the muffin tins and bake until browned (30 minutes).

Tips for Meal Prep:

1. Cool thoroughly on a wire rack.
2. Arrange in a plastic container or freeze to enjoy later.

Lunch: Arugula Salad

Yields Provided: 4

Ingredients for Prep:

- Arugula leaves (4 cups)
- Cherry tomatoes (1 cup)
- Pine nuts (.25 cup)
- Pepper & salt (as desired)
- Grated parmesan cheese (.25 cup)
- Large avocado (1 sliced)
- Rice vinegar (1 tbsp.)
- Olive/Grapeseed oil (2 tbsp.)

Method of Prep:

1. Rinse and dry the leaves of arugula.
2. Slice the cherry tomatoes into halves and grate the cheese.
3. Slice the avocado.

Tips for Meal Prep:

1. Combine the arugula, tomatoes, pine nuts, and cheese into four salad containers.
2. Either place the slices to the side in another container or a divided container for storage.
3. When it is time to serve, add the oil and vinegar with a shake of pepper and salt.

Dinner: Jalapeno Popper Burgers

Yields Provided: 4

Ingredients for Prep:

- Ground beef (1.33 lb.)
- Finely chopped jalapeno (1)
- Cream cheese - reduced-fat (2 tbsp.)
- Mustard (2 tsp.)
- Worcestershire sauce (2 tsp.)
- Shredded cheddar cheese (.5 cup)
- Kosher salt - divided (.5 tsp.)

Method of Prep:

1. Combine all of the burger fixings. Divide into six patties and wait about 10 minutes before cooking for the flavors to mix.
2. Grill to your liking (four to six min. per side suggested). If you prefer, use a frying pan, and cook for five to six minutes for each side.

Tips for Meal Prep:

1. Let the burgers thoroughly cool. Store in the fridge for about three days.
2. When ready to eat, warm the burgers and serve with the desired garnishes.
3. Freeze in plastic containers with other meal items (veggies) or freeze individually in freezer bags.
4. *Note*: You can also use ground turkey.

Snack: Peanut Butter Power Granola

Yields Provided: 12

Ingredients for Prep:

- Pecans (1.5 cups)
- Almonds (1.5 cups)
- Sunflower seeds (.25 cup)
- Almond flour or Shredded coconut (1 cup)
- Swerve sweetener (.33 cup)
- Vanilla whey protein powder (.33 cup)
- Butter (.25 cup)
- Peanut butter (.33 cup)
- Water (.25 cup)

Method of Prep:

1. Set the oven at 300° Fahrenheit.
2. Prepare a rimmed baking tin with a layer of parchment paper.
3. Process the almonds and pecans in a food processor and add to a large bowl.
4. Fold in the sunflower seeds, sweetener, shredded coconut, and protein powder.
5. Place the butter and peanut butter in the microwave to melt. Pour over the nut mixture. Toss lightly. Mix in the water.
6. Spread the mixture evenly onto the baking sheet.
7. Bake for 30 minutes. Stir about halfway through the cycle.

Tips for Meal Prep:

1. Cool before storing in an airtight container and serve anytime.

Day 5

Breakfast: Greek Yogurt Pancakes

Yields Provided: 14 (5-inch pancakes)

Ingredients for Prep:

- Nonfat plain Greek yogurt (2 cups)
- Baking soda (2 tsp.)
- All-purpose flour (1 cup)
- Slightly beaten eggs (4)
- Salt (1 tsp.)
- 1% Low-fat milk (.5 cup)
- Vanilla (1 tsp.)

Method of Prep:

1. Use an electric mixer stand and scoop the yogurt and remainder of the dry fixings into the mixing dish, blending until just incorporated.
2. Whisk the milk, vanilla, and eggs. Combine everything.
3. Prepare the batter in a griddle pan or sprayed skillet until golden. When the bubbles begin, it's time to flip. Serve and enjoy.

Tips for Meal Prep:

1. Prepare the pancakes and cool them completely.
2. Store in the fridge if you are using them within a day. Otherwise, it's best to freeze them in closed containers or zipper-type freezer bags.

3. Begin by placing two pancakes on a microwave-safe plate. Microwave at 100% power or high power for 1 to 1.5 minutes or until warm, turning once.
4. Add butter and syrup, and breakfast is served!

Lunch: Tomato Soup

Yields Provided: 4

Ingredients for Prep:

- Olive oil (1 tbsp.)
- Onion (1)
- Garlic (3 cloves)
- Carrots (3)
- Roasted tomatoes (15 oz.)
- Tomato paste (1 tbsp.)
- Veggie stock (1 cup)
- Tomato sauce (15 oz.)
- Dried basil (1 tbsp.)
- Black pepper (1 pinch)
- Dried oregano (.25 tsp.)
- Coconut cream (3 oz.)

Method of Prep:

1. Chop the onion, garlic, and carrots.

2. Heat a soup pot using the medium temperature setting. Pour in the oil to heat until hot. Toss in the onion and garlic to sauté for about five minutes.

3. Pour in the tomato sauce, tomato paste, carrots, stock, tomatoes, basil, oregano, and black pepper.
4. Stir the fixings well and continue cooking for another 15 minutes.

Tips for Meal Prep:

1. Cool the soup and pour it into a large container until time to eat.
2. When it is time to eat, pour in the cream, and blend using an immersion blender.
3. Portion the tomato soup into serving bowls and serve.

Dinner: Turkey Sloppy Joes

Yields Provided: 4 -1 cup each

Ingredients for Prep:

- Raw ground 93% lean turkey breast (1 lb.)
- Olive oil (1 tsp.)
- Medium onion (1)
- Garlic (2 cloves)
- Medium red bell pepper (1)
- Sea salt (.5 tsp.)
- Ground black pepper (.25 tsp.)
- All-natural tomato sauce, no salt or sugar added (1 cup)
- Worcestershire sauce, gluten-free (1 tbsp.)
- Raw honey/Pure maple syrup (1 tbsp.)
- Hot pepper sauce (1.5 tsp.)
- Optional: Fresh parsley (to taste)

Method of Prep:

1. Warm the oil in a large frying pan using the medium heat temperature setting.
2. Chop and add the garlic, onion, and bell pepper. Sauté for about one minute and add to a medium bowl. Set aside in a mixing bowl.
3. Add the turkey, salt, and pepper to the skillet. Simmer using the medium temperature heat. Stir often until the turkey is no longer pink (8 to 10 minutes).
4. Mix in the onion mixture, tomato sauce, hot sauce, Worcestershire sauce, and maple syrup.Lower the heat

to med-low, stirring occasionally until the sauce has thickened (15 to 20 minutes).

Tips for Meal Prep:

1. They are good in the fridge for 3-4 days.
2. Cool the *Sloppy Joes* thoroughly in the fridge before you freeze them in labeled freezer bags. Lay them flat in your freezer, so you can stack the frozen meals for three to six months.
3. Chop and sprinkle each serving with parsley before serving.
4. Place on 1 piece of whole-wheat toast or romaine lettuce leaves.

Snack: Fried Queso Fresco

Yields Provided: 5

Ingredients for Prep:

- Coconut oil (1 tbsp.)
- Queso fresco (1 lb.)
- Olive oil (.5 tbsp.)

Method of Prep:

1. Chop the cheese into cubes.
2. Warm both of the oils to the smoking point, and toss in the cheese.
3. Fry the cheese, flipping once until well browned.
4. Remove and let the cheese rest to cool.

Tips for Meal Prep:

1. Drain on towels to remove the oil.
2. Store in a closed container to enjoy anytime.

Day 6

Breakfast: Omelet Waffles

Yields Provided: 2
Ingredients for Prep:

- Black pepper (1 pinch)
- Eggs (4)
- Low-fat shredded cheddar cheese (.25 cup)
- Chopped ham (2 tbsp.)
- Chopped parsley (2 tbsp.)

Method of Prep:

1. Warm and lightly grease a waffle iron with a spritz of the cooking oil spray.
2. Combine all the fixings in a mixing container.
3. Empty the mixture into the iron and cook for four to five minutes.

Tips for Meal Prep:

1. Cool the waffles entirely before freezing, so they don't collect ice in the freezer.
2. Place them on a cookie tin, so they do not touch and let them fully freeze. If you want to prepare more, stack the trays for a few hours.
3. Place into resealable freezer bags until needed.

Lunch: Chicken – Apple Spinach Salad

Yields Provided: 4

Ingredients for Prep:

- Onion (.5 cup)
- Spinach (4 cups)
- Chopped toasted pecans (.25 cup)
- Acai dressing or your favorite (.75 cup)
- Cooked breast of chicken (2 cups)
- Granny Smith apples (2 cups)

Method of Prep:

1. Prep the Fixings: Dice the chicken. Chop the apples, pecans, and spinach. Slice the onion.
2. Use individual containers or one large salad dish to prep the salad, beginning with a layer of spinach.
3. Arrange the remainder of the fixings.

Tips for Meal Prep:

1. Note: You can wait to slice the apple if desired.
2. Cover the prepared salad with a lid or a layer of plastic wrap until serving time.
3. Sprinkle with the dressing to serve.

Dinner: Apricot BARBECUE Chicken

Yields Provided: 6

Ingredients for Prep:

- Breasts of chicken (1 lb.)
- Sugar-free BARBECUE sauce (.5 cup)
- Sugar-free Apricot jam (.5 cup)
- Low-sodium soy sauce (2 tbsp.)
- Ground ginger (1 tsp.)
- Onion powder (1 tsp.)
- Garlic powder (1 tsp.)

Method of Prep:

1. Warm the oven temperature at 350° Fahrenheit.
2. Trim away the skin and bones from the chicken. Prepare a baking sheet with foil and add the chicken.
3. Whisk the barbecue sauce, jam, seasonings, and soy sauce together in a mixing container. Pour over the chicken and bake for about 30 minutes.

Tips for Meal Prep:

1. This is a great choice for meal prep. Make this entire recipe and let it cool.
2. Store in the refrigerator for up to two days or freeze for later use.
3. Enjoy with your favorite side dishes.

Snack: Veggie Egg Cups

Yields Provided: 6 (2 each)
Ingredients for Prep:

- Homemade salsa (12 tbsp.)
- Green onions (2)
- Medium red bell pepper (1)
- Mushroom (1 cup)
- Large eggs (12)
- Nonstick cooking spray
- Sea salt and black pepper (as desired)

Homemade Salsa:

- Fresh cilantro (1 bunch)
- Small sweet onion (1)
- Garlic (3 cloves)
- Sea salt (.5 tsp.)
- Medium tomatoes (3)
- Medium jalapeno (1)

Method of Prep:

1. Prepare the salsa. Roast the jalapeno with the veins and seeds removed. Chop the cilantro with the stems removed. Finely chop and combine the jalapeno, tomatoes, garlic, onion, cilantro, and salt in a medium mixing container.
2. Prepare oven to 375° Fahrenheit. Spray a muffin tin with cooking spray.

3. Add the eggs, salt, and pepper in a large mixing bowl and whisk until blended. Finely chop and mix in the mushrooms, green onions, and bell peppers.
4. Fill each muffin cup evenly with the egg mixture.
5. Bake in the oven until a toothpick inserted into the center of the cups comes out clean (15-20 min.).

Tips for Meal Prep:

1. Freeze for Later: When completely cooled, put them in a gallon-sized freezer bag or container, squeeze out any air, seal, and freeze for up to 3 months.
2. Prepare from Frozen: Thaw overnight in refrigerator or pop into the microwave for a quick defrost.
3. To Serve: Top each egg cup with 1 teaspoon of homemade salsa.

Day 7

Breakfast: Banana Oat Pancakes

Yields Provided: 8 (2 pancakes each serving)

Ingredients for Prep:

- Extra-virgin coconut oil (.5 tsp.)
- Old-fashioned rolled oats - dry (2 cups)
- Sea salt (1 dash)
- Ground cinnamon (.5 tsp.)
- Baking powder (1 tsp.)
- Large ripe banana (1)
- Large eggs (2)
- Unsweetened almond milk (1 cup)
- Pure vanilla extract (1 tsp.)
- Fresh mixed berries (3 cups)

Method of Prep:

1. Combine the almond milk, salt, baking powder, cinnamon, eggs, banana extract, and oats in a blender. Blend until it's creamy.

2. Pour the oil in a frying pan using the med-low heat setting.

3. Pour ¼ cup of batter into the skillet and cook for two to three minutes. The edges of the pancake will bubble when they're ready to flip. Cook for another 1.5 minutes.

4. Repeat the process until all of the batters are gone.

Tips for Meal Prep:

1. The pancakes that are not eaten can be frozen and reheated in a toaster.
2. Cool thoroughly, and place in freezer bags for longer storage.
3. When ready to eat, top with fresh mixed berries.

Lunch: Ham Salad

Yields Provided: 4

Ingredients for Prep:

- Mango chutney (1 tbsp.)

- Onion powder (2 tsp.)

- Light mayonnaise (2 tbsp.)

- Dried mustard (2 tsp.)

- Plain Greek yogurt - Nonfat (2 tbsp.)

- Cooked - chopped ham (1 cup)

Method of Prep:

1. Pulse the fixings (omit the ham or not) in a processor until creamy smooth.
2. Put the container in the fridge for 30-45 minutes or until needed.

Tips for Meal Prep:

1. For meal prep, place the salad into four individual bowls.
2. Leave in the refrigerator and enjoy on-the-run.

Dinner: Baked Chicken Fajita

Yields Provided: 4

Ingredients for Prep:

- Chicken breasts (1 lb.)
- Bell pepper (1)
- Onion (1 medium)
- Tomato (1 ripe)
- Cumin (1 tbsp.)
- Garlic powder (2 tsp.)
- Salt (1 tsp.)
- Black pepper (1 tsp.)
- Onion powder (1 tsp.)
- Chili powder (.5 tsp.)

Method of Prep:

1. Slice or chop the veggies. Slice the chicken into strips making sure to remove all of the skin and bone fragments.
2. Combine all of the seasonings in a mixing container and add the chicken. Toss.
3. Set the oven temperature at 375° Fahrenheit.
4. Use a misting of cooking spray on the casserole dish and add the prepared chicken in a single layer. Top with the veggies.
5. Bake 35-40 minutes.

Tips for Meal Prep:

1. This is yet another great option for meal prep.
2. Prepare as above and let it cool thoroughly.

3. You can put it into four separate containers for storage or freezing.
4. Enjoy with some salsa, cheese, on a tortilla, or any way you like it.

Snack: Mini Crustless Quiche

Yields Provided: 12

Ingredients for Prep:

- Large eggs (15)
- Plum tomatoes (3)
- Pepper jack cheese (.5 cup)
- Mozzarella cheese (1 cup)
- Sweet onion (.33 cup)
- Pickled jalapenos (.33 cup)
- Salami (1 cup)
- Heavy cream (.5 cup)
- Also Needed: Muffin tins - 11x15-inch

Method of Prep:

1. Warm up the temperature in the oven to 325° Fahrenheit.
2. Prep the veggies. Dice the tomatoes, onions, jalapenos, and salami. Shred the cheese.
3. Spritz the muffin tins lightly with a misting of cooking oil.
4. Whisk all of the fixings together and split the batter in the muffin tins.
5. Bake for 25 minutes.

Tips for Meal Prep:

1. Cool thoroughly and slice the quiche into 12 portions.

2. Wrap it in plastic wrap.

3. When ready to eat, microwave from frozen, using the high setting at 30-second intervals - probably no more than one minute.

4. If you don't slice it, cover it in foil. Place the prepared dish into an oven-proof container, and heat for 20 minutes using a 350° Fahrenheit oven.

Week 2

Day 8

Breakfast: Veggie Egg Scramble

Yields Provided: 6

Ingredients for Prep:

- Diced tomato (1)
- Large eggs (6)
- Baby spinach (3 cups)
- Minced garlic clove (1)
- Red or purple diced onion (half of 1)
- Freshly cracked black pepper and kosher salt (1 tsp. each)
- Olive oil (1.5 tbsp.)
- 2% sharp cheddar cheese - ex. Cabot (.5 cup)

Method of Prep:

1. Whisk the eggs, pepper, and salt.
2. Warm up the oil in a skillet. Toss in the spinach, onions, tomato, and garlic. Simmer until done or 5 to 7 minutes.
3. Pour in the eggs and simmer 3 to 4 minutes – stirring occasionally.
4. When set, let the container become room temperature and take it away from the burner.
5. Sprinkle the cheese. Serve and enjoy.

Tips for Meal Prep:

1. Prepare the eggs and set aside to cool.
2. Place in the fridge and take the fixings with you to work tomorrow for a healthy breakfast.

Lunch: Asparagus Soup

Yields Provided: 6

Ingredients for Prep:

- Cooked chicken breasts (2)
- Salt & black pepper (1 pinch each)
- Carrots (2)
- Chopped asparagus spears (12)
- Yellow onion (1)
- Spinach (4 cups)
- Minced garlic cloves (3)
- Low-sodium veggie stock (6 cups)
- Lime (half of 1)
- Olive oil (1 tbsp.)
- Chopped cilantro (1 handful)

Method of Prep:

1. Cook the chicken and remove the skin and bones. Finely chop the asparagus, yellow onion, and carrots. Mince the garlic cloves.
2. Use the medium heat setting on the stovetop, and add the oil to a soup pot.
3. When hot, toss in the onions and sauté for five minutes.

4. Next, toss in the garlic, asparagus, and carrots. Continue cooking for an additional five minutes.
5. Toss in the spinach with a dusting of the pepper and salt. Add the chicken and stock. Continue cooking for about 20 minutes.

Tips for Meal Prep:

1. Chill thoroughly before placing it in the fridge.
2. When it is time to eat, toss in the lime zest and cilantro.
3. Stir well and ladle the soup into serving dishes.

Dinner: Asian Glazed Chicken

Yields Provided: 4

Ingredients for Prep:

- Coconut aminos (.33 cup)
- Chicken thighs (8)
- Garlic (3 tbsp.)

- Balsamic vinegar (.5 cup)
- Olive oil (.25 cup)
- Black pepper (1 pinch)
- Garlic chili sauce (3 tbsp.)
- Green onion (1 tbsp.)

Method of Prep:

1. Set the oven temperature at 425° Fahrenheit.
2. Discard the bones and skin from the chicken. Mince the garlic and chop the green onion.
3. Prepare a baking sheet with a spritz of cooking oil spray.
4. Add oil to the pan along with the chicken, vinegar, aminos, chili sauce, onion, black pepper, and garlic.
5. Toss well and bake for 30 minutes.
6. When done, serve with the sauce.

Tips for Meal Prep:

1. This is super for meal prep since all you do is let it thoroughly cool.
2. Arrange the chicken into individual freezer bags or another type of storage container.
3. Be sure to label its contents and freeze.

Snack: Veggie Snack Pack

Ingredients for Prep:

- Foster Farms <u>Bold Bites Pouch</u>
- Cherry tomatoes (5)
- Red bell pepper (.25 of 1)
- Sugar snap peas (.33 cup)
- Baby carrots (.5 cup)
- English cucumber (.33 cup)
- Hummus (2 tbsp.)

Method of Prep:

1. Rinse all of the veggies.
2. Discard the seeds from the pepper and slice.
3. Slice the cucumber.
4. Measure out the rest of the fixings.

Tips for Meal Prep:

1. Fill a small reusable dipping sauce container with two tablespoons of hummus. Secure the lid and place it into the container.
2. Arrange the prepared vegetables into portions (bell peppers, cucumbers, tomatoes, carrots, and peas) and close the container.
3. Place in the fridge until you need a quick on-the-go snack. Serve with one package of *Bold Bites*.

Day 9

Breakfast: Spinach – Feta & Egg Breakfast Quesadillas

Yields Provided: 5

Ingredients for Prep:

- Olive oil (2 tsp.)
- Red bell pepper (1)
- Red onion (half of 1)
- Eggs (8)
- Milk (.25 cup)
- Black pepper and salt (.25 tsp. each)
- Spinach leaves (4 handfuls)
- Feta (.5 cup.)
- Mozzarella cheese (1.5 cups)
- Tortillas (5)

Method of Prep:

1. Warm the olive oil in a skillet using the medium temperature setting.
2. Dice the onion and peppers. Toss into the pan to sauté for 4-5 minutes.
3. Whisk the eggs, salt, pepper, and milk. Stir often and toss in with the onions and peppers until the eggs are done.

4. Fold the feta and spinach into the eggs, stirring until the spinach is wilted. Take the pan from the burner.

5. Spray another frying pan with a spritz of cooking oil and warm using the medium temperature setting. Add the tortilla and spread ½ cup of egg mixture on one side of the tortilla. Garnish with ⅓ cup of the mozzarella and fold over the tortilla. Cook until browned (2 min.).

6. Flip it and cook another minute. Continue until all are done. It should take no more than 25 minutes from start to finish.

Tips for Meal Prep:

1. Cool thoroughly on a rack and wrap in plastic or store in a resealable container.

2. Reheat on top of a paper towel in the microwave for 30 to 60 seconds.

3. Crisp on a grill or in a frying pan for two to three minutes.

Lunch: Salmon Vegetable Frittata

Yields Provided: 6

Ingredients for Prep:

- Eggs (6)
- Mushrooms (2 cups)
- Green onion (.25 cup)
- Butter or margarine (1 tbsp.)
- Smoked salmon (4 oz.)
- Skim milk (1 cup)
- Paprika (.25 tsp.)
- Pepper (.25 tsp.)

- *Also Needed*: Ovenproof skillet

Method of Prep:

1. Warm up the oven to reach 350° Fahrenheit.
2. Chop the onions and mushrooms. Sauté in melted butter in the pan for about three to five minutes.
3. Whisk the eggs with the milk, pepper, and paprika with a wire whisk until mixed.
4. Dice the salmon into small chunks. Fold into the egg mixture with the cooked onions and mushrooms. Toss well.
5. Bake for 30 minutes.

Tips for Meal Prep:

1. Carefully transfer the pan to the stovetop to cool.
2. Slice into six wedges and store in the fridge.
3. *Option #1*: You can individually wrap the frittatas or leave them in the pan to enjoy for a full meal.
4. Option #2: Portion the frittata into sealed containers with your favorite veggies for another meal.
5. Freeze after the first or second day.

Dinner: Thai Peanut Chicken

Yields Provided: 6-8
Ingredients for Prep:

- Chicken thighs (2 lb.)
- Minced garlic (2 tsp.)
- Coconut milk (14 oz. can)
- Creamy peanut butter (.5 cup)

- Lime juice (3 tbsp.)
- Ginger (1 tbsp. - grated)
- Tamari or soy sauce (2 tbsp.)
- Honey (3 tbsp.)
- Toasted sesame oil (1 tbsp.)
- Garam masala (1 tsp.)
- Curry powder yellow (2 tsp.)
- Cumin (1 tsp.)
- Red pepper flakes (.5 tsp.)

Method of Prep:
1. Trim and discard the bones from the chicken.
2. This is a great prep recipe since you put it together and freeze it to pop into a slow cooker at a later date.
3. In a medium container, mix the coconut milk, lime juice, ginger, tamari, honey, sesame oil, garlic, curry powder, cumin, garam masala, peanut butter, and red pepper flakes.
4. Whisk it all together until smooth. Add the chicken.
5. To Eat Now: Add the chicken and sauce to a crockpot and cook.

Tips for Meal Prep:
1. Transfer chicken and sauce to a labeled container or freezer bag and freeze.
2. From thawed or freshly made, transfer the chicken and sauce into a slow cooker. Cook using the low setting for six hours or the high setting for four hours.

Snack: Beef & Cheddar Roll-Ups

Yields Provided: 1

Ingredients for Prep:

- Cheddar cheese (half of 1 slice)
- Thousand Island yogurt/Regular dressing (1 tbsp.)
- Tomatoes & onions (as desired)

Method of Prep:

1. Thinly slice and lay the roast beef onto a preparation surface.
2. Place the cheese, dressing, and veggies on top.
3. Roll it up and secure with toothpicks.

Tips for Meal Prep:

1. When you are ready to eat, cut them into halves.

Day 10

Breakfast: Breakfast Bowls

Yields Provided: 6

Ingredients for Prep:

- Yukon gold potatoes (2 lb.)
- Green pepper (1)
- Onion (1)
- Olive oil
- Seasoned salt
- Eggs (12)
- Freshly shredded cheddar cheese (4 oz.)
- Green onions (3)
- Optional Toppings: Salsa - tortilla & avocado
- Individual-sized glass containers with lids or Tupperware type (6)

Method of Prep:

1. Dice the cucumber, onions, and potatoes into 1-inch cubes. Deseed and chop the green peppers.
2. Warm the oven at 425° Fahrenheit.
3. Prepare a baking tray with a drizzle of oil and add the onions, potatoes, and peppers. Dust with the pepper and seasoned salt.
4. Split the veggies onto two baking trays and roast for 30-40 minutes. Rotate and toss the potatoes about halfway through the baking cycle.
5. Whisk the eggs pepper and salt until smooth.

6. Prepare a skillet using the medium temperature setting with a spritz of cooking oil. Lower the heat to the low-temperature setting, cooking until the eggs until barely incorporated.

Tips for Meal Prep:

1. Divide the fixings evenly into two containers. Cool thoroughly and sprinkle with green onions and cheese. Place a lid on each container.
2. Eat the meal within three days or freeze.
3. When ready to reheat from frozen, set the microwave at 50% power, and set the timer for 1.5 minutes. Stir until fully heated. Top to your liking.

Lunch: Chili Con Carne

Yields Provided: 12

Ingredients for Prep:

- Ground chuck (5 lb.)
- Large onion (1)
- Green and red bell pepper (1 each)
- Garlic cloves (2)
- Chili powder (.5 cup)
- Cumin (2 tbsp.)
- Chipotle (1 tsp.)
- Pinto/kidney beans (2 - 15 oz. cans)
- Tomato paste (10 oz. can)
- Tomato sauce (2 - 10 oz. cans)
- Black pepper (1 tbsp.)
- Salt (2 tsp.)

- Water (2 cups or as needed)
- Cayenne (as desired)

Method of Prep:

1. Gather the fixings. Drain the beans in a colander. Seed and dice the peppers. Mince the onion and garlic.
2. Add the ground beef to a large pot using med-high heat. Cook it until browned. Drain the grease and mix in the onions, bell peppers, and garlic. Simmer for about three minutes.
3. Toss the remainder of the fixings into the pan. Simmer using the low-heat temperature setting (lid off) until the meat is tender or

about one hour. Add more water as needed. Adjust the spices and serve hot.

Tips for Meal Prep:

1. Scoop the chili (1 cup) into a container or a plastic freezer bag. Seal, leaving ½ inch of empty space at the top.
2. Label it with the date you made it and also the time you placed it in the freezer. Usually, chilies that are frozen are good for one week.
3. Place each bag of chili at the end of the freezer, as this is the coldest part of the freezer.
4. To Eat: Thaw the chili in the refrigerator for 1 hour. Place it in a pot over medium heat (rolling boil). Keep the pot covered to retain moisture.
5. Upon boiling, lower the temperature. At this point, it's necessary to season it because the flavor has diminished a little during the freezing process.
6. Serve it piping hot.

Dinner: Cajun Chicken

Yields Provided: 4-5

Ingredients for Prep:

- Chicken breast (1 lb.)
- Black pepper (1 pinch)
- Olive oil (1 tbsp.)
- Dried oregano (.5 tsp.)
- Low-sodium vegetable stock (.25 cup)
- Cajun seasoning (1 tbsp.)
- Chopped green onions (4)
- Cherry tomatoes - cut in half (2 cups)
- Minced cloves of garlic (3)
- Coconut cream (.66 cup)
- Sweet paprika (.5 tsp.)
- Lemon juice (2 tbsp.)

Method of Prep:

1. Heat a skillet using the med-high temperature setting.
2. Once the oil is hot, toss in the chicken and portion of pepper. Cook on each side for five (5) minutes.
3. Pour in the stock, oregano, lemon juice, cream, paprika, garlic, green onions, and the Cajun seasoning.
4. Simmer for about ten minutes. Divide into serving bowls and enjoy.

Tips for Meal Prep:

1. Let everything cool.
2. Portion the fixings into storage containers to freeze.

Snack: Fruit Snack Pack

Yields Provided: 3 packs

Ingredients for Prep:

- Raspberries (.5 cup)
- Sliced oranges (¼ of 1)
- Strawberries (4)
- Grapes (1 cup)
- Trail mix (2 tbsp.)
- Foster Farms <u>Bold Bites</u> Pouch (1)

Method of Prep:

1. Slice the orange before you begin.

Tips for Meal Prep:

1. Add the trail mix to a reusable dipping container.
2. Fill a small reusable dipping sauce container with 2 tablespoons of the trail mix. Close the top tightly and transfer to a single- compartment container.
3. Arrange the prepared fruit (orange, strawberries, grapes, raspberries) within the container and cover.
4. Serve with 1 pouch of your favorite Bold Bites and store in the fridge until ready to enjoy.

Day 11

Breakfast: Carrot Muffins

Yields Provided: 5
Ingredients for Prep:

- Whole wheat flour (1.5 cups)
- Stevia/your preferred sweetener (.5 cup)
- Baking soda (.5 tsp.)
- Cinnamon (.5 tsp.)
- Baking powder (1 tsp.)
- Natural apple juice (.25 cup)
- Egg (1)
- Olive oil (.25 cup)
- Freshly picked cranberries (1 cup)
- Grated carrots (2)
- Chopped pecans (.25 cup)
- Grated ginger (2 tsp.)
- Cooking oil spray (as needed)

Method of Prep:
1. Warm the oven to reach 375° Fahrenheit.
2. Drain the cranberries.

3. Sift or whisk the stevia, flour, cinnamon, baking soda, and baking powder in a mixing container.
4. Pour in the apple juice, whisked egg, oil, cranberries, carrots, pecans, and ginger. Stir thoroughly.
5. Lightly grease a muffin tray with a spritz of cooking oil spray. Divide the mix and to each of the containers.
6. Bake for 30 minutes. When ready, take out of the oven.

Tips for Meal Prep:

1. Leave in the muffin pan for 5 to 10 minutes to cool.
2. Remove each muffin from the pan and thoroughly cool before storing it in the refrigerator. Freeze for longer storage.
3. If frozen, leave them on the countertop to defrost for about 30 minutes.
4. You can also add them in a lunchbox for a quick pick-up at work.

Lunch: Classic Stuffed Peppers

Yields Provided: 6

Ingredients for Prep:

- Green peppers (6 large)
- Lean ground beef (1 lb.)
- Onion (.25 cup)
- Diced tomatoes (16 oz. can)
- Tomato sauce (16 oz. can)
- Basil (1 tsp.)

- Oregano (1 tsp.)
- Black pepper & salt (as desired)
- Instant white rice (1 bag)
- Shredded cheddar cheese (1 cup)

Method of Prep:

1. Warm the oven in advance to reach 350° Fahrenheit.
2. Brown the beef and finely chopped onion in a large skillet using the low-temperature setting.
3. Slice the tops off of each pepper, discard the seeds, and arrange in a lightly greased baking dish.
4. Prepare the rice according to package instructions and drain.
5. In a large mixing container, combine the tomato sauce, basil, oregano, salt, black pepper, rice, and diced tomatoes. Stir in the cooked beef and onions with a few chopped peppers if desired.
6. Spoon the mixture into each shell. Bake for 35 minutes.
7. Remove and add a portion of cheddar cheese on top. Place back into the oven. Bake until the cheese has melted (5 min.).

Tips for Meal Prep:

1. Cool thoroughly and wrap each pepper in plastic wrap. Place into freezer zipper bags or individual containers to keep for up to six months.
2. Defrost them in the microwave when desired. Reheat them for five minutes. Remove the dish from the microwave and sprinkle with a portion of fresh cheese. Serve when ready.

Dinner: Cilantro Lime Chicken

Yields Provided: 6

Ingredients for Prep:

- Chicken breast (1 lb.)
- Orange juice (1 cup)
- Chicken broth (1 cup)
- Juice (2 fresh limes)
- Garlic (2 tsp.)
- Cilantro leaves (.5 cup)
- Black beans (1 can)
- Frozen corn (2 cups)
- Ground cumin (1 tbsp.)

Method of Prep:

1. Rinse and drain the beans, mince the garlic, and chop the cilantro leaves. Remove the skin and bones from the chicken.
2. This is great to prepare and set aside for those days when you are pressed for time. Add all ingredients to a gallon-sized freezer bag or container.

Tips for Meal Prep:

1. From thawed or freshly made, transfer into a slow cooker. Cook on high for three to four hours or low for six hours.
2. Serve as a homemade burrito bowl. Just add rice, sour cream, guacamole, and cilantro for a super delicious meal. Tacos and nachos are great ways to serve this as well.

Snack: Avocado Hummus Snack Jars

Yields Provided: 4 jars

Ingredients for Prep:

- Chickpeas (1 can)
- Tahini (.5 cup)
- Avocado (1)
- Garlic (2 cloves)
- Lemon juice (1 tbsp.)
- Salt (.5 tsp.)
- Water (.25 cup)
- Optional Toppings: Sliced sun-dried tomatoes/antipasto
- Celery, cucumber & carrot sticks
- Assorted chips & crackers

Method of Prep:

1. Rinse and drain the chickpeas. Dice the avocado and garlic. Cut the carrots, celery, and cucumber into wedges/sticks.
2. Toss all of the fixings (omit the optional/final toppings) into a Vitamix.
3. Blend using the lowest speed setting for about 30 seconds. Stir as needed until full mixed (5 min.).

Tips for Meal Prep:

1. Scoop into jam jars, and top with antipasto or sundried tomatoes.
2. Serve alongside cut-up veggies, crackers, chips, or whatever other snacks you're craving.
3. Enjoy within the first two to three days after preparation.

Day 12

Breakfast: Buckwheat Pancakes

Yields Provided: 6

Ingredients for Prep:

- All-purpose flour (.5 cup)
- Buckwheat flour (.5 cup)
- Baking powder (1 tbsp.)
- Sugar (1 tbsp.)
- Egg whites (2)
- Fat-free milk (.5 cup)
- Sparkling water (.5 cup)
- Fresh strawberries (3 cups)
- Canola oil (1 tbsp.)

Method of Prep:

1. Slice the berries. Whisk the oil, eggs, and milk in a small mixing container.
2. Use another dish to blend the sugar, baking powder, and each of the flours. Blend in the egg white mixture along with the water until barely moist.
3. Using the medium heat setting to prepare a nonstick griddle or skillet, and spoon the batter in ½ cup increments.
4. Continue cooking for about two minutes (bubbles will appear on the top).
5. Flip and continue to cook for about one to two more minutes.

Tips for Meal Prep:

1. Either serve now or cool for storage.
2. Store in freezer bags until ready to serve.
3. Place the frozen pancakes in a heated 375° Fahrenheit oven for 8-10 minutes.
4. Garnish each one with 1/2 of a cup of sliced berries and serve.

Lunch: One-Tray Caprese Pasta

Yields Provided: 2
Ingredients for Prep:

- Pasta (2 cups - cooked al dente)

- Onion (.75 cup)

- Marinara sauce (1 cup)

- Fresh basil (.33 cup)

- Black pepper and salt (1 tsp. each)

- Optional: Mozzarella cheese

- Also Needed: Aluminum foil (2 sheets @ 12 by 12)

Method of Prep:

1. Set oven to 400° Fahrenheit.
2. Chop the veggies and shred the cheese.
3. Stack the sheets of foil on top of each other.
4. Fold one side of the foil about ⅓ of the way across the sheet, repeat for the opposite side.
5. Pinch the corner to form a point and then flatten it to the short side of the foil, forming a raised corner. Repeat for all four sides (make 4).
6. Add all of the ingredients to the foil boats and stir.

7. Bake for 12 minutes.

Tips for Meal Prep:

1. Cool for 10-15 minutes.
2. Refrigerate for no longer than three to five days.

Dinner: Shrimp Taco Bowls

Yields Provided: 4

Ingredients for Prep:

Spicy Shrimp:

- Medium shrimp (20)
- Garlic clove (1 minced)
- Olive oil (1 tbsp.)
- Ground cumin (.5 tsp.)
- Chili powder (.5 tsp.)
- Optional: Onion powder (.25 tsp.)
- Kosher salt (.25 tsp.)

To Serve:

- Brown rice (2 cups - cooked)
- Corn (1 cup)
- Black beans (1 cup)
- Tomatoes (1 cup - diced)
- Cheddar cheese (.5 cup)
- Cilantro (2 tbsp. - minced)

- Lime (1 cut into 4 slices)
- Meal prep containers (4)

Method of Prep:

1. Drain and rinse the corn and black beans.
2. Peel and devein the shrimp. Toss them into a medium mixing bowl.
3. Whisk the olive oil, salt, cumin, garlic, chili powder, and onion powder. Fold in the shrimp and toss gently.
4. Cover and pop into the fridge to marinate for at least ten minutes or up to 24 hours.
5. Heat a large heavy-duty or cast-iron skillet using the high heat temperature setting for two minutes. Add the olive oil and shrimp.
6. Cook the shrimp in a skillet over med-high heat until pink and cooked thoroughly (5 min.)

Tips for Meal Prep:

1. Divide the brown rice into four containers (.5 cup each). Top with five shrimp, corn, tomatoes, a scoop of black beans, cheese, cilantro, and a lime wedge.
2. Cover and place in the fridge for a maximum of four days.
3. Time to Eat: Warm the bowls in the microwave for two minutes or until heated thoroughly. Top with salsa, sour cream, or guacamole to your liking along with a drizzle of lime juice.

Snack: Vanilla Cashew Butter Cups

Yields Provided: 12 large or 24 small cups

Ingredients for Prep:

- Dark chocolate or chocolate chips (7 oz. - chopped)
- Cashew butter (1 cup)
- Honey/maple syrup for vegan (2 tbsp.)
- Vanilla (1 tbsp.)
- Sea salt (1 pinch)
- Flaky sea salt - for the tops
- Also Needed: 12-count or 24-count muffin tin with liners

Method of Prep:

1. Line the muffin tin with liners.
2. Place about two-thirds of the chocolate in a pan using the low-temperature heat setting. After it's mostly melted, remove it from the heat and add the remaining chocolate. Stir a few times while the residual heat melts the chocolate.
3. Working one at a time, add slightly less than a tablespoon of the melted chocolate to one of the cupcake liners. Tip it on its side and rotate it so that the chocolate comes one-third of the way up the side of the liner. Repeat until all the liners have a chocolate coating then place them in the fridge to harden.
4. Add the cashew butter, honey, vanilla, and salt to a medium- sized bowl. Gently fold them together. Once the chocolate cups have hardened, divide the cashew butter between the cups. Use your finger to press it down into the cups.
5. Pour the remaining chocolate over the tops of the cashew butter cups, then pop them back into the fridge to harden.

6. Sprinkle a little flaky sea salt on top to make them irresistible.

Tips for Meal Prep:

1. In a microwave, melt the chocolate for 20 to 30 seconds. Drizzle and serve.
2. Cashew butter can be pricey. You can make your own with a food processor or high-powered blender and about ten minutes. You'll need two cups of raw cashews plus one tablespoon of coconut oil to make 1 cup of cashew butter.

Day 13

Breakfast: Corn & Apple Muffins

Yields Provided: 12

Ingredients for Prep:

- All-purpose flour (2 cups)
- Packed brown sugar (.25 cup)
- Yellow cornmeal (.5 cup)
- Baking powder (1 tbsp.)
- Salt (.25 tsp.)
- Egg whites (2)
- Apple (1)
- Corn kernels (.5 cup)

Method of Prep:

1. Peel and coarsely chop the apple.
2. Use a 12-cup muffin pan and line the containers with foil or paper liners.
3. Set the oven temperature to reach 425° Fahrenheit.
4. Mix the brown sugar, cornmeal, salt, flour, and baking powder completely in a big container.
5. Use a separate mixing container to beat the egg whites and milk. Blend in the corn kernels and apple bits.
6. Whisk again and pour the batter into the flour mixture. Continue to gently stir the fixings until slightly moistened.
7. Fill the cups 2/3 of the way full. Bake for about 30 minutes.

8. Test the muffins for doneness by gently pressing the center. They should spring back.

Tips for Meal Prep:

1. Cool thoroughly before placing the muffins into a storage container.
2. Store in the fridge for longer storage times.

Lunch: Smoked Sausage & Orzo

Yields Provided: 6-8
Ingredients for Prep:

- Jennie-O Hardwood Smoked Turkey Sausage (16 oz.)
- Olive oil (1 tbsp.)
- Yellow onion (1 small)
- Red bell pepper (1 small)
- Garlic (3 cloves)
- Cajun seasoning (1 tbsp.)
- Crushed red pepper flakes (.5 tbsp.)
- Chicken broth - Low-sodium (14.5 oz. can)
- Crushed tomatoes (15 oz. can)
- Uncooked orzo pasta (8 oz.)
- Medium zucchini (1 shredded)
- Kosher salt (.5 tsp.)
- Freshly cracked black pepper (as desired)
- For the Garnish: Flat-leaf parsley

Method of Prep:

1. Slice the sausage diagonally and add to a large skillet with olive oil. Dice and toss in the onions, bell peppers, garlic, kosher salt, black pepper, Cajun seasoning, and pepper flakes.
2. Pour in the chicken broth, orzo, and tomatoes. Wait for it to boil.
3. Reduce the heat setting to med-low and cover. Set a timer for 8 minutes, or until the orzo is tender.

Tips for Meal Prep:

1. Pour the fixings into resealable plastic bags or shallow airtight containers for up to three to five days.
2. Time to Eat: Stir in shredded zucchini, freshly chop flat-leaf Italian parsley and a sprinkle of Cajun seasoning.

Dinner: Chicken & Broccoli

Yields Provided: 4
Ingredients for Prep:

- Breasts of chicken (4)
- Olive oil (1 tbsp.)
- Red onions (1 cup)
- Garlic cloves (2)
- Oregano (1 tbsp.)
- Coconut cream (.5 cup)
- Broccoli florets (2 cups)

Method of Prep:

1. Cut the skin and bones from the chicken breasts.
2. Mince the garlic cloves. Chop the red onions and oregano.
3. Heat a skillet to warm the oil using the med-high heat setting.
4. Arrange the chicken breasts in the pan and simmer for about 5 minutes per side.
5. Toss in the onions and garlic. Stir and cook for approximately 5 more minutes.
6. Add in the broccoli, cream, and oregano. Continue cooking for 10 more minutes.
7. When ready, portion into the plates and serve.

Tips for Meal Prep:

1. It will keep for 3-5 days in the fridge.

2. For further prep time, cover with foil and place in a freezer bag or container.

Snack: Protein Snack Pack

Yields Provided: 3

Ingredients for Prep:

- Foster Farms <u>Bold Bites</u> Pouch
- Hard-Boiled egg (1)
- Chopped cheese (.25 cup)
- Avocado (half of 1)
- Chickpeas (.5 cup)
- Hazelnuts/your preference (2 tbsp.)

Method of Prep:

1. Chop the cheese into cubes.
2. Fill a dipping sauce <u>container</u> with two tablespoons of hazelnuts.
3. Close the top and place it into a storage container alongside the rest of the fixings.

Tips for Meal Prep:

1. Arrange the egg, chickpeas, cheese, and avocado within the storage container and securely close the lid or use plastic wrap.
2. Place in the fridge until needed. It's best used within 24 to 48 hours.
3. When it is time to eat, serve with a pouch of the bold bites.

Day 14

Breakfast: Veggies & Eggs

Yields Provided: 4

Ingredients for Prep:

- Large eggs (8)
- Broccoli crowns (2)
- Small head cauliflower (half of 1)
- Bell peppers (2)
- Garlic powder (1 tsp.)
- Black pepper (as desired)
- Salt (.5 tsp.)
- Avocado/coconut oil (3 tbsp.)
- Water (.25 cup)
- Optional: Cheese of choice
- Sprouted bread slices (2 toasted)
- For Serving: Salsa

Method of Prep:

1. Coarsely chop the broccoli and cauliflower. Dice the peppers.
2. Warm a large ceramic skillet using the medium temperature heat setting and swirl two tablespoons of oil to coat. Toss in the broccoli and cauliflower. Cover and cook for two to three minutes. Stir, cover, and cook for another two to three minutes.
3. Meanwhile, in a small dish, whisk the eggs, water, pepper, and ¼ teaspoon of salt. Whisk well and set aside.

4. Add the bell pepper, rest of the salt, garlic powder, and black pepper to the skillet with the vegetables. Stir and cook for two to three more minutes.

Tips for Meal Prep:

1. Divide between four plastic or glass meal prep containers, add a small container of salsa, 1/2 slice of toast, and sprinkle of cheese if desired.
2. Refrigerate for up to 5 days. Heat in a skillet on the stovetop.
3. Swirl one tablespoon of oil into the pan and pour in the egg mixture. Cook until it's scrambled, stirring (folding) constantly.

Lunch: Starbucks™ Protein Bistro Box

Yields Provided: 8
Ingredients for Prep:

- Hard-boiled eggs (8)
- Grapes (2 cups)
- Large apples (2)
- Mini Babybel cheese - Reduced-fat (4)
- Multi-grain flatbread sandwich thins (2 cuts in quarters)
- Honey-Roasted Peanut Butter (portioned into 2 oz. containers)
- Optional: Freshly squeezed lemon juice
- Freshly cracked pepper and kosher salt (as desired)

Method of Prep:

1. Rinse the apples and grapes. Brush the apple slices lightly using the juice to prevent browning.

2. Boil and peel the eggs. Cool and dust eggs using salt and pepper to taste.

Tips for Meal Prep:

1. Assemble the protein bistro boxes and store refrigerated.
2. It is recommended to store the eggs whole.

Dinner: Sweet & Sour Meatballs

Yields Provided: 8-12

Ingredients for Prep:

- *The Meatballs*:
- Ground chuck (1.5 lb.)
- Water chestnuts (3-4 tbsp. - chopped)
- Quick oats (.75 cup)
- Garlic powder (.5 tsp.)
- Onion powder (.5 tsp.)
- Salt (.5 tsp.)
- Egg (1 beaten)
- Milk (.5 cup)
- Soy sauce - reduced-sodium (.5 tsp.)
- *The Sauce:*
- Brown sugar (1 cup)
- Beef bouillon (.5 cup)
- Vinegar (.5 cup)
- Cornstarch (2 tbsp.)

- Reduced-sodium soy sauce (2 tsp.)
- Pineapple tidbits - drained (8-9 oz. can)
- Chopped bell pepper - green (.5 cup)

Method of Prep:

1. Combine the meatball fixings preparing them into one-inch balls.
2. Brown, drain the grease and set aside.
3. Whisk the sugar, vinegar, bouillon, cornstarch, and soy sauce in a Dutch oven or large deep skillet, bringing it to a boil.
4. Simmer the sauce mixture until thickened. Drain and stir in the pineapple, peppers, and meatballs.
5. Continue cooking for about half an hour.

Tips for Meal Prep:

1. Cool the meatballs until thoroughly chilled.
2. Measure your required number of meatballs per serving into a freezer bag.
3. Pop the package into the freezer for a quick meal.
4. Be sure to label it with its contents and date to ensure you don't overlook it.

Snack: Ham – Swiss & Spinach Roll-Ups

Yields Provided: 1

Ingredients for Prep:

- Uncured organic deli ham/your preference (1 slice)
- Hummus (1 tbsp.)

- Swiss cheese (half of 1 slice)
- Baby spinach leaves (4-5)

Method of Prep:

1. Spread hummus onto the slice of ham.
2. Top that with swiss cheese and spinach leaves.
3. Roll them up.

Tips for Meal Prep:

1. Prepare as many snacks as you want to prep.
2. The roll-ups can be made 1-2 days ahead of time.

Chapter 4:
Keto Diet

What Is the Keto Diet?

The term keto in ketogenic comes from ketones. Ketones are small fuel molecules produced in the body. These molecules provide an alternative source of fuel for the body when there's a short supply of glucose in the blood.

When you consume very few carbs, your body will not have sufficient glucose or blood sugar needed to power the cells. Since glucose is unavailable, the body will reach into its fat reserves to produce blood sugar.

The ketogenic process takes place in the liver. It is the liver that produces ketones from fat stores in the body. These ketones then

provide the necessary fuel needed throughout the body and mostly for the brain. The brain is an organ that is continuously working and has a high demand for energy. However, it cannot run on fat. It only functions on glucose or ketones.

When you consume no carbs, the body will lack glucose to produce energy, and the body will convert the fat that you consume into ketones. This happens when your insulin levels fall drastically. When this happens, fat burning occurs quite fast. Your body can easily access stored fat, including the stubborn fat around the belly and waistline.

The ketogenic process is excellent for weight loss and fat burning. If you are looking to lose weight and shed off the pounds, then the ketogenic diet is highly recommended. However, apart from the benefit of weight loss occasioned by the keto diet, you will also enjoy a host of other benefits as well. For instance, you will lose weight but without the need to fast.

Variations of the Ketogenic Diet Plan

- **Standard Ketogenic Diet:** It's also known as SKD, which is a high-fat, very low-carb, and moderate-protein diet. This diet consists of 20% protein, 75% carbs, and only 5% carbs.

- **Targeted Ketogenic Diet:** The technique used in this dieting phase is similar to the standard keto diet except that it allows variations in carbs intake based on workout demands.

- **Cyclic Ketogenic Diet:** This variation of the keto diet involves varying periods where you enjoy five days of ketogenic diet followed by two days where you have a diet high in carbs; hence, the 5:2 diet.

- ***High-Protein Ketogenic Diet:*** You can also enjoy a high-protein keto diet, which is somewhat similar to the standard keto diet. However, it consists of higher protein levels compared to the SKD diet. The ratios here are 35% protein, 60% fat, and 5% carbs.

Most people follow the standard ketogenic diet and sometimes the high-protein keto diet. For purposes of learning more about the ketogenic diet, we will focus more on the standard version.

Benefits of the Keto Diet

Ketosis has numerous benefits. At the onset, it provides the brain and body an endless supply of energy. This energy is crucial for the brain and helps you to be sharp and focused. This also enhances your physical and mental endurance.

Other benefits of ketosis include the facilitation of effortless weight loss. Ketosis is one of the most efficient weight loss processes known. People who have type 2 diabetes can get relief from the condition. Type II diabetes is aggravated by excessive blood sugar, which is controlled via ketosis. Other conditions, such as epilepsy, can easily be controlled using ketosis even without the use of medication.

Let's see how tasty the foods are in this segment! You'll be surprised!

Week 1

Day 1

Breakfast: Almost McGriddle Casserole

Yields Provided: 8
Total Net Carbs: 3 grams

Ingredients for Prep:

- Breakfast sausage (1 lb.)
- Flaxseed meal (.25 cup)
- Almond flour (1 cup)
- Large eggs (10)
- Maple syrup (6 tbsp.)
- Cheese (4 oz.)
- Butter (4 tbsp.)
- Onion (.5 tsp.)
- Sage (.25 tsp.)
- Garlic powder (.5 tsp.)
- *Also Needed*: 9 by 9-inch casserole dish & parchment baking paper

Method of Prep:

1. Warm the oven temperature to reach 350° Fahrenheit.

2. Use the medium heat setting on the stovetop to prepare the sausage in a skillet.
3. Add all of the dry fixings (the cheese also), and stir in the wet ones. Add four tablespoons of syrup. Stir and blend well.
4. After the sausage is browned, combine everything (the grease too).
5. Prepare the casserole dish using a sheet of baking paper. Dump the mixture into the casserole dish. Drizzle using the rest of the syrup and bake for 45 to 55 minutes.
6. Transfer to the countertop to cool.

Tips for Meal Prep:

1. The casserole should be easily removed by using the edge of the parchment paper.
2. After the casserole has cooled, slice it into eight portions to enjoy for a couple of days.
3. Place the muffins in a storage container or freezer baggie. Store in the fridge for about five days or freeze for later.

Lunch: Caesar Salmon Salad

Yields Provided: 2

Total Carbohydrates: 2 grams

Ingredients for Prep:

- Salmon fillets (2 - 6 oz. portions)
- Bacon slices (4)
- Ghee (1 tbsp. or as needed)
- Pink salt (1 pinch)
- Freshly ground black pepper (1 pinch)

- Avocado (.5 of 1)
- Romaine hearts (2 cups)
- Caesar dressing (2 tbsp.)

Method of Prep:

1. Cook the bacon until crispy for 8 minutes using the med-high heat setting on the stovetop. Drain on a platter using paper towels.
2. Remove the excess water from the fillets. Give them a shake of pepper and salt.
3. Use the same pan to prepare the salmon. Add butter if needed.
4. Cook the salmon for five minutes per side for medium-rare.

Tips for Meal Prep:

1. Break the bacon into bits.
2. Chop the romaine hearts and slice the avocado.
3. Prepare two salad dishes or a closed container for the meal prep with equal parts of romaine, avocado, and the bacon.
4. Place the bacon into separate containers to keep them crunchy.
5. When ready to serve, enjoy with a drizzle of the dressing.

Dinner: Chipotle Roast

Yields Provided: 4

Total Carbohydrates: 1 gram

Ingredients for Prep:

- Diced tomatoes (7.25 oz.)
- Bone broth (6 oz.)
- Diced green chilis (2 oz.)
- Pork roast (2 lb.)
- Chipotle powder (1 tsp.)
- Cumin (.5 tsp.)
- Onion powder (.5 tsp.)

Method of Prep:

1. Combine each of the fixings in the Instant Pot and close the lid.
2. Manually set the timer for 1 hour. Natural-release the pressure.

Tips for Meal Prep:

1. Cool the roast and slice into four portions.
2. Freeze in individual compartment storage containers. Add your favorite vegetable and freeze for later.
3. When it's dinner time, defrost the meat, and heat as desired.

Snack: Peanut Butter Protein Bars

Yields Provided: 12 bars Total

Carbohydrates: 3 grams

Ingredients for Prep:

- Keto-friendly chunky peanut butter (1 cup)
- Egg whites (2)
- Almonds (.5 cup)
- Cashews (.5 cup)
- Almond meal (1.5 cups)

Method of Prep:

1. Warm up the oven ahead of time to 350° Fahrenheit.
2. Combine all of the fixings and add them to the prepared dish.
3. Bake for 15 minutes, and cut into 12 pieces once they're cooled.

Tips for Meal Prep:

1. Store in the fridge to keep them fresh using a closed, airtight container.

Day 2

Breakfast: Jalapeno Cheddar Waffles

Yields Provided: 1

Total Carbohydrates: 6 grams

Ingredients for Prep:

- Large eggs (3)
- Jalapeno (1 small)
- Cream cheese (3 oz.)
- Psyllium husk powder (1 tsp.)
- Coconut flour (1 tbsp.)
- Cheddar cheese (1 oz.)
- Baking powder (1 tsp.)
- *Also Needed:* Immersion blender

Method of Prep:

1. Mix all of the fixings using the blender, except for the jalapeno and cheese.
2. After you have a smooth texture, add the cheese and jalapeno. Blend and pour the batter into the waffle iron.
3. Cook for 5 to 6 minutes. Set aside when done.

Tips for Meal Prep:

1. Let the waffles cool off for prep.

2. Put them into a plastic freezer bag and pop them in the freezer until you have the desire for a delicious waffle.
3. To reheat, preheat the oven temperature to 400° Fahrenheit. When it's hot, place the waffles on a baking tin. Warm them up for 5 minutes. Serve and enjoy!
4. *Tip*: It isn't recommended to warm them in a regular toaster.

Lunch: Chicken 'Zoodle' Soup

Yields Provided: 2

Total Carbohydrates: 4 grams

Ingredients for Prep:

- Chicken broth (3 cups)
- Chicken breast (1)
- Avocado oil (2 tbsp.)
- Green onion (1)
- Celery stalk (1)
- Cilantro (.25 cup)
- Salt (to taste)
- Peeled zucchini (1)

Method of Prep:

1. Chop or dice the breast of the chicken. Pour the oil into a saucepan and cook the chicken until done. Pour in the broth and simmer.
2. Chop the celery and green onions and toss into the pan. Simmer for 3 to 4 more minutes.
3. Chop the cilantro and prepare the zucchini noodles. Use a

spiralizer or potato peeler to make the 'noodles.' Add to the pot.

4. Simmer for a few more minutes and season to your liking.

Tips for Meal Prep:

1. Store in a glass container in the fridge. It will remain tasty for 2 to 3 days.

Dinner: Chicken Nuggets

Yields Provided: 6
Total Carbohydrates: 2 grams

Ingredients for Prep:

- Cooked chicken (2 cups)
- Cream cheese (8 oz.)
- Egg (1)
- Garlic salt (1 tsp.)
- Almond flour (.25 cup)

Method of Prep:

1. Set the oven temperature to 350° Fahrenheit.
2. Lightly spritz a baking tray using a misting of cooking oil spray. You can also use a layer of parchment paper.
3. Shred the chicken using a food processor or by hand. (Try using a combination of dark and light meat.)
4. Combine the rest of the fixings and mix well.
5. Scoop the nugget mixture onto the baking tin.

6. Bake until firm and slightly browned (12 to 14 min.).

Tips for Meal Prep:

1. You will love this one. Just prepare the mixture and bake.

2. Store in the fridge for one or two days.

3. Freeze and enjoy at another time for lunch, dinner, or just a snack

Snack: Blueberry Cream Cheese Fat Bombs

Yields Provided: 12

Total Carbohydrates: 1 gram

Ingredients for Prep:

- Unchilled cream cheese (1.5 cups)

- Fresh/frozen berries (1 cup)
- Swerve (2-3 tbsp.)
- Vanilla extract (1 tbsp.)
- Coconut oil (.5 cup)

Method of Prep:

1. About 30 to 60 minutes before preparation time, place the cream cheese on the countertop to become room temperature.
2. Take the stems off the berries and rinse. Pour into a blender. Mix well until smooth.
3. Pour in the Swerve and extract. Blend in the oil and cream cheese.
4. Add the mixture to candy molds and freeze for approximately two hours.

Tips for Meal Prep:

1. Once the bombs are solid, just pop them out.
2. Store in freezer bags or another safe freezer container.

Day 3

Breakfast: Baked Green Eggs

Yields Provided: 6

Total Carbohydrates: 5 grams

Ingredients for Prep:

- Sun-dried tomatoes (.25 cup)
- Feta cheese (.5 cup)
- Oregano (.5 tsp.)
- Chopped kale (1 cup)
- Eggs (12)

Method of Prep:

1. Warm up the oven to reach 350° Fahrenheit.
2. Cover a baking tin with a layer of foil and a spritz of nonstick cooking spray.
3. Whisk the eggs and combine with the rest of the fixings. Stir well and pour into the pan to bake for approximately 25 minutes.
4. Transfer to the countertop to entirely cool and slice.

Tips for Meal Prep:

1. Place the package in the refrigerator to use within four to five days in an airtight container.

2. You can also place them into individual containers for convenience.

Lunch: Mushroom & Cauliflower Risotto

Yields Provided: 4

Total Carbohydrates: 4 grams

Ingredients for Prep:

- Cauliflower (1)
- Vegetable stock (1 cup)
- Chopped mushrooms (9 oz.)
- Butter (2 tbsp.)
- Coconut cream (1 cup)
- Pepper and Salt (to taste)

Method of Prep:

1. Pour the stock in a saucepan. Boil and set aside.
2. Prepare a skillet with butter and sauté the mushrooms until golden.
3. Grate and stir in the cauliflower and stock.

Tips for Meal Prep:

1. Simmer and add the cream, cooking until the cauliflower is al dente. Serve.
2. Let it cool before placing it in the fridge for storage.

Dinner: Chili Lime Cod

Yields Provided: 2

Total Carbohydrates: 3 grams

Ingredients for Prep:

- Wild-caught cod (10-12 oz.)
- Coconut flour (.33 cup)
- Egg (3)
- Lime (1)
- Garlic powder (1 tsp.)
- Cayenne pepper (.5 tsp.
- Salt (1 tsp.)
- Crushed red pepper (1 tsp.)

Method of Prep:

1. Heat the oven temperature to reach 400° Fahrenheit.
2. In separate dishes, whip the egg, and remove any lumps from the flour.
3. Let the fillet soak in the egg dish for one minute per side. Dip it into the flour dish, and then add it to a baking sheet.
4. Sprinkle the spices and drizzle the lime juice over the cod, and bake it for 10 to 12 minutes or when it easily flakes apart.

Tips for Meal Prep:

1. Cool the fish entirely once it is like you like it.
2. Use foil to keep the fish safe for a day. Freeze and enjoy later.

3. Once it is time to eat, just drizzle with some Sriracha if you wish, and enjoy.

Snack: Coffee Fat Bombs

Yields Provided: 15

Total Carbohydrates: 0 grams

Ingredients for Prep:

- Unchilled cream cheese (4.4 oz.)
- Powdered xylitol (2 tbsp.)
- Instant coffee (1 tbsp.)
- Unsweetened cocoa powder (1 tbsp.)
- Coconut oil (1 tbsp.)
- Unchilled butter (1 tbsp.)

Method of Prep:

1. Put the butter and cream cheese on the countertop for about an hour before it's time to begin.
2. Use a blender/food processor to blitz the xylitol and coffee into a fine powder. Add the hot water to form a pasty mix.
3. Blend in the cream cheese, cocoa powder, butter, and coconut oil.
4. Add to ice cube trays and freeze for a minimum of one to two hours.

Tips for Meal Prep:

1. Use zipper-type bags to keep them fresh in the freezer.

Day 4

Breakfast: Vegan Gingerbread Muffins

Yields Provided: 5
Total Carbohydrates: 2 grams

Ingredients for Prep:

- Non-dairy milk or water (.75 cup)
- Granulated sweetener - your preference (.25 cup)
- Ground flax seeds (.5 cup)
- Melted coconut oil or MCT oil (2 tbsp.)
- Vanilla extract (1 tsp.)
- Coconut flour (.5 cup)
- Freshly grated ginger (1.5 tsp.)
- Allspice (.25 tsp.)
- Cinnamon (1.5 tsp.)
- Ground cloves (.25 tsp.)
- Nutmeg (.25 tsp.)
- *Also Needed*: Standard-size muffin pan with paper liners

Method of Prep:

1. Heat the oven to 375° Fahrenheit.
2. Line five of the wells of the pan with a layer of parchment baking paper.

3. Combine the sweetener, flax seeds, oil, milk, and vanilla. Whisk well and set aside for approximately five minutes for the seeds to rest.
4. In another mixing container, whisk the remainder of the fixings until the mixture has thickened.
5. Empty the batter mixture into the muffin pan.
6. Bake until the tops are firm to the touch (30-35 min.).

Tips for Meal Prep:

1. Remove and transfer to the countertop to cool in the pan for at least 15 minutes.
2. Once cool, the muffins should easily pop out of the pan.
3. Place the container in the refrigerator for the best storage results.

Lunch: Spicy Beef Wraps

Yields Provided: 2

Total Carbohydrates: 4 grams

Ingredients for Prep:

- Coconut oil (1-2 tbsp.)
- Onion (¼ of 1)
- Ground beef (.66 lb.)
- Chopped cilantro (2 tbsp.)
- Red bell pepper (1)
- Fresh ginger (1 tsp.)
- Cumin (2 tsp.)

- Garlic cloves (4)
- Pepper and salt (as preferred)
- Large cabbage leaves (8)

Method of Prep:

1. Dice the bell pepper, onion, ginger, and garlic.
2. Heat a frying pan and pour in the oil.
3. Sauté the peppers, onions, and ground beef using medium heat.
4. When done, add the pepper, salt, cumin, ginger, cilantro, and garlic.

Tips for Meal Prep:

2. Cool the burger entirely and add to storage containers.
3. *Time to Eat:* Prepare a large pot of boiling water (3/4 full).
4. Cook each leaf for 20 seconds, plunge it in cold water and drain before placing it on your serving dish.
5. Reheat the beef mixture.
6. Scoop the mixture onto each leaf, fold, and enjoy.

Dinner: Asparagus & Chicken

Yields Provided: 8

Total Carbohydrates: 4 grams

Ingredients for Prep:

- Chicken breasts (4 lbs.)
- Avocado oil (1 tbsp.)

- Trimmed asparagus (1 lb.)
- Sun-dried tomatoes (4)
- Thick-cut bacon slices (4)
- Salt (1 tsp.)
- Pepper (.25 tsp.)
- Provolone cheese slices (8)
- *Also Needed*: 1 baking pan

Method of Prep:

1. Slice the chicken into eight thin pieces. Chop the bacon and tomatoes into one-inch pieces.
2. Warm up the oven temperature to 400° Fahrenheit.
3. Add the oil to the baking pan along with the chicken and asparagus. Top it off with the tomatoes and bacon. Sprinkle some pepper and salt for seasoning.
4. Bake until the chicken reaches 160° Fahrenheit internally - or about 25 minutes.
5. Toss in the asparagus and cheese.
6. Garnish with some bacon and tomatoes. Bake another three to four minutes until the cheese has melted.

Tips for Meal Prep:

1. Prepare the chicken and store it in the fridge for several days.
2. Place into plastic bins or freezer bags until ready to use.
3. Prepare the asparagus when ready to eat and combine with the cheese. Garnish and serve.

Snack: Mocha Cheesecake Bars

Yields Provided: 16

Total Carbohydrates: 3 grams

Ingredients for Prep:

- Vanilla extract (2 tsp.)
- Unsalted butter (6 tbsp.)
- Large eggs (3)
- Almond flour (1.5 cups)
- Hershey's Baking Cocoa (.5 cup)
- Erythritol (1 cup)
- Salt (.5 tsp.)
- Instant coffee (.5 tbsp.)
- Baking powder (1 tsp.)

The Cream Cheese Layer

- Erythritol (.5 cup)
- Softened cream cheese (1 lb.)
- Large egg (1)
- Vanilla extract (1 tsp.)
- Also Needed: 8 by 8-inch baking pan

Method of Prep:

1. Heat the oven to 350° Fahrenheit. Lightly grease or spray the pan with a spritz of oil cooking spray.
2. Combine the wet fixings, starting with the vanilla, butter, and eggs.

3. In another container, combine the dry fixings and whisk with the wet ones. Reserve .25 cup of the batter for later. Pour the mixture into the pan.

4. Mix the cream cheese (room temperature) with the rest of the ingredients for the second layer. Spread it on the layer of brownies.

5. Use the reserved batter as the last layer (will be thin). Bake it for 30 to 35 minutes.

Tips for Meal Prep:

1. When cooled, slice the cheesecake bars.

2. They will store in the refrigerator for several days or freeze in containers or freezer bags for extended use. Be sure to date and add the name of the contents.

Day 5

Breakfast: Egg Loaf

Yields Provided: 6

Total Carbohydrates: 0 grams

Ingredients for Prep:

- Eggs (6)
- Water for steaming (2 cups)
- Unsalted butter (for the bowl)

Method of Prep:

1. Prepare a heat-proof container with the butter.
2. Break the eggs into the dish (yolks intact) and cover with a sheet of aluminum foil. Set aside.
3. Add the trivet and two cups of water into the Instant Pot cooker. Arrange the bowl in the cooker.
4. Secure the lid and choose the manual pressure cooker function for 4 minutes using the high-temperature setting.
5. When the egg loaf is done, quick-release the pressure, and remove the pot.

Tips for Meal Prep:

1. Let it cool slightly and place in the refrigerator for up to four days.
2. Chop to your liking and mix with a little egg for salad or a little butter, pepper, and salt.

119

Lunch: BARBECUE Pork Loin

Yields Provided: 4

Total Carbohydrates: 3 grams

Ingredients for Prep:

- Pork loin (1 lb.)
- Tomato paste (4 tbsp.)
- Worcestershire sauce (1 tsp.)
- Avocado oil (2 tbsp.)
- Smoked paprika (.5 tsp.)
- Minced garlic (.5 tsp.
- Chopped onion (1 tbsp.)

Method of Prep:

1. Whisk the minced garlic, chopped onion, paprika, tomato paste, and Worcestershire sauce. Use the rub to prepare the pork and wrap it in foil.
2. Marinate the pork loin in the fridge for at least 1/2 hour for the spices to be absorbed.
3. Add the trivet to the Instant Pot and pour the water into the cooker. Secure the lid.
4. Set the timer for 60 minutes. Natural-release the pressure, when it's done.

Tips for Meal Prep:

1. Open the lid and let it cool slightly.
2. Let the pork completely cool.

3. Place into individual containers along with your favorite prepped veggie.
4. When it's time to eat, just thaw the container.
5. Warm it up and serve as desired.

Dinner: Short Ribs

Yields Provided: 4

Total Carbohydrates: 2.5 grams

Ingredients for Prep:

- Keto-friendly soy sauce (.25 cup)
- Beef short ribs (6 - 4 oz. each)
- Fish sauce (2 tbsp.)
- Rice vinegar (2 tbsp.)
- Red pepper flakes (.5 tsp.)
- Sesame seeds (.5 tsp.)
- Onion powder (.5 tsp.)
- Salt (1 tbsp.)
- Minced garlic (.5 tsp.)
- Ground ginger (1 tsp.)
- Cardamom (.25 tsp.)

Method of Prep:

1. Mix the fish sauce, vinegar, and alternative soy sauce.

2. Arrange the ribs in a dish with high sides. Add the sauce and marinate for up to 1 hour.
3. Combine all of the spices together. Take the ribs from the dish and sprinkle with the rub.
4. Warm up the grill (med-high) and cook for three to five minutes per side.

Tips for Meal Prep:

1. Put the ribs in a platter to cool.
2. Place in freezer bags or into plastic containers (4 portions) until it's time to serve and enjoy.

Snack: Delicious No-Bake Coconut Cookies

Yields Provided: 20

Total Carbohydrates: 0 grams

Ingredients for Prep:

- Melted coconut oil (1 cup)
- Monk fruit sweetened maple syrup or sweetener of choice (.5 cup)
- Shredded unsweetened coconut flakes (3 cups)

Method of Prep:

1. Prepare a cookie tray with a layer of parchment baking paper.
2. Combine all of the fixings. Run your hands through some water from the tap and shape the mixture into small balls. Arrange them in the pan around one to two inches apart.
3. Press them down to form a cookie and refrigerate until firm.

Tips for Meal Prep:

1. Prepare these into individual bags if you're an on-the-go kind of person.
2. The cookies will remain fresh covered for up to 7 days at room temperature.
3. Store in the fridge for up to a month.
4. If you choose, you can freeze the cookies for up to two months.

Day 6

Breakfast: Spinach Quiche

Yields Provided: 6

Total Carbohydrates: 0 grams

Ingredients for Prep:

- Chopped onion (1)
- Olive oil (1 tbsp.)
- Frozen & thawed spinach (10 oz. pkg.)
- Shredded muenster cheese (3 cups)
- Organic eggs – whisked (5)
- To Taste: Black pepper and salt
- Also Needed: 9-inch pie plate

Method of Prep:

1. Heat the oven at 350° Fahrenheit. Lightly grease the dish.
2. Use the medium temperature setting to warm a skillet with the oil.
3. Toss in the onion and sauté for 4-5 minutes. Raise the heat setting to med-high.
4. Fold in the spinach. Sauté for about two to three minutes or until the liquid is absorbed. Cool slightly.
5. Combine the rest of the fixings in a large mixing container, and toss with the cooled spinach. Dump into the prepared dish. Set a timer to bake for 30 minutes.

6. Take the quiche out of the oven to cool for at least ten minutes.

7. Slice into six wedges.

Tips for Meal Prep:

1. Add the cooled pieces into plastic baggies.

2. It will store in the fridge for two to four days.

3. To warm up, prepare in the microwave for one minute on the high setting before serving.

Lunch: BLT Salad in a Jar

Yields Provided: 8

Total Carbohydrates: 7 grams

Ingredients for Prep:

- Romaine lettuce (2 cups)
- Iceberg lettuce (2 cups)
- Chopped scallions (2)
- Diced tomatoes (2)

Method of Prep:

1. Combine all of the dressing components.

2. Slowly pour into the jars.

Tips for Meal Prep:

1. Tightly close each of the jars.

2. Place in the refrigerator and enjoy it within three days.

Dinner: Buffalo Chicken Burgers

Yields Provided: 2 burgers

Total Carbohydrates: 1 gram

Ingredients for Prep:

- Cooked chicken breasts (8 oz.)
- Room-temperature cream cheese (2 oz.)
- Shredded mozzarella cheese (.5 cup)
- Frank's Red-Hot Sauce or your choice (2 tbsp.)
- For Frying: Ghee or Coconut oil

Method of Prep:

1. Either chop or shred the prepared chicken and combine it with the rest of the fixings.
2. Place the fixings in the microwave for 15 to 20 seconds to help compact the ingredients. Form two medium patties and place them on a plate. Store in the freezer for about 15 minutes.
3. Heat a skillet using the high heat setting. Add the fat and patties. Prepare the burgers for 2 to 3 minutes per side.
4. Serve when crispy brown.

Tips for Meal Prep:

1. Prepare the chicken and shape the mixture into patties.
2. Freeze, or cook and freeze the patties.

Snack: Spice Cakes

Yields Provided: 12

Total Carbohydrates: 3 grams

Ingredients for Prep:

- Eggs (4)
- Baking powder (2 tsp.)
- Almond flour (2 cups)
- Salted butter (.5 cup)
- Nutmeg (.5 tsp.)
- Allspice (.5 tsp.)
- Ginger (.5 tsp.)
- Cinnamon (.5 tsp.)
- Erythritol (.75 cup)
- Ground cloves (.25 tsp.)
- Vanilla extract (1 tsp.)
- Water (5 tbsp.)

Method of Prep:

1. Set the temperature in the oven to 350° Fahrenheit. Prepare a cupcake tray with liners (12).
2. Mix the butter and erythritol with a hand mixer. Once it's smooth, combine with two eggs and the vanilla. Mix and stir in the remainder of the eggs, stirring until creamy.
3. Grind the clove to a fine powder and add with the rest of the spices. Whisk into the mixture. Stir in the baking powder and

almond flour. Blend in the water. When the batter is smooth, add to the prepared tin.

4. Bake for 15 minutes. Enjoy any time.

Tips for Meal Prep:

1. Cool thoroughly for the prep.

2. It's recommended to place them in the refrigerator for a few days or in the freezer to enjoy later.

Day 7

Breakfast: Morning Hot Pockets

Yields Provided: 2

Total Carbohydrates: 4 grams

Ingredients for Prep:

- Shredded mozzarella - not fresh (.75 cup)
- Almond flour (.33 cup)
- Scrambled eggs (2 large)
- Ghee or unsalted butter (2 tbsp.)
- Slices of bacon (3 cooked)

Method of Prep:

1. Cook the bacon and eggs. Prepare the dough by melting the shredded mozzarella (stovetop @ low heat or in a microwave). Fold in the almond flour. Stir until the dough is well-combined.
2. Arrange the bacon strips in a large pan. Add two to three tablespoons of water. Steam-fry using the med-high heat setting until the water starts to boil.
3. Lower the temperature setting to medium. Simmer until the water evaporates and bacon fat is rendered. Reduce the temperature setting to low. Continue cooking until the bacon is crispy.
4. Grease the same skillet with half of the butter/ghee and add both eggs. Simmer using the med-low temperature until done,

stirring continuously. Transfer to the countertop and add the rest of the butter.

5. Roll the dough out between two sheets of parchment paper (A silicone mat and silicone rolling pin are useful).
6. Place the bacon slices and scrambled eggs along the center.
7. Fold over and seal the dough. Make several holes for releasing the steam while baking.
8. Set the oven temperature to 400° Fahrenheit. Bake for about 20 minutes, or it is firm to the touch.

Tips for Meal Prep:

1. Transfer the hot pockets from the oven and let them cool.

2. Wrap in foil and toss into a freezer bag. Place on a baking tin to freeze solid.
3. *Note*: It is advisable to not leave in the refrigerator for storage.

Lunch: Greek Salad

Yields Provided: 1

Total Carbohydrates: 8 grams

Ingredients for Prep:

- Red onion (.25 cup)
- Tomato (.25 cup)
- Cucumber (.25 cup)
- Bell pepper (.25 cup)
- Feta cheese (.5 cup)
- Olive oil (3 tbsp.)

- Olives (1 tbsp.)
- Red wine vinegar (.5 tbsp.)

Method of Prep:

1. Dice the tomato, chop the olives, and slice the onion, cucumber, and pepper.
2. Combine the bell pepper, tomato, cucumber, crumbled feta cheese, and onion.

Tips for Meal Prep:

1. You can prepare the salad and pop into the fridge until time to eat.
2. Spritz using the oil and vinegar with a shake of salt and black pepper to your liking.
3. Toss until all of the ingredients are well mixed before serving.

Dinner: Buffalo Sloppy Joes

Yields Provided: 8

Total Carbohydrates: 2 grams

Ingredients for Prep:

- Coconut oil (1 tbsp.)
- Celery stalk (1 medium)
- Baby carrots (.25 cup)
- White onion (1 small)
- Garlic powder (1 tsp.)

- Red hot sauce (.5 cup)
- Mayonnaise (.25 cup)
- Ground chicken or turkey (1 lb.)

Method of Prep:

1. Pulse the baby carrots, celery stalk, and onion using a food processor. (You can also finely chop the veggies.)
2. Heat a skillet using the med-high temperature setting.
3. Pour in the coconut oil to heat. Toss in the minced veggies. Sauté for five to eight minutes. When it's ready, the carrots and onions will be fork tender.
4. Fold in the ground chicken. Continue to sauté until the chicken is thoroughly cooked.
5. Adjust the heat setting to low. Stir in the hot sauce and garlic powder.
6. Simmer for another five minutes. Remove from the burner.

Tips for Meal Prep:

1. Cool the chicken completely. Add to eight containers or freezer bags.
2. Store in the freezer until needed.
3. Defrost the portions needed to thaw.
4. Once it's dinner time, stir in the mayonnaise.
5. Note: Be sure the mixture is cool, or mayonnaise could curdle.
6. Spoon into your wrap or bun to serve.

Snack: Brownie Muffins

Yields Provided: 6

Total Carbohydrates: 4.4 grams

Ingredients for Prep:

- Salt (.5 tsp.)
- Flaxseed meal (1 cup)
- Cocoa powder (.25 cup)
- Cinnamon (1 tbsp.)
- Baking powder (.5 tbsp.)
- Coconut oil (2 tbsp.)
- Large egg (1)
- Vanilla extract (1 tsp.)
- Pumpkin puree (.5 cup)
- Sugar-free caramel syrup (.25 cup)
- Slivered almonds (.5 cup)
- Apple cider vinegar (1 tsp.)

Method of Prep:

1. Set the oven temperature to 350° Fahrenheit.
2. Use a deep mixing container—mix all of the fixings and stir well.
3. Use six paper liners in the muffin tin, and add ¼ cup of batter to each one.
4. Sprinkle several almonds on the tops, pressing gently.

5. Bake approximately 15 minutes or when the top is set.

Tips for Meal Prep:

1. Cut the brownies into six portions.

2. Store in plastic baggies for the fridge or freezer bags if you want to have them last longer than three to four days.

Week 2

Day 8

Breakfast: Avocado Eggs

Yields Provided: 2

Total Carbohydrates: 9 grams

Ingredients for Prep:

- Eggs (2)
- Avocado (1 ripened)
- Black pepper and salt (to your liking)
- Optional: Hot sauce

Method of Prep:

1. Warm up the oven until it reaches 425° Fahrenheit.
2. Slice the avocado in half and discard the pit. Use a metal scoop to remove about one to two tablespoons of the fleshy insides.
3. Arrange the halves in a small baking pan. Crack an egg into both halves and season with some pepper and salt.
4. Bake for 15-20 minutes.

Tips for Meal Prep:

1. Let the fixings cool and store for a day or so in the refrigerator to enjoy the next morning or for a snack.
2. If you want to spice it up a little, sprinkle in a portion of keto-friendly hot sauce on the second day.

Lunch: Tuna Salad

Yields Provided: 2

Total Carbohydrates: 6 grams

Ingredients for Prep:

- Fresh lemon juice (half of 1)
- Olive oil (1 tbsp.)
- Large chopped boiled eggs (2)
- Tuna packed in oil (2 cans - 15 oz. each)
- Cucumber (half of 1)
- Medium red onions (2)
- Cilantro (half of 1)
- Salt (1 tsp.)
- Mayonnaise (2 tbsp.)
- Dijon mustard (2 tsp.)

Method of Prep:

1. Whisk the oil, lemon juice, mayo, and mustard in a container.
2. Thinly slice the cucumber and onions.
3. Drain the tuna and combine it with the remainder of the ingredients in another bowl.
4. Place each container in the fridge.

Tips for Meal Prep:

1. Add the dressing to the salad and toss to serve.

Dinner: Bacon & Shrimp Risotto

Yields Provided: 2

Total Carbohydrates: 5 grams

Ingredients for Prep:

- Bacon (4 slices)
- Daikon winter radish (2 cups)
- Dry white wine (2 tbsp.)
- Chicken stock (.25 cup)
- Garlic (1 clove)
- Ground pepper (as desired)
- Chopped parsley (2 tbsp.)
- Cooked shrimp (4 oz.)

Method of Prep:

1. Peel and slice the radish, mince the garlic, and chop the bacon. Remove as much water as possible from the daikon once it's shredded.
2. On the stovetop, heat up a saucepan using the medium heat temperature setting. Toss in the bacon and fry until it's crispy. Leave the drippings in the pan and remove the bacon with a slotted spoon to drain.
3. Add the stock, wine, daikon, salt, pepper, and garlic into the pan. Simmer for 6-8 minutes until most of the liquid is absorbed.
4. Fold in the bacon (saving a few bits for the topping), and shrimp along with the parsley. Serve.

5. *Tip*: If you cannot find the daikon, just substitute it using shredded cauliflower.

Tips for Meal Prep:

1. This delicious treat can be cooled and stored in the fridge for a day or two.
2. Save the bacon and shrimp in separate containers until ready to serve.

Snack: Pumpkin Pie Cupcakes

Yields Provided: 6

Total Carbohydrates: 2.9 grams

Ingredients for Prep:

- Coconut flour (3 tbsp.)
- Baking powder (.25 tsp.)
- Salt (1 pinch)
- Baking soda (.25 tsp.)
- Pumpkin pie spice (1 tsp.)
- Large egg (1)
- Pumpkin puree (.75 cup)
- Swerve Granular/Swerve Brown (.33 cup)
- Heavy whipping cream (.25 cup)
- Vanilla (.5 tsp.)

Method of Prep:

1. Warm up the oven to 350° Fahrenheit. Prepare the baking pan.

2. Whisk the coconut flour with the baking powder, pumpkin pie spice, baking soda, and salt.

3. In another container, whisk the pumpkin puree with the cream, sweetener, vanilla, and egg until well combined.

4. Whisk in the dry fixings. If the batter is too thin, whisk in an additional tablespoon of the coconut flour.

5. Portion into the muffin tins. Bake until puffed and barely set (25 to 30 min.).

6. Transfer the pan to the countertop (in the pan) to cool. Store in the fridge for a minimum of one hour before it's time to serve.

7. Top it off using a generous helping of whipped cream.

8. Note: They will sink when you let them cook. It will be that much tastier with the serving of whipped cream!

Tips for Meal Prep:

1. After they are cooled, store in the fridge until you want one to eat.

2. Top it off using the whipped cream.

Day 9

Breakfast: Tomato & Cheese Frittata

Yields Provided: 2

Total Carbohydrates: 6 grams

Ingredients for Prep:

- Eggs (6)
- Soft cheese (3.5 oz./.66 cup)
- White onion (half of 1 medium)
- Halved cherry tomatoes (.66 cup)
- Chopped herbs - ex. Chives or basil (2 tbsp.)
- Ghee/butter (1 tbsp.)

Method of Prep:

1. Set the oven broiler temperature to 400° Fahrenheit.
2. Arrange the onions on a greased - hot iron skillet. Cook with either ghee or butter until lightly browned.
3. In another dish, crack the eggs and flavor with salt, pepper, or add some herbs of your choice. Whisk and add to the pan of onions, cooking until the edges begin to get crispy.
4. Top with cheese (such as feta), and a few diced tomatoes. Put the pan in the broiler for five to seven minutes or until done.
5. Enjoy piping hot or let cool down.
6. Note: You can purge all of the leftover veggies into the recipe (if you wish).

Tips for Meal Prep:

1. Divide into two equal portions. Place in separate containers until you're ready to enjoy a healthy breakfast.

2. Enjoy this readily prepared frittata that you can serve either hot or cold.

3. The deliciously prepared frittata will remain good to serve for up to five days. So, prep enough for several days.

Lunch: Beef & Pepperoni Pizza

Yields Provided: 4

Total Carbohydrates: 2 grams

Ingredients for Prep:

- Large eggs (2)
- Ground beef (20 oz.)
- Pepperoni slices (28)
- Pizza sauce (.5 cup)
- Shredded cheddar cheese (.5 cup)
- Mozzarella cheese (4 oz.)
- Also Needed: 1 Cast iron skillet

Method of Prep:

1. Combine the eggs, beef, and seasonings and place in the skillet to form the crust. Bake until the meat is done or about 15 minutes.

2. Take it out of the oven and add the sauce, cheese, and toppings. Place the pizza back in the oven for a few more minutes until the cheese has melted.

Tips for Meal Prep:

1. After it's cooled completely, slice the pizza into four equal portions for freezing.

2. You can also leave it whole and freeze. Add it to a freezer bag until it's time to serve and enjoy.

Dinner: Chicken & Green Beans

Yields Provided: 3
Total Carbohydrates: 4 grams

Ingredients for Prep:

- Olive oil (2 tbsp.)
- Trimmed green beans (1 cup)
- Whole chicken breasts (2)
- Halved cherry tomatoes (8)
- Italian seasoning (1 tbsp.)
- Salt and pepper (1 tsp.)

Method of Prep:

1. Heat a skillet using the medium heat temperature setting. Pour in the oil.
2. Sprinkle the chicken with pepper, salt, and Italian seasoning.

3. Arrange in the skillet and fry for 10 minutes on each side or until well done.

Tips for Meal Prep:

1. Let the chicken cool. Place in a container until it's time to use.

2. Add the tomatoes and beans. Simmer another 5 to 7 minutes and serve.

Snack: Amaretti Cookies

Yields Provided: 16

Total Carbohydrates: 1 gram

Ingredients for Prep:

- Coconut flour (2 tbsp.)
- Cinnamon (.25 tsp.)
- Salt (.5 tsp.)
- Erythritol (.5 cup)
- Baking powder (.5 tsp.)
- Almond flour (1 cup)
- Eggs (2)
- Almond extract (.5 tsp.)
- Vanilla extract (.5 tsp.)
- Coconut oil (4 tbsp.)
- Sugar-free jam (2 tbsp.)
- Shredded coconut (1 tbsp.)

Method of Prep:

1. Cover the tin with a sheet of paper.

2. Warm up the oven to reach 400° Fahrenheit.

3. Sift the flour and combine all of the dry fixings.

4. After combined, work in the wet ones. Shape into 16 cookies.

5. Make a dent in the center of each one. Bake for 15 to 17 minutes.

Tips for Meal Prep:

1. It is important to let them cool for a few minutes.

2. Add a dab of jam to each one and a sprinkle of coconut bits.

Day 10

Breakfast: Blueberry Pancake Bites

Yields Provided: 24 bites

Total Carbohydrates: 7.5 grams

Ingredients for Prep:

- Baking powder (1 tsp.)
- Water (.33 - .5 cup)
- Melted ghee (.25 cup)
- Coconut flour (.5 cup)
- Cinnamon (.5 tsp.)
- Salt (.5 tsp.)
- Eggs (4)
- Vanilla extract (.5 tsp.)
- Frozen blueberries (.5 cup)
- Also Needed: Muffin tray

Method of Prep:

1. Set the oven to reach 325° Fahrenheit. Use a spritz of coconut oil spray to grease 24 regular-sized muffin cups.
2. Combine the eggs, sweetener, and vanilla, mixing until well incorporated. Fold in the flour, melted ghee, baking powder, salt, and cinnamon. Stir in .33 cup of water to finish the batter.
3. The mixture should be thick. Next, divide the batter into the prepared cups with several berries in each one.

4. Bake until set (20 to 25 min.). Cool.

Tips for Meal Prep:

1. Store in an airtight container; preferable cool also.
2. It will be good for 8 to 10 days.
3. Freeze for 60 to 80 days.

Lunch: Buffalo Chicken Burgers

Yields Provided: 2 burgers

Total Carbohydrates: 1 gram

Ingredients for Prep:

- Chicken breasts (8 oz. cooked)
- Unchilled cream cheese (2 oz.)
- Shredded mozzarella cheese (.5 cup)
- Frank's Red-Hot Sauce or your preference (2 tbsp.)
- Coconut oil or ghee - for frying

Method of Prep:

1. Either chop or shred the prepared chicken and combine it with the rest of the fixings.
2. Place the fixings in the microwave for 15 to 20 seconds to help compact the ingredients. Form two medium patties and place them on a plate. Store in the freezer for about 15 minutes.
3. Heat a skillet using the high-temperature setting. Add the fat and patties. Prepare the burgers for 2 to 3 minutes per side.
4. Serve when crispy brown.

Tips for Meal Prep:

1. Prepare the chicken and mix to form patties.

2. Freeze, or cook and freeze the patties.

Dinner: Roasted Leg of Lamb

Yields Provided: 2

Total Carbohydrates: 1 gram

Ingredients for Prep:

- Reduced-sodium beef broth (.5 cup)

- Leg of lamb (2 lb.)

- Chopped garlic cloves (6)

- Fresh rosemary leaves (1 tbsp.)

- Black pepper (1 tsp.)

- Salt (2 tsp.)

Method of Prep:

1. Grease a baking pan and set the oven temperature to 400° Fahrenheit.

2. Arrange the lamb in the pan and add the broth and seasonings.

3. Roast 30 minutes and lower the heat to 350° Fahrenheit. Continue cooking for about one hour or until done.

4. Let the lamb stand about 20 minutes before slicing to serve.

5. Enjoy with some roasted brussels sprouts and extra rosemary for a tasty change of pace.

Tips for Meal Prep:

1. Cool and wrap any leftovers to use later.

2. Wrap well in plastic wrap and store in a freezer bag.

Day 11

Breakfast: Blueberry Essence

Yields Provided: 1

Total Carbohydrates: 3 grams

Ingredients for Prep:

- Blueberries (.25 cup)
- Coconut milk (1 cup)
- Optional: Whey protein powder (1 scoop)
- Vanilla Essence (1 tsp.)
- MCT Oil (1 tsp.)

Method of Prep:

1. For a quick burst of energy, add all of the fixings into a blender.
2. Puree until it reaches the desired consistency.

Tips for Meal Prep:

1. Store in the fridge until ready to enjoy.
2. Add several chunks of ice if you like.

Lunch: Italian Tomato Salad

Yields Provided: 2

Total Carbohydrates: 6 grams

Ingredients for Prep:

- Minced garlic clove (1)
- Freshly chopped basil (.25 cup)
- Balsamic vinegar (1 tbsp.)
- Olive oil (2 tbsp.)
- Pepper and salt (as desired)
- Sliced ripe tomatoes (2 medium)
- Fresh arugula (2 cups)
- Cubed mozzarella cheese (3 oz.)

Method of Prep:

1. Combine the oil, vinegar, basil, garlic, black pepper, and salt into a blender. Mix until it's creamy smooth.
2. Toss the rest of the fixings in a salad container.

Tips for Meal Prep:

1. Combine the salad and add the dressing mixture or add it to individual containers for an on-to-go method.
2. You can store this way for up to one day.

Dinner: Bacon Cheeseburger

Yields Provided: 12

Total Carbohydrates: 0.8 gram

Ingredients for Prep:

- Low-sodium bacon (16 oz. pkg.)
- Ground beef (3 lb.)
- Eggs (2)
- Medium chopped onion (half of 1)
- Shredded cheddar cheese (8 oz.)

Method of Prep:

1. Fry the bacon and chop to bits. Shred the cheese and dice the onion.
2. Combine the mixture with the beef and blend in the whisked eggs.
3. Prepare 24 burgers and grill them the way you like them. You can make a double-decker since they are small. If you like a larger burger, you can just make 12 burgers as a single-decker.

Tips for Meal Prep:

1. Let the cooked burgers cool.
2. Separate them into freezer bags for later use anytime you need a quick meal or snack.

Snack: Strawberry Cream Cheese Bites

Yields Provided: 12
Total Carbohydrates: 2 grams

Ingredients for Prep:

- Diced strawberries (1 cup)
- Vanilla extract (1 tsp.)
- Coconut oil (.25 cup)
- Unchilled cream cheese (.75 cup)
- Also Needed: 12-count muffin cup tin

Method of Prep:

1. Prepare a muffin tray with liners or grease with a spritz of cooking oil spray.
2. Toss the berries into the blender and mix until pureed.
3. Add in the rest of the fixings and mix until it's all smooth.
4. Scoop into the cups and freeze until solid (2 hrs.).

Tips for Meal Prep:

1. After they are frozen, your job is done.
2. Pop them out and store them in a freezer bag and enjoy any time you desire!

Day 12

Breakfast: Pancakes & Nuts

Yields Provided: 2

Total Carbohydrates: 9 grams

Ingredients for Prep:

- Almond flour (10 tbsp.)
- Baking soda (.5 tsp.)
- Ground cinnamon (1 tsp.)
- Large eggs (3)
- Almond milk (.25 cup)

Method of Prep:

1. Whisk all of the fixings in a container. Let the batter sit for 5-10 minutes so the flour will thicken.
2. Warm-up a greased skillet (low-medium).
3. Measure out .25 cup portions of the batter in the frying pan. Cook for two to three minutes per side.

Tips for Meal Prep:

1. Let the pancakes cool.
2. Pour the nuts into a baggie or plastic container. You can add the nuts in the containers together or separately.
3. You can store the pancakes for 5-7 days in the refrigerator.
4. *Time to Eat*: Heat the pancakes and serve with the prepared almond butter drizzle.

Lunch: Pulled Pork for Sandwiches

Yields Provided: 8

Total Carbohydrates: 2.2 grams

Ingredients for Prep:

- Boneless pork shoulder (3 lb.)
- Chopped white onion (1)
- Bay leaves (3)
- Smoked paprika (1 tsp.)
- Garlic powder (2 tsp.)
- Pink Himalayan salt (3 tsp.)

Method of Prep:

1. Warm a slow cooker using the low setting. Combine the paprika, salt, and garlic powder. Slice the pork into chunks and rub into the spices.
2. Chop the onion and toss it into the cooker along with the pork.
3. Add the bay leaves and close the lid. Cook for 10 hours on low.
4. When ready, shred, and let cool.

Tips for Meal Prep:

1. Add the shredded pork to individual bags for the freezer or into compartmentalized dishes to await a veggie.
2. Be sure to date the containers and label with the name of its content.

Dinner: Shrimp Alfredo

Yields Provided: 4

Total Carbohydrates: 6.5 grams

Ingredients for Prep:

- Raw shrimp (1 lb.)
- Salted butter (1 tbsp.)
- Cubed cream cheese (4 oz.)
- Whole milk (.5 cup)
- Salt (1 tsp.)
- Garlic powder (1 tbsp.)
- Dried basil (1 tsp.)
- Shredded parmesan cheese (.5 cup)
- Baby kale or spinach (.25 cup)
- Whole sun-dried tomatoes (5)

Method of Prep:

1. Warm the butter using the medium heat temperature setting in a skillet.
2. Toss in the shrimp and lower the heat to med-low. After 30 seconds, flip the shrimp and cook until slightly pink. Blend in the cream cheese.
3. Increase the heat and pour in the milk. Stir frequently.
4. Sprinkle with the salt, basil, and garlic. Empty the parmesan cheese in and mix well.
5. Simmer until the sauce has thickened. Cut the sun-dried tomatoes into strips.

6. Lastly, fold in the kale/spinach and dried tomatoes. Serve steaming hot.

Tips for Meal Prep:

1. Cool thoroughly and store in the fridge to enjoy in a day or two.

Snack: Coconut Macaroons

Yields Provided: 40 cookies/20 servings

Total Carbohydrates: 1 gram

Ingredients for Prep:

- Water (.33 cup)
- Low carb sweetener (.75 cup or less to taste)
- Sea salt (.25 tsp.)
- Sugar-free vanilla extract (.75 tsp.)
- Large eggs (2)
- Unsweetened shredded coconut (3-4 cups)
- *Optional*: Sugar-free chocolate chips
- Nonstick cooking oil spray

Method of Prep:

1. Set the oven to reach 350° Fahrenheit.
2. Lightly spray the cookie tin with the oil spray.

3. Combine the sweetener, water, vanilla extract, and salt in the pan.
4. Bring to a boil using the med-high temperature setting. Stir well and remove from the burner.
5. Combine the coconut flakes and egg in a food processor. Pour in the syrup and pulse. Scoop the dough onto the prepared cookie tin (one-inch apart).
6. Bake for eight minutes, rotating the cookie tin in the oven.
7. Continue baking until lightly browned or approximately four additional minutes.
8. Cool on the rack. Garnish with the melted chocolate as desired.

Tips for Meal Prep:

1. Note: Start with 3 cups of dried coconut shredded coconut.
2. You can add more as needed for the desired consistency, depending on taste preference.
3. After they are cooled, melt the chocolate, and serve.

Day 13

Breakfast: Cinnamon Smoothie

Yields Provided: 1

Total Carbohydrates: 5 grams

Ingredients for Prep:

- Cinnamon (.5 tsp.)
- Coconut milk (.5 cup)
- Water (.5 cup)
- Extra-virgin coconut oil/MCT oil (1 tbsp.)
- Ground chia seeds (1 tbsp.)
- Plain/vanilla whey protein (.25 cup)
- Optional: Stevia drops

Method of Prep:

1. Pour the milk, cinnamon, protein powder, and chia seeds in a blender.
2. Empty the coconut oil, ice, and water. Add a few drops of stevia to your liking.

Tips for Meal Prep:

1. Store in the fridge until ready to enjoy.
2. Add several chunks of ice if you like.

Lunch: Pita Pizza

Yields Provided: 2
Ingredients for Prep:

- Marinara sauce (.5 cup)
- Low-carb pita (1)
- Cheddar cheese (2 oz.)
- Pepperoni (14 slices)
- Roasted red peppers (1 oz.)

Method of Prep:

1. Set the oven to 450° Fahrenheit.
2. Slice the pita in half and put on a foil-lined baking tray. Rub with a bit of oil and toast for one to two minutes.
3. Pour the sauce over the bread, sprinkle with the cheese, and other toppings. Bake for an additional five minutes or until the cheese melts.

Tips for Meal Prep:

1. Remove the pizza from the oven and cool it thoroughly.
2. Store in the fridge for a couple of days.
3. Freeze to enjoy later using a freezer bag.

Dinner: Roasted Chicken & Tomatoes

Yields Provided: 2

Total Carbohydrates: 5 grams

Ingredients for Prep:

- Olive oil (1 tbsp.)
- Plum tomatoes (2 quartered)
- Chicken legs – bone-in with skin (2)
- Paprika (1 tsp.)
- Ground oregano (1 tsp.)
- Balsamic vinegar (1 tbsp.)

Method of Prep:

1. Set the oven temperature setting at 350° Fahrenheit. Grease a roasting pan with a spritz of oil.
2. Rinse and lightly dab the chicken legs dry with a paper towel. Prepare using the oil and vinegar over the skin. Season with the paprika and oregano.
3. Arrange the legs in the pan along with the tomatoes around the edges.
4. Cover with a layer of foil and bake one hour. Baste to prevent the chicken from drying out.
5. Discard the foil and increase the temperature to 425° Fahrenheit.
6. Bake 15 to 30 minutes more until browned and the juices run clear.
7. Serve with a side salad.

Tips for Meal Prep:

1. If you plan to use this for meal prep only, stop at step 4. Put in a zipper-type freezer bag.
2. Freeze the contents until another time. Proceed by baking.

Snack: Pecan Turtle Truffles

Yields Provided: 15

Total Carbohydrates: 1

Ingredients for Prep:

- Swerve or your preference (.33 cup)
- Melted butter (.5 cup)
- Vanilla extract (.25 tsp.)
- Caramel extract (.5 tsp.)
- Vanilla protein powder -o- carbs (.33 cup)
- Finely ground pecans (1 cup)
- 85% chocolate - Lindt or your choice (4 squares)
- Pecan halves (15)

Method of Prep:

1. Combine the sweetener, butter, vanilla extract, caramel extracts, finely ground pecans and protein powder in a mixing container.
2. Roll into 15 truffles and place them on a sheet of parchment or waxed paper.

3. Melt the chocolate in a baggie in the microwave for one minute. Snip the corner and squeeze the chocolate over the prepared truffles.
4. Garnish each truffle with a pecan half. Chill and enjoy any time.

Tips for Meal Prep:

1. Store in the fridge for the truffles to remain fresh.

Day 14

Breakfast: Bacon Cheese & Egg Cups

Yields Provided: 6

Total Carbohydrates: 1 gram

Ingredients for Prep:

- Large eggs (6)
- Bacon (6 strips)
- Cheese (.25 cup)
- Fresh spinach (1 handful)
- Pepper & Salt (as desired)

Method of Prep:

1. Warm up the oven to 400° Fahrenheit.
2. Prepare the bacon using medium heat on the stovetop. Place on towels to drain.
3. Grease 6 muffin tins with a spritz of oil.
4. Line each tin with a slice of bacon, pressing tightly to make a secure well for the eggs.
5. Drain and dry the spinach with a paper towel. Whisk the eggs and combine with the spinach.
6. Add the mixture to the prepared tins and sprinkle with cheese. Sprinkle with salt and pepper until it's like you like it.
7. Bake for 15 minutes. Remove when done and cool.

Tips for Meal Prep:

1. Prepare the cups and store them in airtight containers.

2. Reheat when ready to eat. It keeps in the fridge for 3-4 days.

Lunch: Caprese Salad

Yields Provided: 4
Total Carbohydrates: 5 grams

Ingredients for Prep:

- Grape tomatoes (3 cups)
- Peeled garlic cloves (4)
- Avocado oil (2 tbsp.)
- Mozzarella balls (19 pearl-sized)
- Fresh basil leaves (.25 cup)
- Baby spinach leaves (4 cups)
- Brine reserved from the cheese (1 tbsp.)
- Pesto (1 tbsp.)

Method of Prep:

1. Use a sheet of aluminum foil to cover a baking tray.

2. Set the oven temperature at 400° Fahrenheit.

3. Arrange the cloves and tomatoes on the baking pan. Drizzle with oil. Bake for 20 to 30 minutes until the tops are lightly browned.

4. Drain the liquid (saving one tablespoon) from the mozzarella. Mix the pesto with the brine.

5. Arrange the spinach in a large serving bowl. Transfer the tomatoes to the dish along with the roasted garlic.

Tips for Meal Prep:

1. Cool the ingredients thoroughly. Place in closed containers until time to use.
2. Drizzle with the pesto sauce. Garnish with the mozzarella balls and freshly torn basil leaves.

Dinner: Enchilada Skillet Dinner

Yields Provided: 4

Total Carbohydrates: 7 grams

Ingredients for Prep:

- Small yellow onion (1)
- Ground beef (1.5 lb.)
- Red enchilada sauce (.66 cup)
- Chopped green onions (8)
- Diced Roma tomatoes (2)
- Shredded cheddar cheese (4 oz.)
- Optional: Freshly chopped cilantro (as desired)

Method of Prep:

1. Use a wok or skillet to sauté the yellow onion and meat. Drain the juices and add the green onions, tomato, and enchilada sauce.

2. Once it starts to boil, simmer for about 5 minutes. Sprinkle with the salt and cheese. Continue cooking until the cheese has melted.

3. Stir in the cilantro. Serve over chopped lettuce and serving of sour cream. Add the extra carbs and enjoy.

Tips for Meal Prep:

1. If you have any leftovers, omit the cilantro, lettuce, and sour cream.

2. Wrap each portion tightly in plastic wrap and then in foil. Freeze.

3. Remove from the freezer and bake at 350° Fahrenheit until the cheese is melted, and the dinner is warmed.

Chapter 5: Meal Prep
for Kids

You will find these quick and easy recipes are easy to prepare in a short time!

Special Smoothie Options: Smoothies are included for children who don't always like veggies or some fruits. All that is required is a freezer-safe container or a push-up popsicle mold to make a special snack.

You can make a unique pack using 2 cups of fruit, 1 cup of optional greens, and a sliced banana. When you're ready to eat, place 1 cup of liquid into the blender (or half yogurt and half water), add the fruit, and mix. Day 2 and 4 are using the mango base with additional boosters to make it a meal.

Week 1

Day 1

Breakfast: Apple Banana Muffins

Yields Provided: 12
Ingredients for Prep:

- Baking powder (1 tsp.)
- Whole wheat flour (1.33 cups)
- Salt (.25 tsp.)
- Baking soda (.5 tsp.)
- Egg (1)
- Olive oil (3 tbsp.)
- Unsweetened applesauce (.5 cup)
- Vanilla extract (1 tsp.)
- Ripe bananas (1.5 cups)

Method of Prep:

1. Set the oven temperature at 375° Fahrenheit.
2. Heavily grease a muffin tin.
3. Whisk the egg and mashed bananas. Fold in everything except the flour.
4. Lastly, stir in the flour, using caution not to overmix.
5. Portion the batter into each of the tins.
6. Bake for approximately 20-25 minutes.

168

Tips for Meal Prep:

1. When the muffins are done, transfer them to the countertop, leaving them in the pan for about five minutes. Arrange them on a cooling rack to thoroughly cool before proceeding.
2. Place the muffins into a freezer bag or another type of storage container.
3. Store in the fridge for about five days or freeze for later.

Lunch: Cranberry Tuna Salad

Yields Provided: 5
Ingredients for Prep:

- White tuna - packed in water (16 oz. can)
- Low-fat mayo (3 tbsp.)
- Salt and pepper (as desired)
- Light sour cream (3 tbsp.)
- Celery (.5 cup)
- Red onion (.25 cup)
- Lemon juice (1 tbsp.)
- Dried cranberries (.25 cup)
- Apple (1 diced)

Method of Prep:

1. Drain the tuna.
2. Chop the celery and mince the onion. Measure out the rest of the fixings.

3. Combine and mix all of the ingredients.

Tips for Meal Prep:

1. Place a cover on the salad.
2. Store in the refrigerator to enjoy for breakfast or brunch.

Dinner: Hawaiian Chicken Kebabs

Yields Provided: 8

Ingredients for Prep:

- Chicken breasts (1 lb.)
- Yellow & Red bell pepper (half of 1 each)
- Purple or red onion (half of 1)
- Pineapple chunks (1.5 cups)
- Pineapple (.5 cup)
- Orange (.5 cup)
- Teriyaki sauce (.25 cup)
- Salt (1 tsp.)
- Ginger (.5 tsp.)
- Onion powder (1 tsp.)
- Black pepper (1 tsp.)
- Garlic powder (1 tsp.)

Method of Prep:

1. Soak the wooden skewers in water for one hour.
2. Slice the peppers and onions into 1-inch pieces.

3. Prepare the marinade (orange juice, teriyaki, and pineapple). Marinate the chicken for one to two hours.
4. Prepare the skewers. Alternate the chicken and veggies (2 to 3 of each veggie and 3 to 4 pieces of meat).
5. Combine the spices in a small container (black pepper, salt, ginger, onion, and garlic powder). Sprinkle over the kebabs.
6. Cook on the grill (med. flame) 5 to 6 minutes on each side.
7. Take the goodies from the skewers and enjoy the feast.

Tips for Meal Prep:

1) You have two options.

2) *Option 1:* Go through step 3 to prepare the skewers,

3) Cover the skewers with foil and cook the following day.

4) Continue the recipe.

5) *Option 2:* Prepare and cook the kebabs. Remove from the skewers if desired.

6) Store in the fridge. For best results, enjoy the next day or two

Snack: Apple Pie Cookies

Yields Provided: 24

Ingredients for Prep:

- Sugar-free yellow cake mix (1 box)
- Applesauce - unsweetened (.5 cup)
- Eggs (2)
- Diced apples (1 cup)
- Cinnamon (.5 tsp.)

Method of Prep:

1. Warm the oven temperature at 375° Fahrenheit.

2. Prepare a baking tin with a silicone baking mat or a piece of parchment paper.
3. Combine all of the fixings, mixing well. Scoop out and make one-inch balls. Arrange in the pan about two inches apart.
4. Bake until they're done to your liking or about 10 to 12 minutes.

Tips for Meal Prep:

1. Prepare the cookies and let them cool.

2. Store in an airtight container until desired.

Day 2

Breakfast: Mango Smoothie Base & Oats

Yields Provided: 1

Ingredients for Prep:

- Frozen mango chunks (1.5 cups)
- Liquid: Coconut water, dairy milk, almond milk, or water (1 to 1.5 cups)
- Optional: Chia seeds (1 tbsp.)

Method of Prep:

1. Combine the fixings in a blender until creamy smooth.
2. Use these optional nutrient boosters as desired:
   a. Ground flax (1 tbsp.)
   b. Hemp seeds (1 tbsp.)
   c. Coconut oil (1 tbsp.)
   d. Avocado (¼ of 1)
   e. Goji berries (1 tbsp.)
3. Add .25 cup of oatmeal to finish the smoothie with the boosters and base.

Tips for Meal Prep:

1. Freeze the prepared smoothie.
2. The night before, you can place the container in the fridge to defrost.

3. You can also put it into a lunchbox with a straw to be defrosted for lunches or a quick treat.

Lunch: *Buffalo Chicken Tenders*

Yields Provided: 6

Ingredients for Prep:

- Chicken breasts (1 lb.)
- Panko breadcrumbs (1 cup)
- Flour (.25 cup)
- Eggs (3)
- Red hot sauce (.33 cup)
- Brown sugar (.5 cup)
- Garlic powder (.5 tsp.)
- Water (3 tbsp.)

Method of Prep:

1. Set the oven setting to 425° Fahrenheit. Lightly prepare a baking sheet with a spritz of cooking oil.
2. Slice the chicken into strips and pound into a ½-inch thickness for even cooking and tenderness. Toss into a zipper-type baggie along with the flour. Shake well.
3. Add the breadcrumbs in one dish and the eggs in another.
4. Place the sliced pieces of chicken in with the eggs, then the breadcrumbs. Arrange on the prepared pan. Lightly spray with a misting of cooking oil.
5. Bake 20 minutes.
6. Prepare the sauce with the rest of the fixings in a small saucepan.

Tips for Meal Prep:

Let the chicken strips and sauce cool completely.

1. Wrap the chicken and place it in an airtight container. Add the sauce to another dish and store both in the fridge.
2. When ready to eat, warm the fixings.
3. Prepare any veggies you want as a side dish.
4. Enjoy the tenders with the sauce and your favorite side of veggies.

Dinner: Chili & Mac 'n' Cheese

Yields Provided: 6

Ingredients for Prep:

- Cooked ground beef (.5 lb.)
- Box - your favorite Mac 'n' cheese (1)
- Red kidney beans (1 cup)
- Green, canned chili (1 can - 4 oz.)
- Grated cheddar cheese (.25 cup)
- Chili powder (2 tsp.)

Method of Prep:

1. Prepare the box of macaroni and cheese.
2. Cook the ground beef until done.
3. Combine all of the fixings and serve.

Tips for Meal Prep:

1. You can divide the leftovers into individual containers to use over the next few days or leave it in one bowl for the next dining meal.

Snack: *Pumpkin Cupcakes*

Yields Provided: 24

Ingredients for Prep:

*   100% Pumpkin puree (15 oz. can)
*   Water (1 cup)
*   Sugar-free yellow cake mix (1 box)
*   Also Needed: 2 dozen muffin tins with liners

Method of Prep:

1. Set the oven temperature setting to 350° Fahrenheit.
2. Prepare the muffin tins.
3. Combine all of the fixings. Pour into the prepared cupcake holders
4. Bake until lightly browned or about 22 minutes.

Tips for Meal Prep:

1. Transfer the cupcakes to the countertop and cool on a rack.
2. When they are fully cooled, store in the fridge.
3. Freeze to use anytime.

Day 3

Breakfast: Banana Almond Pancakes

Yields Provided: 4

Ingredients for Prep:

- Banana (half of 1)
- Large egg (1)
- Cinnamon (.125 tsp.)
- Ground almond flour (1 tsp.)
- Olive oil (2 tbsp.)

Method of Prep:

1. Whisk the egg and mix with the cinnamon and flour.
2. Mash the banana using a fork and combine it with the rest of the fixings.
3. Warm the oil in a skillet. Pour the batter to the pan. Flip once during the cooking process.
4. You'll have delicious pancakes in 20 minutes from start to finish.

Tips for Meal Prep:

1. Cool thoroughly and store in freezer bags according to how many servings you will use at one time.
2. Place the frozen pancakes onto a microwave-safe dish.

3. Microwave using the high setting for 1- 1.5 minutes.
4. Garnish with your favorite toppings.

Lunch: Colored Iceberg Salad

Yields Provided: 4

Ingredients for Prep:

- Iceberg lettuce (1 head)
- Bacon (6 slices)
- Sliced green onions (2)
- Sliced radishes (6)
- Shredded carrots (3)
- Red vinegar (.25 cup)
- Minced cloves of garlic (3)
- Olive oil (.25 cup)
- Black pepper (1 pinch)

Method of Prep:

1. Prepare the bacon in a skillet until crispy. Arrange on paper towels to drain the grease.
2. Use a large-sized salad bowl or individual dishes to prepare the salad.
3. Combine the torn lettuce leaves with the black pepper, garlic, carrots, green onions, bacon, oil, vinegar, and radishes.

Tips for Meal Prep:

1. This is a great one for the kids to get healthy veggies by using delightful colors.
2. Cover with plastic lids or plastic wrap until time for lunch.

Dinner: Delicious Meatloaf

Yields Provided: 6

Ingredients for Prep:

- 93% lean ground beef (2 lb.)
- Almond flour (2 tbsp.)
- Coconut flour (2 tbsp.)
- Garlic powder (1 tsp.)
- Onion powder (1 tsp.)
- Black pepper (.25 tsp.)
- Salt (1 tsp.)
- Egg (1)
- Worcestershire sauce (1 tbsp.)
- Regular or almond milk (1 tbsp.)
- BARBECUE sauce (.5 cup + more for serving)
- Also Needed: 9x5 loaf pan

Method of Prep:

1. Warm the oven at 350° Fahrenheit. Prepare the pan in

2. Note: You can also place the loaf pan on a baking tray to prevent spillovers in the oven.
3. Whisk the salt, pepper, garlic powder, and both flours in a mixing container.
4. In another container, mix the egg, barbecue sauce, milk, Worcestershire sauce, and ground beef.
5. Combine everything and place it in the pan.
6. Bake for 45-65 minutes (depending on its thickness).
7. After it has baked for about halfway (20 min.), add barbecue sauce to the top and continue baking until the internal temperature reaches 155 Fahrenheit.
8. Serve and prepare the rest for freezing.

Tips for Meal Prep:

1. Cool thoroughly and place in a storage container and freeze for another time.

Snack: Whole Grain Banana Bread

Yields Provided: 14

Ingredients for Prep:

- Millet flour (.5 cup)
- Quinoa flour (.5 cup)
- Rice flour (.5 cup)
- Tapioca flour (.5 cup)
- Amaranth flour - brown (.5 cup)
- Baking powder (.5 tsp.)
- Salt (.125 cup)
- Baking soda (1 tsp.)

- Grapeseed oil (2 tbsp.)
- Raw sugar (.5 cup)
- Mashed banana (2 cups)
- Egg whites (.75 cup)
- Also Needed: 1 loaf pan - 5 by 9-inch

Method of Prep:

1. Lightly spray the loaf pan with a spritz of cooking oil. Sprinkle with a little flour and set aside.
2. Heat the oven temperature setting to reach 350° Fahrenheit.
3. Combine each of the dry fixings in a large mixing container - omitting the sugar.
4. Whisk the egg, mashed banana, oil, and sugar in another bowl. Thoroughly mix, adding the fixings to the loaf pan.
5. Bake for 50-60 minutes.

Tips for Meal Prep:

1. Transfer the loaf pan to the countertop to cool.

2. When cooled, place the entire loaf in a freezer bag. You can also slice and store the bread in the fridge or freezer for individual servings.

Day 4

Breakfast: Mango Smoothie Base & Greens

Yields Provided: 1

Ingredients for Prep:

- Liquid: Almond milk, coconut water, dairy milk, or water (1 to 1.5 cups)
- Frozen mango chunks (1.5 cups)
- Optional: Chia seeds (1 tbsp.)

Method of Prep:

1. Combine the smoothie fixings in a blender until creamy.
2. Use these optional nutrient boosters as desired:
   a. Hemp seeds (1 tbsp.)
   b. Ground flax (1 tbsp.)
   c. Avocado (¼ of 1)
   d. Coconut oil (1 tbsp.)
   e. Goji berries (1 tbsp.)

Tips for Meal Prep:

1. Add a scoop of protein powder with the boosters and base to finish the smoothie. Jazz it up to suit your youngster.
2. Store the smoothie in the freezer.
3. The night before, place the container in the fridge to defrost.

4. You can also add it to a lunchbox with a straw to be defrosted for a quick treat.

Lunch: Tuna Melt

Yields Provided: 4

Ingredients for Prep:

- Chunk white tuna – packed in water (12 oz. can)
- Coleslaw – packaged or homemade (1.5 cups)
- Green onion chopped (3 tbsp.)
- Mayonnaise – fat-free (3 tbsp.)
- Dijon-style mustard (1 tbsp.)
- English muffins – split in half (4)
- Cheddar cheese, reduced-fat – shredded (.33 cup)

Method of Prep:

1. Warm up the barbecue grill, broiler, or toaster oven.
2. Mix the drained tuna, coleslaw, and onions.
3. Whisk the mayo and mustard. Mix well.
4. Stir in the tuna mixture and combine well.

Tips for Meal Prep:

1. Place a lid on the tuna dish and store it in the fridge.
2. When it's mealtime, cut the muffins into halves.
3. Spread the tuna mixture on the muffins and arrange on a broiler pan.

4. Place on the rack about four inches from the burner. Broil for 3-4 minutes.
5. Toss the cheese over the top to melt and broil for about one to two minutes.

Dinner: Loaded Bacon Mac & Cheese

Yields Provided: 4-6

Ingredients for Prep:

- Mac 'n' Cheese (1 box)
- Cooked bacon (1 cup)
- Grated Monterey Jack cheese (.25 cup)
- Grated mozzarella cheese (.25 cup)

Method of Prep:

1. Make the macaroni and cheese and prepare the bacon.
2. Combine all of the fixings to serve now.
3. Note: It is noted by some that the powdered cheese is not as tasty as the creamy options.

Tips for Meal Prep:

1. You can prepare the mac 'n' cheese and bacon but store them individually until time to serve or use.
2. It will not store well in the freezer but should be good for several days.

Snack: Banana Oatmeal Cookies

Yields Provided: 36 cookies

Ingredients for Prep:

- All-purpose flour (1.5 cups)
- Ground nutmeg (.25 tsp.)
- Salt (.25 tsp.)
- Baking soda (1 tsp.)
- Butter (.25 cup or .5 stick)
- Ripened mashed bananas (2-3 medium or 1 cup)
- Brown sugar - Firmly packed (1 cup)
- Egg (1 large)
- Applesauce (.5 cup)
- Vanilla (1 tsp.)
- Old-fashioned rolled oats (2.5 cups)
- *Optional:* Chopped nuts (1 cup)

Method of Prep:

1. Combine the nutmeg, salt, flour, and baking soda. Set aside for now.
2. Beat the butter and brown sugar in a large mixing container using the medium setting of an electric mixer until well blended.

Fold in and mix the vanilla, egg, applesauce, and mashed bananas.

3. Using the low-speed setting, combine with the flour until just combined. Stir in the oats and nuts. Mix until just incorporated.

4. Place the container in the fridge for 10 minutes or up to six hours.

5. When ready to bake, just warm up the oven to 350° Fahrenheit.

6. Prepare the baking pan with some cooking spray. (Tip: Bake on a parchment paper-lined pan or silicone liner for the best results.)

7. Spoon the dough onto the tins about three inches apart and bake 15 to 17 minutes. Remove while they're still soft on the top.

8. Let them rest in the pan a few minutes before moving with a spatula to a cooling rack.

Tips for Meal Prep:

1. Make this batch any time your snacks are getting low.

2. Once they are moved to the cooling rack; cool thoroughly.

3. Store in a closed container to use later.

Day 5

Breakfast: 2-Ingredient Pancakes

Yields Provided: 12-inch pancake (1)

Ingredients for Prep:

- Eggs (2)
- Ripe banana (1)
- Cinnamon
- Vanilla

Method of Prep:

1. Mash the bananas and whisk two eggs.
2. Use some cooking spray to grease the skillet/griddle. Scrape in the batter.
3. No syrup is needed for these tasty treats. Add a little cinnamon or vanilla if desired.

Tips for Meal Prep:

1. Prepare these deliciously quick and easy pancakes.
2. You can do this the night or day before you want them.
3. Either freeze or let it chill in the fridge for a day.

Lunch: Pear & Banana Breakfast Salad

Yields Provided: 2

Ingredients for Prep:

- Asian pear (1)
- Banana (1)
- Lime (half of 1)
- Cinnamon powder (5 tsp.)
- Toasted pepitas (2 oz.)

Method of Prep:

1. Core and cube the pear. Peel and slice the banana. Toast the pepitas. Juice the lime.
2. Combine all of the fixings into two dishes.

Tips for Meal Prep:

1. Store in the fridge until time to serve.
2. Toss well and serve it onto serving platters for breakfast.

Dinner: Chicken Fried Rice

Yields Provided: 6

Ingredients for Prep:

- Cooking oil spray (2 squirts)
- Scallions (.5 cup)
- Carrots (.5 cup)
- Frozen-thawed green peas (.5 cup)
- Cooked regular or instant long-grain brown rice (2 cups)
- Garlic cloves (2)
- Egg whites (4 large)
- Soy sauce - low-sodium (3 tbsp.)
- Chicken breasts (12 oz.- ½-inch cubes)

Method of Prep:

1. Chop the green and white parts of the scallion and dice the carrots and garlic. Remove all of the skin and bones from the chicken. Scramble or cook the egg to your liking for the mixture.
2. Prepare a skillet with the spray and set the temperature to med-high.
3. Toss in the garlic and scallions to sauté for two minutes.
4. Stir in the carrots and chicken and sauté about five more minutes.
5. Fold in the prepared brown rice, cooked egg whites, peas, and soy. Sauté for about one minute.
6. Let it cool entirely.

Tips for Meal Prep:

1. Your kids will love this.

2. Cooked chicken can stay in the fridge for <u>3-4 days</u>. After that, you'll need to toss it. You can also freeze it for longer prep times.

- *Option 1:* Heat the rice using the microwave. Add a few tablespoons of broth or water per one cup of rice. Cover to create a steaming effect as it reheats.
- *Option 2:* Stir-fry the rice: Use a sauté pan or large wok to heat canola or peanut oil using the high-temperature setting.

Snack: Apples & Dip

Yields Provided: 4

Ingredients for Prep:

- Chopped peanuts (2 tbsp.)
- Unchilled fat-free cream cheese (8 oz.)
- Vanilla (1.5 tsp.)
- Brown sugar (2 tbsp.)
- Orange juice (.5 cup)
- Apples (8 small or 4 medium)

Method of Prep:

1. Chop the peanuts well and place them in a storage container.
2. Take the cream cheese out of the fridge for about 5 minutes to soften at room temperature.
3. Combine the cream cheese with vanilla and brown sugar until smooth.

Tips for Meal Prep:

1. Store the mixture in the fridge.

2. Time to Eat: Remove the core from the apples and slice.

3. Fold the nuts into the cream cheese mixture.

4. Serve the dip with sliced apples and a drizzle of juice on top.

Day 6

Breakfast: Mango Smoothie Base & Tofu

Yields Provided: 1

Ingredients for Prep:

- Frozen mango chunks (1.5 cups)
- Liquid: Dairy milk, almond milk, coconut water, or water (1 to 1.5 cups)
- Optional: Chia seeds (1 tbsp.)

Method of Prep:

1. Combine the fixings in a blender until smooth. Store in the freezer until time to use.
2. Use these optional nutrient boosters as desired
   a. Coconut oil (1 tbsp.)
   b. Hemp seeds (1 tbsp.)
   c. Avocado (¼ of 1)
   d. Goji berries (1 tbsp.)
   e. Ground flax (1 tbsp.)
3. Add 3 ounces of tofu to the chosen fixings and mix until it's the desired consistency.

Tips for Meal Prep:

1. Freeze the prepared smoothie in a freezer bag or freezer-safe jar.

2. The night before, you can put the container in the fridge to defrost.
3. Add the frozen smoothie into a lunchbox with a straw. It will defrost by lunchtime.

Lunch: Chicken Salad

Yields Provided: 6

Ingredients for Prep:

- Shredded chicken breast (2 cups)
- Mayonnaise (1 tbsp.)
- Nonfat sour cream (.25 cup)
- Nonfat Greek yogurt (.5 cup)
- Bell pepper (2 tbsp.)
- Gala apple (half of 1)
- Garlic powder (1 tsp.)
- Dill pickle relish (1 tsp.)
- Onion powder (1 tsp.)
- Freshly cracked black pepper (.5 tsp.)
- Paprika (.5 tsp.)
- Salt (.5 tsp.)

Method of Prep:

1. Combine all of the fixings with a sprinkle of the pepper and salt as desired.

Tips for Meal Prep:

1. Prepare the salad and store in the refrigerator using a glass container with a lid.
2. Serve it any time for a snack or lunch on your choice of bread, veggies, or crackers.

Dinner: Cheesy Beef Egg Rolls

Yields Provided: 8

Ingredients for Prep:

- Egg roll wrappers (8)
- Cheddar cheese stick - cut in half (4)
- Cooked roast beef - chopped (2 cups)
- Creamy style horseradish (.25 cup)
- Frying oil

Method of Prep:

1. Warm a deep fryer or oil in a pan to approximately 350° Fahrenheit. Prepare an egg roll wrapper, placed in a diamond shape.
2. Place a small amount of horseradish sauce in the center. Lay down ¼ cup of shredded beef. Arrange a cheese stick (half) over the beef and fold in the two sides. Take the bottom point and fold it like an envelope.
3. Wet the top side of the wrapper with water along the edge.
4. Roll from the bottom to form the stick into the shape of a cigar.

Tips for Meal Prep:

2. Cool and use within a day or so. You can also freeze and prepare later.
3. Bake for 12-15 minutes at 400° Fahrenheit.

Snack: Banana Roll-Ups

Yields Provided: 2

Ingredients for Prep:

- Whole wheat bread (1 slice)
- Medium peeled banana (.5 of 1)
- Salt-free chunky peanut butter (1.5 tsp.)

Method of Prep:

1. Use a rolling pin to flatten the bread.
2. Apply the peanut butter to one side of the bread. Add the banana.
3. Roll it up and slice into three to four segments.

Tips for Meal Prep:

1. After you roll up the bananas, just store them in the fridge in a closed container.
2. Enjoy anytime.

Day 7

Breakfast: Berry Monkey Bread Cinnamon Rolls

Yields Provided: 6

Ingredients for Prep:

- Refrigerated orange rolls (2 cans)
- Berries (2 pints)
- Optional: Softened cream cheese (3 oz.)
- Basil (3 tbsp.)

Method of Prep:

1. Chop the orange rolls and scatter them onto the bottom of a greased bundt pan.
2. Sprinkle with half of the berries, and repeat.
3. You can also press a dollop or two of cream cheese in the dough and berries with a sprinkle of basil.
4. Bake for 20 minutes. Wait a few minutes and turn it over and out.
5. Drizzle with the orange spread if you are using it the same day.

Tips for Meal Prep:

1. If these are for prep, wait on adding the spread until it's time to eat.
2. Leave the rinsed berries in a container also until mealtime.

Lunch: Strawberry Sandwiches

Yields Provided: 4

Ingredients for Prep:

- Stevia or favorite sweetener (1 tbsp.)
- Softened cream cheese - low-fat (8 oz.)
- Grated lemon zest (1 tsp.)
- Whole wheat English muffins (4 toasted)
- Sliced strawberries (2 cups)

Method of Prep:

1. Slice the strawberries. Set the low-fat cheese out to soften. Grate the lemon.
2. Use a food processor and combine the stevia, cream cheese, and lemon zest.

Tips for Meal Prep:

1. Once combined, cover with foil or plastic wrap.
2. When it's breakfast time, toast the muffins.
3. Use a butter knife to spread the cheese mixture onto the toasted muffin halves. Add the berries and serve.

Dinner: Air-Fried Parmesan Chicken

Yields Provided: 4

Ingredients for Prep:

- Chicken breasts (2)
- Reduced-fat mozzarella cheese (6 tbsp.)
- Seasoned breadcrumbs (6 tbsp.)
- Olive oil/melted butter (1 tbsp.)
- Marinara sauce (.5 cup)
- Grated parmesan cheese (2 tbsp.)
- Cooking spray (as needed)

Method of Prep:

1. Warm the Air Fryer at 360° Fahrenheit for nine minutes. Chop the chicken in half to make four servings.
2. Combine the parmesan and breadcrumbs in one dish. In another dish, melt the butter. Lightly brush the butter over the chicken and dip in the mixture.
3. When the fryer is hot, just add two of the pieces in the basket and spray a layer of oil over the top of the chicken. Cook for six minutes and flip each piece. Chop each piece with 1 tablespoon of sauce and 1.5 tablespoons of the cheese.
4. Cook three more minutes and set aside to prepare the other two.
5. Repeat the process. Serve and enjoy or store for later.

Tips for Meal Prep:

1. Prepare the chicken and let it cool.
2. Store in a wrapper of foil.
3. Serve for one to two days and freeze at that time for the best results.

Snack: Baked Pumpkin Pie Egg Roll

Yields Provided: 4

Ingredients for Prep:

- Pumpkin puree (.75 cup)
- Greek yogurt (.25 cup)
- Pumpkin pie spice (1 tsp.)
- Brown sugar (2 tbsp.)
- Egg roll wrappers (4)
- Cooking spray
- Cinnamon
- Fat-free Cool-Whip

Method of Prep:

1. Set the oven temperature to 350° Fahrenheit.
2. Whisk the pie spice, brown sugar, pumpkin, and yogurt – mixing well.
3. Spread about ¼ cup of the pumpkin mixture in the middle of the wrapper.
4. Fold the bottom corner and run a line of water across the rest of the sides to act as glue. Prepare and close each of the rolls.
5. Arrange the rolls on a greased baking sheet, pizza stone, or parchment-lined pan.
6. Give the tops a spray of the cooking oil and bake until crispy (11 to 13 min.).

Tips for Meal Prep:

1. This super easy recipe is great anytime.
2. Let the cookies cool and store in an airtight cookie jar for later.

Week 2

Day 8

Breakfast: Overnight Oats with Bananas & Walnuts

Yields Provided: 1

Ingredients for Prep:

- Ground cinnamon (.25 tsp.)
- Low-fat or nonfat milk (.5 cup)
- Rolled oats (.5 cup)
- Mashed ripe banana (1)
- Chopped walnuts (2 tbsp.)
- Optional: Sweetener of choice as desired
- Also Needed: 1 mason jar

Method of Prep:

1. Fill the mason jar with the oats, cinnamon, banana, and walnuts.
2. Pour in the milk and place it in the fridge.

Tips for Meal Prep:

1. Let it sit overnight while you sleep or about 8 hours.
2. When serving, add more milk as desired.

Lunch: Heirloom Tomato & Cucumber Toast

Yields Provided: 1

Ingredients for Prep:

- Persian cucumber (1)
- Heirloom tomato (1 small)
- Olive oil (1 tsp.)
- Dried oregano (1 pinch)
- Black pepper and salt (to your liking)

For Serving:

- Low-fat whipped cream cheese (2 tsp.)
- Whole Grain Crispbread or another favorite (2 pieces)
- Balsamic glaze (1 tsp.)

Method of Prep:

1. Dice the cucumber and tomato.
2. Combine all of the fixings except for the cream cheese and glaze.

Tips for Meal Prep:

1. Store the prepared mixture in a closed container until ready to serve.
2. Smear the cheese on the bread, and add the mixture (step 1).
3. Top it off with the balsamic glaze and serve.
4. Note: Increase the ingredient portions to suit your needs.

Dinner: Drumsticks with Apple Glaze

Yields Provided: 4

Ingredients for Prep:

- Apples (2)
- Molasses (.25 cup)
- Ground ginger (.5 tsp.)
- Apple butter (.25 cup)
- Salt (.5 tsp.)
- Freshly cracked black pepper (.25 tsp.)
- Lemon - juiced (half of 1)
- Chicken drumsticks (4 skin-on or skinless)

Method of Prep:

1. Core and slice the apple into 8 pieces. Sprinkle using the lemon juice.
2. Combine all of the components for the marinade. Add the drumsticks to the mixture. Marinate in the fridge for 15 minutes.
3. Warm the oven broiler. Prepare the broiler pan with foil. Arrange the drumsticks in the pan and broil for 12 to 15 minutes. Turn a couple of times and baste with the marinade.
4. Serve with sliced apple wedges.

Tips for Meal Prep:

1. Cool the chicken and add it into freezer bags for storage unless you will be eating it in the next day or two.

2. Wait to slice the apple until serving time.

Snack: Pumpkin Cookies

Yields Provided: 6

Ingredients for Prep:

- Whole wheat flour (2 cups)
- Baking soda (1 tsp.)
- Coconut sugar (1 cup)
- Old-fashioned oats (1 cup)
- Pumpkin pie spice (1 tsp.)
- Egg (1)
- Melted coconut oil (1 cup)
- Pumpkin puree (15 oz.)
- Roasted pumpkin seeds (.5 cup)
- Dried cherries (.5 cup)

Method of Prep:

1. Warm the oven to reach 350° Fahrenheit.
2. Prepare a baking tin with a sheet of aluminum foil.
3. Combine all of the fixings in a mixing container.
4. Mix well and shape into medium cookies.
5. Place each one on the baking tin.
6. Bake for approximately 25 minutes.

Tips for Meal Prep:

1. Move the pan to a cooling rack before storing or serving.
2. Enjoy whenever you want a healthy treat.

Day 9

Breakfast: Pineapple Oatmeal

Yields Provided: 4

Ingredients for Prep:

- Chopped walnuts (1 cup)
- Cubed pineapple (2 cups)
- Old-fashioned oats (2 cups)
- Nonfat milk (2 cups)
- Grated ginger (1 tbsp.)
- Eggs (2)
- Stevia or your favorite sweetener (2 tbsp.)
- Vanilla extract (2 tsp.)
- Also Needed: 4 ramekins

Method of Prep:

1. Set the oven temperature at 400° Fahrenheit.
2. Combine the oats with walnuts, pineapple, and ginger. Stir well and divide into the ramekins.
3. In a mixing container, combine the eggs with the milk, vanilla, and sweetener. Empty the egg mixture over the oats.
4. Arrange the ramekins in the oven and set a timer to bake for about 25 minutes.

Tips for Meal Prep:

1. Serve when ready or cool for storage.
2. Cover the ramekins with plastic wrap or foil
3. and place in the refrigerator until it's
4. mealtime.
5. Remove the wrap. Pop it into the microwave for 30 seconds with a splash of milk if needed. Serve.

Lunch: Baked Sweet Potatoes

Yields Provided: 3
Ingredients for Prep:

- Sliced onion (1)
- Sweet potatoes (3 diced)
- Freshly cracked black pepper & salt (.5 tsp. each)
- Cinnamon (5 tsp.)
- Olive oil (2 tbsp.)

Method of Prep:

1. Warm a skillet on the stovetop and pour in the oil. After it's heated, toss in the sliced onion and sauté for one to two minutes.
2. Set the oven temperature to 355° Fahrenheit.
3. Combine the potatoes with the onion and the remainder of the fixings.
4. Set a timer to bake for 30 to 35 minutes. Serve and enjoy!

Tips for Meal Prep:

1. Cool and store in the fridge for 2-3 days.
2. Warm in a 350° Fahrenheit oven.

Dinner: Lean Cheeseburgers

Yields Provided: 2

Ingredients for Prep:

- Whole-wheat hamburger buns - with seeds (4)

- 95% lean ground beef (1 lb.)

- Quick-cooking oats (2 tbsp.)

- Steak seasoning blend (.5 tsp.)

- Low-fat cheese - ex. cheddar or American (4 slices)

- Optional: Lettuce leaves & tomato slices

Method of Prep:

1. Split the burger buns in half.

2. Dump the oats into a plastic zipper-type baggie and securely seal. Squeeze out all of the excess air and use a rolling pin to crush the oats until they're a fine texture.

3. Mix the oats with the beef and steak seasoning. Shape into four - ½-inch patties.

4. Have the charcoal grill prepared until the coals are ash covered.

5. Place a lid on the grill to cook for 11 to 13 minutes, or you can use the medium heat setting on a gas grill and cook for 7 to 8 minutes. The thermometer inserted horizontally into the center should read 160° Fahrenheit.

6. Prepare the bun with lettuce and tomato if you're using it and top it off with a burger and a slice of cheese.

7. Close the sandwich and serve.

Tips for Meal Prep:

1. Follow all of the steps to step six.
2. Let the burgers cool thoroughly and wrap in plastic wrap. Place in freezer bags for storage.

Snack: Chocolate Pudding

Yields Provided: 4

Ingredients for Prep:

- Nonfat milk (2 cups)
- Salt (.125 tsp.)
- Cornstarch (3 tbsp.)
- Sugar (2 tbsp.)
- Cocoa powder (2 tbsp.)
- Vanilla (.5 tsp.)
- Chocolate chips (.33 cup)

Method of Prep:

1. Whisk the cornstarch, cocoa powder, salt, and sugar together. Stir in the milk.
2. Cook using the medium heat setting until it starts to boil and thicken.
3. Transfer to the countertop. Stir in the vanilla and chocolate chips.
4. Serve and chill until set using a layer of plastic wrap over the top of the bowl.

Tips for Meal Prep:

1. So easy, just prepare and scoop into individual dishes until you are ready to eat them.

Day 10

Breakfast: Cinnamon-Apple French Toast

Yields Provided: 4

Ingredients for Prep:

- Liquid egg whites (1.33 cups)
- 1% milk (1 cup)
- Eggs (4)
- Cinnamon (2 tsp.)
- Apples (2)
- Low-calorie bread (8 slices)
- *Also Needed*: 9x13 casserole dish

Method of Prep:

1. Peel and dice the apples. Grease the baking dish with cooking spray. Prepare the oven temperature to 350° Fahrenheit.
2. Use a microwavable dish to combine and cook the cinnamon and apples for three minutes.
3. Line the baking dish using bread slices and a layer of cooked apples.
4. Whisk the egg whites and milk. Pour over the bread.
5. Bake 45 minutes.

Tips for Meal Prep:

Let the mixture thoroughly cool.

1. Use a layer of aluminum foil or plastic wrap to cover the baking dish.
2. Refrigerate overnight.
3. When you're ready to eat, set the oven temperature at 350° Fahrenheit.
4. Discard the cover of the baking dish.
5. Bake until set and lightly browned.
6. Transfer the dish to the stovetop for 10 minutes.
7. Serve with your favorite toppings.

Lunch: Leftover Turkey Noodle Soup

Yields Provided: 4
Ingredients for Prep:

- Turkey stock – low-sodium canned/homemade (6 cups)
- Bay leaf (1)
- Garlic cloves (2)
- Carrot (1 cup)
- Onion (.75 cup)
- Celery (.75 cup)
- Salt (as desired)
- Freshly cracked black pepper
- Fresh parsley (.25 cup)
- No-yolk egg noodles (3 oz.)
- Leftover shredded turkey (8 oz. - 2 cups)

Method of Prep:

1. Fill a large soup pot with the turkey stock.

2. Dice the carrot, garlic, onion, and celery. Mince the garlic.

3. Add the bay leaf, celery, onion, carrots, salt, and black pepper to your liking. Simmer until the vegetables are softened (10-15 min.).

4. Chop and toss in the parsley, shredded turkey, and noodles. Simmer for about five minutes. Discard the bay leaf and serve.

Tips for Meal Prep:

1. Chill the soup and pour it into four individual containers.

2. Serve as needed over the next day or two.

Dinner: Honey Grilled Chicken

Yields Provided: 2

Ingredients for Prep:

- Margarine (2 tbsp.)
- Minced garlic (1 clove)
- Chicken breast (4 halves)
- Honey (.33 cup)
- Lemon (1 juiced)

Method of Prep:

1. Prepare the grill using the medium heat setting.

2. Use the medium heat setting on the stovetop to melt the margarine. Toss in the minced

garlic and simmer slowly for two minutes. Whisk the juice and honey and spread half over the breasts.

3. Spritz the grill with oil. Arrange the chicken on the grate. Cook for 5-8 minutes per side. Baste with the rest of the sauce at the end of the cooking cycle.

4. The chicken will be firm with clear juices when poked with a fork.

Tips for Meal Prep:

Cool the chicken and place into individual or containers of veggies for a complete meal option.

Snack: Cranberry & Apple Dessert Risotto

Yields Provided: 4

Ingredients for Prep:

- Fat-free milk (3.5 cups)
- Apple (1)
- Dried cranberries (.5 cup)
- Arborio rice (.5 cup)
- Butter (1 tbsp.)
- Apple cider (1.5 cups)
- Salt (1 dash)
- Light brown sugar (2 tbsp.)

Method of Prep:

1. Measure and add the dried cranberries into a bowl of water. Wait for them to plump.
2. Combine the salt, cinnamon, and milk in a saucepan. Once it is hot, transfer the pan to the countertop to steep.
3. Melt the butter in another pan. Add the sliced/diced apple. Stir often until most of the juices are absorbed. Stir in the sugar/milk mixture.
4. Cook until the rice has a creamy texture. Discard the cinnamon stick and drain the cranberries.
5. Stir in the risotto. Serve warm.

Tips for Meal Prep:

1. Cool and scoop into four containers for a quick on the go snack.

Day 11

Breakfast: Oatmeal & Blueberry Muffins

Yields Provided: 12

Ingredients for Prep:

- Unsweetened almond milk (1 cup)
- Canola oil (1 tbsp.)
- Oats (1.5 cups)
- Baking soda (.5 tsp.)
- Salt (.5 tsp.)
- Baking powder (1 tsp.)
- All-purpose flour (.66 cup)

Method of Prep:

1. Use a blender to pulse the oats and soak in the milk for a minimum of 30 minutes.
2. Set the oven temperature to 400° Fahrenheit.
3. Prepare the muffin tins.
4. Whisk the baking soda, salt, baking powder, canola oil, vanilla extract, honey, and applesauce. Mix well.
5. Fold in the brown sugar, soaked oats, and flour. Mix and divide into the prepared tins.
6. Bake about 24 minutes until the tops are nicely browned.

Tips for Meal Prep:

1. Take the muffin tin out of the oven.

2. Set out on the countertop.

3. Once cooled, store them in a plastic bag, seal at room temperature for up to three days.

Lunch: Ravioli Lasagna

Yields Provided: 6-8

Ingredients for Prep:

- Frozen ravioli (1 lb.)

- Pasta sauce (24 oz.)

- Frozen chopped spinach (8 oz. pkg.)

- Fat-free ricotta (15 oz.)

- Minced garlic (1 tsp.)

- Mozzarella (2 cups - shredded)

- Also Needed: 9x13 pan

Method of Prep:

1. Break up the frozen spinach into a small bowl and mix in the garlic and ricotta.
2. Pour a thin layer of sauce over the bottom part of the pan.
3. Lay down the first layer of ravioli, top with half the spinach mixture, 1/3 of the red sauce, then ½ cup of mozzarella. Repeat this layer again.
4. Top with remaining ravioli, red sauce, and mozzarella.

Tips for Meal Prep:

1. Eat it Now or Prep to Freeze: Set the oven at 375° Fahrenheit. Place a layer of foil over the pan and bake for 30 minutes. Discard the layer of foil and continue baking an additional ten minutes until golden and bubbly. Serve.

2. Cool thoroughly and cover with plastic wrap, pressing down to remove as much air as possible, then cover with foil. Label with the date and contents before freezing.

3. Baking from Frozen: Remove the plastic and foil, and cover again with foil. Warm the oven to 375° Fahrenheit. Set a timer and bake for one hour. Remove the foil and bake for ten minutes more minutes until golden, bubbly and all the pasta is cooked through.

Dinner: Ground Pork Loaf

Yields Provided: 4

Ingredients for Prep:

- Red onions (1 small)
- Garlic (2 cloves)
- Olive oil (1 tbsp.)
- Lemon - juiced and zested (1)
- Cherry tomatoes (1-pint)
- Black pepper (as desired)
- Basil (1 tbsp.)
- Low-sodium tomato paste (2 tbsp.)
- Low-sodium vegetable stock (.5 cup)

Method of Prep:

1. Pour the water into a skillet and let it heat up.
2. Mince the garlic. Chop the onions, tomatoes, and basil. When hot, toss in the onion and garlic. Cook slowly for about five minutes.
3. Stir in the tomatoes, stock, lemon juice and zest, tomato paste, black pepper, and the pork. Stir well and cook for 15 minutes.
4. Garnish with the basil and serve when ready.

Tips for Meal Prep:

1. Allow the meat to totally cool.
2. Portion into the chosen freezer container.
3. Defrost and use it as needed.

Snack: Applesauce

Yields Provided: 3-4

Ingredients for Prep:

- Granny Smith apples (1 lb.)
- Water (1 cup)
- Lemon juice (1 tbsp.)
- Sugar (.5 cup)

Method of Prep:

1. Peel, core, and chop the apples.
2. Fill a large pot of water using just enough to cover the apples.
3. Simmer the apples until softened or for about 20 minutes. Add them to a blender or food processor.
4. Pour in the lemon juice and sugar. Pulse until well combined.
5. Add the mixture back into the pot and simmer 4-5 additional minutes.

Tips for Meal Prep:

1. Cool thoroughly and scoop into individual bowls for a quick and healthy on-the-go snack.

Day 12

Breakfast: Cantaloupe Blueberry Breakfast Bowl

Yields Provided: 2

Ingredients for Prep:

- Whole cantaloupe (1)
- Blueberries (1 cup)
- Cottage cheese (1.5 cups)
- Chopped pecans (.25 cup)
- Hemp seeds (2 tbsp.)

Method of Prep:

1. Wash and pat dry the cantaloupe; slice in half.
2. Chop the pecans and add with the hemp seeds in a small container.
3. Store the cantaloupe with a layer of plastic wrap.

Tips for Meal Prep:

1. Time to Serve: Scoop a ¾ cup serving of the cottage cheese into each half.
2. Garnish both portions with the pecans/seed mix and blueberries.
3. Serve and enjoy it immediately.

Lunch: Pizza Logs

Yields Provided: 8

Ingredients for Prep:

- Egg roll wrappers (8)
- Pizza sauce - your healthy option (8 tsp.)
- Italian seasoning (1 tsp.)
- Light mozzarella string cheese sticks (4 - cut into halves)
- Turkey-pepperoni slices (24)

Method of Prep:

1. Warm the oven to reach 425° Fahrenheit.
2. Lightly mist a large baking tray using a spritz of cooking oil spray and set aside.
3. Prepare a dish of water as a fingertip dish.
4. Arrange each egg roll wrapper on a flat surface with the corner facing toward you.
5. Spread 1 tsp. of sauce across the center of the wrapper, leaving 0.5-inch on each side.
6. Sprinkle Italian seasoning, a row of 3 pepperoni slices, and half of a cheese stick.
7. Fold the bottom corner over the fixings and roll. Fold the side corners in and tuck them as you give the filled section another roll.
8. Dampen the edges of the remaining corner of the wrapper. Finish rolling the filled log to close and place on the baking tray.
9. Arrange the wrapped log on the baking sheet. Continue with the remainder of the fixings.
10. Once they're all wrapped and ready on the baking tray, lightly spritz the tops using a portion of cooking oil spray.

11. Bake for 10 to 14 minutes. Flip them over about halfway through the cooking process.

Tips for Meal Prep:

1. Cool and keep in the refrigerator for a few days for the most flavorful results (if they last that long).

Dinner: Lemon Chicken

Yields Provided: 2

Ingredients for Prep:

- Lemon (1)
- Breasts of chicken (2)
- Oregano (1 pinch)
- Olive oil (1 tbsp.)
- Salt & Pepper (to your liking)

Method of Prep:

1. Discard the bones and skin from the chicken. Squeeze juice from the lemons over the chicken.
2. Sprinkle using pepper and salt.
3. Use medium heat to warm up the oil in a skillet on the stovetop. Cook the chicken. As it is cooking, sprinkle with oregano and additional pepper or salt as desired.
4. Poke it with a fork. It's done when the juices in the center of the chicken run clear.

Tips for Meal Prep:

1. Portion into freezer bags and defrost as a quick base for dinner.

Snack: Lemony Banana Mix

Yields Provided: 4

Ingredients for Prep:

- Strawberries (5)
- Banana (4)
- Lemons (2)
- Coconut sugar (4 tbsp.)

Method of Prep:

1. Juice the lemons and slice the strawberries into halves. Peel and chop the bananas.
2. In a mixing bowl, combine all of the fixings.
3. Toss well and serve cold.

Tips for Meal Prep:

1. Serve over the next couple of days.
2. Store in a covered container or individual dishes.

Day 13

Breakfast: Cherries & Oats

Yields Provided: 6

Ingredients for Prep:

- Water (6 cups)
- Almond milk (1 cup)
- Cinnamon (1 tsp.)
- Old-fashioned oats (2 cups)
- Vanilla extract (1 tsp.)
- Cherries (2 cups)

Method of Prep:

1. Remove the pits and slice the cherries.
2. Combine all of the fixings in a small pot.
3. Bring the pot to a boil using the medium-high heat setting.
4. Cook the mixture for 15 minutes and divide it into serving containers or in one dish.

Tips for Meal Prep:

1. Wait for the oatmeal cool to touch (about one hour).
2. Cover tightly and place in the fridge.
3. If using individual jars for oatmeal storage, microwave for two to three minutes until hot.

Lunch: Turkey & Pear Pita Melt

Yields Provided: 1

Ingredients for Prep:

- Sliced pear (1)
- Deli turkey – low-sodium (3.5 oz.)
- Mixed greens (1 cup)
- Shredded cheddar cheese (1 tbsp.)
- Large whole wheat pita (half of 1)

Method of Prep:

1. Slice the pear and rinse the greens.
2. Stuff the pita with the turkey, cheese, and pears.
3. Place in a toaster oven if you have one, or use the main oven.
4. When warm, add the greens to the hot pita and enjoy the remainder of the pear slices on the side of the dish.

Tips for Meal Prep:

1. Prepare the pita, but don't toast it until it is time to eat.
2. Store in the fridge until mealtime.

Dinner: Pork Chops & Apples

Yields Provided: 4

Ingredients for Prep:

- Low-sodium chicken stock (1.5 cups)
- Pork chops (4)
- Black pepper (as desired)
- Yellow chopped onion (1)
- Minced garlic cloves (2)
- Chopped thyme (1 tbsp.)
- Cored & sliced apples (3)
- Olive oil (1 tbsp.)

Method of Prep:

1. Heat the oven until it reaches 350° Fahrenheit.
2. Pour the oil into a pan. Set the temperature on medium-high.
3. When hot, add the pork chops and sprinkle with the pepper.
4. Cook for five minutes per side.
5. Add the garlic, onion, lime, apples, and the stock.
6. Toss well and add the mixture to a baking dish. Set a timer and bake for 50 minutes.
7. Serve when ready.

Tips for Meal Prep:

1. Prepare the dish until ready. Set aside to thoroughly cool.

2. Store in a sectional container or individual container and pop into the freezer.

Snack: Delicious Apple Pie

Yields Provided: 8

Ingredients for Prep:

For the Crust:

- Dry rolled oats (1 cup)
- Ground almonds (.25 cup)
- Whole wheat pastry flour (.25 cup)
- Packed brown sugar (2 tbsp.)
- Water (1 tbsp.)
- Canola oil (3 tbsp.)

For the Filling:

- Frozen apple juice concentrate (.33 cup)
- Tart apples (6 cups or 4 large)
- Cinnamon (1 tsp.)
- Quick-cooking tapioca (2 tbsp.)

Method of Prep:

1. Heat the oven to reach 425° Fahrenheit.
2. Prepare the Pie Crust: Combine the dry fixings in one mixing bowl and the dry in another. Combine the two until a dough is

formed. Blend together until the dough sticks together. You may need more or less water.

3. Press the dough into a nine-inch pie plate. Set aside.

4. Prepare the Filling: Peel and slice the apples. Mix all of the fixings. Let it stand for about 15 minutes. Stir and place into the pie crust.

5. Bake for 15 minutes at 425° Fahrenheit, reducing the heat for the last 40 minutes at 350° Fahrenheit.

Tips for Meal Prep:

1. You have about two days to enjoy your pies unchilled at room temperature.

2. If the pie has been sliced, place them into a container and loosely cover loosely using plastic wrap. The pie will keep for another two to three days in the fridge.

Day 14

Breakfast: Tropical Breakfast Pie

Yields Provided: 4

Ingredients for Prep:

- Granulated sugar (.5 tsp.)
- Unsweetened shredded coconut (2 tbsp.)
- Refrigerated biscuit dough (7.5 oz.)
- Fresh pineapple (1 cup)
- *Also Needed*: 8-inch-square casserole dish

Method of Prep:

1. Warm up the oven in advance to 350° Fahrenheit.
2. Lightly coat the casserole dish with a splash of cooking spray. Break apart the dough into ten portions and slice into quarters.
3. Load a zipper-type bag with the sugar and coconut. Shake and add the dough bits. Shake gently, but thoroughly to coat.
4. Place the biscuits into the dish and garnish with the diced pineapple.
5. Bake for 25 minutes.

Tips for Meal Prep:

1. Transfer to the counter to cool before placing it in the refrigerator.
2. Serve yourself whenever you need a quick and healthy breakfast dish.

Lunch: Baked Macaroni with Red Sauce

Yields Provided: 6

Ingredients for Prep:

- Diced onion (.5 cup)
- Whole-wheat elbow macaroni (7 oz.)
- Spaghetti sauce - reduced-sodium or homemade (15 oz.)
- Extra-lean beef (.5 lb.)
- Parmesan cheese (6 tbsp.)

Method of Prep:

1. Set the oven to 350° Fahrenheit. Spritz a casserole baking dish with cooking oil spray.
2. Sauté the onions and beef in a frying pan until the onion is fragrant. Drain the grease out of the pan.
3. Fill a pot with water and prepare the pasta until tender or about 10 to 12 minutes. Empty the mixture into a mesh colander to drain.
4. Combine the pasta with the meat and add the sauce. Stir and scoop into the prepared dish. Bake for 25 to 35 minutes.
5. Serve and enjoy each serving with 1 tablespoon of the cheese.

Tips for Meal Prep:

1. Properly stored in closed containers, homemade pasta, and the sauce will last for 2 to 3 days in the fridge.
2. Freeze it in heavy-duty freezer bags.

Dinner: BARBECUE Ranch Chicken Bites

Yields Provided: 4-6

Ingredients for Prep:

- Ranch dressing (.66 cup)
- BARBECUE sauce (.33 cup)
- Chicken breasts (2 lb.)
- Optional: Finely chopped fresh chives (1 tbsp.)
- Skewers (10 - 9 to 12-inch)

Method of Prep:

1. If you are using wooden skewers, soak in water for at least 15 minutes. Prepare a rimmed baking sheet using a sheet of foil and spritz with a misting of cooking spray.
2. Pour the ranch dressing and BARBECUE sauce in a large mixing bowl. Stir to combine. Transfer half to a small serving bowl, cover, and refrigerate. Remove the skin and bones from the chicken, cut it into 1-inch chunks, and add it to the remaining sauce. Toss to combine.
3. Marinate for about half an hour on the countertop or cover and refrigerate for up to 24 hours. (The ideal time is about 2 hours. At 24 hours, the chicken is very tender but starts to break down slightly.)
4. When ready to cook, arrange a rack 4 to 5 inches from the heating element and warm the oven to broil.
5. Thread the chicken onto the skewers, 6 to 7 pieces per skewer. Place the skewers (not touching) on the baking sheet. Broil until charred in spots and cooked through, or about 8 minutes. Top with chives, if using, and serve with the reserved sauce for dipping.

Tips for Meal Prep:

1. After the chicken is prepared, either store in the fridge for 3-4 days or put into individual freezer bags until needed.

Snack: Wacky Chocolate Cake

Yields Provided: 6

Ingredients for Prep:

- Whole wheat pastry flour (3 cups)
- Unsweetened cocoa powder (3 tbsp.)
- Sugar (1 cup)
- Salt (.5 tsp)
- Baking soda (2.25 tsp.)
- Vinegar (2 tbsp.)
- Vanilla (1 tbsp.)

231

- Hot water (2 cups)
- Canola oil (.5 cup)

Method of Prep:

1. Warm up the oven to reach 350° Fahrenheit.
2. Likely spritz a baking dish with cooking oil spray.
3. Whisk the baking soda, salt, sugar, and cocoa powder.
4. Stir in the oil, vinegar, and vanilla.
5. Slowly pour in the water as you whisk the mixture for about 2 minutes.
6. Dump the batter into the baking dish and set a timer to bake for 30 minutes.
7. When cool, slice into 18 squares and serve.

Tips for Meal Prep:

1. Cool the cake and store it in a closed container.
2. It should be good for three days.

Chapter 6: Delicious Snacks Dips & Spreads

Black Bean Brownies – Vegan

Yields Provided: 12

Ingredients for Prep:

- Black beans (1.5 cups)
- Unsweetened applesauce (.25 cup)
- Blackstrap molasses (.25 cup)
- All-purpose flour (.25 cup)
- Unsweetened cocoa powder (.33 cup)
- Salt (.5 tsp.)
- Baking powder (.5 tsp.)

233

- *Also Needed*:
- 8x8 casserole dish
- Cooking spray
- Food processor or blender

Method of Prep:

1. Set the oven in advance to 375° Fahrenheit. Spray the dish with the spray.
2. Drain and rinse the beans and add them to the blender. Pulse until fairly smooth. Dump into a container with the molasses and applesauce. Stir.
3. Sift in the salt, flour, cocoa powder, and baking powder. Mix well.
4. Pour into the prepared dish and bake 35 minutes.
5. Perform the toothpick test for doneness. If it's clean when inserted into the center of the brownies, it's done.

Tips for Meal Prep:

1. Let the brownies cool after they are done.
2. Make a double batch; store one and freeze one!

Breakfast Cookies

Yields Provided: 12 Cookies

Ingredients for Prep:

- Rolled oats (2 cups)
- Large bananas (2 mashed)
- Chocolate chips (.75 cup)

Method of Prep:

1. Warm the oven to 350° Fahrenheit.

2. Stir the oats and bananas until they are thoroughly combined.

3. Stir in chocolate chips.

4. Roll the cookies into 2-inch balls, and then flatten to make the cookie shape.

5. Bake on a parchment paper-lined cookie sheet for 12 minutes.

Tips for Meal Prep:

1. Cool thoroughly and store in closed containers until ready to eat.

Chocolate Biscotti

Yields Provided: 15

Ingredients for Prep:

- Large egg (1)
- Monk fruit sweetener or erythritol (.25 cup)
- Stevia concentrated powder (.25 tsp.)
- Softened butter (.25 cup)
- Vanilla extract (.5 tsp.)
- Almond flour (1.75 cups)
- Xanthan gum (.25 tsp.)
- Unsweetened cocoa (.5 cup)
- Baking soda (.5 tsp.)
- Sea salt (.25 tsp.)
- Cinnamon (1 tsp.)
- *Optional:* Sugar-free chocolate chips

- *Optional:* Chopped nuts

Method of Prep:

1. Set the oven to reach 325° Fahrenheit.
2. Mix the butter with the egg, stevia, granular sweetener, and vanilla.
3. In another container, sift or whisk all the dry fixings and mix until well incorporated.
4. Combine the wet and dry fixings, stirring as you go. Chocolate chips or nuts can be mixed in at this time.
5. Prepare the ball of dough. Arrange the dough ball on a layer of parchment baking paper, silicone baking mat or cookie sheet. Shape the dough into a long flat log.
6. Bake for approximately 18 to 20 minutes. Transfer from the oven and lower the heat setting to 275° Fahrenheit. Cool for about 10 minutes. Slice into thin strips about .5-inch wide.

Orange Cream Cheese Cookies & Nuts

Yields Provided: 18

Ingredients for Prep:

- Softened butter (.75 cup)
- Eggs (3)
- Coconut flour (.5 cup)
- Baking powder (1.5 tsp.)
- Monk fruit sweetener (.75 cup)
- Baking soda (.25 tsp.)
- Sugar-free dried cranberries (.25 cup)
- Macadamia nuts chopped (.5 cup)
- Dried grated orange zest (1.5 tsp.)

Method of Prep:

1. In a mixing container, beat the sweetener with the eggs and butter until well combined.
2. Whisk or sift the coconut flour, baking powder, and soda. Beat on the low setting or with a spoon until fully mixed.
3. Fold in the berries, orange zest, and nuts.
4. Shape into rounds and arrange on the cookie sheet.
5. Arrange the cookies a minimum of one inch apart for baking on a parchment-lined cookie sheet. Press each mound down slightly to flatten.
6. Bake at 350° Fahrenheit until edges have started to brown or for eight to ten minutes.

Tips for Meal Prep:

1. Cool on a cooling rack.
2. Enjoy right out of the fridge for a week, or they can be frozen for longer storage.

Peanut Butter Bites

Yields Provided: 2 bites

Ingredients for Prep:

- Rolled oats (1.5 cups)
- Natural peanut butter - for nut-free use sunflower seed butter (.5 cup)
- Honey or maple syrup (3 tbsp.)

Method of Prep:

1. Add the oats to a food processor or blender. Blend until oats reach a flour consistency.
2. Next, add the peanut butter and honey or maple syrup. Process until the fixings are well combined and come together to form a dough ball. You may need to scrape the sides once or twice.
3. Roll into round bites – about a scant tablespoon per bite. If the dough isn't holding together, add one to two tablespoons more of the peanut butter.
4. If the dough starts to stick to your hands, oil them with coconut oil or cooking spray.

Tips for Meal Prep:

1. Store the *Peanut Butter Bites* in an airtight container in the fridge for up to 2 WEeks.

Cookies Scout

Yields Provided: 12

Ingredients for Prep:

- Vanilla wafer cookies (12)
- Chocolate chips (.5 cup)
- Creamy peanut butter (3 tbsp.)
- Coconut oil (.25 tsp.)

Method of Prep:

1. Spread the peanut butter on the wafers and place them on a parchment paper-lined cookie tin.
2. Place the chocolate chips in the microwave at 15-second intervals until melted. Add a splash of coconut oil to make the chips smoother.

3. Dip the wafers into the chocolate to cover and place it on the paper-lined pan.

Tips for Meal Prep:

1. Cool thoroughly and place it in the fridge to set.
2. Cover and eat as desired.

3 Ingredient Reese's Fudge

Yields Provided: 24

Ingredients for Prep:

- Vanilla frosting - not fluffy (1 container)
- Mini Reese's Pieces (10 oz. bag)
- Peanut butter cups (10 oz.)

Method of Prep:

1. Discard the foil wrapper from the frosting and microwave the container for 30 seconds.
2. Add the peanut butter chips in another container and microwave for one minute.
3. Stir it all together and toss in about ¾ of the bag into the mixture.
4. Grease the baking tin and add the fudge.

Tips for Meal Prep:

1. Before slicing into squares for storage, be sure it is thoroughly cooled (about 30 minutes.

Movie Night Popcorn Galore

These are a sure way to enjoy movies on a budget! Just choose the desired flavors.
Prepare the popcorn in advance and combine the chosen topping from these:

Birthday Cake Popcorn

Yields Provided: 4
Ingredients for Prep:

- Melted white chocolate chips (1 cup)
- Biscoff spread (1 tbsp.)
- Betty Crocker ™ candy sprinkles (2 tbsp.)
- Popcorn (8 cups)

Method of Prep:

1. Melt the chocolate chips and mix in the Bischoff spread.
2. Drizzle over the prepared popcorn and top with the sprinkles.
3. Cool before serving.

Caramel Apple Popcorn

Yields Provided: 10

Ingredients for Prep:

- Popped popcorn (12 cups)
- Brown sugar (1 cup)
- Light corn syrup (.25 cup)
- Salt (.5 tsp.)
- Baking soda (.5 tsp.)
- Vanilla (1 tsp.)
- Cinnamon chips (1 cup)
- Toffee bit (1 cup)
- Whole pecans (1 cup)
- Dried apple chips (1 cup)
- Butter (1 tbsp.)

Method of Prep:

1. Place the brown sugar, light corn syrup, salt, and butter in a microwave-safe bowl.
2. Microwave for about 1 minute, just until the butter is melted, then stir together until well mixed.
3. Return to the microwave and cook for 2 minutes, stir, then cook for an additional 2 minutes.
4. Add the baking soda and vanilla to the caramel. Stir until well mixed.
5. Place your popped popcorn in a large bowl and drizzle the caramel over the popcorn.
6. Sprinkle the cinnamon chips, toffee bits, pecans, and dried apple chips over the popcorn. Toss lightly. Allow cooling before serving.

Chocolate Coffee Peanut Butter Pretzel Popcorn

Yields Provided: 4

Ingredients for Prep:

- Popcorn (8 cups)
- Instant coffee grounds (.5 tbsp.)
- Crushed peanut butter pretzels (.5 cup)
- Chocolate bars - melted (2 bars/4 oz.) or Dark chocolate chips (1.5 cups)

Method of Prep:

1. Melt the chocolate and stir in the grounds of coffee.
2. Drizzle and toss over the popcorn with the pretzels.
3. Let the chocolate harden (room temp) before serving.

Cool Ranch Popcorn

Yields Provided: 4
Ingredients for Prep:

- Melted butter (.25 cup)
- White cheddar mac & cheese powder (2 tbsp.)
- Dry ranch dressing mix (2 tbsp.)
- Smoked paprika (.5 tsp.)
- Popcorn (8 cups)

Method of Prep:

1. Drizzle the prepared butter over the popcorn.
2. Whisk and sprinkle with the spice combo (paprika, cheddar & ranch powder).
3. Toss gently and serve.

Sriracha Popcorn

Yields Provided: 4

Ingredients for Prep:
- Melted butter (.25 cup)
- Sriracha (2 tbsp.)
- Garlic (1 clove)
- Popcorn (8 cups)

Method of Prep:
1. Mince the garlic and melt the butter.
2. Whisk the garlic, Sriracha, and butter to pour over the popcorn.
3. Enjoy immediately.

Dips & Spreads

Baked Potato Dip

Yields Provided: 8

Ingredients for Prep:

- Crispy crumbled turkey bacon (2 strips)
- Chives (1 tbsp.)
- Shredded 2% cheddar sharp cheese (.33 cup)
- Onion powder (.125 tsp.)
- Black pepper (.125 tsp.)
- Garlic powder (.125 tsp.)
- Salt (.125 tsp.)
- Fat-free sour cream (1 cup)

Method of Prep:

1. Brown the bacon until it's crispy and combine with the rest of the fixings.
2. Cool in the refrigerator for a minimum of one hour.

Tips for Meal Prep:

1. Be sure to let the dip cool completely.
2. Store in the refrigerator.
3. Serve with a tray of tasty veggies.

Italian Basil Pesto – Vegan

Yields Provided: 8 Servings - 2 tbsp. each
Ingredients for Prep:

- Tightly packed basil leaves (1 cup)
- Garlic cloves (2 large)
- Lemon juice (1 tbsp.)
- Lemon zest (1 tsp.)
- Toasted pine nuts (2 tbsp.)
- Olive oil (1 tbsp.)
- Water (.25 cup)
- Sea salt and freshly cracked pepper (to your liking)
- *Also Needed*: Food processor

Method of Prep:

1. Toss the pine nuts, lemon juice and zest, basil, and garlic into the processor. Blend until smooth, yet fairly chunky.
2. Pour in the oil and water to process until almost smooth.
3. Remove and place in a serving dish with a sprinkle of salt and pepper to your liking.
4. Stir and let the flavors blend for about ½ hour before serving.

Tips for Meal Prep:

1. Prepare the pesto as described.
2. Pour the mixture into a mason jar and serve any time.

Jalapeno - Bacon & Corn-Cheese Dip

Yields Provided: 3

Ingredients for Prep:

- Parmesan cheese (.25 cup)
- Shredded cheddar cheese (2 cups)
- Softened cream cheese (8 oz.)
- Drained corn (2 cans - 15 oz. each or as desired)
- Diced jalapenos (.25 cup)
- Bacon strips (8 cooked and crumbled)

Method of Prep:

1. Set the oven temperature to 400° Fahrenheit.
2. Prepare a cast iron skillet with a portion of cooking spray.
3. Combine all of the fixings, mixing well, and add to the pan.
4. Bake 20 minutes and serve.

Tips for Meal Prep:

1. Prepare the mixture for the dip and let it cool.
2. Store in the fridge in an airtight dish.
3. Serve as a delicious snack.

Pea Guacamole with Tortilla Chips

Yields Provided: 1

Ingredients for Prep:

- Avocado (¼ of 1 medium)
- Frozen green peas (.25 cup - thawed)
- Fresh lime juice (2 tsp.)
- Chopped uncooked red onion (2 tsp.)
- Cilantro (1 tbsp. - chopped)
- Table salt (.125 tsp.)
- Fresh tomatoes (1 tbsp. - chopped)
- Chips (7)

Method of Prep:

1. Use a blender or mini food processor to puree the lime juice with the peas and avocado.
2. Once it's smooth, stir in the onion, salt, and cilantro.

Tips for Meal Prep:

1. Store in the fridge until needed.
2. Serve with a portion of cilantro, onion, and tomato. Serve with a side of chips.

Spiced Smoky Red Pepper Dip

Yields Provided: 8 Servings /.25 cup each

Ingredients for Prep:

- Roasted red peppers - packed in water (32 oz.)
- Walnut oil (2.5 tsp.)
- Smoked variety paprika (1.25 tsp.)
- Finely chopped garlic (1 medium clove)
- Ground cumin (.5 tsp.)
- Table salt (.25 tsp.)
- Fresh oregano or chopped parsley (1 tbsp.)

Method of Prep:

1. Rinse and drain the peppers.
2. Puree all of the fixings, except for the oregano or parsley, in a blender or food processor.

Tips for Meal Prep:

1. Store in a glass container until time to serve.
2. Garnish with fresh herbs and serve.

Conclusion

I hope you have enjoyed your new collection of recipes in the *Meal Prep Cookbook for Beginners*. I hope it was informative and provided you with all of the tools you need to achieve your goals, whatever they may be.

The next step is to prepare a list of the cooking equipment and ingredients you will need to get started using your new techniques for meal prep.

Emotional Eating

Complete Guide to Lose Weight and Build a Joyful Relationship with Food Through Mindfulness-Based Eating Solutions — Stop Compulsive Overeating, Sugar Addiction, and Eating Disorders

---

by ALAN DIETER

Table of Contents

Introduction

The following chapters will discuss a variety of topics—all relating to how you can improve your eating habits and overall health. You will be able to have more control over your emotional eating habits and start implementing healthy habits. You will be able to understand your physical and mental health better and take care of yourself.

You will learn what emotional eating is. It is important to understand the physical and mental causes of emotional eating, as well as some of the physical symptoms of it. It is also crucial to understand what physical and mental health entails. Your mental health can have a great effect on your eating habits. Poor physical health can also lead to poor eating habits. Similarly, one's physical health will affect one's mental health (and vice-versa). You must understand how you can improve your physical health. Food and sugar addictions are important to understand, as well as how to combat them. Setting goals is important so that you may treat your body properly. Thus, you must know how to plan, set these goals, achieve these goals, and ease into better habits.

There are several mindsets to understand—a mindset for achieving goals, staying motivated, having a healthier body, avoiding addiction, and having a healthier mind. Mastering mindfulness can help with food cravings, compulsive overeating, and enjoying your food.

Understanding intuitive eating and how to implement it can have numerous positive effects on the body. Detoxes are great to learn about. Sugar detoxes are important to understand and implement, as there are many benefits.

You will learn about how to take care of your mental health by becoming more aware of your emotions, learning what makes you happy, improving your self-talk, practicing self-care, loving yourself, and practicing both self-care and self-compassion. You will also learn how to repair your relationship with food. It is important to know what the signs of an unhealthy relationship with food are, how to build a healthy relationship with food, how to love food without overeating, as well as how to learn to value your health. You will learn about eating disorders—the signs, symptoms, causes, and types of them. Additionally, you will learn how to overcome eating disorders. Finally, you will receive some additional tips and tricks about how you can improve your health overall, how to adopt healthier eating habits, how to be happier and healthier, as well as how to manage poor eating habits.

There are many topics covered, as the emotional eating is a larger-scale problem than simply fixing your diet. Mental health is what drives emotional eating, and overall physical health may be improved. When you improve your mental health, you will be able to begin establishing healthier habits for yourself and value yourself even more. This will allow you to be more motivated to take care of yourself and your health. It is also crucial that you understand the causes of your actions. If you can identify the source of your issues, you will be able to understand yourself more. Understanding why you do what you do will really help you to improve your habits. You can better prevent certain habits of yours from occurring.

There are plenty of books on this subject on the market—thank you again for choosing this one! Every effort was made to ensure it is full of as much useful information as possible. Please enjoy it!

Chapter 1: What Is Emotional Eating?

We are often cautioned not to give in to emotional eating. It is tempting to alleviate any physical or emotional pain with delicious foods to distract oneself from these issues. Food is necessary for life, and humans have developed more and more ways to enjoy food. Whether that be from eating out at restaurants to sweet treats to purchase from the store, eating has become a hobby for many. It is an enjoyable activity that increases one's happiness.

However, emotional eating is widely regarded as a bad habit. It could also have serious consequences for the individual. It is crucial to understand what emotional eating is, what may cause one to eat emotionally, and what may happen to the body when one does eat as a result of their emotions. By understanding these, the individual may recognize what they are doing to their body, as well as why they may want to stop doing so to improve their health.

Of course, we all treat ourselves to an unhealthy snack every once in a while. There may be times where one uses food to make themselves feel better. This is normal. For those with a sore throat due to a cold or such, a popsicle or ice cream might be a nice treat to ease the throat. After a gym session, it may be necessary to refuel and consume food with protein in it. These are examples of normal eating habits. An occasional treat from time to time is okay. However, when it turns into an addiction, a bad habit, or a way of maintaining one's mental health, it can become a problem. If one relies on food (especially unhealthy food) to maintain their happiness, and they develop a dependency on food, this can prove extremely harmful.

On the other hand, emotional eating may be caused by the opposite. Some may feel the need to reward themselves with food constantly. If individuals find themselves motivating themselves by means of food, this may be a sign of an unhealthy relationship with food. Although it is normal to occasionally celebrate with food (i.e., birthdays, holidays, etc.), there is a point where one is making too many excuses for their unhealthy habits. For instance, one may motivate themselves at work by eating a sweet every time they complete a task. This can lead to a strong dependency on food and a subsequent unhealthy relationship with food. The person has become reliant on food for their daily tasks.

There are several signs of an emotional eater. One may eat because they are simply bored. One may eat out of negative feelings such as anger, sadness, loneliness, frustration, or others. One may also eat as a way of coping with stress. Eating out of positive emotions may also be a sign of an emotional eater. Eating as a response to emotions and situations is not healthy. It is important to understand that any unnecessary excess of food is unhealthy, especially when it occurs often. If a person eats until they have stuffed themselves every time or simply eats "for fun" instead of when they are hungry, this is another sign of an unhealthy relationship with food. There may be addictions associated with certain foods or types of foods as well, which is also unhealthy. If one feels guilty or embarrassed about food and feels the need to hide their eating habits, this is also a sign. There may be other, not-so-obvious signs of an emotional eater. These people tend to hide their problems from others and suppress their emotions. They may also choose to not engage in normal activities that they used to enjoy. They may feel poorly about their bodies and create a cycle that causes further guilt and unhealthy habits. These people may also have higher stress levels and fail to understand or execute healthy coping mechanisms. It may be more common in those who live "at the moment," as food only serves as a temporary cure.

Physical Causes

So, what causes one to eat emotionally? Of course, there is the mental aspect of it. One will eat based on their emotions. However, there are several other reasons that one may have the tendency to eat based on their emotions or when certain situations occur in their lives.

One cause may lie in a false hunger or an actual physical hunger that may be cured. The individual should learn the difference between physical hunger and emotional hunger. Physical hunger occurs when the body needs more fuel to power its processes. The body will signal that it needs food, typically by either a stomach that feels empty or by means of stomach growls. The body may also feel weak or out of energy. One may feel shaky or lightheaded. This hunger will be resolved by eating food. This hunger must also not be confused with the craving of a certain food. Cravings may also be satisfied when that certain food is consumed, yet physical hunger may be satisfied with any food. The individual may not be certain whether they are actually hungry or just desire food out of boredom, emotions, or any mental aspects.

It is important to listen to the body instead of the mind. It is also crucial to eat when one is hungry and stop when one is full. Emotional eating may also result in stuffing oneself, which is not necessary or healthy. By training one's body to eat when they are hungry and eat the perfect amount to satisfy that hunger, a healthier relationship with food will be developed. This may be fine-tuned by training oneself to listen to their body's cues and be more in tune with their body.

One may also genuinely feel physically hungry very often. This excessive hunger can result from poor eating habits and further unhealthy habits. This can be due to a number of reasons. If a person does not consume a proper amount of protein, fiber, or fat, they will not stay full for long. Additionally, one who consumes too many refined carbohydrates will not stay full for long. An improper amount of sleep may also result in poor appetite control, as a proper amount of sleep is needed to regulate one's ghrelin (appetite-stimulating hormone) levels. The individual may also simply be dehydrated (either by too little water or too much alcohol).

Both hunger and dehydration have similar physical feelings, and they can be confused quite easily. For this reason, it is important to drink water constantly throughout the day. One may try drinking water when they are hungry to test if it is true hunger or simply dehydration. Exercise also plays a huge role in one's hunger. More energy is used; therefore, more is needed to fuel the body. This may also lead to overeating, as one may justify their habits by exercising more to allow themselves to eat more. Although it is important to drink a lot of water, one may experience more hunger with a primarily liquid-based diet. This is due to the faster digestion of liquids than solids. There may also be medical reasons for the increased hunger, such as medication or a medical condition or disease that one may have.

Mental Causes

A huge aspect of emotional eating is the emotional and mental aspect of it. Humans, throughout time, have developed more of a liking to food. Instead of working for it and using it as fuel for one's body, it has become a source of entertainment, a meaning of socializing, and a hobby to enjoy. Each day, new recipes are concocted, restaurants are built, and food items are stocked in stores. This cultural revolution that celebrates food has led to serious consequences for humans. The tasting festivals, holiday gatherings, and other food-related events all celebrate delicious food and lead to an association between food and happiness.

For those who struggle with their mental health, feel stressed, or otherwise have less control over their emotions, food serves as an escape from negativity. Because it's associated with happiness, it can also be used as a sort of bribe to motivate one or as a means of celebration. This association between food and happiness can take a toll on one's health. Some may use it as a way to literally and figuratively fill the hole in their stomach and heart, respectively. It serves as a way to comfort one and to incur positive emotions.

This process becomes cyclical, as the individual will most likely feel guilty for consuming an excess of food unnecessarily. This guilt may cause further shame and negative emotions, which will lead to the further consumption of food to cope with these emotions, leading yet again to guilt and shame. This overall will affect one's perception of themselves and lead to poorer mental health.

The negative emotions that one feels that will cause them to eat emotionally can result from a number of factors. Those that struggle with depression, anxiety, and the like may eat as a way of coping with their mental struggle. Some may simply eat when they have a tough day at work. They may deal with heartbreak or relationship issues by turning to food. It may be caused by financial stress. There are many reasons that one may feel emotionally unwell and turn to food to aid their emotional well-being.

One may also eat more often because of poor eating habits, which can cause the brain to think that one is hungry even when they are not. For instance, one who eats while distracted will not mentally register the food that they are putting into their bodies. The brain will not truly consider the food that was consumed, as it was focused elsewhere. The same goes for those who eat their food too quickly. The brain does not have time to register the amount of food that was consumed in such a short period of time. There may also be individuals that don't associate certain foods with fullness. For instance, one may view a certain food as simply a snack and feel the need to eat more to make up for the food that they didn't previously consume. Those with high-liquid diets can experience this more frequently, as the meal may be mentally regarded as just a beverage as opposed to a full meal, despite any additives that may reside in it. One may also have no other hobbies or pleasures to look forward to. Perhaps the person neglects themselves from others and doesn't make plans that excite them. The person may feel bored with their job. Food may be the only source of happiness in their life. If one goes too long without eating, they may also subject themselves to improper eating habits, as they will eat whatever they can get their hands on. There is also the possibility of "oh well."

Perhaps someone slipped up in their diet and thinks that they have already messed up, so why not just continue? This can lead to a domino effect and a continued pattern of poor eating. Instead of going back to their diet, the person will continue the bad eating because they slipped up once and think that continuing won't hurt them anymore. However, one must be able to have an overall healthy relationship with eating and should care about what they are putting into their bodies. After all, food is the source of energy for animals and must be the proper source of energy to help the body run most effectively.

Physical Symptoms

It's no surprise that emotional eating will take a toll on the body. Of course, there will be mental consequences, too. However, the body will not be able to function as well under this sort of treatment from the individual. Overeating and the consumption of unhealthy foods can lead to many consequences and side effects for the emotional eater. Because they are eating not out of hunger but due to triggers (whether that be emotional or situational), the individual is not treating their body the best that they can. Additionally, overstuffing oneself may lead to additional side effects and health issues.

Those who overeat may experience nausea. This is due to eating a large quantity of (typically unhealthy) food at once, especially if it is much more than normal. The individual will experience nausea and may have stomach pain, diarrhea, and other digestive issues occur. One may also feel bloated frequently and may even feel tired as a result of the extra work that their digestive system must undergo to digest the larger amount of food that they consume.

Another common consequence of emotional eating is weight gain. This can lead to obesity and being overweight, which can cause anything from muscular and skeletal problems to heart issues. It can lead to diabetes, high blood pressure, and fatigue. This is, of course, caused by regular emotional eating. It will be more severe with those who frequently overeat as a result of emotional eating. For instance, someone who binges each time they are stressed (and becomes stressed quite often) will see a more apparent weight gain than one who only rarely eats based on their emotions.

However, emotional eating will take a toll on the body, regardless. It is an unhealthy relationship for one to have with food. It is also typical for

261

one to eat foods that are high in carbohydrates, sugar, and calories when they are stressed. These foods are lower in nutritional value and can hinder one's bodily performance. It may lead to lethargy and an inability to function as well, especially when performing cardiovascular activities and exercises.

Mental Symptoms

Although the body will suffer from emotional eating, one's mental health will also suffer. Because it is used as a way to cope with emotions, one may develop an inability to otherwise cope with their emotions and any stress that they may experience. As a result of turning to food for comfort and relief, the person may abandon other and healthier ways of treating their mind and body better.

One may also develop negative thoughts and feelings as a result of their emotional eating. For instance, one may feel guilty about their habits. They may also feel guilty about their health and body as a result of the way they treat themselves. This can lead to poor self-confidence and even the withdrawal of oneself from social situations. This neglect can further lead to loneliness, causing even greater stress, sadness, and anxiety. Emotional eating has a domino effect in that it furthers problems that further other problems. This can even lead to other mental health issues such as depression.

Emotional eating can truly hurt the individual. It is triggered by emotions or situations, whether those are positive (using food as a reward) or negative (using food to procure happiness). It can be caused by a variety of emotions and by a sense of false hunger. Emotional eating can cause one's mental health to decline. It may also cause one's physical health to decline. Overall, emotional eating causes many consequences and is the result of poor health.

Chapter 2: Mental Health and Physical Health

Mental and physical health are closely related. When one has great mental health, their physical health tends to be greater. When one's mental health suffers, one's physical health tends to suffer, too. One with greater physical health tends to have greater mental health. Similarly, one with poor physical health tends to suffer from poor mental health. Negative emotions and overall poor mental health can lead to hunger and the tendency to overeat and simply eat poorly. Poor physical health can also contribute to hunger and poor eating habits. It is also important to maintain one's physical health to improve one's mental health. It is also important because one's physical and mental health influences their hunger and digestion, and it further helps one's overall health. Taking care of oneself is more than just diet and exercise, although those are two crucial aspects of the individual's health.

Mental Health and Poor Eating Habits

Mental health or negative emotions have a strong connection with proper eating habits and hunger. Hunger can cause mental health issues, and poor mental health can contribute to a false sense of hunger due to some sort of emptiness that one experiences. Poor mental health can also lead to additional poor eating habits and a poor relationship with food.

For those who don't have access to nutritious food or who struggle to have sufficient funds to support the purchase of an adequate amount of sustainable food, food insecurity can result. They will become hungry and produce more cortisol, which causes the person to become stressed. In the long-term, this can be linked to depression, anxiety, and further mental disorders. It can even lead to suicidal thoughts, especially in teens. Hunger can lead to a lack of concentration, which can make it much more difficult to pay attention, leading to further frustration, as one will struggle to focus. Studies have concluded that those with food insecurity issues are much more likely to experience mental health issues than those who do not struggle with food insecurity. This link between food insecurity and mental health highlights the importance of consuming the right amount of the proper foods to feed oneself. By not doing so, one is hurting their mental health.

For those who fail to feed their body the proper amount of the right type of food, further issues can result. The individual will feel stressed and lethargic, leading to greater sadness, frustration, or overall dissatisfaction with their health. These negative emotions can lead to further poor habits, as the person will cope with these emotions by eating more foods that lack the nutrition they need. When one does not receive enough food, they will feel weak and have less motivation. This can lead to a cause of poor mental health, as one will not enjoy activities that they normally would. They may lack the energy or motivation to do what they love typically. Additionally, one who puts improper foods into their body will feel guilt and shame. This will cause them to think of themselves poorly and develop further issues that need to be coped with. If they continue to cope with these issues in an unhealthy manner, however, they will further their issues.

These issues can be multiplied in mothers and youth. There are typically more mothers that struggle with food insecurity as a result of the financial obligations that they must meet. For those who are pregnant, this is very harmful to their developing baby, which must be given the proper nutrients to develop in a healthy manner. It is also important for the mother, whether pregnant or not, as they must keep their energy up to support their child. Mothers must maintain their mental health to be

264

able to support their child properly, yet this can be difficult if faced with food insecurity. As the children grow, they may struggle to pay attention in school and focus on their studies.

Bad Physical Health and Poor Eating Habits

In addition to affecting one's health, poor eating habits can take a toll on the body. One's physical health can suffer as a result of hunger and other poor eating habits. Studies have found links between hunger and health issues such as high blood pressure, heart disease, and diabetes.

It can greatly affect children, who need a proper amount of food to develop healthily. In children, development can be slowed or hindered as a result of hunger. It can also cause health issues such as asthma and anemia. It can also cause issues with kidneys, vision, and nerves. Food insecurity has been found to be linked with obesity, which can lead to many health issues itself, such as heart disease, high blood pressure, and musculoskeletal issues. Children who are malnourished experience slowed brain development as well as slower development of their muscles and bones. This can also weaken the body's immune system. Those who are malnourished will also have health issues with their teeth, gums, and skin. Food insecurity in children can occur, and it typically involves compromises being made. Instead of receiving the right amount of healthy food, children may be forced to eat less food than they need to thrive. They may also have to compromise when it comes to the nutritional value of their food. Because it often costs more for nutrition-packed food, children may have to eat unhealthy foods in order for their parents to be able to afford to keep them fed.

Pregnant mothers can really suffer from malnutrition. Not only will their babies struggle to develop properly, but they will feel weak from the lack of food in their bodies. Pregnant mothers need to be nourished even more while pregnant to ensure that they and their babies are healthy. Babies of malnourished mothers tend to have a lower birth weight, which can lead to long-term development issues.

Those who are hungry for short periods of time will certainly feel the short-term effects of hunger. One's stomach will growl, they may feel lethargic and weak, and they may also feel empty. One may even start shaking or develop a headache. Those who are hungry will feel their bodies give them signs that it is time to eat. For those who go hungry for the long-term, more serious effects will occur. The individual may become "immune to eating." They may be hungry but not wish to eat. If they do eat, they may even become sick from that. They will also experience other symptoms from not eating. They may struggle to sleep and feel tired constantly. It will be harder to stay focused. Malnutrition will lead to further fatigue and dizziness. It can also lead to a weakened immune system, subjecting the individual to an increased risk of sickness. The individual may also become infected more easily. Ear infections are more common in those who are malnourished and hungry. More frequent infections can lead to the development of diseases in those who experience food insecurity.

Poor Mental Health Leads to Poor Physical Health

Those who are mentally sound tend to feel more motivated to do what they love and to take care of themselves. One who is mentally stable will find it easier to set a proper eating and exercise routine for themselves and will be able to stick to it. Those who struggle with their mental health will have a harder time staying motivated to take care of themselves. They may also find it more difficult to stick to their goals and treat themselves the way they should. Those who have low self-confidence or self-worth may find it more difficult to treat themselves well. One who has low self-worth (perhaps as a result of low self-confidence) will not see themselves as worth taking care of, and they may neglect healthier habits in favor of less healthy habits. One with low self-confidence may withdraw from certain situations. They may feel embarrassed about their health and as a result, will not wish to go to the gym or exercise outside (or anywhere others may see them). They may also begin to slowly neglect themselves from others and avoid social situations when possible. This can lead to further unhealthy habits and worsen one's mental health. Those with depression and anxiety may also avoid social situations and treat themselves badly for similar reasons. Those who don't keep active will experience physical health issues and may not be as motivated to eat well as a result of already doing harm to their physical health.

There is a very real link between physical and mental health. Those with poor mental health are more likely to make unwise decisions when it comes to their physical health. Those with mental health issues are less likely to stay physically active. The main cause is a lack of motivation. Those with poor mental health are also more likely to develop poor and unhealthy eating habits. They may skip meals, overindulge, choose options that aren't the most nutritional, or eat very quickly. Those who struggle with mental health may find themselves starving themselves or not having a large appetite. Individuals with less-than-optimal mental health may also have a greater dependency on tobacco and alcohol. Those with mental health issues are more likely to develop smoking and drinking habits, which are typically used as ways to cope with their troubles. For those affected by stress, psoriasis may develop and present itself on the skin.

It has been found that those with mental health issues have shorter lifespans as a result of both suicide and physical health issues that arise as a result of their mental health issues. Their respiratory and circulatory systems suffer as a result of additional stress that is placed on their body from internal struggles. When one experiences difficulties with their mental health, they tend to be less likely to seek help for their issues. They don't feel the need to take care of themselves as much and will skip on routine checkups that would be able to detect health concerns before it is too late.

Poor Physical Health Leads to Poor Mental Health

Those with poor physical health will increase the likelihood of having poor mental health. Those with physical health problems are likely to feel less self-confident. They will not feel as confident doing activities that others wouldn't have a problem with. They recognize that they may not take the best care of their bodies. This can lead to feelings of guilt and shame about one's body and the way they treat it. Those individuals may also feel less socially included. They may withdraw themselves because of their condition, whether that be staying home to rest (due to fatigue), avoiding situations that involve physical activity (because of an inability to keep up with others), or neglecting themselves from others (as a result of embarrassment). Regardless of the reason, social withdraw can lead to serious mental health issues. One will feel lonely and will not get the socialization that they need to remain mentally sound.

Physical health issues can also cause one to feel stressed. They may feel overwhelmed by the severity of their situation, the costs associated with it, or treatments that they must undergo. For those that receive a diagnosis of a health issue, the mental reaction could be even worse than the physical issue itself. The individual may feel stressed about possible lifestyle changes that they must make. Perhaps they must change their diet or exercise routine. No matter the reason, the individual may experience more stress and anxiety from the situation. If the diagnosis is for a serious health issue, they may become worried or depressed due to the severity of the situation.

Certain physical issues have serious mental health effects. Those with heart disease are much more likely to develop depression. These individuals may feel more stressed and less at ease because of their condition. Additionally, they may seek proper physical treatment for their problems and think that it is adequate. They often fail to consider, though, how important treatment is for their mental health issues as well. They may focus primarily on their physical issues and neglect their mental issues in the process. Many individuals check on their physical health regularly, yet it is not as common to stay in tune with how one's mental health is. Most doctors fail to consider how one's mental health is when they are considering how healthy they are overall. One may feel physical pain. This is a constant reminder for that individual to seek help and receive treatment. Mental health isn't as obvious, however. Although one may experience metaphorical pain, they are less likely to seek proper treatment when they feel any sort of mental issue arise in themselves.

Those who receive an inadequate amount of sleep also subject themselves to a great number of mental health issues. They are more likely to feel fatigued and unmotivated as a result. They may also develop emotional instability as a result of an improper amount of energy that is needed for the individual to function.

How to Improve Physical Health

Commonly, it is said that one should "eat healthily and exercise" to be healthy. Of course, this is true. However, there is more to it than just this. One must exercise the proper amount so that they are working their body enough while also getting the rest that they need. They should also do the right types of exercise. It is important for one to practice cardiovascular exercises for improved heart health. It is also important to practice strength exercises to build the strength of one's muscles and bones so they may move more freely without trouble. One must also develop proper eating habits. This includes getting the proper amount of the right foods to fuel one's body. It also entails eating at the right times so that the individual is fueled throughout the day. They must also avoid processed foods and foods that lack proper nutrition as much as possible.

It is important that one drinks enough water. The best solution is to avoid sugary drinks and to get the proper amount of water for one's weight, height, age, and activity level. This will vary from person to person, and there are online calculators available, as well as the advice of a doctor. It is also crucial for the individual to receive a proper amount of sleep. This will also vary from person to person, although it is mostly based on one's age. Receiving too much and too little sleep will both negatively affect one's body.

When an individual does fail to take care of their physical health, their mental health will suffer. On the other hand, an individual who neglects their mental health will experience physical health issues. Similarly, one who is hungry and has poor eating habits will experience both physical and mental health problems. These issues are all closely related, and one will affect the other. There are several ways to improve one's physical health, which will also work to improve that individual's mental health. By improving both of these, the individual is making it easier for themselves to be able to develop proper eating habits.

Chapter 3: Addictions

Many addictions can occur in individuals. Addictions can result in anything. Some may be addicted to a hobby they have, such as running or watching television. Addictions can start out as a passion for a certain activity, yet they can turn unhealthy once it becomes an obsession for the individual. There can be "healthy" and "unhealthy" addictions. For instance, one may be addicted to running. This is highly regarded as a healthy activity, yet it can be unhealthy if it becomes excessive and is harmful to the individual. People can develop an addiction to alcohol or to drugs, which can lead to serious damages to their physical health. It is also possible to become addicted to certain foods or to food as a whole. This can lead to several consequences for the individual, yet it can be overcome. It is important to understand the causes of these addictions.

What Causes Food Addictions?

When one is addicted to food, they have an uncontrollable impulse to eat. They don't eat to live—they live to eat. It is typically a response to an emotional or situational trigger. Although the body depends on food for its survival and uses it as fuel, those who are addicted to food typically become dependent upon a certain type of food. This can be especially detrimental to the body if the food is unhealthy, such as sweets, chips, or certain grains. This addiction can occur similarly to how one will develop a dependency on cigarettes or alcohol. The brain will depend on the release of chemicals (like dopamine) that the food allows them to have. When one eats the food, it satisfies this craving for it and will release dopamine, making the individual happy. It is pleasurable to the body. The lack of this food (whether the person has yet to eat it or does not have access to it) can lead to serious distress and will cause desperation for this food. Until one satisfies their craving, their body will yearn for that food.

Research suggests, however, that food addictions differ from substance addictions such as cigarettes or alcohol. This is because these are substance addictions. The properties in these substances are addictive themselves. However, food can be a behavioral addiction. Eating becomes a regular habit, and even a hobby, for some individuals. Although it is important to eat enough food to maintain one's energy, there is such a thing as an excess of food, especially when that food lacks nutritional value.

There are certain foods that one is more likely to become addicted to. The most common foods are high in sugar, fat, and starch. Foods such as chips, French fries, sweets, and white bread are the most common foods to become addicted to. These foods taste good and satisfy one's craving. They also tend to be lower in nutritional value, which can further one's health issues. These foods, known as highly palatable foods (which are high in sugar, fat, and salt), are more likely to trigger the sections of the brain that addictive drugs do. They trigger the same reward and pleasure parts of the brain that those drugs do. Consuming such foods will trigger chemical releases that lead to pleasure in people. Because of this happiness associated with eating such foods, individuals with food addictions want more so that they may experience that pleasurable sensation again. This feeling of happiness might cloud one's ability to perceive fullness and satisfaction with what they have already consumed. This leads to a loss of control and a subsequent need to frequently consume such foods and feel the pleasure associated with it.

There are several signs that one may have a food addiction. One may have obsessive food cravings that are uncontrollable and may even interfere with the individual's daily life. They may experience obsessive thoughts about food that interferes with their ability to concentrate until they consume such food. They may have binging episodes or eat compulsively. They may try to stop overeating but find themselves unable to. It may be hard to control portion sizes and the frequency of eating. This can even take a toll on their social life and finances. They may try to hide food from others or feel embarrassed and guilty when

272

eating. They may also depend on food for their emotional well-being. It is also possible that the individual will have lower self-confidence and self-worth. They may try to restrict themselves from eating and starve themselves after a binging episode. They may try to exercise compulsively to make up for their binging. They may even force themselves to vomit after an episode of overeating occurs.

Combatting Food Addictions

If left untreated, those with food addictions can face several consequences. They may have food interfere with their daily lives. It may be difficult to concentrate until they satisfy their craving and give in to their addiction. They may need to leave events in order to satisfy their craving. It can interfere with one's social life and any romantic, family, or friendly relationships. If one begins to build their day around food, this can really become troublesome, as they must give in to their craving and potentially ignore other scheduled events. It may harm one's work or academic life if it impairs cognitive function. Food addictions can further lead to health issues. One may become overweight or obese as a result of their addiction and the potential to overeat. Although not all with food addictions are overweight, it can occur as a result. Some may have a metabolism that allows them to eat more than necessary without any weight gain. Some may also self-induce vomiting or excessively exercise to attempt to counteract the excess of food that they consume.

It is important to combat food addictions, as they can deteriorate one's physical and mental health. There are several ways to do so. Before seeking professional help, one may try to make small changes to improve their lifestyle and the situation of their addiction. One may try to replace their unhealthy foods gradually with better alternatives. For instance, one may replace candy with berries. This will still allow for one to enjoy the sweetness of the food, yet there will be greater nutritional value in it. There are many small switches to make. Another is with beverages. Instead of consuming sweetened beverages, one may gradually incorporate water into their diet. Soda is crucial to replace. The individual may gradually incorporate more water and less sweetened beverages into their diet. They may also reduce the caffeinated and alcoholic beverages that they consume, replacing those with water as well. It is important to drink the right amount of water every day. There are certain eating habits that may also prove highly beneficial to those with food addictions. For instance, one may start gradually replacing meals at restaurants with home-cooked meals. They may focus more on their food and less on other distractions. By eating slowly and truly registering everything that they are eating, the individual may develop a greater sense of self-awareness. The individual may also schedule their meals and stick to it. Some may prefer much smaller meals throughout the day, while others prefer three sustainable meals. This is up to personal preference and the advice of one's medical professional. While shopping, it is important to stick to one's grocery list. It can be tempting to weave in and out of the aisles out of the grocery store. There are also many tempting sales (such as buy one get one free). When shopping, one should also eat before. By sticking to the grocery list, the individual may be more aware of what they are putting into their bodies and make wiser choices regarding what will be accessible to them in their homes. The pantry and refrigerator will be filled with more favorable options. It is also possible for one to track every food that they consume. There are many digital applications to track one's calories and macronutrients. It will greatly help one to realize what exactly it is that they are putting into their bodies and how it is for their health. This can help with portion sizes and for understanding what certain foods will do to the body.

While adjusting one's eating habits can greatly help, there are other ways to allow one to make better decisions about their eating habits. By

274

receiving enough sleep, one will not feel the need to supplement their diet with unnecessary foods to make up for their lack of energy. Exercising on a regular basis will encourage one to take care of their body further so that their progress is not lost. However, one must appropriately fuel up for their workouts and avoid the mentality of allowing themselves to overeat because they exercised. It is also important that the individual makes strides towards improving their mental health, as this can lead to the need to eat emotionally in the first place. By reducing stress and developing healthier ways to deal with their emotions, the individual will help themselves greatly.

What Causes Sugar Addictions?

These days, sugar is added to almost everything. Seasonal beverages at coffee shops are loaded with sugar. Desserts line the aisles at grocery stores. Soda has become a social drink. There are even food items with sugar that one wouldn't even expect! It's tough to avoid sugar, as it's in almost everything. Most people consume way beyond the recommended amount of sugar each day. One may even develop an addiction to sugar, making it even harder to avoid. The individual may develop an emotional or psychological dependence on sugar, causing their body to "need" it. It makes it even harder to avoid when one eats mostly processed foods and refined grains, which create additional sugar once digested. This is one way that it may be more difficult for one to recognize their sugar addiction. Sugary foods like donuts and ice cream are more apparently filled with sugar. However, those with a sugar addiction may crave more than just sweets; refined carbs are a common addiction of those with a sugar addiction because of the glucose produced when those refined carbs are metabolized. Although sugar can occur naturally in many foods, such as fruit, an excess of sugar (especially added sugar) can prove harmful to the body. For this reason, sugar addictions should be dealt with appropriately. One must first recognize what causes an individual to develop an addiction to sugar.

After consuming sugar, one will likely experience a "sugar high." This is a spike of energy in the body that allows one to combat possible fatigue that they may feel. It is typically accompanied by a rise in one's happiness as a result of the dopamine that is released after one consumes sugar. Sugar has often been compared to addictive drugs such as cocaine. Those who overindulge in sugar will also increase their chances of diabetes, obesity, and heart disease.

There are several types of people that may be more at risk for developing a sugar addiction. Those with anxiety, depression, and increased stress levels may be more tempted to reach for sugary foods to increase their happiness and suppress any negative emotions. Those who struggle with constant fatigue may also be more likely to reach for sugar due to the endorphins that are released and the subsequent increase in one's energy. They will use sugar to cope with their emotions and depend on it to maintain their energy levels. When this dependency occurs, one has developed an addiction to it.

There are several signs that one may be addicted to sugar. They may fill their diet with sugar-rich foods and experience frequent cravings for such foods. They will emotionally eat foods that are rich in sugar to cope with certain emotions or situations that may occur in their lives. They may even have binging episodes involving sugary foods and find it hard to control themselves around sugar. This can lead to mental consequences such as feeling helpless or having poor self-esteem and self-worth.

Combatting Sugar Addictions

There are several ways to break free from sugar addiction. Once one recognizes that they have a sugar addiction, they may take steps towards helping themselves to overcome that addiction. Before seeking professional medical help for sugar addiction, one may consider easier remedies that they can do themselves. It can be difficult to break an addiction, but there are ways to help one to overcome that addiction more easily.

One may gradually replace their sugary favorites with healthier alternatives. Replacing refined carbohydrates for whole-grain options is a quick and simple switch. Instead of snacking on chips and other salty snacks, one may find popcorn that is natural and doesn't have added sugar or sodium. It is important to gradually replace any sugary beverages in one's diet with water. By making small switches here and there gradually, it will be easier for one to develop proper eating habits without relapse. It is important not to cut out all sugar completely right away. This will only lead to a later binge of the food and a loss of motivation. By gradually switching one's diet to be healthier, it will make it much easier for the individual to transform their diet into one that is more sustainable. Products must be researched, however.

Some food products claim to be "healthy" but just contain alternatives to sugar that are worse than sugar itself. For this reason, one must inspect the ingredients before purchasing the product. When in doubt, it is better to go for more "whole" foods. This way, the individual knows just what they are putting into their bodies. If one can't pronounce an ingredient in the product, it may not be the best chemical to put in the body. It's best to know just what one is eating. For instance, an apple is simply that: an apple. When one purchases cheesy puffs, however, this can get more complicated. There are many more ingredients, most of which are unknown to the general population. It's better to be aware of what is going into the body.

One quick and easy fix is not to surround oneself with tempting foods. This can quickly be done by cleaning out one's pantry and refrigerator and ridding oneself of the foods that are not nutritionally sufficient. However, one must not bring in new foods that will cave in to their addiction. By setting a proper shopping list and sticking to it, this can be done more easily.

By sticking to an eating plan, one may combat their sugar addiction. Instead of eating out, one may make food at home. It's wise to prepare meals ahead of time. This way, there's food that is already made. The excuse of eating out for convenience can't be used. This also helps with preparing foods that are based on what's best for the body, not the taste buds. When one is hungry, they are more likely to eat foods that are not the best for them nutritionally. This eliminates that issue.

Seeking Professional Help for Addictions

If there have been several steps taken to attempt to combat the addiction, but no results are seen, it may be time to seek professional medical help for the addiction. Although this may be costlier and take extra time, it is necessary if the individual has put in the effort to combat their addiction themselves but is unable to take control of their bodies and food cravings. Otherwise, they face serious health consequences, especially if left untreated for a long period of time. There are several ways that one may seek help and receive treatment for their food or sugar addiction.

One may try cognitive-behavioral treatment (CBT). This helps to identify thought patterns and change them to create a new coping mechanism for the individual that doesn't involve eating.

One may try medication for their mental issues. It is also a possibility to try solution-focused therapy. This aims to find solutions for triggers of overeating and emotional eating. Trauma therapy may be used for those who eat as a result of past trauma. One may use eating as a coping mechanism for this trauma, and they should seek help for coping with that trauma and any emotions associated with it. One may seek the help of a nutritional counselor or dietary planner, who may create an individualized plan for the person and come up with meals that they may eat each day in order for them to be nutritionally satisfied.

There are also 12-step programs, which involve meetings with others who share the addiction to food. This can help one to feel less lonely and meet others that also struggle with their issue. Typically, one will receive a sponsor to truly help them to develop a plan to combat their addiction. There are also commercial treatment programs, which may cost more but will still offer beneficial information and effective solutions to those who struggle with food addiction. One may also visit a psychiatrist to discuss their issues and receive medication that will help them to feel better and eliminate the need for using food as a coping mechanism.

When one experiences emotional troubles, they need a way to cope with those issues. For those that turn to food, addictions to certain foods or sugary foods can become quite common. There are several ways to recognize and treat these addictions. One may first try to solve their problems themselves. If that is ineffective, though, they may need to seek professional help for their addiction.

Chapter 4: Setting Goals

It's always important to set goals. It's crucial to constantly set goals to improve oneself and work towards being happier and healthier. It is especially important to set goals regarding health. Everyone gets off the path to success once in a while, and it is important to constantly check in to ensure that the proper steps are taken to maintain the best body and mind possible. By being more aware of which aspects of one's self can be improved, it will be easier to work towards being the best person possible.

Determining the Proper Way to Treat Your Body

Before setting goals, one must determine which aspects of their health that they wish to most improve. It may help to keep a log of one's daily activities and the foods they consume (as well as water that they drink). This will help put into perspective what improvements must be made to help with the individual's health. There are several aspects that the

280

individual may make improvements to. Of course, diet and exercise are common ways to improve one's health, yet other aspects should also be considered to maximize the individual's health.

One aspect that may be improved upon is improving the types of foods that one puts into their body. They may limit themselves to only consuming certain foods on holidays or birthdays. This goal will depend on the person, as some individuals will have more improving to do than others. For instance, one that consumes seven donuts a week may try to first dwindle that number down to one per week, eventually having only a few per year or cutting that out altogether. There may be a certain type of food that the individual wishes to reduce in their diet or replace it with another food. They may also wish to incorporate more nutritious foods into their diet. There are several food-related goals. One may wish to adopt a vegan, vegetarian, or plant-based diet. They may wish to switch from refined grains to whole grains. They may also wish to switch to healthier fats.

In addition to improving the types of foods that one eats, they may also wish to set goals for their eating habits. For instance, portion sizes may have to be reduced. It may also be wise to set a schedule to stick to regarding meals to eliminate binging episodes and excessive snacking. One may also set goals regarding eating with fewer distractions and taking more time to eat so that their brain properly registers the foods that they will consume. The individual may also set the goal of not eating past fullness.

For many, fitness is also a common category in health-related goal-setting. There are different ways to set goals regarding fitness. One may wish to exercise for a certain amount every week. They may wish to set goals in a specific activity, such as running for 3 miles at 6 mph without stopping (or running a 6-minute mile). They may also wish to visit the gym a certain amount of times per week. It may involve an event, such as running a 5k. There may also be a certain category for the exercise, such as incorporating more cardio or more strength into workouts. Fitness goals may even be as simple as improving one's posture. This can help muscles to be healthier. They may even set simple goals such as walking or biking instead of driving or using the stairs instead of an elevator.

Along with diet and exercise, the individual may wish to aim for a healthier weight or slimmer waist size. A doctor should be consulted to determine the ideal weight based on the person.

Sleep is very important. Without proper sleep, one is more likely to develop poor eating habits and suffer mental health issues. One may wish to set a schedule for their sleep, such as going to bed at 10 each night and waking up at 5 each morning. They may also set a goal for the number of hours of sleep every night. One may also make the goal of sleeping through the night, which may be accomplished by consulting a medical professional and taking supplements. The individual may also set goals for their nightly routine, making sure to unwind before bed and reducing poor nightly habits.

Water is also an important goal to set. One typically will set goals increasing the amount of water they drink on a daily basis so that they consume the proper amount. This may also involve replacing other beverages with water.

One may wish to set goals regarding the elimination of poor habits. One may wish to eliminate or reduce the amount of tobacco or other drugs that they use. This can help reduce the risk of lung cancer (for smokers) and decrease potential health problems. Another goal may be to eliminate or reduce the amount of alcohol that the individual consumes. This may also be replaced with water to ensure that the individual is staying hydrated and not consuming unnecessary beverages. One may choose to limit the number of drinks they consume or how often they drink.

Social goals are important to set to ensure that one's mental health stays in check. If the individual has found themselves neglecting themselves from others, it may be time to set some social goals. Perhaps the individual wishes to make plans with friends at least once per week. They may set the goal of finding two clubs to join or an organization to volunteer with and sticking to that. They may set a number of times per month that they wish to volunteer or attend meetings. They may also set goals to spend more time with family members. This may also involve technology goals. Perhaps one wishes to cut out or reduce social media usage in favor of face-to-face socialization. They may also wish to reduce the amount of time that they spend on certain devices.

One may also set mental goals. This will help to keep one's emotions more stable, and their mental health will be improved as a result. One may wish to practice gratitude by writing in a journal each day. The individual may also set the goal of relaxing for a certain time each day or week. It is important to take time for oneself. This can be done by going for walks, reading, meditating, writing, creating, or whatever else is relaxing. One may also set spiritual or religious goals to attend services, pray, or learn more about one's faith. This can also help.

One may also set medical goals. They may wish to regularly visit a therapist, dentist, doctor, or other medical professional regularly and stick to their appointments.

Setting Goals

There is a certain way to set goals for oneself. Although many set the goal of "being healthier," what does this mean? It's hard to determine if one has met that goal because it is not clearly defined. Once the individual has determined what aspects of their health that they would like to improve, they must set proper goals accordingly. These goals must be strong objectives that will allow the goal-setter to monitor their progress towards achieving these goals. These goals must be SMART, which is an acronym for being specific, measurable, achievable, relevant, and time-bound.

Specific

The goal must be specific. This means that it must be clear and well-defined what exactly the goal is. This will make it easier for both the individual and any others that will encourage that individual to take steps towards achieving that goal. The individual should know what they are doing, how they would like to impact themselves, and what the action is. For instance, instead of setting the goal of simply losing weight, the individual may wish to lose 10 pounds by replacing sugary foods with more nutritional options and by visiting the gym.

Measurable

The goal must be measurable. Instead of simply saying that one will visit the gym, they can set the goal of visiting the gym for an hour three days a week. This allows the individual to measure if they are making progress towards their goal.

Achievable

The goal must be achievable. Although losing twenty pounds in a week may sound great to some, this is not realistic, nor is it healthy. Going to the gym for two hours, seven days a week, is also not realistic or healthy, as rest is needed. Time, supplies, and health should be considered when setting goals that are realistic.

Relevant

The goal must be relevant. This means that the goal should have importance to the individual. Otherwise, it will be difficult to find the motivation to work towards that goal. For instance, one that wants to incorporate more cardiovascular exercises into their routine but hates running should not set the goal of running three miles each morning. They may instead choose to focus on another exercise, such as dancing, biking, or swimming. Goals should be exciting. The individual should look forward to improving themselves and working towards their goal. Otherwise, it will be quite easy to abandon the goal set.

Time-Based

The goal must be time-based. Otherwise, it is hard to measure them, and there will be room to slack off. If one's goal is to lose 24 pounds in the next year, it can be much easier to work towards. This makes splitting the goal easy. Instead of looking at it as losing a total of 24 pounds, the individual can see it as losing only 2 pounds per month, which does not sound as difficult. By splitting the goal into smaller goals based on the time period, it will be easier to measure and not seem as overwhelming as looking at the whole goal.

Planning Those Goals

It's one thing to come up with the goals for one. However, it is important to truly take action and plan how to go about accomplishing those goals. There are several ways to do so. There are also ways to make it easier to accomplish those goals and to find additional motivation to work towards those goals. The individual may prioritize their goals, split them up, start a blog or journal, accomplish goals in a group, or even seek professional help for working towards their goals.

Prioritizing Goals

The individual should prioritize their goals. This is important to ensure that they are working towards what is most important to them. This step may also involve eliminating goals that are irrelevant or unimportant. It may also involve combining certain goals. For instance, instead of eating better and exercising more, the individual may set the goal of losing weight by eating better and exercising more. Typically, it is best to stick to one to three goals. It's difficult to keep track of more than this, and it makes it easier to place greater importance on achieving these goals.

Setting Goals

When setting goals, it's important to split them up. This will make it much easier and realistic to go about achieving. For instance, if one wishes to run 40 miles in a month, they may instead look at it as (assuming that a month has four weeks) ten miles per week. They may further split that up and run 2 miles 5 days per week. Two miles seems much more achievable than forty. Goals may be split up into smaller daily, weekly, or even monthly goals. If the goal is measurable, this should be quite easy to accomplish, and the progress towards achieving that goal will be easy to track.

Starting a Journal

One way to make accomplishing goals easier is to start a journal or log. This will make it simple to track progress and even write how one feels about their goals. It can help with maintaining motivation. It's a great way to remind oneself why they are working towards this goal. These can also be used as a scheduling tool to help the individual to come up with a plan for their goals. They may combine this with prioritizing to determine what is important and use the goal-splitting to write a plan.

Seeking Help from Others

One may also seek help from others. It is really beneficial when one sets goals with others. That means that all people involved may hold each other accountable, encourage each other, and remind each other why these goals are important. They may find a friend to go to the gym with or otherwise be active with. They may have each person living with them start eating healthier foods. The individual may join a club for those with similar goals. They may even seek the help of a professional in guiding them to success. The professional will have more knowledge about proper goals and how to achieve them.

Easing into Better Habits

There are many ways to make small changes that will have a big impact on one's life. Of course, one can make progress towards their goals each and every day. They may split up their goals and tackle a portion daily, working towards the bigger goal and making their body the healthiest they can. However, there are many small changes that one may make to improve their health. These small habits can have a great effect on a person's body, mind, and overall health. By incorporating these habits into one's lifestyle, they are truly helping themselves.

Trying Challenges

One fun way to go about making healthier choices is to try challenges. There are many 30-day challenges out there, most of which have a schedule to follow each day and are already planned out. These usually involve doing a bit each day or starting a new habit and sticking to it for thirty days. By committing for thirty days, the individual is training their brain to think of the new habit as normal. It also allows the individual to follow a plan that already has goals that are split up and easier to follow. These goals are also measurable.

These challenges can be for anything. They may even be for a different length of time (such as a week). By looking at the goal as a fun challenge instead of a goal to work towards, it will be more fun and seen as a sort of game to play. The individual may set a goal to do yoga, meditate, go without eating certain foods or drinks, drink enough water, only have three meals per day, or do a certain exercise a certain way. These are all small habits to make one healthier and to improve their body and mind.

Slightly Changing Routines

Another great way to incorporate healthy habits is by slightly changing morning and night routines. For instance, one may choose to have a glass of lemon water within thirty minutes of waking up every morning. They may also reserve a certain time, such as eight a.m., for exercising for an hour. By starting off the morning on the right foot, the individual is setting themselves up for success. This will start the day off well and motivate the individual, as they have already accomplished something at the beginning of their day. Nighttime routines are also important, as this is a way to unwind and prepare the individual for sleep. One great habit is shutting off all electronics an hour before bed. Setting a sleep schedule, creating a skincare routine, reflecting, setting goals for the next day, and reading are all great habits to incorporate into one's nighttime routine.

Setting goals are crucial for improving one's health. It is important to know what goals to set, how to set them, how to accomplish them, as well as how to incorporate healthier habits into one's life. By following these steps, the individual is setting themselves up for success in achieving their health-related goals in life.

Chapter 5: Mindset

Adopting the proper mindset is crucial for one's success. Without the proper mindset, the individual will not have the motivation to work towards and achieving their goals. It is important to have the proper mindset for achieving goals so that they may work towards them. There is a certain mindset necessary for remaining motivated when one gets hit with issues to face. One must adopt the right mindset to avoid unhealthy addictions. There is a proper mindset for improving one's physical health and having a healthier body. The proper mindset is also necessary for better mental health and a healthy mind.

Mindset for Achieving Goals

When one wishes to take steps towards achieving their goals, a certain mindset must be adopted. It is crucial that one sticks to their goals and works towards them every day. To do so, certain aspects regarding one's mindset may need some tweaking to help them to achieve their goals.

Developing a "Change" Mindset

The first mindset adjustment is to change. In order to better oneself, change is necessary. This may be difficult for some. Some individuals stay with jobs that they don't enjoy despite knowing that better options are available because they settle for what's comfortable to them. In order to achieve one's goals, however, a change must be made. Whether that's a change in routine, scheduling, or behavior, change is necessary to work towards achieving a goal. One must recognize that change, although it may be nerve-wracking at first, is beneficial and should be viewed as advancement towards becoming a better person.

Developing a Detail-Oriented Mindset

It's also important to develop a detail-oriented mindset. When working towards goals, it's important to take into account every action that is taken and what may be improved upon. This will really help one to track progress towards achieving goals. It will also help the individual to know what exactly it is that they want. When one becomes clearer about what their goal is and why they have set it, it will be easier to work towards. This will also help with scheduling exact ways to make progress towards the goal and will help when the individual is recording their daily progress.

Developing a "Constructive Criticism" Mindset

Another mindset that must be adopted is the constructive criticism mindset. If working towards a goal, the individual must already be aware that some change must be made in their life. Although it isn't always enjoyable to be criticized, it is necessary to use constructive criticism to one's advantage. This means taking it from both others and from oneself. When crafting the goals to accomplish, one must realize what it is that they need to improve about themselves. They must also be willing to hear what others see, as this will give an outsider's perspective. This can also be helpful while working towards those goals. One must constantly check in with themselves and determine if there is any way that they may be able to achieve their goals more efficiently and effectively. It takes a strong person to be able to acknowledge that they may be slacking off with working towards their goals. However, the sooner that it is recognized, the sooner the individual may go back to working towards their goals and bettering themselves.

Developing a "Progress" Mindset

The final mindset that is important for achieving goals is that progress is just as important as achieving the goal. Often, people adopt an "all or nothing" mentality. This can prove detrimental, as progress is what drives results. It is still helpful even if a person only slightly improves their health. Many smaller changes lead to a great change and an improvement in health.

Mindset for Staying Motivated Despite Obstacles

There are several adjustments that are beneficial to one's mindset when trying to stay motivated despite obstacles. There will always be inconveniences that arise or negative influences that hinder one's performance. For instance, holidays may be a time that can be tempting to cave in to overeating tendencies. When one is sick and has a sore throat, they may be tempted to binge on ice cream. Friends may want to go out to eat and go drinking. These are all ways that the individual may be swayed towards making a choice that they wouldn't make otherwise.

Adopting a Disciplined Mindset

To remain motivated, one must adopt a disciplined mindset. They must be able to practice self-control. It is okay to give in to unhealthy choices every once in a while. Although it would be ideal for eating perfectly nutritious meals all the time, this is not realistic. One must enjoy themselves every so often. However, this shouldn't be taken too far. Perhaps the individual has chosen to allow themselves one cheat meal per week. This is adequate, provided that they remain disciplined. Although it's fine to eat that meal out and choose foods that wouldn't usually be consumed, the individual shouldn't overstuff themselves or eat beyond what they should. They must remain disciplined and stick to their original plan.

Rewarding Oneself

It is important to reward oneself. When progress has been made, it is important to recognize that and to celebrate one's success. Every step forward should be viewed as progress towards achieving the goal. However, the individual shouldn't stop and celebrate every tiny bit of progress that is made in a way that will interfere with other goals. They must also not give up or stop just because they have made progress. Even though progress is good, the individual should keep working towards their goal.

Penalizing Oneself

Along with rewarding oneself, it is crucial to adopt the proper mindset concerning punishing oneself. It is not beneficial to punish oneself for making mistakes or for getting off track with one's goals. It is important to acknowledge that the mistake has been made, determine why that mistake was made, and determine how to avoid making the same mistake in the future. However, one should not punish themselves for making a mistake; imperfection is inevitable. The individual must move on. Similarly, the individual should not "domino" once they make a mistake. One should not abandon their goals as a result of one mistake. For instance, one may eat fries on a day where they shouldn't (perhaps they've already had their unhealthy foods for the week and reached their capacity). Although this decision may not have aligned with their goals, they shouldn't have the mindset of not caring. Often, people will do so and think they've already made a mistake. What's the harm in making more mistakes? It's already been messed up. They will then proceed to drink soda, have a cheeseburger, and go back to the same pre-goal mindset. However, this should not be the case. When a mistake has been made, the individual should go right back to their goals. They should not stray farther off the path, as this can lead to further damage and possible abandonment of the goals altogether.

Mindset for a Healthier Body

One must adjust their mindset for a healthier body. To achieve a healthier body, one must have a passion for improving their physical health. This is crucial for success. Although one may enjoy eating potato chips and watching television all day, the individual with a proper mindset will be able to take care of themselves properly and have the motivation to help themselves to become better. There are a few factors to adjust when changing one's mindset.

Developing a "You Are What You Eat" Mindset

One must first consider the "you are what you eat" mindset. Although this is a common phrase that is typically not given much meaning, it is very true. If one consumes healthy, nutritional foods, their body will be healthy and full of nutrition. If one does not watch the health of the foods they consume, their body will not be healthy. It is important to understand the reasoning for eating well. What an individual puts in their body will directly affect their health. By not caring about one's diet, the individual is increasing their risk of a number of health problems. This can cause short-term and long-term issues for that individual and for their health.

Developing a "Fitness" Mindset

A similar mindset is necessary regarding fitness. Although it may be easy to avoid exercising, it is highly beneficial for the individual to exercise. The individual's fitness level also directly corresponds to their health. One who eats well but doesn't exercise is missing half of the equation and will be unable to unlock their full potential. It is important to stay in motion so that the individual may move properly, especially into older age.

Developing a "Work-Life Balance" Mindset

Another mindset to adopt is that rest is just as important as work. Although it isn't okay to use sleep as an excuse for not watching one's health, the individual must ensure that they are receiving a proper amount of sleep each night. This will help to allow the body to rest from exercise. It will also help the individual to have the proper amount of energy and not to eat to make up for that lost energy. Getting too much sleep is also just as bad as receiving too little sleep. The individual must place a high value on sleep, as it is necessary for one's health.

Developing an Overall Positive Mindset

An overall positive mindset is required for those who wish to have a healthy body. Although there may be many "what if" questions, the individual should have a positive outlook and believe in themselves. Mistakes are inevitable. What matters not is if mistakes are made, they will be. It matters more about how the individual handles themselves after they make a mistake. One may also be tempted to think of negative things when reflecting on their past. Although there may have been mistakes made, the individual must think about the future and how to improve it. They should not dwell on their past mistakes; they are working towards improving their present and future selves. An "everything happens for a reason" mindset is also beneficial when it comes to a healthier body. Some that are overweight or obese may think that they "weren't blessed" with an ideal body. They may think that they are meant to live in the body that they have. By approaching it from an "everything happens for a reason" mindset, the individual may see that there is hope for them. They had that body, and now, it is time to improve that body. By improving themselves so greatly, the individual will have an even greater appreciation for their new body and all of the great progress that they made. There will be a great appreciation for all of the hard work that went into the formation of their newer and better selves.

Mindset for a Healthier Mind

Those who want to be healthier overall must also realize that the mind is just as important as the body. Although it is important to pay attention to physical health, mental health can be just as important (if not, more important). This is because one's mental health directly affects one's physical health. If one is not in the right mindset, they will not work towards improving their physical health and may feel a barrier separating them from their current self to an improved version of themselves. Often, when people speak of health, physical health is what first comes to mind. However, individuals must not neglect mental health, as it shapes who they are. If one's mental health is inadequate, they will not have the motivation to take care of their physical health. They will not have the motivation to work towards their goals and improve themselves, as they will be stuck in the negative emotions that they are feeling.

Taking Care of Oneself

Another important mindset switch regards taking care of oneself. Society constantly seems to force individuals to put everything before themselves. Mothers must put their children before themselves. Giving is more important than receiving. It's important to put in the effort with friends even if they do not put effort into themselves. Although this is a great mindset to have, as it is kind and will be appreciated, one must also watch their own health. It's okay to take time for oneself. It's okay to spend money on oneself. It's okay to indulge in a treat once in a while. There are many ways to pamper oneself, and it should not be an activity to feel guilty about. It is necessary to take time to be alone and relax. When a stressful situation occurs, it is important to step back from the situation and take time to deal with it in a healthy manner. When one does not do so, unhealthy coping mechanisms surface, one of which is emotional eating.

Surrounding Oneself with Other People

In order to improve one's mental health, the individual should also recognize that it is crucial to surround themselves with the proper people. It is okay to distance the self from those who don't make them the best person possible. People that bring negativity into the individual's life should not be given that power. The people that one surrounds themselves with should encourage them to be the best possible person that they are. They should motivate the individual to make progress towards their goals in life.

Being in an Environment in Which One Thrives In

It is also crucial for the individual to reside in an environment that they thrive in. If one does not take care of their surroundings, they will constantly feel overwhelmed and find it difficult to focus on themselves. One way to make this happen is by having a clean environment that is free of distractions or any negative influences. A person's home and workspace should be kept clean in order to maximize their productivity and to improve their mental health. This may also involve creating a "safe space." This is a place that the individual may visit when they need time to be quiet, reflect, and take time to themselves. This may be a room, a favorite place to visit, or simply a chair to read in. No matter where it is, the individual should find the space that best suits them for this purpose. This will really help to improve the individual's mental health, as they will be able to cope better by visiting this space. This is a much healthier way to deal with any stress or issues that may come up in the individual's life. It will allow them to find peace and quiet. Instead of eating emotionally, for example, the individual may take time in this space.

Mindset for Avoiding Addiction

For those with addiction, a certain mindset must be adopted. It is crucial to overcome addiction, as it can take a serious toll on one's

298

health. When overcoming addiction, one must have a positive mindset and be willing to change themselves. It will be difficult, and the individual must be willing to overcome obstacles to rid themselves of the addiction and to help to be a better person. They must also avoid addiction in the future and discipline themselves well enough to prevent relapse from occurring. This is possible with the proper mindset.

Recognizing When Help Is Needed

The individual must be able to recognize when help is needed. Although independence is important, they should not look to others as ones to depend on. Others are there to support and help. It is one's own goals that they are working towards. Sometimes, it is truly beneficial to seek the help of others. The individual must be able to motivate themselves, although they must also recognize when it would be more beneficial to seek the help of others. Perhaps a professional is needed to guide the individual towards their goals. Perhaps it would be beneficial to have a friend or group that shares similar goals. This individual may find it beneficial to receive motivation from others and be able to discuss their progress or exchange tips with others on ways to reach their goals.

Having a Balance Between Cutting Oneself Slack and Staying Motivated

There must be a balance between cutting oneself slack and staying motivated. Although it is important to be able to allow oneself to make mistakes without punishing themselves or becoming overly frustrated, it is also important to not let everything slide. There must be a distinction between trying and actually doing. One must not reward themselves when they have not worked towards their goals. Simply trying is not enough; you must actually put in the effort and make progress towards your goals.

Not Giving Up Along the Way

Similarly, when working towards your goals, it is important not to let the past get in the way. Perhaps a certain strategy has not worked. Perhaps you have tried every diet out there, every workout routine possible. You've joined groups, started a journal, or a number of other attempts. Everyone works differently. Although certain strategies may not have led you to accomplish your goals in the past, it is important to keep making an effort. You must not give up just because you messed up once. Everyone has their own way of motivating themselves. There are thousands of possible ways to better your health. If you've tried dozens of ways, there are still thousands out there waiting for you to try. This mindset is crucial to your success.

Staying Motivated

Those with goals must adopt the proper mindset for achieving such goals. There is also a certain mindset necessary for remaining motivated despite possible obstacles in the way. If one wishes to have a healthy body, one must adopt the proper mindset. Similarly, one who desires improved mental health must also adopt the proper mindset. A proper mindset is also required for those wishing to overcome and prevent future unhealthy addictions for themselves.

Chapter 6: Mindfulness

Practicing mindfulness can be beneficial for the body and mind. One that practices mindfulness will be more aware of their emotions and their hunger. One may practice mindful eating to solve certain issues. One may use mindfulness to prevent themselves from giving in to food cravings. Mindfulness may also be used to help one struggling with compulsive overeating. Practicing mindfulness will allow one also to learn how to enjoy the food that they eat. This can help one to overcome certain food addictions and to prevent compulsive overeating. Mindfulness will additionally help one's mental and physical health to be improved.

What Is Mindfulness?

Mindfulness is all about being aware. It means that the mind is aware of what's happening and what is occurring in the surrounding environment. Oftentimes, especially with the increase of dependence upon technology, we are distracted. There are constant messages to read, people to talk to, and places to be. However, it is important to live in the moment and check-in with oneself. We must learn to live in the present instead of dwelling on the past or worrying about the future. This will truly help improve one's physical and mental health.

Mindfulness is about relaxing, not reacting. Stress can lead to overwhelming emotions, yet we must take time to ourselves and listen to our bodies. No matter what is going on, it is important to take time to unwind and listen to your body. It's important to know how you are truly feeling physically and mentally. If there is something bothering you, being mindful will help you to pinpoint what it is that's bothering you. It is important to practice mindfulness at least every once in a while to tune in to your feelings and emotions. This will allow you to treat your body properly.

One common way to practice mindfulness is through meditation, although there are many ways that one may practice mindfulness. It is possible to write down one's feelings, perhaps in a journal, to truly understand what's going on. One may choose to talk to someone, whether that be a friend or a professional. This is a great way to see what's on the mind and what may need to be fixed. One may also choose to have some quiet time to themselves. They may go for a walk, simply sit down, or do whatever it takes for them to have some time to themselves.

It isn't difficult to practice mindfulness. Although many choose to add meditation to their mindfulness exercises, mindfulness may be practiced anywhere by anyone. It doesn't require great change; it simply involves taking the time to be more aware of oneself and one's thoughts. It may also provide those who practice it with several benefits. One will reduce the stress in their life, have more motivation, see their goals more clearly, and gain insight into one's mind. It will also help one to become more aware of their thoughts and increase one's ability to focus on themselves and on others. It may also make certain issues clearer that the individual would have missed otherwise.

Mindfulness for Food Cravings and Compulsive Overeating

Mindfulness can help with a number of issues, some of which are food cravings and compulsive overeating. When one practices mindfulness, they may occupy their mind with topics other than that of cravings. This provides short-term memory with a distraction, therefore interrupting cravings. When practiced in the long-term, mindfulness can work to eventually stop cravings and prevent them from occurring in the future. Mindfulness has been found to help with addictions to food, drugs, and alcohol. This is a method to try for those struggling with cravings and addictions.

Cravings result from an intense desire at the moment to fulfill some "need." For instance, one may have an intense craving for food. This craving will typically subside if the individual waits it out. However, cravings can be so intense that the individual can't wait; they must give in and fulfill their craving. If one practices mindfulness, however, they may be able to recognize that this craving is only temporary and is not caused by any logical reason. It is simply the body wanting what it can't have. It is especially helpful if the individual recognizes that this craving is not something that they need. This can be particularly true for highly unhealthy cravings, such as foods high in sugar, salt, and fat. Cravings may result from a particular emotion or situation that triggers it. If the individual can pinpoint the origin of this craving, they may help themselves more. For instance, the individual may reflect on their feelings and determine that they are feeling stressed. Instead of giving in to their craving of a dozen donuts, they may realize that they are stressed and do an activity that relieves such stress instead.

Mindfulness may also be used for compulsive overeating. Instead of continuing to shove food in your mouth, you may be more mindful. It is necessary to get used to the feeling of when you are full so that you may understand when it is time to stop eating. During meals, take the time to register how you are feeling. When you are full, don't continue eating. Perhaps listen to your body and determine why you think you should continue eating. Is it a feeling of guilt? Perhaps you don't want to waste food. If this is the case, develop a smart and easy way to save food. Perhaps you don't even realize that you are full because you eat without thinking. This is why it's crucial to check in with yourself throughout the meal to determine if you are eating to fuel your body or if you are eating mindlessly. This is important to determine so that you may prevent yourself from overeating. When you are mindful, you will be more aware of how your body feels. You will be able to determine if you are full. If so, you will know when it's the proper time to stop eating.

Incorporating Mindfulness into Your Life

When one thinks of mindfulness, they may imagine the stereotypical meditator—burning a candle, legs crossed, soothing music, eyes closed, and maybe even humming. Although meditation is a great way to practice mindfulness and train the body to relax while the mind focuses; this is not the only way that one may practice mindfulness. There are several exercises and strategies for becoming more mindful. It doesn't have to be difficult to start with, and there are many options so that anyone may enjoy the process of becoming more mindful and having a more relaxed and focused mind.

To be mindful, one must be quiet and listen to their body. There are many apps out there that allow one to enjoy guided mindfulness sessions. This is a simple way for a beginner to start their mindfulness journey without having to worry about learning to guide themselves; they must simply listen to the guide. There are also many videos on the Internet with guided mindfulness sessions. This is a great way for a beginner to start. For an Internet-free option, one may choose just to sit and breathe. This can be for an extended period of time or simply a couple of minutes. While breathing, the individual should focus on their breath and be aware of their body's reaction to that breath. If the mind wanders, the individual should bring it back to their breath. This has the greatest benefit when the individual truly carves out their time for this experience. Otherwise, they will feel rushed and unable to focus on being mindful. Mindfulness can't be rushed. Instead of viewing it as something that must be done before moving on with the day, it must be viewed as an important part of the day. This will give it greater importance.

One may practice mindfulness while they eat. This means paying attention while one is eating. One may practice mindfulness while walking and focus on the movement of their body and their surroundings. One may practice mindful breathing, really focusing on the effect of breathing on the body. Connecting with the senses every once in a while is another way to be mindful. The individual may focus on what they are seeing, smelling, touching, tasting, hearing, and feeling at the moment. Mindful listening is crucial for both gaining knowledge and building better relationships. Instead of focusing on one's surroundings or on anything but the present, the individual should listen to the speaker and what they have to say. Full listening is much more mindful than thinking of what to say next or letting the mind wander to other topics. Taking little pauses throughout the day is also a great way to be mindful of the little things in life. One may also pause to consider their current thoughts and emotions. One may also take mindful showers and baths, truly enjoying the sensation of water on the skin. Yoga is a great way to be mindful, as it teaches the individual to focus on their breathing while being aware of the body. Of course, a very common way to practice mindfulness is by meditating.

Learning How to Enjoy Your Food

One who eats mindfully can really help themselves. Mindfully eating can keep one fuller for longer, reduce cravings, prevent overeating, and simply help the individual to enjoy their food and mealtime in general. It helps one to take control of their eating habits.

Freeing Oneself of Distractions

While eating, one should free themselves of distractions. Often, we eat while on our phones, watching television, or otherwise while distracted. One who eats mindfully will rid themselves of distractions and instead focus on the present. This means truly taking the time to appreciate the look of the food, the smell of the food, and the taste of the food. One will begin to view food as a blessing, something that is truly worth appreciating. When we don't take the time to appreciate our food truly, the brain won't register it. This is a common reason for overeating. We don't realize how much food we are putting in our bodies, so we keep putting more in. Instead of doing this, it is crucial to register every bite that we take and to really think about the food as we eat it.

Focusing on Hunger

Another way to eat mindfully is to focus on hunger. One should only eat when truly hungry. This means paying attention to the body's hunger cues. Instead of eating for fun or when one is bored, one should only eat when they are truly hungry. Listening to the body's cues will help with this. Additionally, one should only eat until they are full. Overstuffing oneself is an easy way to overeat. This can be prevented by really listening to the body's cues and determining when it is time to stop. The body will no longer give hunger cues.

Before eating, one should pay attention to their emotions. Are they eating as the result of a certain emotion, or is it due to hunger? One should notice how they feel about eating, too. Is there anxiety regarding eating? While eating, one should remain focused on their feelings and how the food makes them feel. What are the effects of food on the body and mind? The foods that one eats should not make them feel guilty or anxious, and they should make the body feel good. A person experiencing guilt or anxiety about the foods they consume or noticing a negative impact on their body and mind should make a dietary change to improve how they feel.

Mindfulness can prove highly beneficial for individuals. Mindfulness is the practice of being quiet and paying attention to one's mind and body. It can help with one's eating habits. It can help those who struggle with compulsive overeating or with hard-to-handle food cravings. It is quite easy to incorporate mindfulness into one's life, and there are several ways to do so. One may also try mindful eating, which is becoming more aware of their food while they eat. Practicing mindfulness is helpful for the body.

Chapter 7: Intuitive Eating

Intuitive eating is another way to improve one's health. It is important for one to understand what intuitive eating is so that they may incorporate it into their life. One may also learn how to practice intuitive eating to improve their health. There are certain intuitive habits that one may also begin to improve their health. It is important that one also sets intuitive goals to maximize their potential as a person. There are many benefits of intuitive eating, and there are several positive effects that it will have on the person who practices eating intuitively.

What Is Intuitive Eating?

Intuitive eating and mindful eating are often used interchangeably, yet their functions and practices differ. Mindful eating is being aware of the whole eating experience. It requires one to focus on their food and their feelings. However, intuitive eating relies more on one's intuition. One must really pay attention to the gut instinct they have. They must learn to eat for physical reasons instead of emotional reasons. This really relies on one's ability to understand their internal hunger and satiety cues. Although mindfulness can assist with understanding these concepts, one must rely on their intuition to really feel this. Mindfulness is the process of understanding how to use these concepts. Intuitive eating is the concept itself and may be used alongside mindfulness.

Intuitive eating is not about restricting oneself to a certain diet. It's not about counting calories, weighing yourself every day, or worrying about macros. In fact, those may actually contribute to overeating and emotional troubles. When doing this, one is just disconnected from themselves. They think more about numbers than how they actually feel. Although they may have an ideal waist size, look fit in photographs, or weigh their ideal weight, they may not be truly happy.

Intuitively eating requires the individual to pay attention to their hunger, not their boredom. It teaches people not to feel guilty about enjoying themselves and eating their favorite food. This helps to promote emotional wellness. It's important to not think about the numbers or any foods that make one feel guilty. It is more about listening to the body, which is the natural way to eat and live. It relies on internal cues as opposed to external cues. This will help the individual determine how much they should eat, what foods their body needs, and when to eat. On the other hand, those who undergo a diet are likely to be unhappy. They will restrict themselves to eating certain foods. When this occurs, they are likely to crash at some point.

While dieting, people are following what works for others' bodies. However, each individual's body differs. Everyone has different wants and needs, and those must be fulfilled differently for each person. People may eat certain foods because they're generally regarded as "good" or "healthy," but it is important to eat what makes the body feel good. One should let go of any anxiety or grief over certain foods and find out what really helps to provide them with energy and happiness.

How to Eat Intuitively and Implement Intuitive Habits

To eat intuitively, one must abandon the "dieting" mentality. One must learn to not focus on weight loss or on numbers in general. They must not feel guilty for their lack of progress towards losing weight. You may have books or magazines with dieting tips; get rid of them. Diets are just fads. They contribute to gaining weight more often than losing weight. Rid yourself of dieting influences. If you follow any dieting pages on social media, unfollow them. Take control of your life instead of letting diets take control of your life. Surround yourself with positive messages regarding health and food. Cut out any negative people in your life that bring you down. Instead, surround yourself with positive health influences. Stop trying to chase after diets with the same results. Start out fresh and reset your body and mind.

Truly listen to your body's sense of hunger. This is a naturally-occurring process that signals when it is time to eat. Eating is necessary for life. It is necessary to keep your energy up. You must be able to really learn when your body needs to be refueled. Much like a car's gas light may go on, your body will start to send you apparent signals when it must be refueled. If you ignore these signals, your body will respond. As time passes, your body will become more desperate for food and begin craving some foods. You may also feel the need to binge or otherwise overeat to compensate for this prolonged hunger. By feeding yourself at the proper time, you are allowing your body to be fueled properly.

Similarly, you should understand the concept of fullness. You shouldn't feel obligated to eat when you don't want to or need to. You should also not feel guilty for leaving any food uneaten. Listen to your body and understand when you are full and have had enough. It is also important to distinguish between fullness and satisfaction. You may be full but not satisfied. Often, we will crave a certain food and will still be "hungry" until we finally eat that food. Instead of listening to our bodies, we will usually try to "feed" that craving other foods. The body, however, will still be hungry because it is not satisfied. Satisfying that craving can often prevent one from this overeating that occurs, and it will usually take less food to satisfy yourself.

You must also make peace with all the food. Eating one donut won't take you from a healthy weight to obesity. When you restrict yourself to certain foods, your body will crave the off-limits foods even more. You may feel trapped and will feel guilty about consuming any of the "taboo" foods. By disallowing oneself to have certain foods, you will feel deprived and begin developing deep cravings for these foods. When you do finally consume that food, you will likely overeat and feel guilty once more. You should not categorize foods into what is good or bad. This will only lead to guilt. Eating should be an enjoyable experience, yet it

310

can become an activity that causes anxiety when one labels their food or criticizes themselves.

With intuitive eating, one must also pay attention to their emotions. Emotional eating occurs as a result of these emotions. Instead of coping with emotions using food, you should find another and healthier way to handle these emotions. Although the food may help with emotions, it may not be such a great idea. Often, it won't actually help. It is just a temporary distraction for a bigger issue. It is also really unwise to use eating as one's primary coping mechanism. There should be a variety of ways to help yourself feel better.

Reject vanity. With intuitive eating, one is focusing on how their body feels. If you only care about how your body looks, you may not even be truly healthy. You should not criticize your body or dislike yourself.

A healthy body comes along with intuitive eating and exercise. However, one should not change their habits purely out of vanity purposes. It is important to recognize how much it matters to treat your body well. You're only given one body in your life, so you must honor it. The same is true for exercise. Not all of us are supposed to be (or want to be) bodybuilders. It's okay if you don't like running. You should build a fitness routine that you like. That way, you'll enjoy exercising and will even look forward to it! This means that working out will become a fun activity instead of seeming like a chore. You should also pay attention to how exercising makes you feel. This is why to do it. You will have more energy, you may sleep better, and you will have more motivation.

Intuitive eating is all about abandoning the typical ways that one loses weight. You don't have to follow a certain diet. There's no "perfect" workout routine. It's all about you. It's about what you like. It's about what makes you feel good. You should pay attention to your body and how everything you do makes you feel. Although there are certain foods out there that are higher in nutritional value, you should go off of how you feel. Are the foods you eat satisfying? Are the foods you eat tasty? Of course, you may want to try putting more nutritious foods into your diet.

However, you shouldn't do so because you feel obligated to or because you would feel guilty otherwise. It should be because you want to. It should be because you feel good after eating them. You must also recognize that your diet as a whole is what matters. Over time, your diet should make you feel good. It isn't all or nothing. Having some French fries or soda here and there is okay. Allow yourself to love what you eat and not feel so guilty about what you eat.

Intuitive Eating Effects

Intuitive eating has a number of positive effects on the body. It will lead to higher self-esteem and better body image. This is because instead of being fixated on your weight, waist size, or the foods that you eat, you will pay attention to how you feel. You will feel good and therefore know that you're treating your body well. You will feel much better about yourself after intuitive eating than you could ever feel with any diet or exercise routine. You'll follow the right path for your body, not the path that someone else created for themselves.

You will feel more satisfied with life. In general, you'll learn how to pay attention more to what you really want in life. In addition to your physical health, you will know what makes you happy and what doesn't. This will help you to feel much better about your life. The idea of not feeling guilty for doing what others are doing will truly help you to be more satisfied with your life. You'll stop comparing yourself to others and paying attention to numbers. Life will be more about how you feel, and if you're happy, not what others think it should be.

You will become more optimistic.

In addition to feeling more satisfied with life, you will feel happier overall because you are doing what you like. You won't pay attention to negativity. You'll be surrounding yourself with those who are also positive and optimistic. Life will be more about enjoying yourself instead of following someone else's blueprint. You will view life as something that you are excited about, not something you should be better at.

Intuitive eating will greatly help your mental health. You will become better at coping and will develop better coping mechanisms for your emotions. This will also lead to a lower rate of emotional eating.

Those who implement intuitive eating also see physical results. Lower body mass indexes have been found with those who eat intuitively. It works! The right body will come with emotional eating. Those who eat intuitively also notice higher HDL cholesterol levels and lower triglyceride levels. Those who eat intuitively will also decrease their amount of cravings and decrease the likelihood of overeating. Because one will learn how to fill and satisfy their body, they won't feel the need to compensate by bingeing or by overeating in any way, giving in to cravings.

It is important to understand intuitive eating. Implementing it can have great effects on the body. There are several ways to implement intuitive eating into your life. You will be able to recognize when you are hungry and when you are full. Your physical and mental health will both receive a boost from intuitive eating. It can be combined with mindfulness and mindful eating to help your body to become the best that it possibly can. Your mental health will also receive a boost, and you will become much happier with yourself and with your life. Intuitive eating is truly beneficial for one's health.

Chapter 8: Detoxing

We've all heard of detoxing. It's used to rid the body of toxins and as a way to reverse any damage that we've caused to it. It's typically the result of one feeling unhappy with the way their body feels. They seek a solution to that nasty feeling and go on a detox as a result. There are many ways to detox and many foods that one may seek a detox from. Typically, one thinks of a juice cleanse when they hear the word detox. This is not the only way to detox, however.

What Is a Sugar Detox?

One way to cut one's sugar intake is to go on a sugar detox. This is when you cut out sugar for a certain period of time, and your body learns how to survive without it. It isn't easy for many, as we are surrounded by a great number of sugary options each day.

Most people consume more sugar each day than they are supposed to (four to five times the recommended maximum). Even if the sugar detox isn't permanent, it can train the body to survive without sugar and begin to ease sugar cravings. The health benefits of reducing sugar in one's body are numerous. By decreasing the amount of sugar in your diet, you are lowering your risk for medical conditions and improving

314

your mental health. You will also experience several physical benefits by doing so. However, it can be quite difficult at first. We crave sugar and are surrounded by so many options with much-added sugar.

Sugar is quite addictive. It has been shown to affect the same parts of the brain that nicotine, cocaine, and morphine do. It makes us happy to eat it, and we look forward to it. Although this doesn't seem detrimental, this is not good when sugar affects the body negatively. The body also needs more sugar as time passes, as it becomes tolerant to the sugar and needs more of it to allow for the same effects to occur to the body. When one consumes sugar, they experience a rush of energy, which can feel good and uplifting. One that cuts out sugar, however, will not be getting the same rush, and their body will have intense cravings for sugar and the rush that comes with it.

With sugar, detoxes may calm the effects of sugar withdrawal. When this occurs, one may experience a number of side effects as a result of cutting out sugar from their diet. One may experience cravings, may have difficulty focusing, may have depression or anxiety, and may find it difficult to get proper sleep. One may also experience headaches, low energy, light-headedness, dizziness, nausea, tingling, and fatigue. This will make it difficult for the person undergoing detox at first. One may typically get past these feelings if they stick with it for ten days. However, most that attempt sugar detoxes don't realize this and think that their bodies still need sugar. This is not true. The body must simply go through an adjustment phase before being comfortable without sugar.

How to Sugar Detox

Before beginning a sugar detox, you should plan for it and determine how you will do it. Although you can try a sugar detox for a long period of time, such as thirty days, it is typical to detox for three to ten days. This will help you to go cold turkey and completely eliminate sugar for that period of time. This will give your body time to adjust, yet it won't seem like so long that it is unrealistic for you. For this period of time, you will completely cut out any added, refined, artificial, and natural sugars. It is highly beneficial to seek help from a medical professional while on a sugar detox. They may give you any advice based on your health. This advice can be personal, and you should seek the advice of a medical professional before beginning a detox in case of any health conditions that would prevent you from doing so. The professional will also ensure that your diet remains balanced while on the detox. Although you are cutting out sugar, you should still be well-fed and be getting all the proper vitamins and nutrients while you are on the detox. You may also try easing into a sugar detox. You may decide to do this in a few ways. You may first decide to focus on one meal, such as improving your breakfast. Then, you can work at lunch. Then, you can improve your dinner. You may also work on cutting out sugary snacks and desserts. You may also ease into it by cutting out certain foods and cutting out more each week until you reach a level of sugar-free goodness. You may first work on beverages and then move to foods.

Some people may benefit more from easing into a sugar detox. This can occur over a certain period, such as over four weeks. You may divide the detox into four stages to make it more realistic for you.

It's also important that you take care of the mental aspects of going on a sugar detox. You may want to journal to have a place to jot down your feelings. You should remind yourself why you are going on a sugar detox. It is important to remind yourself of the health benefits of going on a sugar detox to know that you are helping your body and mind by embarking on a sugar detox journey.

Benefits of Sugar Detoxes

Sugar detoxes provide those who go on them with a number of benefits. Sugary foods tend not to have great nutritional value. Replacing those foods with more nourishing foods can really help the body to function better. The body's digestion, metabolism, and overall health will be improved. The body will be able to produce and use energy much more efficiently and effectively. Plus, the body won't experience crashes that it does when filled with sugar.

One will also enjoy the benefit of weight loss that comes with sugar detoxing. Cutting sugar is a great way to shed some pounds. Sugar helps the body to store more fat. By eliminating sugar, the body will decrease its stored fat. This will help you to have more energy and decrease your risk for health problems. Those who are overweight or obese have an increased risk of health issues, especially that of heart disease. Additionally, losing weight will help you to have more energy and be able to move more easily. You will also have higher self-confidence and self-esteem.

You will experience mental benefits by cutting sugar. You will regenerate the mind by detoxing. Instead of using glucose to fuel your brain, your mind will rely on more sustainable sources of fuel. Instead of crashing and becoming sluggish, you will be able to focus and concentrate better. Your mind won't be foggy from all of the extra sugar anymore. It will be easier for you to pay attention to what you love instead of being dragged down by sugar. Your cognitive function will be improved. Instead of being easily distracted, you will be able to think again. You will have more energy again. This will help with both thinking and moving. When consuming sugar, you may have a spike of energy that's quickly followed by a crash. When you crash, your body hits a low. You don't have any energy, and you are unable to concentrate. Eliminating sugar eliminates the crash that comes with it, allowing you to think better and have more energy.

You will see an improvement in your appearance. Your teeth and gums will be healthier after cutting out sugar. You will also improve the health of your skin, as acne can be caused by a surplus of sugar. Water retention will be reduced, so the appearance of bloating and swelling will improve. This can occur in the stomach, arms, legs, and fingers.

You will also decrease your risk of certain health problems. By decreasing the amount of sugar in your diet, you are decreasing your risk of developing heart disease. Your body will also be able to manage Type 2 Diabetes more efficiently and effectively. Reducing sugar will reduce your risk of non-alcoholic fatty liver disease, too. Your risk for Polycystic Ovarian Syndrome will also be reduced. You can really help your health by decreasing your sugar intake.

Detoxing Tips

It can be difficult to go on a sugar detox. There are a few ways to make it a bit easier for yourself, though. There are several strategies for making your transition from your normal diet to going on a sugar detox. It can be a tough adjustment for your body, especially since your body will still crave sugar at first. You may seem depleted of energy, and your body will try to overcompensate for the decreased amount of sugar by giving you intense cravings, especially for sugary and high-carb foods. One way to make detoxing easier for yourself is by quitting completely and quickly. Instead of trying to ease into a diet with less sugar, it is better to "shock" your body. Although you may experience more intense cravings and side effects, you won't experience these for as long. Your body will be forced to get used to it quickly, and your withdrawal symptoms will subside more quickly. It's like jumping into a cool pool instead of easing in. Your body will be forced to get used to it more quickly. Instead of feeling a little cool and going back on your decision, you will get used to it more quickly. This way, you'll be used to it before you even have the chance to second-guess yourself. It is best to simply cut out all sugary prepackaged foods, sweetened beverages, and white flour all at once. That way, you also won't be tempted to rely on one food for your sugar intake. For instance, if you only cut out sweetened beverages at first, you may be tempted to eat white flour and sugary foods to compensate for that. You may even justify worsening some habits as a result of improving others.

It is beneficial to increase your water, protein, and fiber intake. Protein will help your body to stay full for longer and keep your energy levels up. Fiber will help you to keep full for longer and regulate your blood sugar. This will help to decrease the likelihood of headaches, nausea, and cravings. You should drink more water as well. Staying hydrated will help you to avoid overeating. Since hunger and thirst feel similar, drinking water will help you not to mistake thirst for hunger. Staying hydrated will also help with digestion and will help minimize cravings.

It is best to avoid artificial sweeteners. Although it may seem beneficial to replace sugar with alternatives, it can impede your progress. These sweeteners will lead to sugar cravings and will leave your body dependent on sugar still. It gives the body false hope that sugary foods are still allowed.

It's also important to manage your overall health. There are aspects besides your diet that you must pay attention to. Managing your stress and dealing with your emotions in a healthy way is a great way to help with minimizing sugar cravings. It's also crucial to exercise. This can help assist with cravings, low energy levels, and fatigue. Ensuring that you are receiving a proper amount of sleep will also help with cognitive function, energy levels, and improved food choices.

Going on a sugar detox can be truly beneficial for your health. By cutting out processed foods, artificial sweeteners, sugary beverages, and grains for even just ten days, your body will get a chance to reset. You'll start off on a fresh slate; this will allow you to go in any direction with your diet. You will feel much better and experience great physical and mental health benefits from going on a sugar detox. It is important to understand what it is and why to do it before doing a detox.

Chapter 9: Taking Care of Your Mental Health

Taking care of your mental health is just as important as taking care of your physical health. Oftentimes, we neglect our mental health and only view "health" as physical health. However, your mental health can have a direct effect on your mental health. When you neglect your mental health, your physical health will suffer as a result. You must become more aware of your emotions, learn what makes you happy, stop negative body-talk, start practicing positive body-talk, practice self-care, love yourself, and learn how to practice self-respect and self-compassion. Doing these will really help you to improve your mental health.

Becoming More Aware of Your Emotions

It's crucial to become more aware of your thoughts, feelings, and emotions so that you have a better grasp of how you're feeling. You will understand as well how you can handle yourself when you feel a certain type of way. You must be able to tune in to these thoughts and choose an appropriate way to respond to them. Your body may give you some more obvious hints that you feel a certain type of way. For instance, you may tear up when sad, yell when angry, and smile when happy. However, you can easily be sad and not cry. You don't have to yell to feel angry. It's important to develop an awareness of your emotions. It's best to control your emotions, not let your emotions control you. You can change your mindset and even direct your emotions.

One way to become more aware of your emotions is to look for patterns. Perhaps you feel similarly around a certain person, after performing a certain task, or after visiting a certain place. Jot down everything that makes you upset. There are probably patterns when it comes to this. Perhaps you feel the same stress each time you have a shift at work longer than nine hours. You should reflect on this and understand what triggers certain emotions.

Throughout the day, check-in with yourself. Understand what you are feeling and try to understand why you are feeling that way. It will help to realize what causes certain emotions. Learn how you handle certain emotions, too. When you feel angry, do you tend to take it out on others? When you're stressed, do you eat certain foods or eat more than usual?

Notice the habits associated with your feelings so that you may gain a better understanding of your responses.

Try to have certain activities that you use as reflecting activities throughout the day. Perhaps you can reflect on your feelings while in the shower. Going on a walk is a great way to allow yourself some time to think. You spend all day paying attention to the needs of others and trying to read others' emotions. However, you must take some time to check in with yourself and understand how you are feeling. If it's hard for you to tap into your emotions, consider your behavior. Do certain people, places, or situations cause you to change your patterns? You may see an impact on your productivity, energy levels, or communications with others. These are great ways to identify how you are feeling.

It is necessary also to consider what helps with certain emotions. Perhaps you identify that you are feeling sad. Try to understand what helps you cope with certain emotions. When you're sad, you may find that talking to friends helps you every time. You must not only understand how you are feeling and what caused that feeling, but you must also understand how to cope with the different feelings that you experience throughout the day.

Learning What Makes You Happy

When you identify patterns in your emotions, you will be able to see who and what makes you happy, as well as where you are most happy.

Happiness is evident when you are able to better communicate with others, your energy level is up, and your productivity is increased. You will be able to think more clearly. You will have a more positive outlook on life and will find more enjoyment in the activities you partake in. You may also find yourself living in the moment more, as opposed to dwelling on the past or worrying about the future.

You may already have some ideas in mind for what makes you happy. Identify places that you go that always leave you feeling happier. Understand which people in your life increase your happiness. It's also important to identify certain tasks, situations, and events that make you feel happier. You must key into your own emotions. It may be tempting to see others get happy over certain things, yet those may not make us truly happy. For instance, your aunt may adore cooking, but you may think of it as simply mediocre. Perhaps you really enjoy the experience of eating out at a restaurant. You must not base your happiness on other people, social media, advertisements, popular culture, or anything other than your own feelings.

You can start over with happiness and really take the time to understand how you feel about certain things. Jot down any time that you feel truly happy, worry-free, and energetic. You may make your list more specific to find out what you love. It's possible that you can't stand going to the gym alone, and it feels like a chore to you. However, going to the gym with your cousin may leave you feeling good about yourself and refreshed.

Once you have identified the places, people, and situations that make you happy, incorporate them into your life more. Take time every day to do at least one small thing that makes you very happy. Allocate at least one time each week to do a bigger thing that makes you happy. Perhaps you enjoy writing and take the time to journal every night before bed. You may also enjoy going to the beach, so you may plan a few hours every Saturday to do that and really make the most out of it. If you aren't doing what makes you happy in life, you won't be happy and enjoy life. It's that simple!

Improving Your Self-Talk

Your self-talk is your internal dialogue. It's what you tell yourself inside your head and the way you think about yourself. You may have positive self-talk, which is when you hype yourself up and have a pep talk with yourself. Negative self-talk is when you cut yourself down. You may think you're not good enough or that your body isn't the way you want it to be. You must increase your positive self-talk and decrease your negative self-talk to improve your mental health.

You must lower and stop your negative self-talk and negative body-talk. It is important to identify when you negative self-talk the most. Certain situations may increase your likelihood of having negative self-talk. It is important to identify this and stop it in its tracks. Otherwise, you can doubt yourself, lower your confidence, and feel unworthy. You may not feel good about yourself and judge yourself. However, you must not judge yourself. You must recognize all of the wonderful things about yourself and be proud of who you are. Aside from recognizing how you feel (and when), you should also begin to identify the patterns of your self-talk.

Eliminating negative self-talk is crucial. You can't blame yourself for everything. Everybody makes mistakes, and you must learn from mistakes to become a better person. A positive outlook on life is necessary. Focusing on the negative aspects of people, places, and situations is not okay. You can't let your worries or emotions get the best of you. Of course, not everything goes to plan. However, you can't always expect the worst in every situation. Life consists of many aspects, not just the negative aspects.

You must increase your positive self-talk. This is when you think positively about yourself. You are confident, positive, and motivated. This will help you to build positive thoughts. You will also improve your self-esteem by increasing the frequency of your positive self-talk. You will be more productive, be more satisfied with your life, improve your health, and feel less stressed. It's important to shift your internal dialogue from negative to positive.

It's important to check in with yourself to ensure that you are thinking positively. If you can catch yourself in the act, it will be easier to remind yourself that you are thinking irrationally. You may bring yourself back to where you need to be and switch your mindset. It is important to surround yourself with those who are positive so that you may be encouraged and inspired by them. When you surround yourself with negative people, you will be tempted to adopt the same mindset. They may also bring you down or criticize you, which may decrease your self-worth. Remind yourself how amazing you are, and remember that you can accomplish anything you set your mind to. Identify what makes you think more positively. Perhaps laughter and happiness can lead to positive self-talk. Spending time with a certain person may also help with this. Identify what works for you. You should spend more time doing these tasks and being with these people, especially when you find yourself having negative self-talk.

Practicing Self-Care

Of course, you probably care about yourself. You want to live and care about yourself. However, self-care is more than just caring about yourself. It's about going out of the way to do something for yourself to take care of your mental, emotional, or physical health. It's very important to practice self-care, yet it's typically not done as much as it should be. By practicing self-care, you will improve your health, your mood, and your relationship with yourself. You will also be able to care for others better.

Practicing self-care is doing something that will make you feel better and happier. Although it is about improving your health, it must also be something that you enjoy. It can't be forced. Running may be a great way to get exercise and improve your health. However, it is not self-care to force yourself to run when you don't genuinely enjoy running. When you practice self-care, you will feel better. It is necessary for you to practice self-care often to ensure that you are taking care of yourself.

Many people refuse to practice self-care. Although it is a wonderful trait to care about making others happy and to go out of your way to do so, you must take care of yourself. Some view self-care as a selfish act. It is quite the opposite. You must practice self-care so that you take care of yourself properly. When you practice it, you will feel much better, and your ability to care for others will improve. When you feel happy, you

327

will be able to spread that happiness to others more easily. You can't love someone else if you don't love yourself first.

There are many ways to practice self-care. However, there is a proper way to do it and make it easier for yourself. Although you can go out and get a full spa treatment every week at your local spa, that can be quite costly. You don't have to make self-care expensive, time-consuming, or complicated. It should be able to fit into your routine easily. You must also make the active choice to plan out and set aside time for self-care. It must be thought of as self-care in order for you to truly enjoy it and all of the benefits it offers.

There are many activities and choices that you can make to practice self-care. One way is to cut out the things in your life that you don't enjoy. Don't talk to people who bring you down. Don't attend events that you don't like. Do what you love. Another way is to take care of your diet and exercise. You may get a proper amount of sleep. Exercising (the way that you like to) is a great way to practice self-care. Monitor your health with doctor visits, dentist visits, and therapy sessions (if desired). Take time to relax. This could be in whatever way you choose. Some enjoy at-home spa days; others enjoy meditating. You can try yoga, reading, writing, drawing, or whatever it is that brings you peace. You can also plan to spend time with friends and family. Overall, find activities that make you happy and actively plan for those activities.

Loving Yourself

Loving yourself is crucial for your mental health. You must love and appreciate the person you are. This will help you to feel more confident and increase your positivity. It is important that you realize what a great person you are. You must not cut yourself down or think of yourself poorly. Your self-confidence and self-worth will increase when you love yourself more. You may find it easier to trust others, communicate with others, and form relationships with others. You will develop a better grasp of who you are and what you love in life. It will be easier to take care of yourself, and you will value your health more as a result of loving yourself more. You may also find it easier to work, as your productivity and ability to focus will improve.

There are several ways for you to practice improving your ability to love yourself. This will help you to feel better about yourself and gain independence. Instead of depending on others for love, the love for yourself will be internalized. You will develop a much deeper appreciation for life. You may also find that you learn more about yourself.

To love yourself more, you must enjoy spending time by yourself. Find a hobby or activity that allows you to be alone and enjoy yourself. This can improve your confidence and help you to try new things. Perhaps you commit to learning about a new subject. You may try learning how to bake on your own. Creative hobbies help you to express yourself while having some fun along the way. A great way to gain confidence is by going places by yourself. This will teach you that you don't need anybody else to have fun; you can be your own best friend. Traveling and exploring new places is another way to love yourself. You will also learn more about the world around you and what you really love in life. Practicing self-care is another great way to love yourself.

You must also shift your mindset. It's important to accept yourself for the whole person you are. There will always be aspects of yourself that you can work on improving. You must also accept that you will feel pain. You will make mistakes. Life happens. However, you can't blame yourself for everything that happens to you. You must, however, take responsibility for your actions. This means accepting your triumphs and mistakes. You must also care about your mental, physical, and emotional health. Loving yourself also means taking care of yourself. You must react appropriately to situations based on what you know about yourself. Treat your body and mind properly. It's important.

Practicing Self-Respect and Self-Compassion

It is also important that you practice both self-respect and self-compassion. You must respect your body and mind. Self-respect is having confidence in yourself and having grace, honor, and dignity. It is the respect that you have for yourself. You like yourself, regardless of your performance. Even if you have a bad day or make a mistake, you will still love and respect yourself. It creates a strong and healthy relationship with yourself, which can really help your mental health and will allow you to treat yourself well. You will respect yourself for all aspects of yourself, both your strengths and weaknesses. This will be evident to others, and they will respect you more as a result. You will also recognize your self-worth, and this will disallow others to put you down or use you. You will understand the amount of respect that you deserve, and you won't let yourself or others put you down as a result. You will know who you are, so you won't have to find yourself through other people. You won't need to only be around certain people to "feel yourself" because you'll already know who you are. You won't need to seek love, attention, and respect from others because you will be happy with the person you are. You won't need others to justify who you are. You will also want to treat yourself well and take care of yourself because you know that's what you deserve. You also won't tolerate those who don't treat you the way that you know you deserve to be treated.

Self-compassion is also crucial. It is similar to having compassion for others, yet you are having compassion for yourself. You will take care of yourself, especially when you sense that you are in pain. You will be understanding and kind to yourself. Warmth, care, and helpfulness to yourself will come naturally to you. It is also understood that you won't always be perfect. Suffering, pain, and failure are natural and happen to everyone. Those with self-compassion won't judge themselves for making mistakes. They will instead understand that everyone makes mistakes. When pain and suffering occur, it is important to care for yourself and help yourself to feel better. You will be able to value your health and happiness by being kind to yourself and not judging yourself for any imperfections. You will also recognize how to love yourself yet also allow yourself to love others and experience love from others.

Taking care of your mental health is crucial. It can have just as much of an effect on you as your physical health can, if not more. You must become more aware of your emotions to care about your emotional health. Learning what makes you happier can help you to make yourself happier. You must improve your self-talk. It's important to practice self-love, self-compassion, self-respect, and self-care. It is also crucial to learn to love yourself. These are all ways to improve your mental health and be a better person.

Chapter 10: Repairing Your Relationship with Food

It is important to repair your relationship with food, especially if you have gotten off track with it. You must be able to recognize the signs of having an unhealthy relationship with food. If you identify that your relationship with food is unhealthy, you must be able to find a way to turn that around. It is also important to learn to love food without having to overeat. You must also learn how to value your health. You have one body, and you must treat it properly to have the best health that you possibly can. It's important to take care of yourself.

Signs of an Unhealthy Relationship with Food

You may realize that your relationship with food isn't the best. There are some obvious ways to tell that your relationship with food isn't healthy. Sometimes, it's more difficult to tell that your relationship with food is in need of improvement. There are several signs that you may need to improve your relationship with food.

If you try to hide your eating habits, you may have an unhealthy relationship with food. Perhaps you constantly snack at home and have frequent binging episodes. Around friends, family, and others, you may try to hide these tendencies or make different food choices. This is normal to an extent. Perhaps you feel more motivated to make different choices around different people. If you have a friend who is a vegetarian, you may choose more plant-based options around them. However, if you feel so guilty or ashamed about your eating habits that you feel the need to hide them or pretend that you eat differently, there may be an issue. You may "wear a mask" when it comes to food. You may pretend to eat a certain way while in public. As soon as you get home, you eat completely differently. This is due to the guilt that you feel.

If you exercise according to how much you eat, you may also have an unhealthy relationship with food. Perhaps you ate a 300-calorie donut and can only justify it if you run enough to burn 300 calories. You base your exercise off of how much you eat and try to burn off what you eat. Similarly, you may obsess over your weight. Each time you eat, you step on the scale. If you weigh yourself every day or even several times a day, there is a problem. Developing a fixation on your weight is unhealthy, both physically and mentally. You may end up exercising or starving yourself to get the weight that you desire. It will destroy your self-esteem.

If you are constantly trying new diets, paying for every plan, and trying every new trend, there may be a problem. You constantly try a diet, don't stick with it, and move on to the next one. You will never feel satisfied with your results and will only end up disappointed in yourself. This is a way to develop an obsession with dieting. You may view foods as "good" or "bad," especially when you develop the dieting mentality. This is unwise, as you will restrict yourself and end up craving the foods that you restrain yourself from eating, even more leading to binging episodes. When you constantly switch from diet to diet, you won't make any progress.

Building a Healthy Relationship with Food

After recognizing that your relationship with food needs to improve, you must start rebuilding a healthier relationship with food. Food should not be a source of anxiety or guilt. It is not a coping mechanism. Food is necessary for feeding your body. It should also satisfy your soul. Those with a healthy food relationship will truly enjoy food and the whole eating experience that comes with it.

To begin building a healthy relationship with food, you must accept all types of foods. Although there are foods that have more nutritional value than others, you can't label which foods are "good" and which are "bad." This will only lead to guilt associated with certain foods. It's all about how your body feels. When you begin labeling foods, food will begin to play mind games with you and make you feel bad. If you occasionally have foods with little nutritional value, that is okay. You won't gain ten pounds from a single meal that lacks nutritional value. It's important that you don't punish yourself for eating nutritionally-lacking foods.

To build a healthy relationship with food, surround yourself with good options. Eliminate foods from your home that can be tempting. If there is a certain food that you are trying to stay away from, keeping it in the pantry will certainly not help. Additionally, remind yourself that it's okay to say no. Perhaps your friend gave you some baked goods that they made. It's okay to have a bit and give the rest away. You don't have to eat something just because it's on your plate. If you've already eaten dinner and your family invites you to dinner, you don't have to eat again. Allow yourself to say no.

However, you don't have to say no to everything. You don't have to cut out all "junk food." Allow yourself to enjoy cookies, cake, French fries, and other such foods in moderation. As long as every meal doesn't turn into a cheeseburger and French fries, allow yourself to enjoy the foods you love. Having a salad for breakfast, lunch, and dinner is neither realistic or enjoyable. It isn't all or nothing. If you have an overall healthy day but slip in a little snack that isn't the greatest, that's okay. As long as the majority of what you're putting into your body makes you feel great, that's good.

Try tracking your foods. This doesn't mean that you have to count calories. In fact, it's better not to track calories, as it isn't an accurate measurement of nutritional value. However, it's important to jot down everything you eat (even for a short period of time, such as a week) so that you get an idea of what you really eat throughout the day. Perhaps you don't realize how much you eat or what you eat. This will help to put it in writing and allow you to see it. After doing this, you can analyze it. Are you happy with your eating habits? If so, great! If not, you can make adjustments until you are happy with your eating habits.

Loving Food Without Overeating

Just because you love food, you don't have to eat constantly. You can have an appreciation and love for food without constantly shoving food in your mouth or reaching for another snack. You must appreciate food as fuel for your body. It should be something that makes you feel good. There are several ways to stop yourself from overeating.

One way is by paying more attention to what you're eating. This can be done in several ways. One way to do so is to start keeping a log of what you eat. This will have you think more about what you eat since there will be a record of what you ate and how much of it you ate. You may also minimize distractions while eating. This way, your brain will truly register what you ate. Put away devices and other distractions while you are eating. You can truly appreciate your meal this way.

You may also allow yourself to eat the foods that you truly crave every so often. Instead of depriving yourself of French fries and eventually caving in, you can prevent this. When you deprive yourself of a certain food that you crave, you will most likely end up binging this food and overeating to compensate for the time without this. However, if you occasionally allow yourself to have some fries, you will satisfy your craving and prevent this from occurring.

Another important way to avoid overeating is by regulating your portions. Avoid eating from the container. If you eat chips from the family-size bag, you will likely overeat without realizing it. Eating from a container is an easy way to lose track of how much you've eaten. You may try meal prepping to portion your foods properly and avoid overeating later. It is much better to put no matter how much food you'd like onto a plate or into a bowl so that you avoid eating from the container. When eating out, don't feel obligated to eat the whole meal. Restaurant portions are typically larger than the recommended portion size. It's okay to take home some of your food.

Watch your emotions. By controlling your emotional and mental health, you will greatly reduce your likelihood of overeating. You won't feel the urge to overeat to cope with your stress or other negative emotions. It is also wise to come up with a list of healthy coping mechanisms to go to when you are feeling down. Instead of ordering an entire pizza for yourself, you may choose to go for a walk or talk to a friend. By taking care of your emotional and mental health, you will reduce these binging and overeating episodes and help improve your relationship with food.

Learning to Value Health

It's crucial to value your health. You have one body. It's important to treat your body well so that it can treat you well. When you care about your health, you take care of yourself better. When you take care of yourself properly, you will reduce your likelihood of developing a number of health problems. Taking care of your mental health can help improve your mental and physical health. Taking care of your physical health will improve both your physical and mental health. Additionally, you will feel much better about yourself. Your whole outlook on life will grow to be more positive.

Surround yourself with those who value their health. If you surround yourself with people who lounge all day long, neglect their mental health, and don't take care of themselves, you are likely to be negatively influenced by those people. Surround yourself with people who take care of themselves and encourage you to do the same. This can make a huge difference. You can share goals with those people. You can encourage each other and share your progress towards your goals together. It's great to have people that can push you to be the best person you can.

Make it a point to remind yourself to take care of your health. Each night, set your goals for the next day. Every morning, remind yourself why you are doing what you are doing. Remember why it's so crucial to fill your body with good foods. Before working out, think about why you are doing so. It is good for your body. Schedule time for a little self-care every day. Place a high value on health in your life. If you feel inspired by it, create a dream board, or surround yourself with inspirational quotes. On social media, follow accounts that encourage and inspire you. Make a list of all the benefits of health. When you are healthy, you will be more productive. You will be able to form better relationships and communicate better. You will be able to accomplish more. Your chance for health issues will decrease. You will be able to get more out of life. It'll be more common to experience genuinely happy moments. You will be able to move more easily. The list can go on forever. Remind yourself each day of at least some of these benefits. This will accentuate the importance of caring for your health and valuing it more in life.
It is important to take care of your health. You must understand if you have developed an unhealthy relationship with food. If you have, you must be able to build a healthy relationship with food so that you may enjoy the eating experience. As important as it is to love food, you must also ensure that you are not overeating. It's crucial that you learn to value your health. This way, you can treat your body well. You will be motivated to love your body and really pay attention to your health.

Chapter 11: Eating Disorders

Eating disorders can be serious. They can have serious consequences for your health. It is important to understand the different types of eating disorders. You must also understand the causes of eating disorders to determine the mental aspect behind them. You should also familiarize yourself with the symptoms of eating disorders to identify if you may struggle with an eating disorder. You will also need to understand the proper ways to overcome eating disorders. They can be quite serious. Oftentimes, one won't even be aware that they have an eating disorder. Their actions are normal to them. It is important to educate yourself on eating disorders to prevent and/or overcome an eating disorder.

Types of Eating Disorders

There are several different types of eating disorders. These each has its own characteristics, symptoms, and effects on the body. Eating disorders can be serious, and attention must be given to them to ensure the health of the individual struggling with the eating disorder. One that struggles with an eating disorder will not be able to go on with their daily life due to a constant preoccupation with food. Their concerns about food, weight, and body image will interfere with their life and can result in serious health issues.

Anorexia Nervosa

Anorexia nervosa will result in weight loss (or for children the inability to gain weight). One will not be able to maintain a healthy weight. This is often accompanied by poor self-image. Those with anorexia will prevent weight gain in several ways. They may restrict their diets heavily and count calories. They may exercise compulsively (perhaps working off any "extra" calories). They may prevent themselves from eating certain types of foods. Weight loss may be hidden with loose clothes. They may also purge (either by vomiting or laxatives), and binge eat.

Bulimia Nervosa

When one does binge and purge, this is known as bulimia nervosa. One who struggles with this will be caught up in a constant cycle of bingeing and purging. They may try to hide their bingeing episodes from others and will "undo the damage" by purging it all afterward. A person who vomits after meals may struggle. One who uses diuretics or has evidence of much uneaten food may be struggling with bulimia. They may also drink excessive amounts of water or become seemingly obsessed with breath fresheners. There may be the development of dental issues and calluses on the hands as a result of self-induced vomiting.

Binge Eating Disorder

Binge eating disorder (BED) is characterized by frequent urges to binge-eat. They will not be able to control such episodes and may overstuff themselves to the point of discomfort. Afterward, they may feel guilt, shame, and anxiety as a result of the episode. Those with binge eating disorder will not try to "undo the damage." They will simply eat a large quantity of food in a short period of time. This binge will not be able to control themselves or stop themselves from eating more. They may try to hide food for the purpose of bingeing and will attempt to hide the actual action of bingeing.

Avoidant Restrictive Food Intake Disorder

Those with Avoidant Restrictive Food Intake Disorder (ARFID) will not maintain a proper and healthy weight. They may lose weight very quickly. They limit themselves to very specific foods. This is not due to a desire to lose weight or because of poor self-image, but because they are "picky." The selection of foods to eat is narrow and typically becomes even narrower over time.

They may even begin eating items that are typically not regarded as food and don't have significant nutritional value. When this occurs, it is known as pica. One may eat paper, hair, paint, ice, clay, or other substances. Those with pica may worry about choking or vomiting. They may also increase their risk of health problems as a result of an improper diet.

Rumination Disorder

Those with rumination disorder will regurgitate their food and re-chew or re-swallow their food. When regurgitating their food, the individual will not be upset, stressed, or disgusted. It may even seem natural for one to do so. They may also spit their food out after re-chewing their food up.

Unspecified Feeding or Eating Disorder

Unspecified feeding or eating disorder (USFED) is where one will be affected in their daily life by a disorder significantly. They may be impaired in their social life, occupation, or education (as well as in other areas of their life). They may not have the full symptoms of another eating disorder, yet the eating or feeding disorder will have a significant impact on their life and lead to distress. There may not be enough information to make a more specific diagnosis of the person. However, there will be symptoms of some type of eating disorder present. It may not be certain what type it is exactly, though.

Purging Disorder

Purging disorder occurs when one purges frequently. They will not, however, have the bingeing episodes before that are the key characteristic of bulimia. This will occur when one has a poor self-image or wishes to lose additional weight.

Night Eating Syndrome

Night eating syndrome (NES) is where the individual will eat a significant portion of their meals after their dinnertime meal. They may also wake up throughout the night so that they may eat. Those with night eating syndrome will eat at least a quarter of their daily consumption after their evening meal.

Other Specified Feeding and Eating Disorders

This is the classification for those who have symptoms of other eating disorders but don't quite match another eating disorder perfectly. They may have bingeing episodes followed by purging. They may also binge-eat. Those with OSFED may excessively diet, have poor self-esteem, and exercise excessively.

There are several different types of eating disorders. They all have different symptoms and can all have a serious impact on the individual's health. If left untreated, the individual can develop a number of health problems. It may even be fatal if left untreated for a long period of time. This will depend on the intensity of the eating disorder as well. However, it is important to recognize the symptoms of eating disorders to understand if one may have an eating disorder.

Causes of Eating Disorders

Eating disorders are complex. Each individual will have their own variation of an eating disorder if they have one. There are numerous causes, and the reasoning behind the development of an eating disorder will vary for everyone. However, there are some common causes of eating disorders that may be true for a great number of people. It's important to understand what causes eating disorders so that they may be prevented and understood more. The underlying cause may be helped if it is identified.

Genetics

One reason for the development of an eating disorder is due to genetics. The individual may have an increased risk of developing an eating disorder based on their genes. This is a heredity trait, which means this increased risk can be passed down to one's offspring. Those with a family member with an eating disorder are much more likely to develop one themselves.

Personality

One's personality may also be a contributing factor in the development of an eating disorder. One who frequently experiences obsessive thinking is more likely to develop an eating disorder. This is because the person is more likely to develop an unhealthy obsession with food, weight, body, exercise, and eating in general. An individual who is a perfectionist will want the perfect body and may do anything to achieve that. One who thrives off of rewards and punishments will also be more likely to develop an eating disorder. They will reward themselves when they lose weight or achieve their goal. This may be in the form of a binge or other unhealthy reward. Similarly, they may punish themselves. Perhaps they look in the mirror and don't like what they see. They may purge, starve themselves, or exercise obsessively to change their image. One who is impulsive and excessively persistent may also be more likely to develop an eating disorder.

Trauma

Those with trauma or with past events that had a great effect on them are also more likely to develop an eating disorder. They may feel ashamed of themselves or guilty about themselves and use the eating disorder as a way to express this. They may also wish to harm or punish themselves for the trauma. It may also be the result of their past. For instance, those who were bullied about being overweight may express that pain through an eating disorder. Eating disorders can be an expression of one's pain and emotions.

Coping Mechanism

Similarly, one may use the eating disorder as a coping mechanism. They may lack the ability or knowledge to utilize healthier ways to cope. It may be an outlet for their emotions. This is a way to express one's pain.

Outside Influences

One may also develop an eating disorder as a result of outside influences. Those with unrealistic bodies that are portrayed on television, in magazines, and on the Internet may cause one to believe that their body is not good enough. As a result, they will do whatever they can to change their bodies so that it matches this unrealistic ideal.

Overcoming Eating Disorders

Eating disorders can be dangerous. It's important to understand when you have one. When you identify what you may struggle with an eating disorder, it is important to take care of yourself and overcome the eating disorder that you have. It may not be easy. However, it's important to take the necessary steps to take care of yourself and watch out for your health. Otherwise, you are risking serious consequences. Eating disorders can take a toll on your health. The longer that they are left untreated, the worse that they will become. Your body will suffer if you don't work towards helping yourself.

Listening to Yourself

To overcome an eating disorder, you must listen to yourself. Listen to your thoughts and feelings. You must understand how you feel so that you can treat yourself accordingly. If you sense that you are unhappy, identify why that is and how you can help yourself cope in a healthy manner. You may also identify what triggers you. If you can learn how to stop yourself from reacting to certain situations in an unhealthy manner, you can really help yourself. You must also learn to listen to your body. Your body will send you signals on what it needs.

Learning to Love and Accept Yourself

You must also learn to love and accept yourself. It's important to be patient and understanding with yourself. You will make mistakes. You are not perfect. Your body will not look like others' bodies. You must love and accept yourself for who you are. If you punish yourself for your imperfections, your physical and mental health will seriously suffer. Train yourself to find aspects of yourself that you love. Learn to love your body and surround yourself with people who encourage you. Learn how to avoid comparing yourself to others. Everyone has their own strengths. Learn to appreciate your strengths.

Seeking Help

If you have tried to help yourself with your eating disorder and haven't had luck, it is crucial that you seek help. You can't be embarrassed or feel shameful asking for help. If you don't seek help, you will suffer. You may seek the help of someone close to you. Opening up with someone about your struggle may help you. They may be able to push you in the right direction. Choose someone that you are comfortable with so that you can really open up to them. You may also seek professional help. Seek out a medical professional that you can talk to and receive professional help from.

Understanding the Causes and Symptoms

Eating disorders are serious. There are several types of eating disorders, and it's important that you understand the causes and symptoms of both. You must also understand how you can overcome eating disorders. If you leave an eating disorder untreated, you can face serious consequences on your health. Understanding the symptoms of an eating disorder can help you to consider if you may struggle with an eating disorder. Understanding the causes can also help you understand how you may prevent an eating disorder from developing. Preventing and treating eating disorders is crucial.

Chapter 12: Tips and Tricks

There are some additional tricks that you may learn. There are some simple ways to improve your health. These are simple tricks, yet they can have a great impact on your health. You may also learn how to implement healthier eating habits. By slightly changing your habits, you can really help your health. You may also learn to be happier and healthier overall, which will help you to get more out of life and experience genuine joy in your life. You will also learn some tips and tricks to learn how you can manage any poor eating habits that you may have.

Little Ways to Improve Your Health

There are many quick and simple tips to improve your health. Implementing these in your life can make a huge difference.

Drinking More Water

Make an effort to drink more water. Replacing the sugary beverages that you consume with water can make a huge difference. Even if it's only one drink a day to start off, you will be much better off. Make an effort to minimize or eliminate soda from your diet. Even fruit juice, tea, and lemonade can be loaded with sugar. Water is the best option, as it contains no sugar and hydrates your body. We need water to live, and it helps the body run more effectively and efficiently.

Exercising

Take some time to exercise. Only a little time is necessary. If going to the gym for an hour five days a week seems overwhelming to you, don't worry! You don't have to spend hours upon hours every week working out. In fact, five minutes a day is better than nothing. You can go for a short walk every evening to wind down after work. There are many videos online with short exercise routines that you can accomplish in under ten minutes. Even doing a few push-ups and sit-ups here and there is better than nothing. Carve out some time every day to dedicate to moving around. A great way to incorporate exercise into your routine is by scheduling classes to go to, especially with friends. This way, you can choose something that you like doing, and you will have to go. Your friend will count on you, and you will most likely have to pay.

Having Time for Yourself

You should also schedule a little bit of time each day to devote to yourself. This way, you can relax and unwind. It will give you time to collect your thoughts and focus on your goals. You may also enjoy some mental and emotional stability by doing so. This can reduce your stress, and you will feel more motivated to take care of yourself. Remind yourself of your goals during this time. You may also focus on what you would like to improve with your existing routine. You don't even need to spend a long time each day doing this. Even taking a minute to really relax and breathe can make a huge difference.

Tips for Healthier Eating Habits

Improving your eating habits can be as simple as slightly adjusting your routine. You may do this in a few ways. One way is to rid yourself of unnecessary snacks. Go through your refrigerator and pantry. Get rid of any snacks that you don't need in your life. If you aren't surrounded by unhealthy temptations, then you won't be as likely to reach for them. You may also choose to replace your snacks with healthier options. Start surrounding yourself with more fruits and vegetables. You may even plan out your snacks to ensure that what you are eating is right. Prepare proper portions of healthy options. One example of a potential snack is apple slices and peanut butter. If these are already prepared for you, the excuse of not having enough time to choose a healthier option will be invalid. Bring healthy snacks with you. Whether you put them in your car, in your bag, or bring them to work, it is good to have healthy options with you so that you aren't as tempted to grab a quick bite at a fast-food restaurant instead.

Eating More Fruits and Vegetables

One way to improve your eating is by incorporating more fruits and vegetables into your life. Instead of white rice, try cauliflower rice. When making pasta, shred some carrots into the sauce. Choose broccoli over French fries when eating out. Add some mushrooms to your grilled chicken. Replace chips with dried fruit. There are numerous ways to incorporate fruits and vegetables into your diet, and they can really boost your health and add some nutritional value to your diet. An easy way to boost your diet with fruits and veggies is to make smoothies. This is a great way to pack in your fruits and veggies. Plus, you can make them tasty! You can even make smoothie bowls. Salads are also a great way to load up on fruits and veggies.

Lessening Your Sugar and Salt Intake

Another way to boost your diet is to stop adding sugar and salt to your foods. Most food is already loaded with an excess of sugar and salt. While eating out, resist the urge to use the salt shaker. When cooking, reduce the amount of sugar and salt that you add to your foods.

Choosing Healthier Options

You may replace your foods for healthier options. Start swapping fried food for grilled food. Grilled chicken is a much better option than chicken fingers. Make the switch from refined grains to whole grains. Swap out any meat for leaner options. Reduce the amount of red meat and try to eat more turkey and chicken.

When shopping at the grocery store, make a list ahead of time. Plan out what exactly you need. This will reduce shopping for extra items. Make sure that you stick to your list. It can help you to eat before you go grocery shopping. That way, you won't be tempted to buy the entire store just because you're hungry. Planning ahead can help you to make better and healthier decisions. It may also help to come up with recipes for the meals you plan to make and buy according to that. This will help you be more motivated to cook those meals.

How to Be Happier Overall

Everyone likes to be happy. There are many small habits that you can incorporate into your life that can boost your happiness. When you do this, you are also helping to improve your mental health. When you are happier, you also experience negative emotions less. This will allow your emotional and mental health to improve. When you boost your emotional and mental health, you will be able to make better decisions regarding your health and can take care of yourself better.

Adjusting Your Sleep Schedule

Slightly changing your sleep schedule can make you happier. Simply waking up fifteen minutes earlier than usual can greatly impact your happiness. You can start your day off the right way and set the bar high. Waking up a bit early will allow you more time to enjoy your day. You can have more time to get ready instead of feeling rushed. Instead of waking up and immediately feeling stressed, you are starting the day off with a better mindset. You may take this time to ease into your day. You may also use it to go over your goals for the day and sort out your to-do list. It will change your whole attitude.

Cleaning Up Your House

Cleaning up a bit can make a huge difference. When your space is cluttered, you won't be able to think properly. If your workspace is cluttered, you will struggle to focus, as you will be distracted and overwhelmed by the mess. If your bedroom is a mess, you won't be able to sleep as well. When your kitchen is a mess, you won't make wise choices in what you eat. A cluttered pantry or refrigerator may seem overwhelming. This can be frustrating and lead to a preference for eating out, as you won't want to sift through the mess for food. When you are less stressed, you will be able to enjoy life more and will be happier.

Undergoing Social Media Detox

It is important to take a break from social media. Although social media can be a great way to communicate with others, it can easily become toxic if it is overused. People have a tendency to compare themselves to others, and social media is a prime example of this. You will find yourself comparing yourself to others, yet you must stay on your own path; everyone has different goals. Reduce the time you spend on social media, and you will find your happiness will increase. You may even consider a social media detox.

Expressing Gratitude

One way to be happier is by expressing gratitude. Think about all of the things that you are thankful for, as well as how grateful you are for yourself. At least once a day, remind yourself of one thing that you are grateful for (bonus points if it's something about yourself). By looking for the positives in life, you are shifting your mindset. You will start to see the good in life, and you will be much happier as a result. It's always possible to find joy in life.

Managing Poor Eating Habits

There are many simple tricks for combatting unhealthy habits. You can change your bad habits by slightly switching what you do. Just by making small switches, you can make big differences.

Listening to Your Body

Make sure that you take the time to listen to your body. Understand any emotions that may trigger certain eating habits and learn how you can handle these. Listen to your body to decide when you are hungry and when you are full. Don't keep eating if you're full, and make sure that you feed yourself when you're hungry. If you keep eating after you're already full, you are overeating. Starving yourself will most likely lead to a bingeing episode later. Watch out for yourself and prevent future issues before they even occur.

Reducing Your Food Stock

Reduce the amount of food in your house. Although you can clean your kitchen and make it appear decluttered, you must truly keep it clean. Don't buy what you already have; maintain your kitchen's cleanliness. When you only have the very best foods in your kitchen, you are more likely just to put the very best foods in your body. You should clean out your cupboards and drawers. Make sure the counter is also clean so that you may actually use it for cooking. Once you have gotten your kitchen to the point where all of your foods are of higher nutritional value, make sure that you don't bring back any of the foods that you wished to eliminate in the first place. Put the foods that you really want to eat where you can see them. You can put your "best" foods on display, and you will be more inclined to eat them.

Reducing Distractions While Eating

Remember to reduce distractions when you are eating. In addition to paying attention to your food by not watching any devices or such, you should also eliminate audible distractions. Although you may enjoy listening to music or podcasts, try to make meals special. Set aside that time for eating and eating only.

Regulating Your Portions

Regulate your portions. Choose smaller utensils, bowls, and plates. The smaller bowls and plates will allow you to think that you are consuming more. Smaller utensils will require more bites to eat the same amount of food. When you think that you are eating more, your brain will tell you that you are full sooner. You will be satisfied with less food. Even if the bowl is smaller, a full bowl of food still registers as a full bowl of food, regardless of whether or not it's a bit smaller. You may also consider switching to smaller glasses for beverages besides water.

Having an Eating Schedule

You may establish scheduled eating habits. When you follow the same daily schedule, your body will get used to eating at a certain time. This will also help you to keep track of your eating more easily. Instead of eating more than you should when you are bored, you will know when exactly it is time to eat. You may also have an eating ritual. Do the same task before you eat every time, and your body will be alerted that it is time to eat. You may even enjoy eating more when you have a ritual to look forward to.

There are many tips and tricks to help you out. Improving your health is quite simple. You can improve your health by adding small tasks to your daily routine. The same is true for improving your eating habits. Similarly, happiness may be increased in one's life by making slight switches. You can help make your poor eating habits into better habits by also utilizing some simple tips and tricks. Making improvements doesn't have to be difficult.

Conclusion

Thank you for making it through to the end of *Emotional Eating*! Let's hope it was informative and able to provide you with all of the tools you need to achieve your goals—whatever they may be.

The next step is to implement the habits that you learned. You can continue your research and continue starting healthy habits. After reading this book, you will understand how you can work to improve your eating habits and health overall.

These are key concepts that will help you to improve your health. When you eat better, your body will be happy. Treating your body better will make you feel better. You will experience the physical aspects of this, such as having more energy and being able to move better. You will experience the mental aspects of it. You will be more motivated to take care of yourself and your health. This will also allow you to be more productive and have a better ability to focus. You will also be in better control of your emotions, which will have a great impact on improving your emotional eating habits.

It is important to combat your bad habits once and for all and start implementing healthier eating habits. You need to discover the proper way to actually enjoy the food that you eat. You have to recognize the signs of an unhealthy relationship with food and know how to repair it. You will learn how to value your health.

It is important to work on your mental health. This will help you to control your emotions and get a grip on your emotional eating. Understand what mental health is and how you can work to improve your mental health. By improving your mental health, you will also be helping your physical health to improve. Understand the proper mindsets that you can work to adopt. Identify which mindset or mindsets that you wish to work on. You should learn how to plan and achieve goals, but just goals that are realistic and achievable and how to stay motivated despite obstacles.

Do you need a mental boost with achieving goals, staying motivated when issues arise, having a healthier body, overcoming addiction, or having a healthier mind? This is important to keep in mind. You may also work on mastering mindfulness and incorporating mindfulness techniques into your daily life. Identify why you wish to master mindfulness. Perhaps you have food cravings. Perhaps you struggle with compulsive overeating. You may wish to enjoy your food more. Mindfulness can help with all of these and in other areas.

Emotional eating is eating that is triggered by certain emotions_or situations. It is important that you understand the causes and symptoms of overeating, as well as ways to help eliminate them. You need to learn how emotional eating is caused by more than your emotions. You must monitor all aspects of your health if you want to improve your eating habits. Healthier habits can result from taking care of both your physical and mental health. By learning how you can take care of both of those aspects, you can learn how to help with emotional eating. You can experience all of the wonderful benefits of living a healthier lifestyle as a result.

There are other areas of mental health to work on as well. Understand if you would like to become more aware of your emotions. Perhaps you need to focus more on what makes you happy. You may need to improve your self-talk and practice self-care. You may wish to love yourself more and practice self-care and self-compassion. Make a plan for repairing your relationship with food. If you have identified that you have an eating disorder, start working towards overcoming that.
There are several steps to improving your overall health. You must understand emotional eating. Identify if you are an emotional eater and take steps to improve your habits. You can also learn more about what physical health entails and how you may improve your habits. When you work to improve your physical health, your mental health will also get a boost. Understand if you have an addiction to sugar or to food, in general. Identify your plan for combatting that addiction. Consider going on a detox to get your body used to the idea of thriving without the foods that you are addicted to.

There are other ways that you may work on your emotional eating. It will really help to start a journal. This is a great way for you to write down your emotions. You can plan out your goals and anything else you need to do. You can also track your portions and the types of foods that you consume throughout the day. If you have tried to work on your health on your own but have seen no results, another way that you can improve your health is by seeking the help of a professional. A final way to help yourself is surrounding yourself with good influences on social media, with the people whom you surround yourself with, and in your refrigerator or pantry.

Autophagy

Heal, Detox and Self-Cleanse Your Body. Speed Up Your Metabolism with Intermittent Fasting to Lose Weight Easily.

Keep Healthy and Promote Longevity with Anti-Inflammatory Keto Diet

by ALAN DIETER

Table of Contents

Introduction

Thank you for purchasing *Autophagy*, a book that gives you all the necessary information to attaining excellent physical health and body metabolism. This varies from the definition of autophagy and types of autophagy to the detoxification process and how to lose weight in the most basic way. Are you looking to reduce weight? Are you having trouble with your metabolism? Are you trying to use anti-aging products that have not worked for some time now? Well, if your answer is yes, this book has the right natural procedures and mechanisms that will not only make you look more youthful but also increase your stay here on earth!

Chapter one starts by introducing autophagy, the significant types of autophagy, as well as the formation of this process. The second section deals with the self-cleansing, detoxification, and healing of the body. The third part involves a critical analysis of how individuals can lose weight through the activation of this autophagy process.

Chapter two focuses on how to burn fat in the body, which can be done through intermittent fasting, introducing the consumption of healthy fats and less sugar, as well as undertaking aerobics training.

Chapter three discusses the ways through which we can lower the risks of getting an inflammatory disease. It also talks about the ketogenic diet and gives you a variety of meals that can stimulate the process of autophagy.

Chapter four introduces longevity that can be achieved through the process of autophagy. It ranges from the specific topics that discuss the anti-aging process, types of nutrition that make your cell rejuvenated and younger, the circadian rhythm that can be achieved through the process of autophagy, and the optimization of sleep.

This book is going to interest whoever comes across it to find out more about what autophagy is, what it entails, as well as the procedure to go about it. It is that simple and clear. Get yourself one of these detailed guides to healing, detoxification process, anti-aging, and losing weight—and use it to your benefit.

Chapter One:
What Is Autophagy?

Living creatures—both plants and animals—have complex systems of behavior and physiological procedures to adapt to their ever-changing environment. There are uncountable stimuli that we are susceptible to on our day-to-day activities, and they all send a particular signal to the body. Consequently, this activates a chain response of events that ascertain how your metabolism, nervous system, and psychology react.

Autophagy is part of this reaction, where the body of the organism is responding to specific changes or limitations in its environment Autophagy engages in either an immediate or a deviant part of health. It's most uncomplicated—meaning that autophagy is usually an enormously compounded procedure that results in the change, excess, as well as the injured living macromolecules and the entire cell organs with the use of hydrolytic enzymes found within the lysosome. It is made up of consistent procedures of the autophagy enrolment, the emergence of the precursor autophagosome, its development, as well as its amalgamation with the lysosome, breaking down of the bulk contents, secretion carrying off the degraded outcome to the cytoplasm, and lysosome refinement. In this section, we will discuss the particular work done by autophagy and its underlying procedure.

The Specific Functions of Autophagy

Autophagy involves either an immediate or long-term effect on health and disease. In this section, we are going to look at its function in both health and disease. The tasks of autophagy in health are as follows:

- The control of the embryonic and primary postnatal growth
- Tissue homeostasis and the control of mitochondrial standard
- The protection of the cells against stress
- The response of tissue to nutrient deprivation for survival reasons
- The survival of cellular and physiological death of a cell during growth
- How a cell is involved in death during the treatment of radiotherapy or chemotherapy
- The remodeling of tissues during the evolution
- The tasks played by autophagy in disease include:

- The energy supply, anti-aging, human malignancy, tumorigenesis, maintenance of the tumor, inflammation, ovarian cancer, colon cancer, and melanoma
- The storage of diseases in the lysosome
- Disorders to do with metabolism

- Cardiovascular diseases
- Cardiomyopathy of alcohol
- Myopathy of the skeletal muscles
- Atherosclerosis
- Diabetes
- Complications of being obese
- Degradation of lipid in the liver
- The diseases of the liver that are related to alcohol
- Pancreas diseases
- The management of cellular quality
- Genome protection
- The adaptive and innate responses by microbial pathogens to infection
- Defense of the body opposed to intracellular bacteria, parasites, and viral infections
- The intracellular pathogens' protection and the development of epileptic cells

Autophagy helps fight against infectious diseases. It does this by removing bane, which usually causes a defilement in the body, as well as by aiding to improve the way that the immune system of the body reacts to the banes. Intracellular bacteria and viruses can be removed by autophagy.

Autophagy betters the performance of muscles. By exercising, we usually put stress on the cells, resulting in energy raising; thus, the segments usually get tired quickly. Due to this, the process of autophagy aids in the elimination of damages and also maintains your energy levels.

What science can tell us today is that autophagy works to make your body function better. By cleaning up cellular junk, you will clear the way for cells to rebuild themselves with new parts. Sort of like that biological upgrade—giving an older car a more modern engine, so that it not only keeps running but "corners like it's on rails."

Autophagy Process in the Cells of Mammals

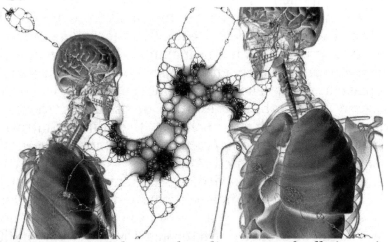

Even though the process moderates the adjustment of cells in various strain situations that involve starvation, this strain is seen as a problem—a multicellular organism cell can be able to solve consistently. The basal level of this process is seen in a lot of cells, hence being authorized to the suppositional detrimental clusters protein, which usually leads to a defective cellular. Consequently, the autophagy process in mammals is basically essential in aiding the cleaning of the intracellular of the injured proteins.

Therefore, the lack of a cleaning process would lead to the transformation of neoplastic. Mentioned earlier, lack of food is not so common in the cells of mammals on ordinary nutrition circumstances. As a result, it is necessary to find out the technique behind the regulation of autophagy under essential nutritional circumstances.

Major Types of Autophagy

There are three types of autophagy in the mammalian body.

I. Macro Autophagy - entire divisions of the cytosol whereby they are all secluded then transported for degeneration in lysosomes. These seclusions occur in the structure of autophagy. This process involves the innate authorized technique of cells that disposes of any defective or unwanted components in an organelle.

II. Micro Autophagy - is the immediate consumption of dispersible cellular components into the lysosome. It relocates the cytoplasmic material into the lysosome for the breakdown process through the direct division of the lysosome limiting membrane. As opposed to the other two, it is moderated in mammals by lysosomal activity, and in plants, it is reduced through vacuolar action (straight submersion of the cytoplasmic load. The cytoplasmic substance is confined in the lysosome by an arbitrary exercise of tissue introversion. In simple terms, microautophagy includes the direct introspection and amalgamation of lysosome/vacuole tissue under nutrient limitation.

III. The Chaperone Mediated Autophagy - is autophagy's conceptual manifestation that exists virtually in many kinds of tissues, including cells. It is distinguished in eukaryotes and not in yeast. For the reason of this specific feature, just the solvent proteins but not the entire organelle can be broken down through CMA. CMA is conditional on the inherent extracted heat shock cognate and recognizes the peptide series of the cytoplasmic parent material. Therefore, it is extra discerning than autophagy in its break down process. CMA performs duties for the stabilization of imbalanced energy and is best started up by metabolic or nutritious and oxidative tension.

Autophagosome Formation

Autophagy is an immensely compounded procedure that involves a series of steps of the inauguration of autophagy, the emergence of autophagosome predecessor, development of a phagosome, the amalgamation of an autophagosome and a lysosomal membrane, breakdown of cargo material, the deluge movement of the broken down content to be delivered to cytoplasm, as well as the refinement of the lysosome.

As for the cells of mammals, the process of autophagy development starts through the evolvement of a nucleus, in which the segregation membranes of diversified originations create phagophores, which then enlarge and merge to create a finished product that has two layers called an autophagosome. They are created at cytoplasm incidental places. After amalgamation with the lysosome, the cargo is broken down through hydrolases, followed by the renewal of lysosome virtually by the Golgi body. The segregation membranes could be produced from many origins—namely, outer mitochondria tissue, Golgi organ, Plasma tissues, and the Endoplasmic Reticulum. However, the Endoplasmic Reticulum origin is more attainable due to its protein synthesis aided by its ribosomes. The existence of a lot of autophagosome proteins near the endoplasmic reticulum also advocates that endoplasmic reticulum engages in a significant position in membrane source for the creation of autophagosomes.

Autophagy is implemented by the existing autophagy-related genes, which could also be connoted as Atg. Amino acid discerning in mammals and even indicators like growing and responsive oxygen breed control the undertaking of the protein kinases mechanistic target of rapamycin and the activated protein kinase. Both usually balance the process of autophagy by derailed addition of phosphoryl to the kinases unc-51-like kinase 1 and also unc-51-like kinase 2, as well as the initiation of autophagy outcome and the stimulation of the ULK kinases.

ULK is a section of the protein compound that contains autophagy-related protein 13, autophagy-related protein 101, and family-interacting protein 200. The unc-51-like kinase stimulates BECN1, which is the additional fragment of the protein network. The autophagy-practical Beclin-1 mixture carries the proteins protein 150—this unc-51-like kinase and the BECN1 multiplex position its location to where the formation of autophagy began.

The Self-Cleansing Process

In majority situations of our life, we have no self-cleaners. But other things demand quality of time and serious attention to get rid of dirt and waste that has piled up over a while. Come to think of it, what would happen if we dint regularly clean things or pieces of equipment? I know the expression you have on reading this is unpleasant. Our cars, desks, and kitchen would become toxic cesspools of dirt, and they would be sickening.

In the same way, this could occur to our bodies. If dirt and toxins are not thoroughly cleaned and thrown away, our cell productivity lowers, causing dull skin color, dark energy, fast aging, and weight loss. This is just what autophagy, your cellular self-cleaner, and talks about. Don't forget that in the literal sense, it means self-eating. This is because it takes up its own toxins and waste to produce younger and healthier cells.

This is how the process mainly works. Notably, our bodies are made up of different parts and organs that affect cellular functions. It is also made up of a lot of cells, each of which plays a significant role in the ways we function and live. A good example is the mitochondria, which is an organelle that gives rise to energy for a cell. Cells also carry proteins that are crucial for the working of a cell. These proteins provide structure to the cells and also carry out chemical reactions in the body. Besides, they act as messengers to relay a variety of information throughout the body.

Even though they're microscopic components, every cell chugs, and churns, manufacturing power, and elements that make your body carry out tasks the way they do, these cells play a role in how we think and feel. It provides the power to send signals, recall lyrics to a song, rational decisions, and even calculate rent payments and anything else you will do on your day-to-day lives. These cells are always operating. At many times they carry out a good job specifically at the early stage. Each item is usually new, and the networks function together in a consonance manner; therefore, everything continues functioning well without any problem. The work is done efficiently by all cells, and this usually results in the body being very healthy and fully energized.

That doesn't mean each cellular system works all the time correctly. Our standard cellular system becomes injured with use over some time through those unavoidable and speeds up Agers explained earlier. The majority of the people assume that wear and tear is a certainty of life and that no matter what we do, our bodies will break down because of aging. Surely, we cannot go against the natural arc of life and death, but we can definitely hinder the impacts of aging. At this point, we are going to see why.

Our cells degrade sections of themselves through segregating them into vacuoles and assimilating them. Consequently, they brought about waste material consisting of dead organelles, injured proteins, and oxidized pieces; this waste has to be eliminated. And not unless the waste is disposed of properly, that dirt stays and piles up in the body. That building up of trash is a critical influence in the rate of aging. The toxins get in the way and cause everything to malfunction. It could sound like jargon from a biology lesson, but in reality, it is when the toxins damage the system of our cells, it is a massive factor in the aging process. It makes your skin look older, your body becomes slow, your energy drops drastically, and the hormones scatter all over. Do you want that? Cause I also don't want that to happen to me.

This is the reason why autophagy is necessary for human health. It's the same as cellular garbage is being disposed of, taking the defective sections and destroying them, so that they wouldn't cause a distraction anywhere else. If it is functioning correctly, then it has undergone self-renewal degrading old useless structures to create space for new ones. The product is a brand new, more young, and energetic structure that would allow us to be more dynamic and look younger.

You can just imagine how that plays out in our day-to-day life. Increased youthful cells mean that you have healthier and softer skin, your body undergoes less fatigue, your metabolism rate being better, this will result in the cells to be able to generate energy all over the body from the muscles to your brain cells to your internal organs.

Many researchers term autophagy as a strategy or mechanism used for survival. In that, it speaks about how a cell would react to specific changes in the environment to ensure the health of a body. This makes sense because all living organisms are out there trying to survive to stay alive.

This knowledge has indeed resulted in the innovation of treatments for aging and finding natural cures for diseases like cancer, diseases like cancer, and infectious diseases. Major labs around the world saw the first known gene responsible for autophagy in mammals. They say the waste-removal function is what keeps us healthy.

Usually, autophagy hums along silently behind the scenes in the maintenance of the body's well-being mode. It suddenly kicks in the high gear during stressful times, acting as a protector to the body when there are limited amounts of food or water. The body stimulates the process of autophagy to slow down the aging of your body, reduce inflammation, and speed up the natural ability of your body to function. It also helps your body fight off disease-causing microorganisms to boost longevity. The human body can naturally activate the autophagy process.

There are a lot of natural ways through which you can increase the autophagy process of your body. To cleanse the cells and lower the rate of inflammation, and in general, retain your body functioning, you need these techniques discussed below. Remember that since autophagy is a response reaction to stressful conditions, you are required to trick your body into thinking it is under some amount of stress. This is how to go about it:

Eat High-Fat and Low-Carbohydrate Foods

I will be emphasizing on the significance of taking in fats to stimulate autophagy fats should be considered as a ruling macronutrient in our diets because it differs from protein. Where the protein could turn into carbohydrates and be sugar, but fats cannot do that. Particularly in the Keto diet, the intake of low carbohydrates and also the intake of high fat will offer your body an edge in as far as autography is concerned. The movement from a glucose burning to ketones that takes place in a Keto diet procedure impersonates the natural occurrence in a fasted state. This grows the chances of the autophagy process.

A lot of people have testified to the benefits of fats being in a replacement of high amounts of sugar for the activation of autophagy. They also argue that once the process began, it was a bit rough, but everything worked out along the way. You get used to the new diet within a week. You will be feeling much healthier

Try Out Protein Fasting

At least twice or thrice a week try to restrict the amount of protein intake to the utilization of 15 to 25 grams of protein every day. This limitation allows your body to be able to reuse proteins, which will lower the rate of inflammation and cleanse your cells without you struggling. Throughout this period of time, while autophagy becomes activated, your body cells are obligated to take up its own toxins and proteins to survive.

Try Out Intermittent Fasting

This usually refers to the habit of eating, whereby a person balances fasting and eating. It mainly focuses on which times you are supposed to eat, not really the types of foods to eat. There are many ways in which you can practice this kind of fasting. The simplest involves doing without breakfast, eating at noon, and the last meal before 8 pm. No food is permitted during the entire fasting period. You are only allowed to drink coffee, tea or water, and any other non-caloric beverages.

By doing this, you heighten your body's innate autophagy process. For example, protein fasting allows your body to close in on all those remaining toxins by cleansing your cells in the form of eating up these toxins to enable new ones to form. The proper disposal of these waste actually builds up a 16-to-28-hour fast. If the timings are irregular, it could cause hormonal imbalance in most women

This is because women are incredibly delicate to changes such as starvation or restriction of calories. So with that said, you can sidestep hiss problem by taking in a big diet breakfast and try to limit proteins and carbohydrates from your meal. While the fat tricks your body that it is not starving, you remain fasting. We are going to discuss intermittent fasting more broadly in the next section. Be sure to check it out.

Try Out Sprint Interval Training

This is another critical way to activate autophagy. Keep in mind that autophagy involves the body's reaction to stress, and in this case, high-intensity exercise puts you in stress spot. It stresses you sufficient enough to start up biochemical reactions. The right effects to make your muscles stronger without injuring your body. It also induces autophagy, which results in a boost in your longevity. Set a target to exercise approximately 20 to 30 minutes each.

Great emphasis is put on the less is more attitude toward exercise to activate autophagy in your body. Lifting weights and resistance training workouts for about 35 minutes each day is the most effective way to stimulate. It involves obtaining severe, temporary stress and allowing the body to take care of itself by disposing of waste substance through autophagy. You can try this out by taking intervals in training between low pace and brisk.

You can garner the good of autophagy when you are sleeping too. Through sleep personality, which is also known as sleep Chronotype, helps you get knowledge of the benefits and effectiveness of sleep. An individual has a single of four sleep personalities that informs the way one functions throughout the night and during the day. Knowing your sleep personality allows you to set your body to stimulate the autophagy process with your circadian patterns or sleep cycle.

Autophagy to Heal and Detox Your Body and Regenerate Your Mind

The term detox is undoubtedly the most misconstrued and misunderstood word in the health and nutrition sector—with the most significant wrongdoers being the vendors of 'detox smoothies.' The majority of the recipes of so-called detox smoothies carry more sugar than is needed in the body. The types of sugars in these mixtures are fructose that actually intoxicates the body.

Fructose metamorphosis is wholly distinct from that of glucose. While glucose is effortlessly metabolized and transformed into energy by almost all the cells in your body, fructose is at best handled in the liver.

So a diet enriched with fructose is a day-to-day practice in the modern world. It deposits excessive amounts of injury to the main detoxifying organs.

Fructose is destructive to the liver as well as other toxic substances such as alcohol. And observing the rate of intake has grown to four hundred percent in the last five decades, it is not astonishing that fatty diseases of the liver have tripled during the same period of time. The majority of American adults suffer from fatty liver diseases that are non-alcoholic. So before you even think about getting smoothies for body cleansing, consider other options.

Your body is under the normal state of renewal. Every minute of the day, your body is degrading old, not useful cells to give space for the growth of new cells that will be reproduced. New proteins are created as others are used up. If a cell gets to the termination of its usefulness, it experiences a process known as apoptosis, famously known as cell death that has been programmed. This is a sequential procedure for the body to get rid of cells that have worn out. The cell is degraded into component sections and from there 'eaten up' by various immune cells when the necessity arises.

There are other times when it is only specific parts of a cell that need replacement, something close to the replenishment of energy battery in your TV remote control. It could not necessarily mean that an entire organelle needs to be replenished. Autophagy refers to the metabolic procedure where weak, broken or old cellular structures get renewed, repaired and reused through a self-cannibalization in the body

Let us see what autophagy does when it comes to detoxing and anti-aging.

This sequential metabolism utilizes structures that dispose of waste known as lysosomes. These organelles degrade and recycle cellular parts. The component sections are then turned into amino acids, which are proteins building blocks, and moved to other parts of the body where they are used to revitalize cells and get rid of waste materials. Now, this is what detox cation truly means at the very profound level means

As this inner cleansing removes cellular clutter, aging is contrasted because what is old is made new again. And the satisfaction of autophagy goes well far and beyond looking and feeling more youthful.

This operation also helps to wipe out pathogens while creating newer and powerful immune cells. A more powerful immune system means excellent resistance to infectious diseases. Additionally, it improves monitoring against mutated cells and safeguards the wholeness of the cell's nucleus that prevent cancer cells from being created in the first place.

Research also reveals that autophagy helps in lowering inflammation, and resistance to insulin can enhance the symptoms and outward look for individuals suffering from an illness like Alzheimer's disease and even Parkinson's disease. Think about autophagy as your body's natural program for recycling. It makes us more sufficient in the ability to remove defective sections, prevent cancerous growths, and halt metabolic dysfunction such as diabetes and obesity.

In this other section, we will see how to make sure your body does not switch off these disease-fighting and detoxification process.

The primary diet that stops Cellular Detoxification includes high taking in of carbohydrates and, consequently, the release of insulin hormone in the body. This means that the fresh juices that are pressed, veggies smoothies that are mainly termed as detox beverages would switch off the autophagy (detox procedure) the same case applies to honey and sweetened desserts praised in the Paleo Blogs.

An individual should also watch out for excessive protein consumption. The majority of people do not know that a single protein can be easily transformed into glucose through a process known as gluconeogenesis. And researches have also conveyed that the amino acid called leucine completely halts the process of autophagy. This supposedly doesn't mean that an individual should limit consumption of protein to the extent that you may restrict carbohydrates intake, although it is vital to understand that diets rich in proteins could trigger powerful insulin reactions in some individuals and slows the healing process of organelles.

Three Ways to Boost the Symptoms of Autophagy

There are three significant ways to increase the activation of these internal detoxification, healing, and regeneration of mind. These vital factors include practicing fasting, the introduction of the Ketogenic diet, and body exercises.

Fasting

The most primary driver is fasting. Especially, intermittent fasting. The autophagy occurs in different degrees and a variety of organelles. Generally, if your blood sugars and level of insulin are low, they will automatically activate the autophagy process. How long exactly do you need to fast?

Following 16 hours of fasting and eating within 8 hours fasting plan on a daily basis can be essential in the stimulation of the autophagy process. The majority of individuals observe an eating window, which is even more compressed. They take in food within four hours and fast the other hours of the day that are left.

Extended fasting provides even more essential benefits to the body. Many scientists' advice on the introduction of quarterly water fast for at least five days is the best thing you could do to maintain the process of healing and detoxification to improve disease resistance process and longevity.

Ketogenic Diet

The second process involves the ketogenic diet introduction to our day-to-day activities. When fasting is considered more valuable in the health sector, the majority of people prefer strictly sticking to a variety of diets that includes paleo and Keto diet. Let's take a look at the ketogenic diet. Keto diet usually involves the consumption of foods or meals that have a high content of healthy fats, moderately low protein, and, last but not least, are low in carbohydrates. By observing the Keto diet, we can trick the body into thinking it is under siege. This way, it activates the lysosome to degrade old and defective proteins in an individual's body. This diet also introduces ketone bodies. These bodies are not only useful in cleansing the body cells but also switch on the chaperone-mediated autophagy mechanism (CMA). This procedure selectively reuses cellular waste, and yet the only thing you needed to activate this process is to limit the consumption of carbohydrates. With the Keto diet, an individual gets the same metabolic changes and significance as fasting without actually fasting.

Finally, there is a third most effective way to heighten the autophagy process. This involves exercise. In research on animals, scholars found that dreadful activity tends to switch on the autophagy process in the cardiac and skeletal muscles. It also consists of the stimulation of autophagy in the pancreas and liver by renewing and reusing significant metabolic tissues.

Some scholars would argue that autophagy is automatically activated after thirty minutes if acute exercises; however, it starts the process of breaking down and self-eating of toxins after about eighty minutes of vigorous exercise. This process substantiates the fact that a shorter duration but high-intensity activity is of high significance compared to the long term and less intensity cardio.

Feasting & Fasting:

Trying to Strike the Perfect Ancestral Balance

Even in real life, there is a saying that says that too much of everything is poisonous. While autophagy is beneficial to the human body, too much or too little of it could be harmful to your body. Therefore, this calls for the ability to balance between both so that you can avoid killing yourself while trying to undergo these severe changes in your day-to-day activities.

Nonetheless, there's substantial evidence that the severity of the autophagy process is something we can adjust to; it is an evolutionary process of reaction to either feasting or famine during stress periods. If not dealt with naturally, these toxins could kill us, so the best outcomes would be seen after getting used to these techniques over a while.

To obtain optimal health and reap the benefits of the nearest thing we have to natural healing and detoxification of the body, we should incorporate the natural lifestyle of our ancestors of feasting and fasting to enable cellular growth when eating and cellular cleansing when we are fasting.

Weight Loss Through Autophagy

The majority of individuals who are practicing fasting are either doing it to reduce diseases causing microorganisms, or to lose weight. Especially people with signs and symptoms of obesity use this mechanism to lose excessive fats. More specifically, to increase longevity and become more energetic.

Intermittent fasting researches have not established an essential benefit over consecutive energy limitation diets. It only works if a person can adhere to it consistently. Unfortunately, most research on IF is poorly constructed and doesn't consider the differences between fasting routines.

However, losing weight isn't the same as fat loss, and it doesn't mean you're getting healthier or activating autophagy. Conventional calorie restriction diets don't guarantee autophagy and may block it completely.

Most of the longevity benefits of fasting are mediated by autophagy. Deficient autophagy promotes aging and disease. Furthermore, autophagy regulates lipid metabolism through lipophagy.

What Are Lipolysis and Lipophagy?

To lose body fat, you have to first "release" it from the adipose stores. This process is called lipolysis. It is the degradation of fatty acids, triglycerides, and cholesterol by autophagy. It contributes to lipid droplet degradation in many cell types.

Lipophagy uses 'acid' lipolysis in lysosomes to degrade cellular triacylglycerols, which store free fatty acids. Lipid stores are metabolized by lipophagy to fuel mitochondrial beta-oxidation and regulated to maintain energy homeostasis. Impaired lipophagy promotes fatty liver and dysregulates body mass.

375

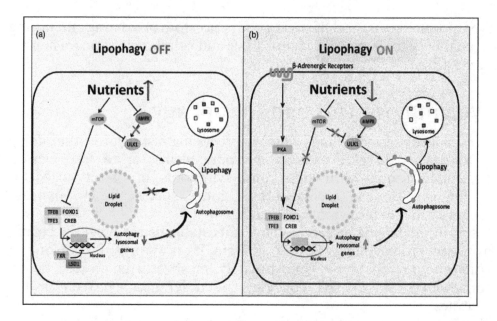

How many lipids get degraded by lipophagy depends on the supply of extracellular nutrients and overall caloric balance. The cells adjust the amount of lipophagy based on their nutritional status.

Autophagy and Ketogenesis

Another pathway related to lipolysis and fat loss is ketosis. It's a metabolic state characterized by elevated ketone bodies, which are energy molecules created from beta-oxidation.

You can be in ketosis without autophagy, and you can have autophagy without ketosis. It's just that, usually, you'd see them together because they follow similar principles.

Autophagy is essential for the synthesis of ketone bodies. Autophagy deficient mice have decreased the production of ketones by the liver.

While inadequate renal autophagy does not impair Ketogenesis, mice with deficient autophagy in both liver and kidneys have lower blood ketones and physical activity under starvation than those who lack autophagy in just the liver. You need autophagy to induce proper Ketogenesis.

If you're on a calorie-restrictive diet, but you don't have autophagy, you'll inhibit Ketogenesis, which lowers the amount of available energy your body has access to it. Body fat is fuel, and you shouldn't feel tired of hungry even when you have sub 10% body fat.

With enough autophagy, you'll enable Ketogenesis to kick in, which raises ketones in your blood and gives more energy to the brain. Most people find it easier to diet and fast when they're in ketosis.

Autophagy and Insulin

Conventional weight-loss diets are anti-autophagic and anti-ketogenic because they promote eating low fat, high protein, high carb at a high eating frequency. This will inevitably interfere with both Ketogenesis and autophagy. If you eat very often throughout the day, then you're preventing the formation of autophagosomes by raising insulin.

The autophagy of the impaired macrophages usually causes the resistance of insulin when it comes to the condition of obesity because the inflammatory adipocytes produce too many reactive oxygen species, which autophagy would frequently clear out. Being obese promotes inflammation, which makes you even more provocative and obese while not being able to heal that inflammation because of suppressed autophagy.

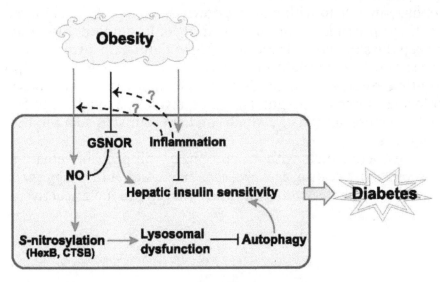

Mice deficient in autophagy show larger adipocytes in the visceral tissues, which are fat, increased liver fat, reduced tolerance to glucose, as well as being resistant to insulin.

So, not only are a ketogenic diet and fasting great for lowering insulin and thus activate autophagy, but they also help to protect against developing insulin resistance.

Autophagy and Loose Skin After Weight Loss

It's said that autophagy can eat up loose skin and tighten it up after you've lost a bunch of weight. However, that's only true to a certain extent.

A 2014 study in Japan found that aging fibroblasts have decreased autophagy. Fibroblasts create collagen in the skin, which causes wrinkles and loose skin.

Another 2018 study from Korea found that aging fibroblasts experience an increase in the production of unwanted materials, which results in skin aging. The researchers said that the role of autophagy is very important, as it aids the counteracting aging process to the skin by keeping the fibroblasts healthy.

Autophagy may help with slowing down the aging of the skin, but it's not eating up wrinkles and loose skin. It only supports the processes that keep the skin more elastic and able to tighten up faster.

In cases of extreme weight loss, fasting and autophagy can help with preventing excess loose skin. You will inevitably have some loose skin after losing a bunch of weight. However, if you lose weight with fasting, you'll have more autophagy, which can help your skin adapt to the new weight quicker.

Calorie restrictive diets without autophagy will probably create much more loose skin because, as we've seen in studies, autophagy is central to at least keeping the fibroblasts and collagen production active.

Does Autophagy Enable You to Lose Fat?

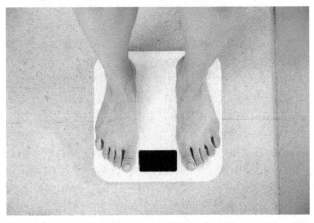

The number of adipocytes is a significant determinant in how much fat mass a person has. Unfortunately, it's said that the total count of the cells that are fat usually remains the same when one becomes an adult or following a loss of weight. About ten percent of the cells that are fat are usually developed every year at all the ages of adults and also the total mass of the body indexes. Autophagy is the process of cellular turnover that increases the rate of cell renewal. Theoretically, increased basal autophagy and specific degradation of adipocytes may enhance this because you'll be breaking down things more effectively.

You're not going to lose fat unless you're at a caloric deficit, even if you have a lot of autophagy. Fasting for three days and then over-eating will still make you gain weight if you consume excess calories.

Autophagy does not make you lose fat directly because your overall energy balance determines it. It's just that autophagy promotes the metabolization of lipid droplets and fatty acids through lipophagy and ketosis.

If you want to know how to start intermittent fasting for autophagy, longevity, anti-aging, and improved body composition, then check out my book.

Three Ways to Activate the Process of Weight Loss

While autophagy occurs throughout the body regularly, there are three primary ways to speed up the process and encourage the body to take its stance against unwanted fat cells. The following three triggers play a key role in weight loss, to begin with, but when used to stimulate autophagy, they take on an entirely new level of efficiency.

Exercise – Exercise stresses the body and can cause small tears in muscle tissue. These micro-tears aren't necessarily harmful, but they take a toll on the body and can increase your risk of injury if not given ample time to heal. This is where autophagy comes in. By helping to clear away the broken and damaged bits of cells associated with the micro-tears, they make way for new cells to form that help to regenerate the muscle tissue.

Autophagy Fasting – Like exercise, fasting creates stress on the body. Intermittent fasting, or going for a few hours a day without eating, may help to control diabetes and minimize a person's risk of developing heart disease. Fasting also works in the brain as well and may help fight neurodegenerative disorders. By eliminating deteriorating brain cells, some studies state that cognitive function may improve when a person uses intermittent fasting. Some people fast for 12 to 18 hours, while others prolong the fast for as long as 36 hours, depending on the results that they hope to achieve.

Decreasing the number of carbs that you consume will also trigger autophagy processes. For this trigger to be active, you would need to fast for up to 18 hours or longer. This forces the body into a state of ketosis. During the other six hours, the use of carbohydrates is minimal, forcing the body to feed on itself for the fuel it needs to function. However, cutting out whole grains to reduce carbs is a risky proposition, with the recent studies connecting low overall grain consumption to cancer (particularly colon cancer).

Chapter Two:

Fat-Burning Strategies

Fat burning refers to the innate utilization of stored fat by the body during certain conditions. It could be either activated or induced in many ways or can naturally happen without us knowing. The burning of fat can be the body's way of surviving in low-energy conditions.

Ways to Burn Fats

Whether you are considering the enhancement of your health, in general, or you want to attain that summer body for a new bikini, the process of burning fats is quite a task. Specific techniques can help an individual to increase the fat burning process on their body. The best ways to burn fat in your body involve:

1. Begin Practicing Training of Strength

This exercise involves a training activity that demands the shrinking of the muscles with another person. It helps to create the mass of muscles and grows your power to be able to pursue work that needs toughness. Nearly all the training of the strength usually consists of weight lifting exercise so as to be able to acquire more muscles. Through the various researches, we are able to understand that strength training produces multiple health benefits like a fat burn and gaining muscles.

Resistance exercise could also assist in the preservation of masses that are free from fat, hence the increase in the level of calories in the body, which usually burns when you are resting. Performing bodyweight training, lifting weights, and using gym resources is one of the simplest ways to begin strength exercise for burning excessive fats.

2. Follow a Diet High in Protein

Inclusive of meals which have a lot of protein is the efficient method which lowers the food appetite while burning a lot of fat. The consumption of increased protein quality is linked to a reduced risk in belly fat. Increasing your protein intake may also heighten your ability to feel full in your stomach because proteins take time to digest in the stomach, thereby reducing appetite and reduction in calorie consumption to help lose weight. The good examples are eggs, seafood dairy products, meat, and legumes, which consist of a lot of proteins.

3. Try to Sleep a Lot

Sleeping at an early time will help you prolong the burning of fats in the body and also the increase of a lot of weight. Several types of research have discovered a link between having a quality sleep period and losing weight. A research conducted on females indicated that the women who were having a sleep period of about five hours in a single night were at the risk of adding more weight compared to the women who had quality sleep of about 8 hours in a single night. A lot of studies found out that deprivation of sleep usually leads to various changes in the hormones of hunger, which will also lead to the appetite of a person to increase and also a person being at risk of having the problem of obesity. Even though every person is different when it comes to the duration of sleep they usually have, a lot of researchers have found out that getting quality sleep of about 7 to 8 hours of sleep period in a single night is very essential, as it will result to losing weight and other benefits which are associated with the health of the body.

A person should be having a single sleeping period pattern something they do every single day, they should decrease the amount of caffeine that is taken just before going to bed and also decrease the level of electronic usage during the time to sleep so as to have a sleeping pattern which is healthier than the ones experienced before. Therefore, one should know that when you get a quality sleep pattern will result in the low chances of increasing your weight.

4. The Diet Should Consist of Vinegar

This is usually because the vinegar is widely proven to contain substances that help increase the health of a person. To add on that, it usually beneficial when it comes to the health of the heart and also the control of the blood sugar levels, and therefore by increasing the level of consumption of vinegar will aid in increasing the burning of fats process, which has been proven by various researchers. Consuming about one to two spoons of the vinegar every day will eventually aid in decreasing the weight of a person. Through the consumption of the vinegar, a person will be able to experience an appetite reduction.

5. The Consumption of Fats That Are Healthy

Through the increase in the consumption of a lot of fats that are healthy will eventually result in weight loss, even though it is viewed as impossible. This is usually because the fats tend to take time to digest and hence aid in the process of stomach emptying in a slow manner, thus causing the reduction of hunger feelings and also the reduction of having an appetite. Various researches indicate that constant following of a diet that consists a lot of fats that are usually healthier which have been extracted from nuts and also olive will result to the weight management of the body whereby a person will have less risk in gaining weight as compared to someone who does not practice this. Many studies have proven that loss of weight can be achieved through the use of vinegar, and therefore, just by taking a spoon of olive oil or even the oil from coconut will eventually be able to lose the weight. Therefore, this process will be very beneficial to a person who is having a diet so as to be able to lose weight.

You should always know that the fats that healthy also contain more calories; therefore, you should be able to balance the consumption level of these fats even though they are healthy. This can be achieved by changing the consumption of taking all fats in general and change to consuming the fats that are healthier. Because fats usually take time to digest; therefore, consuming it will aid in the reduction of your appetite. Thus, its consumption will be beneficial in losing weight in the whole body.

6. Drinking Beverages That Are Healthy

Changing from the consumption of the drinks that are usually high in the levels of sugar to the dinks that are so low on sugar levels will result in the increase of the process of burning of the fats. Therefore, one should avoid drinks the intake of beverages that contain a lot of sugar, for instance, soda, which contains a lot of calories, which usually gives the body a little benefit but a lot of damages. The alcoholic drinks usually consist of a lot of calories, which will also cause the inhibitions in the body to reduce; hence, the person under the influence will be at risk of overreacting to things. Therefore, the consumption of the drinks that usually contain a lot of sugar together with alcoholic drinks will eventually result in gaining a lot of fats around the belly of a person. The limitation of these drinks will be very beneficial, whereby there will be a decrease in the consumption of calories, thus keeping them away from developing the belly fats. You should, therefore, change to drinks which do not contain calories that will help with your health—for example, the drinking of water. Drinking a lot of water every day and more specific around meal times will result in loss of weight. The consumption of green tea is also a good way to help improve your health, whereby it contains caffeine and contains a lot of antioxidants, which will help in the process of burning fats and also increase the rate of metabolism.

7. Increase Fiber Intake

The dissolved fibers usually suck up water and shift through the track of digestion hence aiding a person to feel satisfied for a long period. Therefore, increasing the consumption to consist of a lot of fiber will be very beneficial, as it will guard the body against gaining weight and also the concurrence of fats. Research indicates that the consumption of every ten grams of dissolved fiber will lead to weight loss in between 4 to 5 years, even without following any diet or being involved in any exercise. The consumption of fruits or vegetables will help in the process of burning fats in the body. Therefore, the increase in consumption of a lot of fiber is highly linked to the loss of fats, low consumption of calories, and a general loss of weight.

8. Decrease the Intake of Carbohydrates That Have Been Refined

You should decrease the consumption of the carbohydrates that have been refined hence being able to lose the fats in the body, and this is high because the carbohydrates that are usually refined lose their nutrients in that process hence containing a low level of nutrients and also fiber. Usually, the carbohydrates that have undergone the process of refining have high levels of the glycemic count, resulting in crashes and spikes in the sugar levels of the blood, which will eventually cause high hunger levels. Many types of research indicate that a meal that contains a lot of the carbohydrates that have been refined usually results in the development of fats around the belly. Therefore, the consumption of the carbohydrates that have not been refined will help in the weight loss process in the whole body and, more specifically, around the belly. Many researchers argue that the people who usually consume refined carbohydrates were at risk of getting health problems like the fats around the belly, while the people who consumed the carbohydrates that were not refined were at a lower amount the development of such problems. To be able to do away with such problem you should lower the level of consuming the carbohydrates that have undergone the process of being refined and increase the consumption of the carbohydrates that have not been refined as they contain a lot of nutrients and also have a lot of fiber and reduce the level of hunger in the system and be better health-wise.

9. Raise the Cardio

The exercise of aerobics is a famous type of exercise that is used to train and also exercise the organs of the body, specifically the heart and the lungs. Through doing this will result from increasing the burning of the fats in the body, as it is an operative way of achieving this. Therefore, the increase in aerobics resulted in the burning of a lot of fats, which is around the belly, which can be seen in many types of research. The aerobics can be able to add the mass of the muscles while decreasing the fats around the belly and also the weight loss in the general body. Many professionals have argued that it is important to have aerobics exercises of about 150 to 300 minutes every week. This can be achieved through running and also swimming, including other types of aerobics, which are beneficial to the health of the body. This will also result in lower the total circumference of the waist of the body and also aid in burning off the excess fats in the body, even having a positive effect on the mass of the muscles of the body.

10. Consume a Lot of Coffee

Drinking coffee helps in the burning of fats because caffeine is a very important component that usually speeds up the process of burning the fats in the body. The caffeine, which is included in coffee deeds as the main stimulant, which usually affects the rate of metabolism positively and also encourages the degradation of the acids that are fat in the body. Many research shows that a person can be able to boost energy and even improve the metabolism process through drinking coffee, which contains a lot of caffeine. The high consumption of caffeine is usually linked to the slow gaining of weight. Through drinking coffee, you will be able to benefit a lot, as it also helps in maintaining weight loss in a person. To be able to get the benefits fully through drinking coffee, one should eliminate the sugar and also the cream and, therefore, just drink the coffee in black or add a little milk so as to be able to keep away from the consumption of more calories.

11. Practice the Sprint Interval Training

This is usually a form of practice that joins the first intense of activities which have a small period of recovery so as to be able to increase the rate of the heart. This can be beneficial, as it aids the burning process of fats, as well as it has a positive effect on losing weight. Therefore, through this, you can be able to lose weight in just a week by just practicing it for just 25 minutes a day, and you will be able to see some remarkable changes in your weight. Changes will be vivid, even without altering your lifestyle or what consist of your diet. Through this, one will be able to reduce the fats, which usually accumulate around the belly and even decrease the total circumference of the waist. Through this process, you are also able to burn a lot of calories in just a short period as compared to the others. This process will help you in the burning process of the calories of up to 35 percent, hence being more efficient than the other forms. For the best way to start with the sprint interval training, you should start by balancing between the process of walking and also the action of running slowly for a period of about one minute. You can even choose to balance the exercises—for example, doing a few push-ups and then doing some squats—which will be very beneficial to the person. Therefore, this process is proven to be able to help in the burning of a lot of calories within a small period of time.

12. The Diet Consisting of Probiotics

This is usually a form of bacteria that is usually beneficial to the body of a mammal, and it is located in the digestive tract, and it has been proven to be able to benefit the health of a person. These bacteria, which are in the gut, have been indicated to help big time in many things—for example, the immunity of the body and also the health of the person's mind. Therefore, through the increase in the consumption of probiotics by taking meals that consist of the product, which will benefit the body in so many ways, including the burning process of the fats and also the management of a person's weight. Many types of research have been conducted, and the results are the same whereby the individuals who consumed the probiotics were able to lose weight and more specifically in the reduction of the total percentage of fats in the body but the others they still had a lot of fats and were able to gain a lot of weight. Many types of research indicate that the consumption of the probiotic eke out aided many people who had a diet that consisted of a lot of fats and also a lot of calories, and they were able to the accumulation of fats in the body and also maintained the general weight of the entire body.

13. Add the Consumption of Iron in the Diet

Everyone knows that iron is a very important mineral, as it comprises a lot of functions in the body. The lack of iron mineral in the body will affect the body negatively, whereby it will affect the thyroid gland, which is located on the neck and usually produces the hormones that usually help stimulate the metabolism process in the body. Many types of research indicate that having a diet that is low in iron will result in the thyroid being less effective in performing its duties, as well as the thyroid hormones production will be interrupted. The famous indicators of hypothyroidism, which is viewed as the ineffectiveness of the thyroid will consist of experiencing some form of visibility in the body, some exhaustion of the body, running out of breath, as well as the addition of the bodies weight. Treating the insufficiency of iron in the body will ensure the body functions well and also that the function of the thyroid glands to be more effective; hence, the body will be able to prevent issues like running out of breath and even encourage the activities levels. Research has also discovered that the people who usually get treated for the insufficiency of the iron mineral in the body enjoyed the high level of weight loss. People should start including the right amount of the iron minerals in their diet so as to experience the benefits it comes with. A person should be ready and eager to include the iron mineral in the meals so as to be able to reach the levels of iron that the body really requires so as to be able to maintain the energy levels of the body. This is easy, as you can find iron in dairy products— for example, meat. The insufficient iron in the body will lead to the thyroid not functioning well hence affecting the body negatively in so many ways.

14. Start Fasting

This is usually a diet program that involves the balancing of periods to eat and the periods that you should fast. A lot of researches usually indicates that intermittent fasting aids in the reduction of weight and also being able to lose the fats in the body. Some of the various results of the fasting usually involve the propositional fasting in a day, which is a type of fasting that consists of the alternation of the fasting days and the days of frequently eating. The research I found out that the day alternation fasting of about 3 to 12 weeks resulted in a weight loss of about seven percent and also helped in lowering the level of the fats in the body. Therefore, by eating in between 8 hours of the day also helps to lower the percentage of fats in the body and also maintains the mass of muscles. There exist a lot of methods of fasting, which usually consist of different patterns of eating and also of abstaining from taking any meal. Therefore, you should look for a method that will fit with your schedule and routine to be able to see which of the methods work best. This is because there exist a lot of many methods to aid in the weight reduction process and even improve one's health. The introduction of a new lifestyle that is healthy will be very beneficial.

Intermittent Fasting

It usually refers to the various sequences of eating that surrounds the time that a person eats and fasts. It usually does not portray the food that a person should consume but talks of *when* to consume the food. Therefore, it is not a diet but a guide in giving the direction of when to eat the food. The recognized fasting method usually consists of a person being able to abstain from food in a period of 16 hours and should be practiced within two times a week. Many humans have been practicing fasting since the Ancient Times. The people during these times were not equipped with shops or sophisticated technology. All they had were crude weapons, which helped them survive—but at times, they went to sleep or stayed hungry the entire day. Through this, the humans were enabled to stay for long periods without eating, hence being able to fast over time. Many people have been practicing fasting for religious reasons—for example, the Muslims who usually have a month of fasting. The same case applies to Christians. Though a lot of people usually practice fasting for religious purposes, it is very important to health, as it helps solve a lot of health issues—for example, being obese. There exist various methods of practicing fasting, which usually consists of being able to balance the days of fasting and the days of eating. Therefore, to be able to achieve this, you should eat a small quantity of food or abstain from eating during the days you are fasting. Through this, you will be able to improve your health.

Types of Intermittent Fasting

The following consist of various methods of intermittent fasting:

16:8

The most common one is the fasting of between sixteen hours and being able to eat within eight hours. This method usually consists of missing breakfast and also restricting the consumption habits to a fewer number of hours—for example, 2 to 10 pm—then, abstain from consuming food for almost sixteen hours straight. This will have an impact on your health.

Eat, Stop, Eat

The second method is eating and then stopping and then eating again. This method usually consists of practicing fasting for a full day, which is twenty-four hours in a single week. You should be able to do so one time or repeat the fasting in the same week. This will also have a positive impact on the health of the body.

5:2

The next method is known as the five to ratio two. This method usually consists of the consumption of only five hundred to 600 calories in any given two days in a week, but there is no limit of the remaining days of the week.

Calorie Reduction

The fourth method usually consists of the decreasing consumption of calories, which usually has a positive impact on losing the weight of the body. A lot of people usually suggest that the first method is the simplest and that it is more sustainable, and a person can be able to follow. This method is the most famous type, as many people know about it as compared to the rest, as it is viewed as an easy way to achieve the benefits of fasting.

Effects of Intermittent Fasting

When a person abstains from the consumption of food, a lot of effects are experienced in the entire body. This will be able to change the levels of the hormones so as to be able to access the fats that have been stored. This will also result in the cells stimulating the important process of repairing and also alter the gene-to-protein process. The following are some alterations that usually happen in the body when a person is fasting:

The Hormone Responsible for Growth in Humans

These type of hormones usually increases, and it has many benefits to the body of a person—for example, it usually helps in the fighting the increase of fats in the body and even results to the gaining of the total mass of the muscles. This will be very beneficial to the body, as it makes the body much healthier and being energetic and strong. Therefore, the fasting process usually helps the improvement of the body's health.

Insulin

There are improvements in the sensitivity of the insulin in the body, as well as, the levels of insulin will lower very quickly, thus enabling the body to use the fats that were stored. Therefore, this will improve the accessibility of the stored fats to be reached and used hence promoting the health of the entire body.

The Repair of the Cellular

When a person is fasting, the cells usually stimulate the process of repairing the cellular, which usually consists of the process of autophagy, wherein the cells will be able to undergo the alimentary process and eliminate the proteins which are not functioning and the old ones which usually accumulate in the cells.

The Expression of Genes

These are usually the alterations that usually occur in the duties or roles of the genes which are linked to longevity and guarding the body against getting any diseases. The alterations in the level of hormones, the role of the cells, as well as the expression of genes, are the result of the benefits from fasting, which improves the health of the body. Therefore, when you fast, the hormones which are responsible for growth in humans will increase in number while the levels of the insulin will shift downwards. Due to fasting the cells of the body will alter the expression of the genes and then stimulate the process of repairing the cellular.

Weight Loss

Losing weight is very important, and many people share this, as it has become an issue in society, hence becoming a mutual cause for the individuals to try and fast. Therefore, consuming fewer foods, the process fasting usually leads to a direct lowering of calorie consumption. The fasting process also alters the number of the hormone hence being able to increase the loss of weight in the body. This will also aid in dropping the levels of insulin and boost the levels of the hormones that are responsible for growth in humans and also boosts the discharge of hormones that are responsible for the burning of fats in the body. Due to these alterations in the hormones, hence fasting over a short time period will boost the rate of metabolism in the body. Through the consumption of less and burning calories, the process of fasting usually results in losing weight and thus improves the health of the entire body. Many types of research indicate that the process of fasting can be a beneficial way to lose weight hence being viewed as the best tool for losing weight.

Many types of research prove that through fasting, a person will be able to lose weight, and therefore, the eating sequences can be able to result in a weight loss of about three to eight percent with a given period of about three to twenty-four weeks.

Researches also indicate that people who practiced fasting experience a drop in the total circumference of their waste of about four to seven percent and also illustrated a decrease of the fats around the belly which usually accumulate around the organs of the body and result to diseases which are very harmful to the body. To be able to achieve these, you should be able to consume fewer calories in general. You are advised that when not fasting, you should not consume a lot of calories, as it will hinder the achievement of these benefits.

The process of intermittent fasting will help in the addition of metabolism at the same time, aiding the person to eat fewer calories so as to promote the benefits associated with fasting. Therefore, this method is very useful in helping a person to lose weight and also decrease the fats around the belly.

The Health of the Heart

Through fasting, you will be able to lower the bad low-density lipoprotein cholesterol, which affects the heart.

Cancer Prevention

Through fasting, you can be able to prevent the development of such ailment, which is dangerous for the body.

The Health of the Brain

Through fasting, you will be able to add the level of the brain hormone, which is the brain-derived neurotrophic factor and will enable the growth of cells of the nerve that are new.

Fight Against Aging

Through fasting, you can be able to add on the lifespan as researched on some rats, which enabled them to live longer. Through fasting, you can be able to experience a lot of benefits that are associated with the brain and also the body. This can result in the loss of weight of an individual and also lowers the rate at which a person is at risk of getting type two diabetes and other diseases. This will also play a major role in longevity. People usually view healthy consumption as way too easy, but it usually requires a lot of effort to be able to maintain and make it a daily routine of your life.

If an individual is below a normal weight bracket or has ever experienced disorders when it comes to consuming meals, the person should seek the advice from a professional like a doctor so as to be able to start fasting.

As a result of fasting, a person will experience a lot of hunger and be weak, resulting in the brain not being sharp compared to the normal days that an individual is not fasting. This will take some time for the body to get used to the new lifestyle, which involves abstinence from eating meals for a given period of time. To be able to practice fasting, one should not be included in the categories below:

- People who have any type of diabetes
- People who have a problem with the regulation of sugar in the blood
- People who have decreased blood pressure
- People who are under any medication
- People who are under the general normal weight
- People who are pregnant

Insulin Resistance and Ketosis

The Keto diet usually consists of the consumption of fewer carbohydrates and more fats, and it really helps in weight loss. This is possible, as it alters the metabolism in the body—stimulating the use of fats as energy in lieu of sugar. This will help in promoting the good health of the body.

The Resistance in Insulin

The insulin hormone plays a major role in the body, as it aids the body to be able to control the sugar levels of the blood. If the sugar levels in the blood are above constantly for a long period, it will result in some dangerous health problems through a condition referred to as hyperglycemia. This will increase the risk of getting diabetes. In type one of diabetes, hyperglycemia usually generates due to the lack of insulin production by the pancreas. In type two diabetes, the organs and also the tissues of the body tend to drop their capability, which helps in responding to the insulin produced in the body. The pancreas usually attempts to make it up through the production of even more insulin, but it never enough hence resulting in the occurrence of hyperglycemia.

The general level of sugar in the blood which is usually viewed as the normal level but many researchers have proven it wrong while arguing that what people think is the normal sugar level in the blood is not, as it is more than that hence being higher than what is viewed as the healthy level.

They exist a lot of ways that insulin usually aids in the control of the sugar levels in the blood. This can be achieved through the sending of signals to the liver to cut down on the manufacture of the glucose, and the other is through the absorption of the glucose and then being converted to energy. The resistance of insulin is a complicated disorder that usually has no single source. This will result in the liver becoming resistant to insulin, specifically during the time or period it neglects to lower the manufacture of glucose in the body in reply to insulin. The cells can also resist insulin when they are in need of more quantity of hormones so as to aid them in using glucose. But the major cause in the decrease tolerance of glucose in the Keto diet was high because of the resistance in the liver of the insulin. Many researchers have investigated what causes the resistance of insulin and also type two diabetes, which is not known. The act of the body resisting insulin is the worst news one could get from a doctor, but this can be controlled by the Keto diet, as it aids in altering the way the body usually functions. If an individual observes the symptoms which are associated with the resistance, the best advice so as to be able to fight it is usually the Keto diet, which will help improve the situation whereby the body will be functioning well without any issues.

The Way It Works

The liver usually contains cells, fats, and muscles—and when they fail to help in the absorption of the glucose, which is in the blood, and since the sugar in the blood has nowhere else to go, it results in the blood containing a lot of unnecessary sugar. This will result in the pancreas boosting the production of insulin so as to able to balance the sugar levels in the blood. To be able to moderate the amount of the sugar in the body's blood, the pancreas is responsible for that and also helps in the dealing with the extra sugars but not all the time as the organ gets worn out and fails to give a standard amount of the insulin so as to be able to manage the raised levels of glucose in the body. This will result in the damaging of the architecture of the cells of the body with time, and therefore it fails to take control of the little levels of glucose in the body.

With time, it fails completely, resulting in diseases like diabetes. Due to this, the excess glucose in the body just comes around in the blood with no specific place to go hence resulting in the levels of sugar in the blood to continue to raise, which is dangerous to the health of the body. All of these will result in the body having high levels of sugar in the body's blood and also the increase in the levels of insulin in the body. They are therefore leading to diabetes hence requiring medicine so as to be able to balance the levels of insulin and the glucose levels in the body. In many examples, people usually get to know they are experiencing the resistance of insulin condition very late hence being at the late stages. This will help the person to be checking the levels of sugar and also insulin in the body on a daily basis. If you are found to have these problems, you will require to start the treatment immediately so as to be able to manage the levels of sugar in the body so as to enable the body to function well.

The resistance to insulin is referred to as the condition of diabetes, as this will result in the diabetes disease due to the levels of insulin and also sugar levels in the body. If an individual does not change their lifestyle which comprises of the diet one usually follows, will not help in the management of sugar levels of the body hence resulting to the type two diabetes which is highly associated with having a lot of sugar in the blood and it is resistant to the insulin and also results to various problems which are associated with the issue usually include experiencing stroke or even cancer of any type. These medical problems that are associated with the high levels of the sugars in the blood have resulted in the loss of many lives in the world, and the remaining individuals are also at risk due to the verse lifestyle we usually have. To be able to prevent this, the world should start considering following a diet so as to be able to manage the levels of sugar in the body.

Many types of research indicate that a lot of people in the world usually have the condition of the resistant insulin in the body, but they do not know it yet but will soon learn about it. This is usually because a lot of people in the world do not visit the hospitals for check-ups more often but rather visit the hospitals when they are sick or feeling unwell.

Through the consumption of a lot of carbohydrates and also a diet that usually consists of a lot of sugars due to the lifestyle one is used to. Other reasons include a lifestyle that is usually stationary, which also raises the body's glucose levels because the cells in the body are usually inactive to be able to use the body sugars. This can be dealt with through some exercises so as to be able to use the present glucose in the body. Below are some factors that are responsible for the stimulation of the resistance of insulin in the body:

- Age - the resistance of insulin can be able to affect individuals of all given ages, but it usually worsens when growing older
- Race - many people with the American roots and also the Asian Americas, are usually at high risk of getting this condition
- When a person has high blood pressure
- Experiencing inflammation

Therefore, people should visit the hospital more often to have checkups so as to be able to know the functioning of their bodies. This will lower the chance of it worsening because it was detected late. Therefore, if it is known earlier, you will be put on medication early enough, which will help you more.

Because the body usually attempts to balance the levels of insulin and also the sugar levels in the blood through its own mechanisms hence taking a long time to be able to get the resistant of the insulin. Therefore, a lot of people usually recognize the symptoms when it is at its peak.

More Fat, Less Sugar

For many decades, the nutrition industries have an emphasis on the war against the consumption of fat, making consumers convinced that lowering fats in your diet is vital to losing weight. However, it is advisable to know the contrast between good and bad fats and the effects of sugar consumption on the body.

If you walk down the supermarket aisle, you will discover an endless variety of 'healthy' foods. They may have been branded the fat-free tag or termed as reduced fatty foods. However, these foods could do more damage than good to the body. What the dietary industry does not reveal to a consumer is that these foods are inflated with extra sugars, chemical additives, and preservatives that are used to increase flavor and taste.

Added sugars are more harmful than fats in as far as your weight is concerned, it can also begin to damage about every other aspect of your health. By lowering your fat intake, you could be removing a variety of potential health benefits provided by healthy fats. Many consumers are left in a dilemma asking themselves is it fat or sugar.

Negative Effects of Sugar Consumption

Sugar has been seen to activate the rate of inflammation, which could actually be the root cause of most disease-causing organism survival. Sustenance of high inflammation levels, in the long run, has been connected to an increase in the risks of suffering from conditions such as diabetes, heart diseases, and immune disorders. Recent studies argue that loading up on added sugars may even cause cancer. There's a direct connection between the two, mostly since obesity increases your likelihood to get a variety of cancer types

As you may already know, intake of sugar has also been linked with higher chances of obesity, insulin resistance, and metabolic syndrome, all of which can cause chronic disease.

Additionally, sugar is very addictive and can activate the release of dopamine, which is a neurotransmitter that controls the pleasure and reward centers in the brain — consequently leading to symptoms of sugar withdrawal when you halt the consumption of sugar. Remember that the disadvantageous effects limited mostly to added sugars found in manufactured and processed foods. A good example is soft drinks and sugary sweets.

Good Sugars (and Fats)

There are a lot of healthy foods—for example, fruits carry natural sugars—but they also store a variety of vital nutrients together with fiber lowers the sugar absorption as well as nullify any possible harmful impacts on health. While added sugar is believed to be unhealthy globally, fat is regarded as an essential part of the diet, which has a lot of health benefits.

Advantages of Healthy Fats

Unsaturated fatty acids found in foods like avocados, olive oil, and almonds can actually boost heart health, lower cholesterol levels, and alleviate inflammation. Particular saturated fatty acids, such as coconut oil, may also have health benefits and have been linked to better brain function and increased fat burning (if eaten according to a planned calorie intake). It may be viewed as contrary, the addition of the fats that are healthy will influence the emptying of the gastric thus maintaining your health through making the body feel full for a long period to cut down on having cravings and boost the loosing of weight, however, not all fats are created equal.

The Not-So-Healthy Fats

While fats found in whole, unprocessed foods such as nuts, seeds, and oils are jam-packed with benefits, the fats found in highly processed foods are not at all good for your health. Trans fats, for example, are found primarily in processed foods and hydrogenated vegetable oils that are linked to various ranges of the unfavorable conditions of the health—for example, heart diseases, including diabetes. Steer clear to stick to healthier sources of fats instead to help optimize your health.

Fat or Sugar?

The healthiest and most sustainable way to improve your health is to make minor changes for healthier choices. Sugar is highly addictive and has been associated with some adverse effects on health. Healthy fats, on the other hand, are an essential part of the diet and may actually aid in weight loss, improve heart health, and reduce inflammation. For this reason, it's best to swap the sugar out of your diet and fill up on healthy fats instead.

Please keep in mind that Even if some fats are considered healthy, it's best to eat them in moderation so as to be able to shed weight. Adjusting the calorie consumption crucial for weight loss, and fats, even the healthy ones, have a lot of calories.

If you want to become your healthiest self, opt for the meals which include the oil extracted from the coconut, some fruits like avocados, fatty fish, nutrient-rich nuts and seeds

I also suggest skipping the sugar from processed foods, sugar-sweetened juices, energy drinks or sodas, and other unhealthy sources. If you need to add a hint of sweetness to your favorite baked goods or beverages, do select natural sweeteners like raw honey, stevia, and dates.

Not only can these components provide a bit of extra flavor, but they also carry vitamins, minerals, and antioxidants that make them a much better preference to plain, white, processed sugar.

Aerobic Training

Aerobic training is a process that strengthens your lungs, heart, and your body, in general. It improves the performance of your skeletal muscles. The main aim of aerobics training is to increase sports functions and enhance training response. This specific type of training involves activities that an individual does participate in that raises their heart rate and makes breathing much tricky. The activities must be constant and consecutive.

These activities may be done either indoors or outdoors. Which usually includes print activities which include exercises of walking or even swimming activities and many more. Many exercises are considered to be aerobic when they are done more often in—for example, the sport of tennis. The exercises of the aerobics usually include the forms that are not able to count. Therefore, it is usually done at a level that is balanced over a great duration of time. Therefore, many activities are viewed as aerobic, which helps boost the working of the body physically since, through this, the body will be fit hence ensuring the perfect working of the body. The muscles of the leg are usually involved when it comes to the exercises of aerobics, which usually have a positive effect on the body.

Aerobic vs. Anaerobic Exercise

There are a lot of differences between the aerobic exercise and the exercise that is usually anaerobic, which is highly due to the strength of the training activities and also running short distances. Which will be beneficial to the body. These types of exercises usually differ when it comes to the long period of the exercise and also the shrinking of the muscles and its production of energy inside the muscles. Many types of research have been done on the performance of the endocrine about its role in the shrinking of muscles, and therefore, these exercises are usually practiced so as to be able to boost the transportation of the myokines and also aid in the development of tissues in the body and even have an effect on the reparation of the injured or damaged ones. This also aids in the reduction of inflammation in the body. This is very beneficial since it aids in the prevention of developing various diseases that are infectious. The production of the myokine usually relies on the total quantity of the muscles that have shrieked. Many types of research have found out that both the two exercises usually aid in the secretion of the benefits, which are associated with the endocrine benefits. In a lot of situations, the exercise of the anaerobic is, at times, accompanied by aerobic exercises because the productive anaerobic metabolic process should encourage the aerobic structure highly, as there is a high need for energy, which usually surpasses the capacity of the aerobic structure.

The Improvement of Endurance Through Aerobic Training

The aerobic exercises usually boost the quantity of the oxygen which has been breathed and its transportation from the lungs and also the heart of the body into the blood so as to be used by the muscles of the body. A person who is fit in the aerobic exercises can be able to train for a long period and is wide because the person's body has gotten used to the long hours of training and also the hardship that usually comes with the training. When such an individual does train, their heart rate is usually low, with short rates of breathing, as well as a decrease in the fatigue experienced by the muscles of the body and even increased levels of energy. After the exercise, the recovery period is usually short. The fitness in aerobic can be gauged in the lab through the use of a treadmill and also the use of cycling of the bicycle.

How Long Is the Training Period?

To be able to achieve the benefits that are associated with training of aerobics, a person should have an exercising time for about three to five times in a week, which should be of about twenty to sixty minutes per session of training. To be able to be fit and also increase that fitness, one can achieve it by adding a little time in between the exercises so as to enable the body to get used to the long periods of exercising. This will also enable the person to lose a lot of weight and also the fats which are around the belly. The people who are not yet fit should start with shorter exercising periods so as to also enable their bodies to get used to the training slowly and continue increasing the time span of the exercises over time so as also to enable the improvement of their fitness capabilities. By adding little time in the training plan over time, a person is usually able to prevent many injuries. Through cross-training, a person is able to lower the various risks to a lot of injuries. Through balancing the various exercises of the training will help to prevent these injuries. Therefore, a person should balance the training of activities that are usually vigorous and require a lot of energy with activities which do not require a lot of energy and are less vigorous—for example, walking or even jogging.

A person will be able to increase their persistence in the training by moderating the training levels to be enough. The intensity level of training is usually fun, and it will not lead to various injuries as compared to the training that involves high intensity. The training schedules of aerobics should be planned to be able to fit every person since people are different in terms of their levels of fitness. When training, people should be able to communicate comfortably without experiencing breathing problems. A person should be able to say some words without having any stress and then pause a little bit to breathe and then continue talking without any problem. If a person fails to do this, it shows that they have not trained well. The heart rate also plays a major role in understanding the fitness levels of the individual. The heart rate of an individual should be beating at an average of about 60 to 90 percent.

Through aerobics, a person is able to enjoy a lot of benefits, which is usually associated with the training of aerobics. By doing the aerobics exercises, a person is able to have health advantages, which usually involves the addition in the capability to be able to circulate a lot of air in less time.

Health Benefits

The known benefits that one enjoys by doing aerobics include:

- It aids in making the muscles that are involved in the process of respiration to be strong so as to enable the transportation of air from and to the lungs.
- It helps enlarge the muscles of the heart so as to improve the process of pumping blood.
- It also aids in boosting blood circulation.
- It usually lowers the risk of getting diabetes.
- It helps in adding the number of red blood cells.
- It usually helps in the promotion of mental health.
- It usually helps lower the risk of dying because of the problem linked to cardiovascular.
- It aids in the stimulation of growth of the bones and also lowers the risk of getting osteoporosis.

Effects on Body Performance

The following are the benefits which are associated with the body performance due to aerobic exercise:

•   It aids in raising the storage capacity of the molecules of the energy in the body, which usually include a lot of fats and also carbohydrates.
•   It also aids in the formation of new blood vessels, which enable the transportation of blood in the muscles.
•   It even positively affects the activation of aerobic metabolism in the muscles.
•   It also enables the muscles to be able to use fats as energy when a person is exercising.
•   It usually boosts the rate the muscles will take to recover from the exercises.

Effects on the Brain

•   It aids in boosting the architecture links of the brains.
•   It also adds the density of the gray matter in the brain.
•   It also boosts the growth of the neurons.
•   It also helps the brain to be sharp in terms of memory.
•   It also boosts the general health of the brain.

Disadvantages

•   It is not the best practical way to develop the muscles of the body.
•   It usually leads to a lot of injuries highly due to repetitiveness in the exercises.
•   It is not the best way to burn fats in the body except when done more often.

The benefits, which are associated with both the health and even the performance, usually need the interval—and the rate of the exercises should be greater than the minimum time. Many researchers indicate that allocating an average of about 20 minutes and performed three to four times in a week will be very beneficial.

Exercises That Are Like Aerobics

The raised intensity of exercises usually adds on the resting rate of the metabolism in just twenty-four hours and helps in the process of burning a lot of calories as compared to the exercises that usually contain exercises that are low in terms of intensity. The exercises with a low intensity usually burn a lot of calories during the exercising periods, and this is high because of the time span added. During the period of training, you move large muscles over and over in your legs, hips, and arms. You will observe quick reactions in your body.

Your breathing pattern increases and becomes more profound. This expands the amount of oxygen getting into your blood. This means that your heartbeat rate increases, which consequently heightens the blood flow from your lungs to your muscles and back to your lungs.

In your body, the small blood vessels will widen to ensure the transportation of more oxygen to the muscles is efficient. They deliver back waste products from the tissues such as lactic acid and deoxygenated blood (highly concentrated with carbon dioxide). Your body also generates an enzyme known as endorphins, which act as natural pain relievers which enhance your wellbeing in general.

Take the First Step

Are you ready to get your body energetic in activities? If the answer is yes, then here's a way to get you started on this great journey!

An important strategy in getting started is to start with small steps until your body has adjusted to the rhythm of your exercise—especially if you have been inactive for a long time or have a chronic health condition, you need to start slow. It is also advisable to get your doctor's guidance before you even consider starting this training.

Once you are set to get started, begin with slow walks for about five minutes both in the morning hours and in the evening hours. A preferred activity that consists of the body is usually viewed as beneficial—for example, bicycle riding or swimming. These equally allow you to not only burn calories but also involve your skeletal muscles in healthy exercise.

From there, make sure to add in extra few minutes to each session of the walk, bicycle ride, or swimming. This enables your body to adapt to the physical exercise slowly but surely. Picking up your pace bit by bit consecutively also helps your body fall into the exercise rhythm. Soon enough, you will be comfortable walking or doing vigorous exercise for longer minutes and will notice all the advantages of regular aerobics training. You could reap even more fruits if you do more and more training regularly.

Another potential aerobic exercise could include jogging, dancing, or skiing. Even if you are suffering from conditions that limit you from taking part in full aerobics exercise, you could talk to your doctor for alternative activities that could benefit your general health without harming your muscles or joints.

Chapter Three:
Reducing Inflammation Through Autophagy

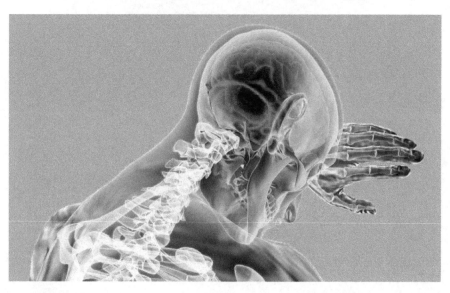

Autophagy is the homeostatic process that is involved in the scrapping of the organelles that are damaged, pathogens that have invaded, as well as the proteins that are denatured. The role played by autophagy in both adaptive and innate immunity is very important, as it influences the pathogens that cause inflammatory diseases. The discovery of autophagy mechanisms usually facilitates autophagy measurement, which is during the periods of pathophysiological and physiological procedures. Autophagy often plays a significant role in inflammation (which is through affecting development), the homeostasis, and the inflammatory cells' survival (which also includes the macrophages and the lymphocytes).

The mechanisms that usually depend on autophagy have been responsible for many inflammatory diseases. Inflammation often plays either a protective or destructive role in an injury. This can be caused by the physical, chemical, as well as biological agents and also include mechanical trauma, exposure to sunlight, through the x-ray and the radioactive materials, the extreme heat or cold levels, bacterial infections, viruses, as well as the corrosive chemicals. The inflammation pathogens include the changes of hemodynamic, leukocytes exudation, chemical mediators' releases, and even the hormonal response. Autophagy usually plays a significant role in the formation and also the pathogenesis of immunity response and inflammation. The process of autophagy interfaces with many cellular responses for stress pathways and also consists of direct interaction between the proteins of autophagy and even the molecules of immune signaling. This is highly brought out that the influenza virus usually triggers the Threonine kinase two, which is used to activate serine, which enhances the autophagy and also controls the activation of the inflammasome.

The critical role played by autophagy in the secretion of interleukin one beta can be seen in the primary human cells, whereby autophagy inhibition leads to an increase in the interleukin one beta production. In humans, the creation of the human tumor necrosis decreased by the inhibition of autophagy, thus suggesting a varying effect of autophagy on cytokines production. When it comes to the impact on autophagy there are essential differences between the humans and mice on the creation of interleukin 1 beta, whereby in mice the result is attributed to the activation or inhibition of inflammasome which is by autophagy while in humans the interleukin 1 beta mRNA transcription is increased when there is an inhibition of autophagy, but there are no effects that are seen on the activation of caspase 1.

Effects of Autophagy on Other Inflammatory Pathways

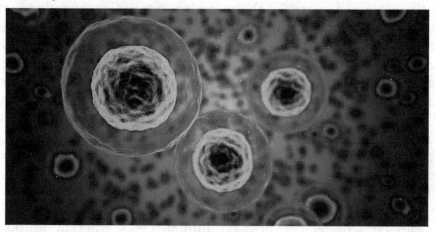

Autophagy usually has inhibitory effects on the activation of the inflammasome but also affects the inflammatory mediators that are independent of the activation of caspase 1. The autophagy restrains the activation of caspase 1, which results in the production of the ROS. Autophagy usually reduces the activation of the nuclear factor kappa B by selective degradation of the B-cell lymphoma complexes. The process is mediated directly through the cofactor of NSFL1C, which is a negative adjustment of the IKBKB, thus acting through the NFKB modulator that has been polyubiquitinated. Therefore, autophagy and inflammation are processes that are intertwined during the defense of the host. The process between the two plays a significant role in the pathogenesis and the treatment of many diseases.

Therefore, autophagy influences many significant components of the responses of immune hence helps in the inflammatory response regulation. Many people have suggested that autophagy developed as a primordial defense mechanism of eukaryote for the host. As this developed, the autophagy has been able to interact with other components of defense for the host like inflammatory reaction.

Anti-Inflammatory Keto Diet

Using a Plant-Based Keto Diet to Reduce Inflammation

If you have been on the food that is ketogenic because of health issues or because you want to lose weight, it might seem to be a little extreme, but it works because many of our health problems usually are caused by inflammation. Therefore, we will feel well if we can reduce inflammation. If one is struggling to shed some weight, experiencing some acne, changes in the hormones, or experiencing chronic pain in the body—but it is not related to any injury—one should know that they have chronic inflammation in their body. When you have injured the direct body fluids to the damaged part of the body to try and heal it.

However, if your diet is causing chronic inflammation in the body, then this means that the body is fighting in opposition to the foods that it is not familiar with. Sadly, several foods that have been seemingly thought to have been healthy, which are modified genetically, have experienced pesticide spraying—or even the animal products that have been improved in an unnatural way can be seen as not being healthy.

417

Inflammation Cut Down by Ketogenic Diet

The ketogenic diet can achieve inflammation reduction by suggesting that one's fat intake should be 70 to 80 percent, while the protein intake should be between 15 and 20 percent, and the carbohydrate intake should be 5 to 10 percent. Something important to remember is that for every gram of the carbohydrates we take, the body claps about four grams of water. This is because a lot of the carbohydrates we take in are usually over-processed, which has negatively affected their nutritional profile. It is, therefore, essential to remember that even carbohydrate that is healthy and is found in their organic set up like oats, the wild rice, the quinoa, the sweet potatoes, the apples, and the bananas usually cause the body to hold a lot of excess fluids. Oftentimes, the people who are on a Keto diet typically remove the foods with high carbohydrates from the menu to be able to have control over the present inflammation in their bodies.

The diets that are against inflammation suggest that one should eat the foods that are high in antioxidants, which will help in fighting the oxidative stress in the body, which is responsible for getting a person fat, tired, or sick. This diet suggests that one should keep away from taking sugars and several other foods that have been processed, which the body was not made to take in. When the body fails to handle the several carbohydrates that a person is eating will result in the carbohydrates being converted into glucose. The glucose will build up in the bloodstream hence causing inflammation and also being kept as fat. If a person takes in a lot of protein, the body will convert the protein that is excessive into glucose through the process known as gluconeogenesis.

Through the intake of a lot of fats instead of carbohydrates, the body can convert the fats into energy instead of converting glucose to power, and the process is known as nutritional ketosis. This process usually occurs when the masses are not getting enough glucose to turn to strength, and this results in the kidney, making a lot of ketones, which is used for fuel. When the body uses fats as fuel instead of the use of glucose as fuel, one will be able to know they are in the ketosis process, and this also helps in promoting loss of weight. Through this one will

418

be able to decrease some a lot of water weight which is extra and also one will be able to adapt to fat. When one is suited to fat, they are getting energy from the use of ketones instead of the use of glucose. Therefore, a person will not need carbohydrates the same way they once did. This will enable a person to be more in control of their appetite since they are not experiencing spikes of blood sugar the entire day since they consume glucose.

By decreasing the number of carbohydrates in the body, the Keto diet will do away with the extra fluids in the body, and hence, ketone Beta-Hydroxybutyrate will increase its levels in the body. The ketone can deactivate the chemicals which cause pain and inflammation in the body, and it does so without hindering the immune functions of the various cells, and this allows the healing process of the body to continue. The Beta-Hydroxybutyrate also positively affects the purposes of the mitochondrial, which usually makes a person healthy at the level of cells. Since the mitochondria are the power center of cells, so when the mitochondria are healthy will result in the whole body being healthy from both the inside and outside. This is because they can resist infections and the various inflammation causes. By the reduction of inflammation, you will be decreasing the chances of getting chronic diseases, as well as you will be able to control and manage the conditions that you already have. The sugar we use is very inflammatory, and in our daily lives, sugar is used in almost everything starting from breakfast. Sad diet usually consists of a lot of sugar, and therefore, when we eat carbohydrates, they will be converted into glucose by the body.

The ketogenic diet was initially formed to help in the treatment of children who had epilepsy, and it has been helpful, as it has enabled the children to function with the illness. Some physicians in the world have started to include the ketogenic diet into the treatment programs for the patients who have cancer, and through this, they have achieved remarkable results. The patients who are suffering from diabetes have been enabled to decrease the number of illness markers through the use of the ketogenic diet, which has helped control their disease.

How a Plant-Based Ketogenic Diet Can Help to Cut Down on Inflammation Further

Many studies suggest that a diet that is based on a plant is usually anti-inflammatory independently. The Keto diet process takes away the fear people generally have from eating dairy products that are full of fats, which is a good habit. This is because our bodies need fats to be able to absorb the vitamins and also minerals and even to be satisfied after the meals. The Keto diet usually encourages the intake of dairy products that are full of fat, as well as it promotes the consumption of dairy products, which are very low in carbohydrates. If after going through the Keto diet for a while and you do not see any changes in the weight loss or you are experiencing health issues that are unexplained chances are that you may have an intolerance on the dairy products which you have not recognized. Many people tend to choose dairy, which grass-fed, and this is because they are healthy. But if your gut lining is being irritated by the dairy, you are advised to remove it from the diet for sometimes hence allowing the healing process of your gut. If you can feel well after eliminating the dairy from your daily diet, you may be able to include it back into the food. The meat, which is usually conventionally raised, is very inflammatory, and this is due to what the animals are eating as they are not eating what will promote their health; hence, the phrase we are what we eat.

If you are taking in too many proteins on your Keto diet, your body will be able to detect it and hence change the proteins to glucose through a process known as gluconeogenesis. Therefore, you may not be reducing inflammation due to the extra stress on your body. You should also make sure that you are furthermore eating foods that are rich in fiber with antioxidants to aid the body in fighting stress. If you are not a vegan and you want to try out a plant-based Keto diet, the following are some suggestions that will aid in the transition. You can be able to eat tempeh, a lot of beans, as well as eggs for proteins. Avocado oil, which too good, the MCT oil, some coconut oil or olive oils, some nuts seeds are also good plant-based sources of fat. The intake of olives, some sprouted beans, the avocados, and non-starchy vegetables will not be dense on the digestive system. Through this, you can save money because they are cheap compared to dairy and meat, which are always expensive. Through this, we can be able to save some cash by taking in a plant-based Keto diet

The expansion of your palate can be achieved through eating a portion of food that is plant-based, and this will help you be satisfied with the many varieties of plants that exist. Since the body usually processes the nutrients, you should eat a variety of some colored foods, and through eating a plant-based diet, this can be achieved. Even though the body does not need a lot of proteins as opposed to what we believe. There is a high possibility that it will increase gut inflammation from just eating a lot of beans than what you are used to on a plant-based keto diet. But by taking in the sprouted seeds, you will be able to limit the degree of inflammation, and you can be able to experience.

If you avoid fish while on a Keto diet, which is plant-based, you will end up having a low amount of fatty acids, which is classified as omega-3, and this is because they are usually found in fish. A fish oil supplement, you should always remember that the nutrients will always be better when absorbed through the foods.

The method of eating in the diet is usually restrictive, and sometimes it can be tough to maintain over a long time. You can be able to eliminate the ingredients from the menu which you suspect are the cause of inflammation for a short period and then you can add one by one after a while to be able to find out if they are the cause of inflammation or they are not. If you are worried that the Greek yogurt, which is usually full of fat or any other dairy products, may probably be causing inflammation, your body will let you know how it feels after abstaining from the consumption of dairy for a short period. The agency will also let you know if you should add the dairy products back into the diet or not.

If you are interested in trying out the Keto diet for vegans for some ethical reasons or some healing, it can be a good option, as well as it is doable. This is because most of the vegan diets are usually consist of a lot of carbohydrates, and the animals typically store fats while the plants do not store fats hence making it a little bit challenging to continue with the Keto diet of a vegan, but it is not impossible. A fully Keto diet for a vegan will limit the various foods that you can consume. This will result in difficulty in consuming the 15 to 20 percent calories from the proteins that are usually suggested on the Keto diet. Most of the protein sources for the vegans generally consist of carbohydrates, which will make it challenging to maintain the intake of carbohydrates levels between 5 to 10 percent of the total calories taken in a day a little confusing. The vegans usually prefer to use the pea proteins or other various vegan powder to be able to supplement their diet and precisely while limiting the intake of carbohydrates.

Beans, at times, have a negative inflammatory effect on the lining of the intestines—more importantly, if the grains are not sprouted. If you add the sprouted nuts and also seeds to your diet, you will increase the nutritional levels and also decrease the effects on the area of the gut. If you have been doing a Keto diet for some time, you will be able to add more carbohydrates in your diet from sources of plants and at the same stay in ketosis. You can also be able to modify random fasting when you feel worried about being in ketosis, which will aid the body in burning its fats rather than looking for glucose to convert it to energy.

The Keto Diet (Introduction and Explanation of the Keto Diet and Its Benefits in Relation to Autophagy)

The Keto diet usually consists of a high quantity of fats, with a sufficient amount of proteins, as well as a low amount of carbohydrates—and it is usually used to treat and manage the negative issues brought by the struggle to be able to control the epilepsy disease in the young people. This is achieved highly because the Keto diet usually forces the body to burn and convert the fats to be used as energy instead of converting the carbohydrates. While usually, the sugars which are found in food are usually changed into glucose, which will be moved across the entire body, and it correctly plays a significant part in fueling the functions of the brain. But if the carbohydrates remain behind, the liver changes the fats into the fatty acids and also ketone bodies. The bodies of ketones usually go in the brain and replace glucose as an energy source. Therefore, an increase in the level of bodies of ketone in the blood, which is referred to as ketosis, usually leads to a reduction in the frequencies of epileptic seizures.

Half of the total of the children and the young people with the problem of epilepsy that has tried this diet has been positive, as it has helped in decreasing by almost half and has been effective even after stopping the diet practices. Many evidence shows that adults who have epilepsy will benefit more from the Keto diet and that the less strict regimes, such as the modified diet of Atkins, which are also similarly effective. The possible effects of this usually include constipation, an increase in cholesterol, slow growth, and even kidney stones.

The original diet used in therapy, which is for pediatric epilepsy, usually provides enough amount of proteins, which aids in the growth and repair of the body and also offers calories, which are sufficient in the maintenance of the correct weight and even height. The therapeutic ketogenic diet was initially formed to help in the treatment of pediatric epilepsy in 1920, and it was widely used in the following decade. The old ketogenic diet usually consists of a 4:1 ratio, which is by weight of the fat to the merged carbohydrates and the proteins.

This can be achieved through eliminating foods with high carbohydrates like the starchy fruits and also vegetables, the bread, some grains, and even sugar, but on the other hand, increase the intake of foods that have high levels of fat—for example, nuts, dairy cream, and even butter. Most of the fats in a diet are usually made of molecules, which are known as long-chain triglycerides. But the medium-chain triglycerides, which are formed by the fatty acids which have shorter carbon chains as compared to the quicker car from long-chain triglycerides, which are usually more ketogenic. A variation of the model diet, which is known as the medium-chain triglycerides ketogenic diet, often uses a type of coconut oil, which generally contains a lot of the medium-chain triglycerides hence help in providing half of the calories. A less amount of fats is required in this form of diet whereby a large number of carbohydrates and also the proteins can be consumed hence allowing a massive way of the food choices.

The plausible therapeutic use for the diet of ketogenic has been researched for several added neurological disorders in which some include the disease of Alzheimer's, the amyotrophic lateral sclerosis, the autism, brain cancer, experiencing headache pain, brain injury, the Parkinson's disease, as well as sleep disorders. The diet of ketogenic is a therapeutic mainstream diet that was created to bring out the success and also eliminate the limitations which are of the non-mainstream through the use of fasting to be able to treat epilepsy sickness. The physicians of ancient Greece were able to treat epilepsy and other diseases by changing the diets of their patients.

During the period of the 1960s, the medium-chain triglycerides were discovered to produce a lot of ketones bodies, which was per unit of energy than the usual dietary fats. The medium-chain triglycerides are usually absorbed more efficiently and are also moved to the liver through the hepatic portal system instead of the lymphatic system. The restriction of carbohydrates of the old ketogenic diet made it a little bit difficult for the parents to be able to make portable foods that the children will be able to tolerate. A physician in 1971 came up with the ketogenic diet whereby about 60 percent of calories usually came from the medium-chain triglycerides oil hence allowing a lot of proteins and also increased the number of carbohydrates by three times the old ketogenic diet. The oil used in the menu was usually combined with skimmed milk, then cooled and then drunk during the meal periods or was mixed with food. The medium-chain triglycerides diet later took over from the old ketogenic diet in several hospitals even though a lot of the implemented diets were the combination of both. By the year 2007, the food of ketogenic was famous and was found around the world, and it consisted of minor restrictive variants—for example, the adults were using the improved Atkins diet.

Diet Changes That Can Boost Autophagy

Autophagy usually means self-eating; therefore, it is understandable that the intermittent fasting and also the ketogenic diets are well known for triggering autophagy. The act of fasting is the best effective way, which is a trusted source that triggers autophagy. The ketosis is a diet that consists of a lot of fats and little carbohydrates, which usually bring out the same advantages of the practice of fasting without fasting, which is seen as a shortcut to implicate the same metabolic changes. This is the best, as it does not overwhelm the body with many external loads, but it usually allows the body a break to be able to focus on its health and also the repair of the body.

In the Keto diet, you will be able to have almost 75% of the total calories you take daily from the fats and also 5–10% of the calories from the carbohydrates. The shift in the sources of calories usually causes the body to move its metabolic pathways. It will start to utilize fat as fuel instead of glucose, which is often gotten from carbohydrates. Due to this restriction, the body will start to produce ketone bodies, which typically have a lot of protective effects. Many studies have suggested that ketosis may also result in starvation, which induces autophagy, which consists of various neuroprotective functions. The low levels of glucose usually occur in the two diets and always associated with low levels of insulin and also high glucagon. And the glucagon level usually affects autophagy.

Through fasting or ketosis, the body usually lows on sugar, which will result in having the positive stress that often wakes up the mode of survival repair. Even through exercises, one can be able to induce autophagy, which is achieved through a non-diet function. According to several studies, physical activities usually induce autophagy in the organs, which are parts of the metabolic regulation procedure. This will include the muscles, the liver, the pancreas, as well as the adipose tissue. If you are interested in the stimulation of autophagy in the body, you should include fasting and also incorporating various exercises into your daily routine. If you are on any medication, you should first consult the doctors for more information. Even if you are pregnant, or if you are breastfeeding, having plans to be pregnant, experiencing some chronic conditions—for example, diabetes—you should not fast without consulting your doctor or without professional advice.

Through the following steps, one will be able to increase the process of autophagy in the body:

By Eating a High-Fat and Low-Carbohydrate Diet

It is imperative to be eating fats to activate the process of autophagy. This is because the fats usually need to be the macronutrient that is dominant in the diet, as it is not similar to proteins. This is because the proteins can be able to turn into carbohydrates and then change to be sugar, but the fat cannot be ready. Especially a Keto diet, which consists of a high level of fat and also a low level of carbohydrate food plan, usually gives you a positive outcome when it comes to the process of autophagy. This process occurs from burning the glucose to ketones, which happens in the Keto diet, usually imitate what usually occurs innately in a fasted mode hence increasing autophagy.

By Abstaining from Proteins

You should be to limit the intake of protein once or even twice a week. This will give the body the entire day to be able to recycle the proteins, thus helping to cut down on inflammation and also aid in cleansing the cells without losing any muscles. At this time, when the process of autophagy is triggered, the body will be forced to absorb its own toxins and also its proteins.

By Practicing Intermittent Fasting

By not having breakfast and arranging to have all your foods within 8 hours, you will be able to increase the process of the essential autophagy of the body. Like fasting on the proteins, the intermittent fasting usually allows your body to be able to reach the lingering toxins through the process of cleaning up. You can be able to eliminate the toxins which typically build up within 16 to 28 hours fast. But if this is not done correctly, the intermittent fasting will be able to affect the women, whereby they cause hormone imbalances negatively. This is because women are usually more sensitive to the signs of starvation or the restriction of calories. Through eliminating the carbohydrates and also the proteins out of the meal, you will be able to remain in a fasting mode hence the body will believe that you are not starving

By Exercising Using High-Intensity Interval Training

Another way to be able to stimulate autophagy is usually through high-intensity interval training, which is very advantageous. You should always know that the process of autophagy is a bodily response to the stress; therefore, the exercise of high intensity usually places the body in excellent tension, and this is because it can stress the person to a point where it results in the change of biochemical. This will result in the body getting impact load, which aids in making stronger muscles is hence inducing autophagy without doing any harm. You can also be able to induce autophagy through lifting weights each day.

By Getting Restorative Sleep

You can also enjoy the benefits that come from autophagy while you are just sleeping. How you function during the day is determined by how you sleep as sleep play a significant role. A person usually possesses one of the four sleep personalities, and therefore, when a person knows which of the sleeping character they have, they will be able to plan themselves to have autophagy between the sleep and wake cycles.

Keto Diet and Inflammation

Most people have been using the Keto diet to aid them in reducing inflammation. Even though the Keto diet is not put up as a diet to fight inflammation, it usually consists of various foods that are anti-inflammatory and less inflammatory foods. The Keto diet often restricts inflammatory foods—for example, the foods that are processed, packed, or refined—as well as highly glycemic foods. The Keto diet usually pays more attention to the foods that are anti-inflammatory—for example, eggs, avocados, coconut oil, as well as low-carbohydrate foods like spinach. The Keto diet will let the body to experience ketosis for a prolonged time frame.

Even though the Keto diet will let a person in the reduction of inflammation through the process of limiting the intake of omega-6s, foods with high glycemic and also the highly processed foods which usually promote inflammation process and encouraging the consumption of omega-3s, various vitamins, absorption of minerals and also the antioxidants which usually calm inflammation hence the levels of inflammation will decrease and the body will begin producing a lot ketones which will aid in the reduction of inflammation. With inflammation described as a number one threat to our health, it can be best defeated through a healthy diet. There exist differences between the acute inflammation and also the chronic inflammation whereby the acute inflammation is usually the swelling and the redness that typically occur after having an injury while the chronic inflammation is the type of inflammation which often destroy the immune system of the body hence increasing its vulnerability to various health conditions. The chronic inflammation is generally associated with multiple diseases, which include the epidemic of cardiovascular, suffering from obesity, have high blood pressure, and many others.

Through the choice of your diet, you can control the levels of inflammation. The cells in the body are usually made of what you always eat. Certain foods can be able to trigger responses of inflammation that typically stress the body, thus weakening your immune system hence preventing the body from functioning normally. The best diet which will eliminate chronic inflammation is a diet that consists of low carbohydrates. The ketogenic diet usually contains substantial anti-inflammatory benefits. The best way to achieve this, you are supposed to remove the refined grains, sugar, as well as other food additives from your diet and replace them with healthy foods, which will reduce inflammation.

Anti-Inflammatory Foods

Turmeric

The turmeric is viewed as an anti-inflammatory product whereby turmeric curcumin has been found to consist of a lot of benefits, which aids in reducing inflammatory. The curry is delicious and also a functional food. The curcumin is usually 154 percent even more effective when it is mixed with the black pepper. When curcumin and the piperine are combined, it will help reduce inflammation very fast, and the curcumin remains in your blood hence giving protection against inflammation. Therefore, you should make the intake of turmeric a daily routine in your life to be able to maximize the benefits of health. Through this, you will be able to achieve the elimination of inflammation as turmeric is one of the best foods which are anti-inflammatory.

Ginger Roots

This type of root is best known to help calm a stomach, which is upset, but at the same time, it contains essential anti-inflammatory properties.

The extract from the ginger usually inhibits the induction of the genes which are associated with the inflammatory response. Thus, ginger can regulate the biochemical pathways which are activated in chronic inflammation. Therefore, you should include more ginger to your meals, which will spice the food and also lessen indigestion and even lower inflammation.

Salmon

The salmon usually contain a lot of fat, whereby 3 ounces of salmon often include 1921 milligrams of the anti-inflammation omega-three fatty acids. Therefore, through the salmon, the body will be able to fight inflammation.

Macadamia Nuts

These nuts are the healthiest because of a lot of reasons, and more important is because they are the fattiest nuts. Macadamia nuts usually contain 75 percent of fat, and the fats included are healthy for the body and also help in reducing the inflammatory effects. Macadamia nuts also contain some magnesium, which aids in turning off the pain signals and also reduces the blood sugar, which are the positive impacts on the effects of inflammation. The magnesium deficiency may result in chronic and reduce inflammation; hence, it is beneficial to be including it in your meals.

Walnuts

The walnuts are usually high in carbohydrates, but as long as you remember to check your consumption, it will be very beneficial. The intake of magnesium is always necessary to prevent chronic inflammation and also lower the pains.

Healthy Fats

A lot of the vegetable oils which are found on the shelves of the groceries—for example, canola oil is sour and also pro-inflammatory. You should eliminate such oils and choose the ones that are healthier

431

like coconut, use of organic ghee, which is obtained from the grass-fed cows and also olive oil.

Green Leafy Vegetables

The green leafy vegetables like kale and spinach are usually rich in anti-inflammatory polyphenols. These green leafy vegetables also contain a lot of antioxidants that regularly repair and also takes care of the damages. They also provide a lot of magnesium, which generally helps fight chronic inflammation. The green leafy vegetables usually contain a lot of nutrients, which helps lower the rate of swelling.

How Fasting Can Stimulate Autophagy

One of the best ways to promote autophagy is by practicing intermittent fasting. Through this method, digestion will be able to provide the nutrients to be able to maintain vital cellular functions, which happen during fasting and even eliminates the cells of organs that are damaged. Many types of research indicate that having an intermittent fast of about 16 hours will result in the autophagy being triggered. This usually consists of the alternations in between the periods of less protein intake and also the periods of moderating to the healthy protein intake. When you are fasting, the levels of insulin and glucose are usually low. Therefore, reducing the level of insulin often triggers the additional glucagon; hence, the body will naturally produce the hormones which will help in the stabilization of the levels of blood sugar.

The link to protein and also the added advantages of protein cycling is that even lowering the levels of protein will also promote the production of glucagon since there is neither both glucose or protein which the body can use as a source of energy. Therefore, as a result, the levels of glucagon will increase hence the increase of autophagy. Without the consumption of the proteins, the body will react by reusing its proteins to be able to extract the amino acids that are usable in the formation of proteins in the future.

Best Foods/Drinks to Stimulate Autophagy Process

Through the use of medium-chain triglyceride in the diet, one will be able to induce autophagy. This is the most abundant natural source of medium-chain fatty acids, which is healthy, and it usually changes into ketone bodies, which is a clean fuel for the brain and also the body. This results in the oil aiding in relieving hunger and also aids in the stimulation of autophagy through the increase of the level of ketone, especially when there are no carbohydrates.

Green Tea

You should try stimulating the pathway of autophagy through the use of polyphenols—for example, the epigallocatechin gallate, which is usually found in the green tea. Therefore, you should try and drink a given amount in a day or otherwise add a teaspoon of the matcha powder in your smoothie in the morning.

Coffee

Even coffee also contains polyphenols, which usually induce autophagy, which is also independent of caffeine. Due to this, several cups of coffee in a day is very beneficial to health and also have low risks even though it has a high amount of caffeine.

Cinnamon

Cinnamon usually contains a lot of antioxidants and is best known for its action in lowering blood sugar hence increasing autophagy. You should find the Ceylon cinnamon since it is regarded as the best quality of cinnamon.

Coconut Oil

Coconut oil is referred to as the best natural source of getting medium-chain fatty acids, which are healthy. It usually aids in reducing hunger and also stimulates autophagy through increasing the levels of ketone, especially when the carbohydrates are absent.

Chapter Four:

Longevity with Autophagy

A lot of longevity-enhancement interventions usually work through the autophagy upregulation. A lot of the existing enhancement interventions for longevity, which have been tested regarding their effects, often suggest an addition in autophagy's cellular maintenance process. The focus point of this research community is the issue of aging.

The cells of the body usually react when there is a lack of nutrients, experiencing extreme heat through maintaining efforts over a long time. If the stress is very severe, it will result in a lot of benefits. The sad thing is that this approach does not have a lot of effects on the increase of the life span. To be able to live a long and healthier life, then you should look at strategies like the rejuvenation biotechnologies, which usually mend the damaged cells and tissues generally responsible for aging.

Through much advancement in the world, the aging molecular signature has been able to be discovered. The extraordinary conservation of the signaling pathways of the cells has been ready to be shown over many of the vertebrates and also the invertebrate species. Autophagy is usually the process of the cellular that came up as a nexus whereby the various pathways can converge. The activities of autophagy have been unveiled to be decreasing with the age of a person. Likewise, Caenorhabditis elegans have been revealed to cause an overall decrease in the activities in a lot of tissues consisting of the intestines and also the neurons. A similar reduction in the functions has also been noticed in many mammals, such as the electron microscopy investigation of the livers of the old mouse.

Many parties have recognized the critical role of autophagy in the effects of longevity, often enhancing mediating. The autophagy inhibiting in a mutant that has lived long usually nullifies the promotion effects of the mutation in survival.

To be able to demonstrate a natural connection between longevity and autophagy, a lot of groups have assessed the various effects of overexpressing the genes of autophagy. A good relationship between the activities of autophagy and the lifespan was shown in Drosophila. The overexpression of the autophagy-related 8a gene by the specific neuron usually results in the increase in the lifespan and also the reduction in the accumulation of the toxic protein aggregates.

Aging usually shows the organism's functional deterioration. The efforts to be able to find the downstream mechanisms in each of the longevity pathways, which often reveal that there are numerous but sets of different factors in each of the longevity pathways even though some of the elements typically work the same way. Recent findings recommend that the process of autophagy is one of the various connecting downstream mechanisms of all the paradigms of longevity. The autophagy activity is usually raised in long-lived, living things, and therefore, it is required for their increased durability.

Dietary Restriction/Reduced mTOR Signaling

The limitation of the diet is the best way that has been proved to aid in slowing the aging process and extend the lifespan in many species. Several molecular mechanisms are said to mediate the various effects of the restrictions of diets on longevity, which include the target of rapamycin also insulin. Through the use of amino acid, you can be able to induce restriction on your diet, which usually increases the autophagy process and even increases the CLS.

The nutrient sensor mammalian target of rapamycin inhibition often raises the CLS, and autophagy and the genes of autophagy are traditionally crucial for the rapamycin in the extension of the lifespan. In the aging of yeast, the role of autophagy is generally complicated. The elimination of autophagy 15, but not including the other autophagy genes which have been tested regularly, disrupts the extension of the RLS, which is always activated by the limitation of glucose, thus another way of restriction of the diet in yeast.

Many ways of restriction of the diet exist like the eat-2 mutants, which usually consist of the receptor of acetylcholine mutation that generally negatively affects the pumping of pharyngeal and also reduces the intake of food. The eat-2 mutants indicate a ban increased level of the green fluorescent protein - immunoglobulin G in the seam cells of the hypodermal. The eat-2 mutants' longevity is usually eliminated when the several genes of the autophagy are usually inactivated. In the eat-2 animals, some of the genes of autophagy are often transcriptionally activated by the several factors of transcription. Some research has shown that the autophagy of the intestines is very significant in the extension of the lifespan during the restriction of the diet. How the existing factors of transcription result to the autophagy and also longevity activation in the spatial and also temporal modes should be outlined.

The use of the TOR mediates the same as yeast the extension of the lifespan, which is activated by the restriction of the diet sometimes, and this is high because the TOR usually inhibits the eat-2 mutant; hence, it does not increase lifespan. The same as this, which is the same as the restricted diet worms, which help in the inhibition of TOR, usually aids in the lifespan extension in the factors of transcription. In the treatment of rapamycin in drosophila often results to a moderate expansion of the lifespan and this also process requires the gene of autophagy hence suggesting that the lowering of the TOR often extends the lifespan in the Drosophila at most through the process of autophagy which is similar to the yeast and also worms the treatments of rapamycin have been revealed to increase thought to the maximum and even the median lifespan of both the male and heterogeneous female mice. Many researchers have illustrated the various positive effects of rapamycin regarding the lifespan in mice through the use of different genetic histories. However, the positive impact of the autophagy process in these mice is not clear.

Germline Removal

The reproduction is usually correlated negatively with longevity in a lot of species. Therefore, the removal of the stem cells of the germline through the use of genetic mutation or by the use of microsurgery usually increases the lifespan in the drosophila. In worms, the mutants that are sensitive to temperature, which generally encodes the notch receptor elegant, indicate the lowering of the stem cells of the germline and also the extension of lifespan. It has been illustrated that the count of the green fluorescent protein-immunoglobulin G puncta is deficient in the germline; hence, the genes of the autophagy and the animals are important for their longevity. In the animal germline insufficient, a lot of the factors of transcription have been illustrated to induce the genes of autophagy. Surprisingly, the specific knockdown of the intestines of the genes of autophagy usually eliminates the longevity of the GLP-1, but it is different in the case of the mutants of daf-2, which shows the contrasts of the regulation of the autophagy in the individual tissues, which are between the conserved paradigms of longevity. The animals of glp-1 usually live long, as they have high lipase activity. Also, the same applies to animals of lipl-4, which aids the animals to live long. The overexpression of the lipl-4 often increases the process of autophagy and the lifespan; thus, the animals require the gene of autophagy to increase longevity. Therefore, the turnover of lipids by the process of autophagy is significant for the promotion of survival.

Reduced Mitochondrial Respiration

The free radical theory suggests that the process of aging is usually the product of damages of the cells through the oxidative process, which is generally over time. The injuries on the molecules are typically caused by the reactive species of oxygen, which created primarily from the respiration of the mitochondrial. Even though the damages caused by oxidation often heightens with age is still not clear if this process has effects on the aging of organisms. By reducing the respiration of the mitochondrial, you will be able to increase the lifespan of various bodies like mice and yeast. For example, in worms, electron reduction usually, transport chain components, which generally extends the lifespan of microorganisms during the larva stage, when they are inhibited. Several mutants of mitochondria, including the ubiquinone synthase mutants, often show longevity. The inhibition of the larva of the gene of autophagy genes often reduces the lifespan of the CLK-1 and also isp-1 mutants. These mutants show generally heighten in the numbers of the green fluorescent protein-immunoglobulin G-1 puncta in the cells of hypodermal during the larval period.

Forced Activation of Autophagy in the Extension of the Lifespan

The loss of the activities of autophagy has been shown to result in premature aging in a lot of species. The process of gene screening, which is involved in the yeast chronological lifespan, usually indicates mutants that have lived shortly, which experienced their mutation in the genes of the macroautophagy. The lifespan decrease in the elegant ATGL can be observed. The same results can be seen in drosophila. Even though the whole body knockouts of the genes of the ATG in mice usually leads to postnatal death and also the conditional knockout of tissue-specific of the ATG7 indicate several phenomena which are associated with age which include the aggregation of the inclusion bodies in the neurons, the lysosomes accumulation which consists of lipofuscin pigments, the disorganized mitochondria, the increased levels of oxidation of the proteins and also lower the mass of the muscles. Through the correlation between autophagy and the process of aging, it is beneficial to test if the forced stimulation of the process of autophagy aids the extension of the lifespan in animals. The same as this, the treatment of the TFEB agonists can help in the expansion of the lifespan in worms and also reduce the metabolic syndromes in the mice. The overexpression of the ATG5 in mice usually extends the lifespan in both the female and male mice. And also, the overexpression of the neuronal of the ATG8 is often enough to aid in the extensions of the lifespan in drosophila.

Pharmacological Activation of Autophagy Contributing to Longevity

Spermidine

The administration of the polyamine (spermidine, in particular), usually provides a lot of benefits for the health in a lot of species and also helps in the extensions of the lifespan of the yeast and other organisms like the mice. The survival of the cultured mammalian cell is usually increased through the treatment by spermidine, which is also included with epigenetic hypoacetylation of the histone through the inhibition of the activities of histone acetyltransferase. This will result in the correlates with transcriptional upregulation of various genes related to autophagy.

Resveratrol

The polyphenolic is usually a naturally occurring resveratrol, which is a compound found in the grapes and also stimulates the NAD-dependent histone deacetylase sirtuin. The administration of the resveratrol can aid in the extension of the lifespan of many organisms and, specifically, the lifespan of any microorganisms. This is specifically for the lifespan of the elegans, which usually depends on autophagy because the resveratrol does not extend the lifespan of the bec-1 of the treated animals. Resveratrol often increases the levels of DsRed-LGG-1 in wild-type animals. The above observations go in line with the findings of the mammalian cells whereby the pharmacological stimulation of the SIRT1 by the resveratrol treatment, which activates autophagy.

Tomatidine

Unripe tomatoes usually contain a natural compound known as cimetidine, which inhibits the age-related skeletal muscle atrophy in the mice. The tomatidine often extends the lifespan and also the health of the elegans. Through the use of the tomatine, many C. elegans behaviors are related to the span and also the health of muscles, consisting of the increase in the pumping of pharyngeal—and even the reduced levels of muscle cells that have been damaged are improved. The imaging of the microarray and the behavioral analyses show that the tomatidine usually maintains mitochondrial homeostasis through modulating the mitochondrial biogenesis process and also PINK-1, which is a dependent mitophagy. Research shows that tomatidine often stimulates the mitochondrial hormesis through inducing the production of ROS, which will activate the pathway of SKN-1 and also the paths of other cellular antioxidant responses hence the increase of mitophagy.

Through all this, we can see how the activation of autophagy plays a significant role in the process of longevity. The neuron-specific knockdown of autophagy after the reproductive period has been seen to be able to extend the lifespan in worms. Therefore, it is essential to understand the spatial and also the temporal regulations of autophagy and even their physiological importance to aging. It is also necessary to determine the process of autophagy contributes to the extension of lifespan and also which of the cargo of the autophagy is essential for aging and even longevity. The clearance of lipophagy and even the mitochondria are related to the aging of the C. Elegans. It is also important to test which of the autophagy stimulators are practical and are even applicable to humans.

Autophagy is the process of cleaning, which aids in fighting stress damages, which are usually created in the cells when they make energy. The protein aggregates often accumulate with effects that are toxic on the cells, which eventually leads to the death of the cells if the damage is not repaired. Therefore, these proteins should be eliminated to be safe, which is through the process of autophagy, which protects the cells against death. Through aiding the removal of oxidative damages, parts of the cells which are responsible for the operation of aging at the cellular level hence increasing the lifespan. Autophagy plays a significant role in the prevention of neurodegenerative diseases, which plays a role in the destruction of the aggregates of proteins that are responsible for these diseases.

The process of autophagy and aging are connected somehow whereby when the genes causing the process of autophagy are inhibited in the mammalian cells, there is degeneration, which looks like the degeneration we observe in the aging process. The aging itself usually

441

comes with reduced autophagy; therefore, when one stimulates the autophagy process, we are mitigating aging. The many strategies used to slow the aging process in model organisms also result in the occurrence of the process of autophagy. When there is inhibition of the autophagy process during some extension of the lifespan—for example, the restriction of calories—it usually erodes the effect of anti-aging. The autophagy shows promise as a fundamental mechanism for maintenance and repair specifically in the process of aging

The Anti-Aging Process Through Ketosis State

Ketogenic diets can slow down aging according to many types of research. Through the intake of low carbohydrates and high consumption of a lot of fats usually prevents the conditions related to age—for example, diseases of the heart and others. During the time of carbohydrates starvation, the body regularly releases a chemical, which is known as the β-hydroxybutyrate, which plays the role of protecting them from the internal stress. The stress is generally connected to the genetic damages in the cells, which causes aging. The Keto diet often forces the body to burn fats instead of carbohydrates for energy, which starves the body of carbohydrates but not the calories.

Through following the intake of fewer carbs and the consumption of high-fat foods, you will be able to prevent conditions related to aging. The restriction of calories usually slows down the process of aging and increase longevity. High concentrations of the bodies of ketone are generally considered to be toxic, and an example is the diabetes of type one, which happens because of an increase in the number of ketone bodies, and this can also be a cause of some life-threatening medical emergencies.

The low level of the collections of the ketone is very beneficial, as it aids in the protection of cells from the oxidation stress, which is a factor contributing to aging. Research indicates that the restriction of calories diet will be able to slow the aging process and also increase longevity. B-hydroxybutyrate is a significant source of energy which is used by the body during periods of fasting, exercises, and even starving.

The B-hydroxybutyrate will block specific enzymes that will promote oxidative stress in the body, which end up contributing to the aging process. The test of the ketogenic diet in mice usually shows an increase in the B-hydroxybutyrate, which blocks the effects of the histone deacetylases enzyme, which generally works by inhibiting the action of two genes.

Nutrition to Make Your Cells Younger

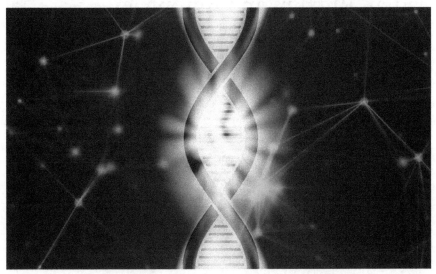

While we typically measure the age in years, the marking of biological aging is cellular aging. Therefore, the DNA of the cells can be able to tell us how much the bodies have aged. The telomeres are structures that are made up of the strands of DNA and proteins. Therefore, every time there is a division of the cells, the telomeres usually shorten until the cells are senescent and finally dies.

Consequently, the length of the telomeres is often the best indicator to show how old a battery is. While the process of shortening the telomere is often a natural process, the accumulated damages in the cells will speed up the process and result in the premature death of the cells. The damaged cells and also the shorter length of the telomere have been linked to chronic diseases and even cancer.

The factors which are associated with damaging the cells are environmental and modifiable. Therefore, you can be able to do something about them. These usually include the diet, the exposure to ultraviolet rays, a lot of alcohol consumption, and the lifestyle; hence, more stress can generally speed up cellular aging, while the practice of exercise keeps the cells young. Overall, researches find a significant association or rather a link between high adherence to any of these diets and longer telomere length.

Circadian Rhythm and Autophagy

The mammalian circadian clock and the connection to the genes of the clock are being discovered and understood as a very important component in various anatomical disease processes that go over the production of hormones, the thermal arrangement, as well as the cycles of sleeping and waking up. A lot of researches indicates that the disruption which is associated with the clinical patterns, which usually consist of the long patterns of the job and even the travel of space, will affect the circadian pattern negatively, which will lead to diseases that will affect the entire systems.

This mammalian circadian clock is usually located at the suprachiasmatic nucleus, which generally lies on the optic chiasm to be able to attain the light through the help of the cells of the photosensitive ganglion, which are located on the eyes. The usually depends highly on the SCN is over gland of the pineal, the nuclei of the hypothalamus also the vasoactive peptide of the intestines to be able to manage various procedures which usually happens like the production of cortisol hormone and also the melatonin hormone, the response stress of the process of oxidative, and even the management of the temperature of the body which is linked to the cycle of the circadian.

The clock of the circadian usually supported by the cellular indications; also, the light got so as to be able to arrange itself with the time of the solar and also being able to period of 24 hours. Circadian Rhythm in Degenerative Disease and Cancer

The disease of the neurodegenerative and the lessen lifespan have been associated with the functions of the various circadian mammalian clock. In the study, the lifespan of the drosophila has been lessened into three choppy mutants consisting of the caladium articulatum, the cyco, and the timo. Specifically, the caladium articulatum mutants included important age-related shortages of locomotor. Through the restoring process, functions were able to help the Drosophila from the shortcomings of locomotor. The rising levels in the oxidative stress were discovered with the phenotype mutants, but the shortages also were seen to be able to agree well with loosing of the neurons of the dopaminergic.

Circadian Rhythm and the Modulation of Autophagy

Autophagy is the process that usually recycles the components of the cytoplasm in the cells for the remodeling of the tissue and also in the elimination of the organelles that do not function. The term macroautophagy usually refers to the classification of autophagy that has the role of recycling the organelles and also consists of the sequestration of the cytoplasmic proteins and the organelles into autophagosomes. These autophagosomes will combine with the lysosomes for the degradation and even recycling process. The microautophagy outlines the invagination of the membrane of lysosomal, which aids in the sequestration and digestion of the cytoplasmic components. The chaperone-mediated autophagy usually uses the cytosolic chaperones to be able to transport the cytoplasmic components across the membranes of the lysosomal.

Therefore, the process of autophagy can be the root cause of a lot of degenerative disorders like the disease of Alzheimer's, Parkinson's disease, Huntington's disease, and diabetes mellitus. The process of autophagy can also have effects on the decline of the cognitive and even the aging processes.

The circadian rhythm dysfunction during the loss of the cognitive and the aging process has been tied to the stimulation of autophagy. The chronic sleep fragmentation can influence the autophagy proteins in the brain, which will alter the recollection ability and also the perception. In addition to this, the autophagy process in the brain is usually not functioning when there are no PER1 circadian clock proteins, which often worsens the pathology of cerebral ischemia.

The loss of a wonderful circadian rhythm will eventually cause an increased risk for having nasopharyngeal carcinoma, cancer of the breast, as well as cancer, which is associated with the metastatic colorectal. The disruption of the clinic behavior, which consists of extended work shifts and even space travel, will negatively impact the circadian rhythm. At the level of the cellular, the management of the autophagy pathways, which usually consists of the wingless related integration site, is usually very crucial due to reasonable anatomical adjustment of the circadian pattern of the body.

Sleep Optimization

Sleep is usually a part that makes us human as we need it. You can argue that as a society, we are getting worse at sleep activity. Many people in the world today usually suffer from a sleep disorder, and only a few people typically get good sleep regularly. This is a very worrying trend that has a lot of negative consequences. Rest is a very important requirement of life; therefore, the quality and the quantity of sleep usually have a direct effect on the health regarding both the physical part and the mental. Deprivation of sleeping over a long period is generally connected to severe health issues like diabetes, suffering a stroke, diseases of the kidney, as well as the heart. Poor quality sleep has also been associated with obesity and also the experience of depression. In some researches show that having a proper sleep can promote longevity. Not only is sleeping necessary to maintain a healthy mind and also body, but it can also be actively used to improve each. Instead of viewing sleep as the inevitable activity of every day, we should be able to optimize it to be able to get the best benefits out of the rest.

When it comes to the health of the body, we usually push sleep aside and then focus on other contributors such as the nutrition and practice of exercise. This is understood as the impact on health is often more apparent. But sleep should be included in all the health plans. We should all know that sleep usually affects the out productivity and also focus. When you have been deprived of sleep, it is challenging to be able to do anything of advantage. Thus, it usually affects the function of cognitive. The ability to be able to solve a problem s, to be able to learn, as well as to be able to think and be more creative is usually affected by the quality of our sleep one typically has. The optimization of sleep is generally not complicated, as it requires some pure self-analysis and also some trials and errors. Our bodies usually respond to the routine of sleeping; therefore, by falling into one, the body will be able to discover when to sleep.

Consequently, this usually means you will be able to sleep comfortably and also have a higher quantity of sleep. The optimization of sleep can be robust. It can also have a positive effect on health and also productivity, and even has the power to be able to change the life. To be able to find the best ideal sleep program might take time, but it usually starts with awareness and practical action-taking.

A diet that usually consists of low fiber and has a high level of saturated fats will result in taking a change in the shutting of the eyes through lowering the quantity of heavy and also the slow sleep, which one can achieve at night. By consuming a lot of sugary staff will cause a lack of sleep, thus leading in the midnight wake-ups. A healthy diet, on the other hand, will help in the fast drifting off, as this kind of diet promotes quality sleep.

Any person with gastroesophageal reflux usually understands how bad it is to be able to go to bed with heartburn. Usually, the individual who is suffering from heartburn does experience sleep problems and other disorders—for example, insomnia, sleep apnea, restless legs syndrome, as well as daytime sleepiness. Through using the best diet, you will be able to create some deviation in the sleep patterns. Then, steer clear of a lot of fried foods or those with a lot of fat, spicy foods, alcoholic drinks, and even carbonated drinks when just about to sleep. For the best sleep at night, you should be able to eat a diet that is balanced which usually emphasizes on the intake of the fresh fruits, some vegetable, the whole grains and also proteins that are low in fat but are rich with vitamins, like fish, meat, poultry, and even the dairy. The B vitamins usually help in the regulation of the melatonin, which is a hormone that generally regulates the sleep cycles.

Through eating well, one can be able to lose weight, which usually helps a person to be able to sleep well, whereby they are able to get quality sleep. The lowering of the excess fats in the body, specifically among the middle parts, usually results in the optimization of rest a little bit easy; hence, there is no struggling to be able to get some sleep.

Nutrition usually has an important part in the health of the organisms, which has been proven through much research. You become what you eat acknowledges the importance of nutrition for the well-being of the body. This concept is usually talking about the addition of the dimension as the research demonstrates the various impacts of diet on optimization of sleep.

Researchers studying both the public health issues have a powerful connection between sleep and disease of obesity, hence there is a strong reason to know and always remember that improving the diet will also improve sleep.

The food and also nutrition usually have a profound effect on sleep. A healthy diet practice and also healthy eating habits typically lead to the promotion of both the higher quality sleep and even more total sleep time.

Researches have long discovered that there are links that exist between poor sleep and poor diet. The people with various types of sleep disturbances usually tend also to have inconsistent or consist of foods that are generally unhealthy. In many of the researches, it is to tell the direction of causality. As it turns out in the investigations, likely, sleep usually affects nutrition, and diet usually affects sleep.

How the body usually processes the food and also the nutrients often depends on what, or when, and how much you eat. Eating at a regular interval stimulates a sequence of reactions in the body, as well as the nature of these reactions, which will influence the ability to be able to fall asleep as well as the architecture of sleep. At the same time, when you get inadequate sleep, you will be able to be at risk of diseases like obesity due to poor diet choices.

The way that people usually respond to food is variable, and it can depend on the person's genetics, the environment, the stress, the activities, the gut microbiome, and other various factors. Researchers have started to deepen their understanding of the compound and also the interrelated network. As a result of this, it might be a little challenging to be able to state exactly how the diet or the food will affect the specific person, but at an overall level, therefore it is vivid that how we eat will directly affect how we usually sleep. This will enable an individual to be

How Diets Affect Sleep

Everyone usually has a diet that refers to what you eat or what your meals typically contain. But when the people are "on a diet" or follow up on a specific diet, it usually means that they follow or have a particular routine of a specific set of rules about what foods to eat and what not to eat. The food intake and how the body usually processes the food will affect the schedule of the sleep. Therefore, the consumption and how the body digests the food will affect the sleep patterns; hence, the different variety of diets that usually restrict some types of foods, or the nutrients will have different impacts on the sleep. In this section, we will outline several popular diets and their possible effects on the sleep pattern. However, you should keep in mind that many systems of the body are usually associated with regulating metabolism and meal processing. Since everyone is not alike, therefore people typically react differently to the same food or the same diet. A nutritionist or the doctor is usually in the best position to be able to give personal advice about the various diet for any individual who is willing to try the foods.

Vegan

The diet of a vegan usually avoids any product which is derived from the animals, which consists of the meats and also dairy products such as cheese, milk, and eggs. And because of the existing considerable restriction which are involved in the diet of a vegan, and it is common for the vegans to plan their meals or what they eat systematically, and this will help in avoiding some of the various negative impacts to the sleep patterns that usually come from overeating or the act of splurging on the extremely fatty or the sugary dishes.

There is no detailed study that has been able to document the effects of the diet of a vegan, but a lot of the vegan diets usually include complex carbohydrates, nuts, as well as fruits that also contain tryptophan and the melatonin which aid in promoting good sleep. A vegan diet regularly avoids some foods which usually disrupt the sleep pattern, such as the heavy meat-based dishes.

Transitioning into a vegan diet is, at times, reported to be able to cause sleep problems or instead disrupt sleeping patterns. This will be part of an adjustment period or will result in a change in the intake of nutrients like the drop in protein or the overall calories, which may make it a little hard to stimulate sleep.

Vegetarian

Vegetarians will not eat the meat products of any type, but they still consume other dairy products—for example, eggs and dairy—which are gotten from the animals. The same as the vegans, the additional planning which will be required to be able to eat a vegetarian diet will aid in adding consistency to a person's menu, which will make it easier for the body to process food without any disruption. The diets of the vegetarian usually include foods that are similar to the foods of the vegans' diet, which will promote sleep, which consists of the almonds, the fruits, and even whole grains. Just like the vegans, vegetarians usually avoid foods like meat consumption, which generally result from the sleeping problem.

Pescatarian

The pescatarian diet usually excludes all the meat products except for fish and other kinds of seafood. The pescatarians can eat other animal products like eggs and also dairy but always rely on fish due to the bulk of their protein. A lot of fish usually have omega-3 fatty acids and also contain vitamin D that will help in the regulation of serotonin and also the promotion of sleep. Even though the researches are still limited, there is some indication that through eating fish you will be able to gain the positive benefits which aid in promoting quality sleep

By avoiding the red meats, a lot of the pescatarians prefer vegetarians, usually include items like yogurt, nuts, and fruits, which will offer useful nutrients hence having a quality sleep.

451

Keto

The ketogenic diet is based around the reduction of the body's net carbohydrate intake to be able to put the body into ketosis process. Ketosis is a state whereby the body uses the stored fat instead of the carbohydrates to be used as energy. Ketogenic diets have recently developed in popularity, but they still require considerable research to figure out their advantages and risks fully. Some people usually describe the "Keto insomnia" or experiencing difficulty sleeping when they first begin this diet. This is typically related to the body's general process of adapting to being in ketosis. Keto diets are usually heavy in the consumption of meat, which, as discussed above, typically results in having several negative impacts on the patterns of sleep. However, a researcher in his finding argued that the study of the ketogenic diet in obese patients did not find any effects on sleep quality. The Keto diet is not the only type of food that consists of low carbohydrates. Many other diets, like the Atkins diet, usually promote the restriction of carbohydrates. There is a link between the diet one chooses and the sleep patterns. The practice of foods with high sugars often supports falling asleep very fast, but at the same, they may reduce the sleep quality or even alter the pattern of sleep; this usually relies on the type of carbohydrates and the period it is consumed.

Paleo

The caveman is also restricted to the types of foods that usually would have been readily available to the early human beings whose food was gotten through the process of hunting of animals and gathering of fruits and roots. This diet profoundly excludes refined sugars, dairy, the agricultural products such as wheat, and other foods that have been processed.

Several people who are on the Paleo diet indicate that their sleep improves while other people have insomnia, specifically at the beginning. The research found out that many people reported the experience of sleeping problems on the Paleo diet. The diet usually consists of nuts and fruits that include melatonin but commonly involves a lot of meat, which will have harmful effects on the patterns of sleep.

452

The Diet Consisting of Raw Foods

This type of diet usually includes the intake or rather the consumption of predominantly uncooked foods—specifically fruits, vegetables, as well as nuts. There is no substantial data from the controlled research studies about the raw food diets and its relation to sleep, and you should remember that the individual experience is different considerably from those who have difficulty sleeping to those who experience their sleep has improved.

The substantial amount of fruits and vegetables will help improve sleep hence promoting the nutrients, but at the same time, there is difficulty in obtaining other crucial nutrients through a raw food diet. Avoiding fatty meats and other heavy meals will help reduce the disruption of sleep.

As the same as the other highly restrictive diets, the raw food diet usually requires significant planning and attention to the detail, as this will add consistency and also avoid the dietary peaks and valleys, which generally interfere with the patterns of sleep.

Foods That Will Help You Sleep

Most of the diets are made up of several individual meals, and the overall diet is what's very crucial for the promoting of the general health. Certain specific foods will be able to aid you to sleep well throughout the night.

- Tart Cherries - the tart cherries usually consist of many specific cultivars of cherries—for example, the Richmond, the Montmorency, and the English Morello, which are generally distinct from the sweeter types of cherries. These cherries usually contain a higher concentration of melatonin and are very useful in the promotion of sleep. The pure tart cherry juice does not mix cherry juice or cocktail juice, as it is an essential way for these fruits to be consumed.

- Kiwi Fruit - Kiwis, which are the small, rounded fruits that are commonly linked with the New Zealand state, have been found to promote sleep when consumed before bedtime. The same machinery is also not known; however, it is linked to the content consisting of the

453

antioxidants, the folate, and the serotonin, which is found in the kiwi fruit.

• Malted Milk - the malted milk is basically linked with James Horlick, who is widely known as its inventor and also a promoter. His recipe consisted of milk, the malted barley, wheat, some sugar, and even an assortment of minerals and vitamins. Studies have found that it helps to improve sleep, and it is also believed that it is related to the vitamins, like vitamin D. The natural, enriched melatonin milk is another milk product which usually gives benefits in the improvement of sleep patterns.

• Oatmeal – A bowl of cereal taken before sleep will be useful in being able to get better sleep. The oats usually contain the tryptophan, an amino acid that is related to sleep, and this is because of how it increases the levels of serotonin and also the levels of melatonin. At the same time, the oatmeal has carbohydrates, which usually help the tryptophan to reach the brain.

• Almonds and Walnuts - The almonds and walnuts are convenient snacks that help in the promotion of sleep highly because of their melatonin content. These nuts usually contain healthy fats hence do not need any advance preparation to have them ready to eat just before bedtime. These nuts may also be taken with other pre-bed foods such as oatmeal.

Foods to Quit Eating Before You Go to Bed

There are specific types of food that, when taken in before you go to bed, would cause insomnia like behavior or just total disruption of your sleep. If you want your sleep to be peaceful and undisrupted, then you are not supposed to consume the following list of foods before bed. It is advisable to do it earlier on during the day.

1. Chocolate - These snacks taste delicious, and to some, it is really addictive; it is made up of caffeine from cacao. Although the intensity of caffeine varies, it is usually highly concentrated in dark chocolates than in milky chocolates. The combination of caffeine and sugar is

known to cause sleeplessness at night. It energizes the brain to be more active; hence, sleep is not in question.

2. Hot Sauce - The majority of professionals' advice against the consumption of spicy meals with inclusiveness to hot Sause before going to sleep. Studies have reported that eating hot Sauce may negatively affect your sleep due to the potentiality of indigestion and to avoid the rise in temperatures at night caused by spicy foods. ·

3. Fried Foods - These types of food naturally contain fats and are massive when it comes to digestion. If you are trying to go to bed, metabolism becomes a considerable problem. Fried foods could also stimulate reflux that disrupts sleep. Additionally, many fried foods are in the form of meat, and consumption of proteins may also cause negative impacts on rest.

4. Candy - Nearly all candies contain substantial amounts of sugar, and a lot of sugar does result in pancreases to produce insulin to control your blood sugars. Sadly, these blood sugars spike combined with insulin before sleeping could really disrupt your sleep at night.

5. Alcohol - A bit of alcohol consumption before going to sleep may make you feel sleepy, but generally, it could cause harm to your rest. Studies have reported that the use of alcohol before you sleep disrupts your sleep architecture and could make you wake up in the middle of the night. Consequently, taking in excessive alcohol results in hangover and drowsiness during the day on the following day.

Nutrition and sleep are highly debated topics, so there are clarifications needed when it comes to the autophagy process and rest. In this book, we will try to clarify some myths that are believed about diets and sleep.

Does Intermittent Fasting Affect Sleep?

Evidence to date is limited but has not shown any clear positive or negative impact of intermittent fasting on sleep.
Intermittent fasting is an approach to dieting that focuses on regular periods with no food intake. Some approaches to intermittent fasting

involve only eating for 8 hours each day, creating daily 14-16 hour fasts. Other ways of doing intermittent fasting may include fasting for one full day for every few days without fasting.

It is believed that intermittent fasting may enhance a healthy circadian rhythm. There is no precise data about intermittent fasting in large part because this is a relatively recent dietary approach and because there are various ways of implementing a diet based around intermittent fasting.

Intermittent fasting may affect hunger levels, especially when first becoming accustomed to this pattern of eating. This may influence sleep onset, as some people struggle to fall asleep when hungry. However, studies of people during Ramadan, a religious holiday that involves eating after sundown, have found no substantial disadvantageous results on sleep.

Burning Fats While Sleeping

The bodies usually burn calories during sleep and also while we are awake. Many people typically assume that we burn more calories during the waking hours, but the deprivation of sleep will lead to the metabolism being affected in ways that will decrease the general burning of calories.

The less sleeping usually seems to promote the appetite and also increases the probability that we overeat. Being deprived of sleep can also impact the moods of a person and will result in experiencing emotional eating. Through this, we can burn calories and fat while sleeping and also get a good sleep, which aids in prime the body for the reduction of fat and the general loss of weight.

Sleeping Well Help in Weight Loss

By getting enough sleep, a person can lose weight, as it is an essential part of the weight loss plan. The people who follow the same diets that usually restrict calories had even worse results, whereby they had a 55 percent reduction in their weight loss due to only sleeping for 5 hours a night relative to the others who slept 8 hours. Therefore, sleep is very important to the wellness of various systems in the body and part in promoting healthy metabolism and also helps in weight loss.

The Foods That Help Babies Sleep

No food can assure that a baby will sleep well, let alone be able to sleep through the night. A feeding shortly before an infant goes to bed is usually an essential part of their routine.

When it is possible, transitioning the baby into solid foods will result in positive impacts on their sleeping patterns. A study which was conducted in the UK showed that the babies who were fed with solid food plus breast milk starting at the age of 3 months were able to sleep longer and experienced fewer instances of crying and irritability. But some organizations are against this, claiming that the introduction of the solid food to babies that young is not advantageous as the babies may experience some hardship in being able to digest the food. Therefore, the parents are encouraged to see the doctors for advice.

Food Allergies Causing Sleep Problems

Some food allergies usually cause some issues which are related to sleep, and this is because of the various effects that they typically have on the body. Like food intolerances and allergies generally result in indigestion, nausea, or even diarrhea, which are often discomforting will interrupt sleep patterns. Research has identified an increase in the rates of sleep disturbance in individuals with an allergy to gluten, which is generally known as the celiac disease. Food allergies are also able to cause sleep disruptions since they can be able to overstimulate the nervous system.

The consumption of spicy foods usually results in a lack of sleep. The intake of foods that are very spicy around the period of sleeping usually leads to the disruption of having a quality sleep. Therefore, a person should desist eating spicy foods before going to bed, and this is high because it usually results in indigestion of food and may also increase the temperature of the body hence disrupting the sleeping pattern; this will affect the health of a person negatively due to lack of enough sleep.

457

This will also affect the function of the body during the day as due to the lack of sleep, the person will be worn out.

The Best Time to Eat

The best time to eat dinner is usually some hours before the sleeping period whereby you eat and give the food some time to digest before heading to bed. A person should also be able to limit the intake of snacks in bed, which is not healthy. Through following such a routine, a person will gain a lot, health-wise. A lot of researches has been done on this, and the findings are that the consumption of food just before sleeping usually results in various consequences that are negative to the promotion of the body's health. This can be seen in the individuals that usually consume food just before going to sleep, which affects them negatively in terms of getting a night of quality sleep. Therefore, a person should eat at least 30 to 60 minutes before going to bed hence resulting in some remarkable results.

The Diet for Sleeping Beauty

This is a diet that usually tries to discourse the problem associated with sleeping—for example, lack of sleep and other disorders that are usually associated with sleep. This strategy pays attention to the phrase that the time used for sleeping is the time taken without the consumption of calories. To be able to achieve this, many people who follow this diet plan usually use some sleeping pills so as to be able to have a night of quality sleep. Some people use even painkillers to be able to initiate sleep quickly and for longer periods. The diet of sleeping beauty is not recommended, as it has not been backed by science. This method usually leads to an individual feeling weak and experiencing fatigue in the whole body and may also result in the development of unhealthy eating disorders, which will boost the addition of body weight. You should remember that it is not advised to sleep when feeling hungry highly because it is not healthy for the body. The use of drugs to assist an individual in sleeping for long is not a good idea, as it is dangerous and also may lead a person being addicted to the drugs, whereby they tend to use it every time hence not being able to function without them.

This diet program shows us how important having a natural quality sleep is and how it helps the body in its daily functions.

Why Choose Sleep Optimization?

Many people today usually sleep less so as to be able to maximize their work, which will not be able to benefit them health-wise. The best way to be able to achieve waking up with energy and also being ready to tackle the day ahead is usually done through sleeping more, which will result in the individual waking up energetic and also feeling rejuvenated. We need to sleep on a daily basis to be able to give the body some time to rest and boost its function. Therefore, sleeping is usually an important process that aids us in becoming more effective and more efficient. We, at times, have the assumption that when we fall asleep, we just lie, and that is all, as there is nothing happening. However, we are wrong because many processes usually happen when we are fast asleep. Since all the individuals usually get to be exposed to a lot of stimuli and even large quantities of information, therefore, the mind needs time to relax and also process the information and the memories. Even when we are sleeping, the brain still works.

Apart from processing the information by the brain, the body also requires rest to recover from all the activities done during the day. Many types of research have proven that the time you sleep is when the muscles usually grow. When we get quality sleep, the immune system is usually made strong, the cells are rejuvenated, and there is the management of the metabolism and the charging process of the body to be able to wake up without any issues. Therefore, the type of sleep one usually gets will determine how their day will be. Thus, it does not add up when people usually sleep for a small duration of time so as to work more, and this is because when a person does not get enough sleep, they will not be efficient in working, as the simple tasks will take way longer than expected. If a person is interested in boosting their sleep optimization, the person needs to sleep for the whole night, and they should not wake up in the middle of the night. A person should start tracking their sleep at the start so as to be able to know when to sleep and when to wake up. For the tracking process, there are applications and software that can aid in recording such periods. The best way for a person to sleep quickly is basically the change of environment in which they sleep in. For example, people are used to sleeping when there is darkness so as to enable them to sleep well without any distractions. Even the temperature of the room also matters, wherein we get to sleep well when the temperature of our sleeping environment is cooler and not having high temperatures. The final method is to employ a good sleeping routine that you always need to follow. Through this, you will be able to sleep well without waking up in the middle of the night.

Conclusion

Thank you for making it through to the end of the book *Autophagy*! Let's hope it was informative and able to provide you with all of the tools you need to achieve your goals—whatever they may be.

You know the perks of being fit, as well as looking and feeling more youthful. The replenishment of cellular structures means that energy is back to a hundred percent.

It is important to have a better understanding of the benefits of healthy fats and less sugar consumption, which allows you to instill it into your day-to-day activities for generations to benefit.

You have learned about the basics of aerobic training, the process involved, its effects on the brain, its effects on the body, as well as activities that you can perform.

Many important strategies that you require to ensure that your body is less at risk of getting inflammatory diseases, like the ketogenic diet, which lets you gain an array of health benefits.

The next step is for you to get out into the world, equipped with this knowledge, and add the missing ingredient for a healthier body, mind, and soul into your life—both personal and professional—and success will be calling in your favor. The trick is always to work *smarter* and not harder. The best way to get results in the activation of the autophagy process is by being consistent with it. I wish you all the best in your future endeavors!

Intermittent Fasting

Step-by-Step Guide to Lose Weight and Eat Healthy with Keto Diet. Heal Your Body with Autophagy.

Use the Best Mindset to Succeed in Fasting Easily for Wellness and Longevity

by ALAN DIETER

Table of Contents

Introduction

Are you looking for the most effective way to lose weight and maintain optimal health? Intermittent fasting is the answer to your search. This book is a great resource if you are interested in combining intermittent fasting and keto but are unsure about where to begin.

Inside this book, you will find invaluable information on how you can use intermittent fasting and the ketogenic diet to bring a turnaround in your life and lose weight as you've never done before.

This book focuses on how you can combine the ketogenic diet and intermittent fasting for the best results. It first begins by looking at intermittent fasting in-depth, followed up by all the basics of the ketogenic diet. We take a look at the different intermittent fasting methods, as well as how to fit the ketogenic diet into intermittent fasting.

Intermittent fasting takes a closer look at both intermittent fasting and the ketogenic diet to give you an exciting solution to weight loss. This looks at the different aspects of both intermittent fasting and the ketogenic diet to help you understand the mechanism of these two diets before you can even think of combining them.

The book particularly looks at the workings of each diet; hence, it will help you to make the decision to lead a life full of vitality. Whether you are interested in losing weight or you simply desire to lead a healthy lifestyle, this book offers you detailed information, complete with how to make a smooth transition so that you're able to adhere to the plan.

Combining a low-carb diet with intermittent fasting will certainly usher you into a new health perspective. By the time you finish reading this book, you will be sufficiently equipped with all the information you need to begin combining intermittent fasting and the ketogenic diet and enjoy all the benefits that it offers. I believe this book will mark the beginning of a new chapter in your lifestyle.

Chapter 1:

What Is Intermittent Fasting?

When you talk about fasting, what comes to mind for most people is starvation. This is a huge misconception because intermittent fasting is actually a lifestyle. It involves going without food deliberately and voluntarily, for a specified duration, and alternating it with a specific window of time within which you can eat. You can practice intermittent fasting for various reasons, although most people who embrace it are motivated by the numerous benefits that result from calorie restriction. What sets intermittent fasting from other forms of fasting like religious fasting or a diagnostic fast is the fact that you are at liberty to take fluids and non-caloric beverages during the fasting window. This makes fasting bearable and easy to follow through while still reaping the benefits.

History of Fasting

Fasting is an age-old practice that has been in existence since the time of the agrarian revolution. At the time, human beings who were mostly hunters and gatherers were forced to fast owing to the scarcity of food. Without cold storage or even modern food preservation technology, they would eat whenever they found adequate food and go without food for long periods in times of scarcity. Yet, others fasted for medical and religious reasons.

Hippocrates, a Greek philosopher and the father of modern medicine, also advocated for fasting for medical reasons. According to Hippocrates, eating while you are sick is equivalent to feeding the sickness because disease-causing microorganisms are able to thrive. He argued that animals didn't eat while they were sick, and this contributed to their speedy healing besides improving their cognitive function. Plutarch and Plato equally advocated for this. Greeks believed that this same principle could apply to human beings. This concept has been integrated into modern medicine; thus, it's a common practice to find patients who are due for surgery being put on compulsory fast hours before the procedure.

Fasting has also been practiced as a spiritual practice in different religions. For instance, Muslims do practice Ramadhan in fulfillment of the fifth pillar of Islam. They take time to pray and reflect. Christians, too, set aside time to pray and fast as a way of seeking spiritual benefits.

History of Intermittent Fasting

Intermittent fasting is not an entirely new concept from ancient fasting patterns. The only new thing about intermittent fasting is the clinical research linking this practice to numerous health benefits and longevity that is driving many people to embrace it. In fact, one of the reasons why intermittent fasting continues to gain popularity is because it's one of the few diets that actually produces results and has the backing of scientific evidence. Intermittent fasting was first popularized in 2012 by BBC journalist and doctor Michael Mosley after sharing the outcome of his two-week journey of the 5:2 protocol. Dr. Mosley shared the benefits of the fasting protocol on his TV program that included rapid weight loss. He went on two write a book, hence making intermittent fasting popular.

To date, millions of people have embraced this practice that continues to produce results. This is partly because of the flexibility of this practice as you get to choose a fasting protocol that is suitable for your lifestyle and needs. Moreover, intermittent fasting is easy to follow since you're simply adjusting your feeding hours, which your body gets accustomed to through time, thus making it doable.

Who Can Practice Intermittent Fasting?

Intermittent fasting is not exclusive to health enthusiasts because we all practice this pattern of eating in one way or the other. Think about the hours you are awake and the number of hours you spend sleeping. These intervals can rightly fit into the fasting and feasting windows keeping in mind the time you have your first and last meal. The only distinguishing factor is the fact that when you practice intermittent fasting, you're more deliberate about the length of your fast.

Generally, nearly everyone can practice intermittent fasting apart from people who have special needs. However, you must make sure that your intermittent fasting plan is well structured if you're to achieve the results you desire. Most importantly, you must be ready to adhere to your intermittent fasting plan. You can practice intermittent fasting if; you are single with no children, you have been watching your food and calorie consumption, you have a good support system, and your job allows you periods of low performance. Although you can also follow intermittent fasting if you are in complete sports, have a performance-oriented job are married with children, you must do so with caution.

Who Shouldn't Practice Intermittent Fasting

Although intermittent fasting is simply a pattern of eating, not everyone can practice it because it can result in some inconveniences or introduce risks that outweigh the benefits for some people. You shouldn't practice intermittent fasting if:

- *You're below 18 years.* The reason for this is simple. At 18 years, you're growing actively; hence, your body requires all the minerals and vital vitamins that promote growth and development. Therefore, intermittent fasting will be counterproductive.

- *You're expectant or nursing.* Nursing and expectant mothers should not practice intermittent fasting because their bodies are providing nourishment for the baby. Besides, your body needs more calories when breastfeeding and during pregnancy.

- *You have gastroesophageal reflux disease (GERD).* Various studies have concluded that intermittent fasting can worsen GERD because when you fast, your stomach will be without food for a couple of hours. Therefore, the gastric juices will not have anything to digest except your stomach lining.

- *You're underweight and malnourished.* It's unrealistic to get into intermittent fasting when you're already underweight or are battling an eating disorder because this can only make a bad situation worse.

- *You suffer from chronic stress or have had a history of disordered eating.* You shouldn't practice intermittent fasting, as this comes with a diet pattern of exercise and diet regiment—that means you will not sleep well.

A Word of Caution

Although intermittent fasting is a pattern of fasting that can be adopted by just about everyone because it's safe, you must approach it with caution for the following reasons:

Not everybody can practice intermittent fasting because of the effect this pattern of eating can have on your physiological functions. Therefore, make sure you talk to a doctor before you begin. This is important because it'll help you to take care of any prevailing health conditions that you may not have been aware existed. Remember, you should not undergo fasting when you're not in good health.

While women are discouraged from practicing intermittent fasting, the reality is that there are certain groups of women who can undergo fasting and reap the benefits of fasting just like their male counterparts. However, you'll need to talk to a doctor, particularly if you're suffering from diabetes, low blood pressure, you're trying to conceive, or have an eating disorder. All these are considered to be risk factors.

What Happens During Fasting?

When you're following the normal eating pattern, your body depends on glucose from the food that you consume. The rest is stored as fat. When you fast, the body goes into a state known as ketosis, where the liver will break down the fat into ketones that are then used as a source of energy. Evidence suggests that ketones are capable of suppressing appetite while also reducing oxidative stress and inflammation levels. However, keep in mind that ketones offer many other benefits other than the production of energy. Fasting reduces risk factors for conditions such as type 2 diabetes and heart diseases.

Why Should You Practice Intermittent Fasting for Fat Loss?

One of the things that have drawn so many people to intermittent fasting is the fact that you can achieve weight loss with this pattern of eating. If you've already practiced numerous diet fads without any results, intermittent fasting could just be the solution you've been looking for as long as you practice it as required. So why should you practice intermittent fasting for fat loss? First, you need to know that intermittent fasting is not a tangible product but a process that involves a lifestyle change, especially with regard to your relationship with food. It's a natural process that lets your body burn fat and lose weight through calorie restriction. However, unlike other diets that require you to count your calories, this diet restricts calories by reducing the duration within which you're allowed to it. So, you will naturally consume fewer calories than you would when following a normal eating pattern. When this happens, you experience a calorie deficit that means that your body must then tap into the fat stores to be able to make up for the deficit. The result of this is the loss of fat because the stored fat is broken down to produce energy for the body.

Secondly, intermittent fasting has continued to gain traction as more and more people across the world share their experiences and results of following this eating pattern. The reason is simple. Unlike many diets that are expensive and difficult to follow through, intermittent fasting is simple, easy to follow, yet it produces results. Anyone can start and follow through intermittent fasting without necessarily having to change your diet. This eating pattern is also not restrictive rather so that you go back to your old eating habits at the end of the diet; rather, it's more of a change in lifestyle, so it's something you can adopt in the long term.

Lastly, intermittent fasting is easy to follow and more relaxed because the only restriction is the window during which you fast and feast. That is, it emphasizes on the number of hours when you need to eat and when you need to fast. However, you'll be allowed to take water and beverages as long as they are calorie-free. This helps in suppressing the urge to eat or crave certain foods. Moreover, you'll be able to burn more fat so that you become healthier and leaner. Intermittent fasting is a holistic way of leading a healthy lifestyle.

Why Should You Start Intermittent Fasting?

If you have heard about intermittent fasting for some time now, you must be wondering whether you should join the bandwagon or not. Well, unless you have a prevailing medical condition, you can be sure to follow intermittent fasting successfully. Your body is well conditioned to handle long periods without food. In fact, you'll be surprised that you can go up to 84 hours without food before you can begin to experience a significant drop in your glucose levels. So many changes occur in the body during fasting, most of which have a positive influence on your overall wellness.

Fasting does pave the way for a number of repair processes that target the genes, hormones, and cells. During fasting, your body's insulin levels decrease significantly while the human growth hormone increases. Intermittent fasting also increases your metabolic health benefits because it improves the number of risk factors and health markers. When you fast, your lifespan also increases because fasting has been found to increase longevity, especially through a process known as autophagy. You can also practice intermittent fasting for the simple reason that it makes your day simple since you no longer have to spend hours preparing meals and eating. While you'd have to prepare up to six meals on any given day, intermittent fasting reduces this time because, in some instances, you may just need to prepare two meals. Most important of all is that the human body has the capacity to adapt to such changes. After all, it echoes the way of life of an early man who ate when there was plenty and fasted during the times of scarcity. There are many reasons why you should start practicing intermittent today. You'll be surprised at the tremendous changes that you'll experience apart from weight and fat loss that are easily noticeable.

Chapter 2:

Common Intermittent Fasting Methods

There are numerous ways to do intermittent fasting. These methods vary in terms of the calorie allowances and the number of days/hours that you can do them. Depending on the method that you choose, intermittent fasting may involve fasting partially so that you only eat for a set amount of time or fasting entirely for a whole day before you can resume eating regularly. Since every person has a different experience with intermittent fasting, different styles will appeal to different people. In this chapter, we discuss the common intermittent fasting methods of doing intermittent fasting.

The 16:8 Method – The Leangains Method

With this method of intermittent fasting, you'll be required to fast for 16 hours and only have an eating window of 8 hours, hence 16:8. It's the most common fasting protocol because most people are already used to going without food for long durations, especially at night. A Swedish nutritionist and bodybuilder, Martin Berkhan, created this method.

This method is easy to adopt, especially if you're already used to a 12-hour fasting period. However, women can do a modification of this method by fasting for 14 hours with a 10-hour feeding window. When followed properly, this method maximizes your muscle while cutting on fat. This method is complemented by a light workout that is mainly strength training. What is even interesting is that the creator of this intermittent fasting method does not only focus on weight loss but also muscle building and body re-composition. The 16:8 Method is not a one-size-fits-all; thus, you're free to adapt it to your needs, especially with regard to meal timing and macro-nutrient breakdown. It's easy to make this method your lifestyle over time.

Following the 16:8 Method

For you to be successful with the 16:8 intermittent fasting method, you must be ready to keep a journal to track your progress. This can be a challenge if journaling is not something you do regularly. Yet this is important in helping you to not only track but also achieve the results you desire. You're free to determine when you will eat and when you will fast. Berkhan suggests that you begin your feasting window in the afternoon all the way to half-past eight because this will ensure that you don't miss out on social gathering where you have to eat. After all, this is when the social scene is active, and it is followed by the first hours of your fast that you will spend while sleeping that you're already accustomed to. The interesting about this method is that you'll have to skip breakfast that has been argued to be the most important meal of the day. Additionally, you have to set aside a time when you will do your workout to which Berkhan suggests the following options; you can opt to do your workout as soon as you wake up or work out after your first meal into the feasting window. You could also opt to work out after your second meal. You should make sure that you target your workouts to focus on strength training while limiting your meal times to three during the 8-hour feasting window. The reason for this is simple. It's not easy to have more than three meals in just about 8 hours. However, make sure you have a large post-workout meal with over sixty percent of your recommended daily calorie intake coming from this meal. The reason behind this is simple; your body is accustomed to converting food into muscle post-workout. Therefore, refrain from practicing fasted training because it's taxing and puts you at risk of suffering from bur out. When this happens, you could end up needing to take supplements, which means you have more things to track. As such, it's better to maintain working out during your feasting window. This also helps you to have quality sleep since your body will be physically tired. Ultimately, make sure you maintain a calorie deficit or just eat at maintenance.

For you to know the number of calories you need, begin by calculating your Basal Metabolic Rate (BMR) so that you're sure about the number of calories you need to maintain your current weight. Make sure you consider your activity level when calculating your BMR. Unless you're sedentary, make sure you pick the level where you're at or go a level lower. Desist from the common mistake of underestimating your activity level because a deficit means five hundred calories less this number, and the maintenance is a similar number of calories. Therefore, when you eat the specified number of calories, you'll be able to maintain your current weight. When you carefully follow the 16:8 fasting method along with the workout, your body will undergo immense re-composition, replacing fat with muscle. Don't be discouraged if you have to lose so much weight in order to reach your healthy weight. You'll definitely begin to see the results over time when you start losing fat, and your muscle becomes dense.

It's also important to think about the food you will be eating as well as the proportions. To do this, take advantage of the online calculators to estimate the size of your food portions and calories you need so you know how to distribute them across the three meals. You also need to determine the proportion of your food that will be carbohydrates and what proportion will comprise proteins. Should you opt to incorporate the ketogenic diet, make sure that you include a higher proportion of fat compared to carbs. You don't have to worry about putting on weight from consuming fats because your insulin levels decrease during fasting, thereby promoting the burning of fat. Carbs are important, especially during your workout, because they help in fueling your muscles. If you realize that you're following through this plan, but you're still not able to realize any significant weight loss, you will have to reduce your daily caloric intake by at least 500 calories and continue journaling the progress.

Making Your 16:8 Intermittent Fasting Method a Success

Although this intermittent fasting protocol is popular, it's not easy to follow through. However, you can follow these tips to be able to post excellent results:

- This program requires that you work out with the emphasis being strength training.

- Make sure you include a sufficient proportion of proteins in the meals you consume during the fasting period.

- Make sure your meals are nutrient-dense while staying away from calorie bombs that add little or no nutritional value.

- Don't consume any calories within the feasting window. This includes anything with the potential of causing your insulin levels to spike. Instead, focus on drinking lots of water and other non-caloric beverages to stay hydrated.

- Avoid eating pre-workout, but instead, have a large post-workout meal.

In conclusion, while intermittent fasting is not about calorie restriction, taking fewer carbs will make the 16:8 Method a huge success.

Pros of the 16:8 Method

- This intermittent fasting pattern tends to offer structure to your day owing to the consistency of the fasting/feasting window.

- This method is planned with physical activity in mind, so it will work well if you lead an active lifestyle.

- The fasting window of this method is not so extreme, like a majority of other fasting diets, making it so easy to stick to.

Cons of the 16:8 Method

- Some people may not want to cycle their carb and calorie intake.

- For optimal results, Berkhan recommends that you need to train when you're in the fasted state. This is impractical for those people who prefer to train later. Even then, you can find different templates on how you can apply this method in various scenarios.

The 5:2 Method – Eat Stop Eat

Eat Stop Eat is the intermittent fasting method that propelled the intermittent fasting method into popularity after Dr. Mosley shared the results of his two-week fast. However, this pattern of eating is originally the brainchild of Brad Pilon, a bodybuilder. This plan is designed to imitate the ancient lifestyle that was practiced by the hunting and gathering communities. Interestingly, you will not find a lot of information on this intermittent fasting plan online. This is in no way meant to mean that this method is not effective because you'll be amazed by the kind of results you'll post with this method of fasting.

Are you wondering what this intermittent fasting method entails? Well, with the eat stop eat method, you get to eat regularly for 5 days and set aside two days of fasting. This means you'll have two 24-hour blocks during which you shouldn't consume any calories. This can be a little difficult for most people, but it can be done because you can still take fluids that do not contain calories. The major misgiving with this intermittent fasting method is that you could end up binge eating after going for 24 hours without food. Even then, studies have discredited this, arguing that the excess calories you'll consume after your fast don't qualify to make it binge eating. All in all, you'll do well to distribute the days you'll be fasting realistically to have a realistic gap so that you don't end up binge eating at the end of the fast.

How to Do the 5:2 Intermittent Fasting Method

Although fasting for 24 hours is not for the faint-hearted, the 5:2 Method can be a good place to start the intermittent fasting lifestyle. The reason is simple; the rules governing this method of fasting are not too harsh. In addition, this method also has minimal requirements, so it's easy for anyone to start on it, including beginners. Although Brad Pilon recommends complimenting this method with exercises, it doesn't have to be HIIT or strength training as long as you're able to break a move and sweat.

You'll do well to know where you stand in terms of maintenance calories, even though this is not a must because you can balance this out on the days when you're not fasting. This is good motivation because beginners can be encouraged to carry on without being under too much pressure yet attain the desired weight loss. However, you need to realize that the weight loss associated with this method is not as rapid as with other intermittent fasting methods. Moreover, you have to follow the guidelines keenly to achieve results. Unfortunately, beginners are often the greatest victims of flouting the guidelines because of lacking a good understanding of the nutritional component resulting in discouragement and eventually abandoning the program. This is also a major shortcoming of this program.

Sample 5:2 Setup

- Monday – Normal eating

- Tuesday – Up to 500 / 600 calories

- Wednesday – Normal eating

- Thursday – Normal eating

- Friday – 500 / 600 calories

- Saturday – Normal eating

- Sunday – Normal eating

The Pros of 5:2

- This method of fasting can suit certain categories of people psychologically.

- You don't have to track your calorie consumption.

The Cons of 5:2

- This method of fasting may not be suitable for people who are in jobs that require them to be active.

- It can be difficult to stick to this plan in the long term.

- Since you have no restrictions on calorie consumption, you can easily overeat on the days when you eat normally.

The Warrior Method

The warrior method of intermittent fasting is relatively extreme of all the intermittent fasting methods because you have to fast for 20 hours and eat for 4 hours. As such, it is recommended for those who have already experimented with the other intermittent fasting methods. Ori Hofmekler, a former member of the Israeli Special Forces who later transitioned into nutrition and fitness, originally created this method. Following this method to the later will change your perspective on the amount of food you need to eat as well as the frequency of meals that you need for the proper functioning of your body. This method is a lot stricter when compared to the Leangains method because it lengthens the fasting window by four hours while shortening the feeding window by 4 hours. As such, it's likely that you will only be able to have one large meal during the feeding window. Although this doesn't seem practical, this diet will get you the results you so much desire.

The only challenge is that you must make sure you stick to this plan to get the results. This is something most people struggle with. However, it's not difficult to get started on this diet as you can find tons of motivation from the online community of people who have either tried it or are doing it now. It is believed to be practiced by those people with a tough personality. Thus, don't be surprised if you don't get any sympathy or even support if you're struggling with adherence. Overall, your success with this plan is mostly psychological and hence has the potential to have a negative effect on your relationship with food.

How to Do the Warrior Diet

Before you can even think about beginning your fast under the warrior diet, you must calculate your BMR so you know the number of calories you should get from fat, proteins, and carbs. You need to determine the amount of protein you need, followed by carbs and fats. You also need to come up with a plan on how you'll be working out, keeping in mind your short feasting window. Although you need to work out during the feeding window, this can be a challenge logistically because the amount of time you need for your work out is just about half of your feeding window. Besides, since you have a large meal portion, you need sufficient time to eat to allow digestion to take place. On the other hand, when you work out during your fasting window, you're unlikely to attain optimum performance that will meet the demand for strength training even if you take supplements. The idea here is that after 24 hours of fasting, your body needs proper nutrition. Therefore, attempting to work out while in the fasted state will increase this need. On the other hand, when you work out after a single meal means you'll have inadequate time to eat. Therefore, you need to balance this by shortening the length of your workout to preserve your muscle mass.

In this case, High-Intensity Interval Training (HIIT) is the most ideal as it can push your heart rate up to 90% of its maximum ability within a short time so that you have a slightly longer duration of rest. You can repeat this within 15- to 20-minute intervals. You can engage in any activity as long as you're doing it with great intensity. This can be anything from sprinting to cycling, pushups, squats and jump rope, and so much more. You just need to make sure that you avoid injuries. You can gradually reduce your resting interval as you get used to this plan. However, you must keep in mind that you can only develop strength up to a certain level. In addition, you can't build muscle beyond a certain point.

Pros of the Warrior Method

- This method will work well for those people who are not hungry during the day, owing to their work schedule, so you find it easier to skip breakfast and eat later in the day.

- Cutting down on your consumption of meals to 1 or 2 meals in a day will help when calories are low.

- This plan mainly emphasizes on eating nutrient-rich, whole foods like vegetables and fruits.

Cons of the Warrior Method

- The set-up of this method of fasting makes it most likely to have to train in the fasted state that might not be practical.

- This method might not be sustainable for most people.

Alternate-Day Fasting – 36/12 Fast

Nutritionist and Dr. James B. Johnson designed the alternate-day fasting method. This intermittent fasting method involves fasting every other day and comes in several variations. This method recommends fasting for 36 hours and feeding for 12 hours, but you can do it. Thus, you can have your three meals during the feeding period. While some people will limit their calorie intake to 500 others, practice complete avoidance of food. Since this method of fasting promotes fasting for an extended duration, it's not suitable for beginners. When following this plan, you must have a higher intake of proteins and fats compared to carbs. This method is silent about working out, probably because of the long fasting period. This method is not as strict because it gives you the freedom to eat anything as long as it's a healthy choice. You'll do well to stick to nutrient-dense foods while avoiding calorie-dense foods.

How to Do the 36/12 Method

Before you start implementing the alternate-day fasting method, you need to begin by defining your feasting and fasting windows. That is establishing when your fasting period will begin and when your feeding window you start. For instance, if your first meal is at 8 am and your last meal at 8 pm on Sunday, you can repeat this schedule at least 4 times each week. Your fasting window typically begins after your last meal of the day.

Many people have posted positive results with alternate-day fasting because it not only promotes weight loss but also contributes to overall well-being. Most people who have strictly followed this plan have recorded weight loss of up to 8 percent within 8 weeks. Other benefits you'll experience with this method of fasting include improved insulin resistance and better cellular energy production. This method is excellent if you want to tap into the benefits of autophagy.

Nonetheless, fasting for 36 hours can be too harsh for the female body; hence, it's recommended that women who want to follow this method have at least 500 calories during the fasting window. You can consider taking smoothies are fruits as these have low calories. Combine this with exercise like strength training to enhance fat burning and obtain better results.

Alternate-Day Fasting Setup

- Monday – Normal eating

- Tuesday – Up to 500 / 600 calories

- Wednesday – Normal eating

- Thursday – Normal eating

- Friday – 500 / 600 calories

- Saturday – Normal eating

- Sunday – Normal eating

Pros of Alternate-Day Fasting

Some of the advantages of alternate-day fasting include the following:

- This method of fasting is handy in improving conditions such as asthma.

- Alternate-day fasting extends your lifespan as well as improving metabolism.

- You'll not experience deprivation because you are allowed to eat anything during the feeding window.

- This method is easy to follow in the long term.

- It's good for your health.

- It doesn't have stringent rules as long as you eat healthy meals.

Cons of Alternate-Day Fasting

- The disadvantages of intermittent fasting include:

- You're likely to experience some unpleasant side effects with this method, such as fatigue, dizziness, and hunger, particularly in the beginning.

- This pattern of eating is not good for those people who have a history of eating disorders such as anorexia.

- This method doesn't say anything about exercising or even the role of working out.

The 12/12 Method

This intermittent fasting pattern is easy to follow because you have an equal length of fasting and feeding duration. That means you're fasting for 12 hours and feeding for another 12 hours. This is quite manageable, keeping in mind that some of those hours of your fasting window will be spent sleeping. Therefore, you hardly get to feel hungry. The only challenge is that you need to limit your meal times to a maximum of three within the 12 hours of feeding. So you can opt for an equal feeding interval, so you don't have to eat snacks in between meals. A 12-hour fast is great because it allows your system sufficient time to rest. Besides, it contributes to a decline in your insulin levels, thus promoting weight loss. Nonetheless, you shouldn't be surprised if you still experience uneasiness, nausea, or a slight headache in the initial stages of fasting because it will take time before your body can adjust. This reaction is usually a result of the withdrawal of sugar, so your body tries to adjust to this change. Like the other intermittent fasting protocols, you need to stay hydrated by taking lots of water and drinks that don't have calories.

Crescendo Fasting

The crescendo method of intermittent fasting was designed for women because of the female body's sensitivity to signals of starvation. For most women, fasting triggers hormonal imbalances that are translated as hunger pangs. Fatigue, mood swings, and weight gain. The crescendo method of fasting is less demanding, making it suitable. When you practice this method of fasting, you don't have to fast daily rather you fast for 12-16 hours per day for up to 3 non-consecutive days weekly. This means that you're still able to maintain your regular feeding plan on those days when you're not fasting. You also must refrain from heavy workouts but consider yoga and cardio. Intense exercises like strength training and HIIT are also recommended.

Pros of Crescendo Fasting

- This method is great when you want to burn fat pockets and slim without having to embrace a demanding routine.

- This method is gentle on the female body; thus, it helps in preserving the hormonal balance that is important for a woman's body.

- Crescendo fasting is an excellent way of preparing your body to handle the complicated intermittent fasting methods like the warrior method and eat stop eat among others.

Cons of Crescendo Fasting

- This method of fasting is not recommended for people with eating disorders because it'll make it worse.

- Practicing this method of fasting could result in an irregular menstrual cycle. In the event that this happens, stop fasting immediately.

Chapter 3:

How to Do Intermittent Fasting in a Healthy and Safe Way

Intermittent fasting is a health trend that is unstoppable because of the evolutionary rationale that drives it. The pattern of eating has been the basis of numerous studies and trials that have sought to investigate the relationship between fasting and its benefits. However, to achieve the benefits, you must practice fasting along with other supporting pillars that include heavy plant nutrition, exercise, mindfulness, and sleep.

One of the concerns of intermittent fasting is how to practice it safely and get to harness all the amazing benefits keeping in mind that you'll be going for long hours without food. A number of intermittent fasting studies done on women have posted overwhelming outcomes of this lifestyle intervention. This is especially true if you're overweight or have a mild metabolic dysfunction like prediabetes and even inflammation. Like any other good thing, too much intermittent fasting can become bad, hence the need to make sure you do it right.

When you talk about doing intermittent fasting in a healthy and safe way, you need to keep in mind that precision is everything. This applies to any other lifestyle intervention as they are all created to be equal and produce a dose-dependent response. When done moderately, intermittent fasting will promote sustainable weight loss, improved lipid levels, reduce inflammation, and improve lipid levels. You'll need to approach intermittent fasting with caution if you are used to engaging in high levels of physical activity. To make sure you're practicing intermittent fasting safely, you need to consider the following:

• *Talk to your doctor or nutritionist.* Anyone can practice intermittent fasting, including people who are living with diabetes. However, you need to make sure you're under the supervision of a medical professional or nutritionist. When you talk to your doctor, you are able to discuss with them the limits so that you know the level you can get to as well as what is off-limits for you. They will also advise you on the fasting method that is best suited for you.

• *Choose a suitable intermittent fasting method.* Once you have been given the green light to proceed with fasting, you need to identify the intermittent fasting method that will work best for you because not all methods are suitable for everyone. One of the things that you need to consider while choosing an intermittent fasting plan is your lifestyle. This includes your work. Choose a plan that compliments your work schedule as well as your goals. While at it, don't be too ambitious as to go for a plan that you can't keep up with because this will only result in you struggling before quitting.

• *Focus on healthy food choices.* Although intermittent fasting doesn't emphasize on the kind of foods you need to eat during the duration you'll be fasting, it's advisable to stick to healthy food choices, especially nutrient-dense foods. These will often leave you feeling full for longer, making it easier to cope with the long hours of fasting. This also makes it possible for you to lose weight if this is your ultimate goal because you will not be feeding on empty calories.

• *Start with the moderate intermittent fasting methods gradually advancing to the more complex plans.* The good thing about intermittent fasting methods is that they have been designed to accommodate the needs of just about every category of people. As a beginner, you will do well by beginning with the friendlier methods of fasting that require you to fast for fewer hours and advance to the more complex methods where you'll be fasting for longer hours.

• *Work out in moderation.* Most of the intermittent fasting methods require you to compliment the fast with workouts. This doesn't mean that you can work out as you would when you are following the normal eating plan. Instead, you should focus your workouts, such that they will coincide with your feeding window, and you can do then in moderation.

• *Keep a positive mindset.* A positive mindset is an important component when you talk about safety in intermittent fasting. When you have the right mentality, you will refrain from the temptation to fast without thinking about your needs.

Can Intermittent Fasting Be Dangerous?

Despite all the evidence put forth in support of intermittent fasting, you must keep in mind that not all types of intermittent fasting are safe or even supported by scientific evidence. Therefore, even for the intermittent fasting methods that have been tested, you must avoid prolonged fasting for an extended duration, especially beyond 36 hours unless you're doing it for medical reasons and have consulted your physician. Some of the intermittent fasting methods have been popularized by people outside the medical and scientific fields, which is dangerous. This includes dry fasting that doesn't have any scientific backing. There are no human studies that have been done to advance dry fasting, and this form of fasting doesn't promote autophagy, either, and hence must be discouraged. If you must practice any form of fasting, you must make sure that it is backed with scientific evidence or clinical trials that prove it to be safe.

Safety Concerns About Intermittent Fasting

The main safety concern when doing intermittent fasting is the possibility of malnutrition or undernutrition. Individuals who are underweight and have a nutritional deficiency or are at risk of such need not to practice intermittent fasting. In fact, they shouldn't practice a fast that lasts more than 12 hours. Women may sometimes experience irregular periods or even have issues with their reproductive health. This is often caused by substantive weight loss, accompanied by excessive exercise. Women who are expecting must also not practice intermittent fasting because their nutritional needs are even more during this time. Ultimately, you need to understand that an intermittent fasting schedule that works for one person may not work for another person. Thus, you will do well to evaluate how you fair with the fasts while paying attention to your overall well-being. Some of the things you can do to practice intermittent fasting safely are:

- Make sure you're well-hydrated and drink up whenever you feel thirsty.
- Adjust your calorie consumption during the feasting window to pack up enough calories to meet your weight loss/maintenance goals.
- Go for fasting schedules that let you eat in the light-dark cycle as within your normal circadian rhythm.
- Don't hesitate to break your fast early whenever you feel nauseous, faint, or dizzy.

Chapter 4:

Benefits of Intermittent Fasting

One of the reasons why intermittent fasting continues to gain popularity is because of the many benefits it offers. Moreover, unlike many diets that promise rapid weight loss but only end up to be fads, you can be sure to experience weight loss with intermittent fasting when you do it properly. Some of the benefits of intermittent fasting include the following:

Intermittent Fasting Prompts Multiple Cellular Processes

Your body is made up of trillions of cells. The cells keep you alive and healthy through a regeneration process. When you fast, your body undergoes a number of physiological processes, including initiation of a cellular regeneration process that is known as autophagy. This process involves metabolization of the broken and dysfunctional proteins that build up within cells over time.

Intermittent Fasting Does Change the Function of Hormones, Genes, and Cells

When your body is deprived of food for an extended duration, a number of processes are initiated. These changes include cellular repair processes as well as changes in your hormonal levels ostensibly to make the stored fat accessible for conversion into energy. Other important changes that occur are a significant decline in your levels of insulin that also promotes the burning of fat. Your body also experiences an increase in the levels of your growth hormones that also promote fat burning as well as muscle gain. Other cellular repair processes that take place include removing waste material from the cells. You could also experience other beneficial changes that take place in molecules and genes relating to longevity as well as protection against diseases.

Intermittent Fasting Leads to a Reduction of Inflammation and Oxidative Stress

Oxidative stress is usually pre precursor to aging as well as most chronic diseases. It involves a number of molecules that are known as free radicals. The free radicals react with other useful molecules causing damage to them. Various studies indicate that intermittent fasting will enhance the body's ability to resist oxidative stress. In addition, it will also help in fighting inflammation that is another major driver of diseases.

Intermittent Fasting Is Therapeutic

The benefits of intermittent fasting go beyond the physical to also offer psychological and spiritual benefits. The physical benefits that you will experience that include a reduction in seizures, an improvement in the symptoms of diabetes, or even a cure for diabetes are well aligned to the spiritual benefits cutting across religions that practice fasting across the globe. When it comes to the psychological benefits, the nature of intermittent fasting prompts you to exercise control of your will power and mind by saying not to food during the fasting window even when you're hungry. This produces a great psychological effect. The ability to exercise restraint and ignore hunger when you're hungry is quite powerful.

Intermittent Fasting Supports the Production of the Neuron Growth Hormone

When you go for a couple of hours without food, your body begins to operate on a cycle that ketone-based. As such, there will be an increase in the production of the Brain-Derived Neurotropic Factor (BDNF). This refers to a type of protein that is responsible for promoting neuron growth in the brain. This protein also ensures the protection of the neurons from other kinds of damage.

Intermittent Fasting Enhances Body Building

Let me begin by acknowledging that this has been under dispute for a while. But here is the reality; when you have a brief feeding window, you can only have so many meals that need to meet your daily calorie intake. In most instances, you'll concentrate your calories in 1 or 2 consistent meals. This approach has been received well by many bodybuilders compared to having to distribute this same number of calories in up to six meals in a day. Therefore, although it's true that you need a certain proportion of proteins to maintain your muscle mass, you need to realize that you can maintain your muscle mass with intermittent fasting. An increase in the growth hormone makes after 48 hours of fasting makes it possible to maintain your muscle mass without having to take protein shakes or even eat proteins.

Intermittent Fasting Results in Increased Energy

Although you'll tend to feel sluggish in the initial days of beginning intermittent fasting, your energy levels will not always below. If anything, you'll be surprised how energetic you'll feel because when you fast, your body doesn't rely on the food you're consuming for energy but your energy reserves. This is meant that you'll always feel energetic for a long period.

Intermittent Fasting Helps to Prevent the Onset of Alzheimer's Disease

Alzheimer's disease is the most popular neurodegenerative disease worldwide. Since this disease has no cure, preventing it is very important. According to a study carried out in rats that also practiced intermittent fasting showed that following intermittent fasting is able to delay the development of Alzheimer's disease. In instances where the disease is already showing, intermittent fasting reduced the severity significantly. Various reports corroborate with this suggesting that a lifestyle intervention that entails short term fasting will improve the symptoms of Alzheimer's disease in nine out of ten patients. Studies that have been conducted in animals show that fasting is capable of protecting against various other neurodegenerative diseases that include Parkinson's disease and Huntington's disease. However, this is not conclusive, hence the need for more studies, especially in human beings.

Intermittent Fasting Contributes to Improved Physical Fitness

Intermittent fasting has a great impact on your digestive system. Having a short feeding window encourages the proper digestion of food. This encourages healthy and proportional daily intake of food and

493

calories. As you used to your intermittent fasting routine, you'll hardly experience hunger. Although most people argue that intermittent fasting slows down metabolism, but this is just a misconception. If anything, intermittent fasting enhances your metabolism so that it's flexible since your body is able to run on either glucose or fat energy effectively. What this means is that intermittent fasting will enhance your metabolism.

Intermittent Fasting Will Help in Synchronizing Your Circadian Rhythm as Well as Fight Off Metabolic Diseases

Your circadian rhythm is basically your sleep and wake cycle. That is, this internal and natural system is designed to regulate feelings of wakefulness and sleepiness over 24 hours. According to research, the benefits of following the intermittent fasting lifestyle are that your body is able to adapt to the natural circadian rhythm, which is good for metabolism. Eating just before going to bed has been associated with sleep disturbance as well as weight gain, particularly where it results in acid reflux. This is linked to insulin sensitivity that is really high during the day and low at night—meaning that likely, it's your body that will store most of the glucose consumed at night, leading to weight gain. That's why experts advise that you go to bed early to provide your body with ample time for self-rejuvenation and repair.

Intermittent Fasting Reduces the Risk of Type 2 Diabetes

The Centre for Disease Control (CDC) estimates that 84.1 million people in the United States are pre-diabetic, a condition that, if left uncontrolled, leads to type 2 diabetes. Intermittent fasting plays an important role in preventing/lowering the risk of type 2 diabetes. This is based on the fact that fasting helps in promoting weight loss that usually has an influence on numerous other factors resulting in a high risk of diabetes. When you lose weight, you'll be insulin sensitive. According to a paper published in the Transnational Research, evidence

494

points to the role of intermittent fasting in reducing the level of insulin as well as blood glucose. This paper further concludes that intermittent fasting will not only help in weight loss but also reducing the risk of diabetes. Adults who practiced intermittent fasting recorded a noticeable decline in diabetes markers like insulin sensitivity in those who are overweight and obese. Thus, it's possible to lower the risk of type 2 diabetes in this demographic since the body will be producing insulin frequently. Intermittent fasting plays a major role in restoring the secretion of insulin as well as promote the generation of insulin-producing pancreatic beta cells.

Intermittent Fasting Helps to Fight Off Diseases

When animals are sick, they tend to stop eating until they recover. This is also true for humans. Intermittent fasting is the gateway to your overall well-being since it helps in preventing numerous diseases and medical conditions. Numerous studies have linked intermittent fasting to better overall health. A study published in the World Journal of diabetes has shown that type 2 diabetes patients who practice intermittent fasting on short term experience a reduction in their bodyweight that comes with improved post-meal glucose variability. The other benefits related to this include reduced inflammation, reduced blood pressure, improved glucose circulation, as well as lipid levels that are likely to result in reduced risk of illnesses.

Intermittent Fasting Helps to Improve Physical Fitness

Besides improved mental performance, intermittent fasting also contributed to improved physical performance. Having an extended fasting period and a short feeding window promotes better digestion resulting in a proportional daily calorie and food intake that is healthy. As you get used to intermittent fasting, you'll most certainly experience hunger at the beginning, but as you fast, your metabolism is enhanced, letting your body run on energy from fats and glucose effectively.

Intermittent Fasting Helps to Lose Belly Fat and Weight

Most people struggle with weight management and weight loss; hence, you may have tried numerous diets before you heard about intermittent fasting. Well, intermittent fasting will drive your weight loss because it lowers your insulin levels. Insulin is the hormone that is responsible for enabling cells to take glucose. When you fast, your body will not have access to glucose for energy. However, when the body enters the fasted state, it breaks down carbohydrates and converts them to glucose that the cells use for energy. Alternatively, they convert it into fat that is then stored. Your insulin level dips when you stop consuming food. This decrease in insulin causes cells to find an alternative source of energy. When you fast repeatedly, you begin to experience loss of weight. This is a shift from what diets are designed to do because most diets get you to avoid certain foods, so when you're done with the diet and must now go back to your normal way of eating, you will end up putting on weight again.

Intermittent Fasting Promotes Enhanced Cognitive Power

Intermittent fasting promotes your neuronal functionality that tends to decrease as you advance in age. As you grow old, there will be a decline in the number of your dendritic spine, which are the small membranous protrusions that are found on the neuron of the dendrite. The dendritic spines play an important role that involves the transfer of information between nerve cells. Even then, the decline of these spines as a result of aging seriously affects the efficiency of neural processes. Intermittent fasting helps to prevent the reduction of the density of these spines. Findings from a study carried out in rats showed a 38% decrease in the dendritic spines of rates that were on a normal eating pattern. On the contrary, rats that were on the intermittent fasting did not have a significant difference in their dendritic spines. Instead, these rats had an improved learning ability. The calorie reduction that is a result of intermittent fasting enhances the process of neurogenesis that involves the formation of new brain cells while protecting neurons from death. Additionally, fasting also stimulated the production of the Brain-Derived Neurotropic Factor (BDNF), a protein that is associated with the increase in neurogenesis. This is essential in slowing down neuron degenerations as well as the eventual cell aging. Neurogenesis also promotes functional recovery and healing of any injuries to the spinal cord in animals regardless of whether intermittent fasting is introduced after or before the injury.

Intermittent Fasting Minimizes the Risk of Cancer

Intermittent fasting helps in slowing down the development as well as the progression of malignant tumors. Rats that were transplanted with a cancer cell line and subjected to intermittent fasting survived longer than those that were free-fed. After ten days, half of the rats that were subjected to intermittent fasting were alive. On the contrary, only 12.5% of the rats in the control group survived. In yet another study involving middle ages rats that were introduced to intermittent fasting and put under observation for four months, there was a notable reduction in the incidence of lymphoma. Although 30% of the mice in the control group got ill, none of those that were on intermittent fasting became cancerous. Intermittent fasting also saw a decline in the development of pre-neoplastic liver surgery and liver nodule, which are usually a result of carcinogenic substances. The rats that ate intermittently also had improved antioxidant activity that results in a reduction in the development of the free harmful radicals within mitochondria. It's important to note that the anti-tumor effect is not a product of calorie reduction because both groups consumed an equal amount of calories.

Intermittent Fasting Enhances Better Heart Health

A study that was done among participants who were non-obese to determine the benefits of practicing intermittent fasting. The findings of the study reveal a decline in triglyceride in men. On the other hand, there was an increase in the levels of good HDL cholesterol in women. This change was recorded 22 days after the participants had taken part in the study. This change was mainly associated with a 4% degradation in body fat. There was an even better improvement in people who were obese as they were able to shed off an average of 5.6 kilograms within eight weeks of intermittent fasting. This was translated to a 21% decline in the levels of cholesterol, a 25% decline in the LDL cholesterol levels, and a 32% decrease in the level of triglycerides. In a similar manner, there was a notable drop in the systolic blood pressure from 124mmHg to 116 mmHg. Besides the reduction in body weight, intermittent fasting will also prompt stress resistance that produces a cardioprotective effect. Studies carried out in mice also show that when there is a heart attack, the area that is affected is much smaller in mice that were subject to intermittent fasting compare to the mice that were normally fed. Moreover, four times fewer did heart muscles die in mice that were fed intermittently.

Intermittent Fasting Contributes to Extending Your Lifespan and Longevity

During intermittent fasting, your body experiences calorie restriction as a result of a shortened feeding window and a longer fasting window. Calorie restriction has the potential of increasing your lifespan considerably. Fasting has also been found to increase the lifespan of various organisms that include yeast and worms. While this pattern of eating's main focus is not calorie restriction, intermittent fasting results in reduced calorie consumption by up to 30%. This promotes enhanced insulin sensitivity a decline in the damage of free radicals and damage to the cellular components that include proteins and DNA, a decrease in the blood pressure as well as heart rate, a decline in the incidence of induced as well as spontaneous tumors and improved resistance to neurodegenerative diseases. Intermittent fasting is a great alternative to calorie restriction that produces a similar effect in the extension of your lifespan and on the aging process in general. Young rats that were subjected to fasting recorded a longer lifespan that exceeded their average lifespan by several months. This same effect is experienced in human beings because fasting sends your body into stress as a result of calorie withdrawal. This is followed by the release of chemicals that cushion you from the effects of fasting. It also helps to fix depression and anxiety. These chemicals also help the body to develop resistance to stress that eventually slows down the aging process.

Chapter 5:

Intermittent Fasting and Autophagy

You cannot talk about intermittent fasting without talking about autophagy. So, what is autophagy? Autophagy refers to the process through which the body gets rid of old cells in a process that involves the regeneration of newer, healthier cells. Autophagy is a term that comes from two words: auto, which means self, and phagy, which means to eat. Therefore, autophagy is the process of self-eating—a self-preservation mechanism that allows your body to eliminate any dysfunctional cells even as it recycles some of the parts of these cells in order to facilitate cellular cleaning and repair.

A Belgian scientist, Christian de Duve, was the first person to come up with the term autophagy following a study he was doing on the roles of glucagon and lysosomes in cell degeneration. This was followed by research on autophagy by researchers, with most of them focusing on cellular autophagy. However, the challenge was that there was scanty information on the importance of this process not just to the human body but the overall well-being as well.

Things took a new twist in 1983 when Yoshinori Ohsumi discovered the gene that played an important role in regulating autophagy in yeast. This was a significant breakthrough because he found that the yeast cells that did not have the said gene did not undergo autophagy. Moreover, they could also not go through the regeneration process. This discovery earned Ohsumi a Nobel Prize in 2016. Among the greatest lessons from Ohsumi's discovery is the manner in which cells respond to a deficiency in nutrients, cellular injuries, an increase in the levels of stress as well as deprivation of energy through an increase in the rate of cellular autophagy. However, when stress is eliminated, the process of autophagy goes back to maintenance mode, which is basically the normal rate. There's a need to carry out more studies to have a better understanding of the autophagy process and its anti-aging properties. This is because it is widely believed that by promoting the process of cell regeneration, autophagy has the capacity to increase your lifespan.

The Process of Autophagy

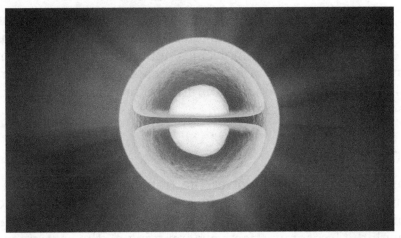

The main goal of the autophagy process is self-regulation and removal of debris, ensuring optimal smooth functioning. This means that it cleans and recycles at the same time. The autophagy process also enhances survival and adaptation as a response to the stressors and toxins that will accumulate inside the cells over time, making them become junky and old, hence requiring a replacement. During this process, both cellular and sub-cellular debris are eliminated. This process occurs when the old cells are sent to the lysosome, which is a special organelle with enzymes that have the ability to degrade proteins. When autophagy takes place, the subcellular parts that are damaged, as well as the unused proteins are isolated for destruction before they can be sent to lysosomes for final processing.

Forms of Autophagy

There are three different types of autophagy—namely, chaperone-mediated autophagy, macroautophagy, and microautophagy. However, the most common of these three is macroautophagy, which is an evolutionary conserved catabolic process involving the formation of vesicles/autophagosomes that engulf macromolecules and cellular organelles.

Chaperone-Mediated Autophagy

In this form of autophagy, the cell makes use of chaperone proteins such as Hsc-70 found in the lysosomal membrane. These proteins will bind on the unwanted protein molecules found in the cell, forming a chaperone complex/substrate. This molecule will then attach onto the wall of the lysosome, making room for the protein molecules to enter the lysosome for disintegration.

Macro-Autophagy

This autophagy process involves the transportation of all the waste material inside a cell via an autophagosome, which is basically a double membrane-bound vesicle into the lysosome. The autophagosome then fuses with the lysosome, effectively emptying all the content and thus creating room for the processing of the waste materials.

Micro-Autophagy

During micro-autophagy, cellular waste, which is supposed to be digested, is wiped out by the lysosomes either by developing cellular protrusions or through the inward folding of a part of the lysosomal membrane.

Although the mechanism is different, the three autophagy processes involve non-selective as well as selective degradation methods that are reliant on organelles or molecules that need to be broken down or recycled. Eventually, each of the cellular components that need to be degraded is mopped from the lysosome, followed by conversion into micro molecules such as glucose, fatty acids, nucleotides, and amino acids. The cell reuses these micro molecules to form larger molecules and new organelles. Such autophagy processes rejuvenate your body's cells, making you feel better, younger, and healthier.

What Does It Take to Activate Autophagy?

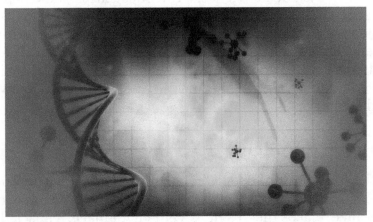

Although everyone wants to tap into the benefits of autophagy, especially longevity, you need to know that not all forms of intermittent fasting are able to activate autophagy. In fact, autophagy is not activated the moment you begin intermittent fasting. It kicks in after hours of fasting. To be more precise, autophagy is mainly activated by nutrient deprivation along with numerous other factors such as your level of activity and the percentage of your body fat. Principally, autophagy depends on the effort you're willing to put in so as to get your body to activate autophagy. Whenever the level of nutrients such as amino acids, glucose, and calories are low, this necessitates autophagy. The reason for this is simple; the body is not motivated to seek alternative energy from alternative sources like body tissues and fat stores. Even then, this can happen under the right conditions. When the body has sufficient nutrients, AMPK and mTOR receive the signal. These cells decide whether they will promote growth or simply switch to intermittent fasting. Other factors that have an impact on autophagy include growth factors such as IGF-1, mechanical muscle stimuli, and insulin.

In general, you need to fast for between 48 to 72 hours in order to activate autophagy. Incidentally, this is the time it also takes for the body to undergo ketosis, where it produces ketones. Although there's no proper way of determining the rate of autophagy, especially in humans, it can be estimated by looking at the glucose ketone index as well as the insulin to glucose ratio. When this ratio is low, various things happen, which include ketogenesis, gluconeogenesis, fat oxidation, and the breakdown of nutrients. The duration needed for autophagy to kick will be determined by your body nutrients, glucose, amino acids, and the presence of nutrients in your ketones. This means that if your body is conditioned not to consume excess fat and protein daily, it will be faster to enter autophagy than someone who has to burn many calories in the initial stages.

Benefits of Autophagy

One of the reasons why people can't stop talking about autophagy is because of the numerous benefits it offers. As various metabolic activities take place, the result is cellular damage, especially to the human body. The rate of the occurrence of cellular damage is aggravated by a poor diet, exposure to radiation, and stress, among other things. Thus, autophagy helps to clean out the old and damaged cells that are no longer active. This process helps to purge the body from pathogens that cause diseases. It also gives rise to a number of benefits that include the following:

Decreases the Risk of Cell Death

In certain instances, the cells in your body may be degraded so much that they can longer be regenerated or replaced, and the only option left is cell death that is also referred to as apoptosis. This is not good because the cells that are spared when cell death occurs are usually irreparable, so losing them means a total loss. Autophagy comes in to prevent such a scenario as well as prevent diseases that are associated with cell death.

Extends Lifespan

While there are a number of techniques and methods that guarantee you an improvement of health along with other benefits, autophagy is the most outstanding in this respect. Since cells are the building blocks of life and autophagy plays a critical role in eliminating waste from the cells, the removal of substances that are perceived to be toxic will help to promote the cell metabolic efficiency. The cellular regeneration and degeneration that is triggered by autophagy will help you in staying more youthful than you are. This is especially great for your skin that is often exposed to harsh elements and pollutants, resulting in wrinkles as well as a decline in your skin quality.

Regulates Inflammation

The process of autophagy can either improve or minimize your immune response by preventing or promoting inflammation. When there is an invade, autophagy will boost inflammation by alerting your immune system to attack. It can also decrease inflammation by eliminating all the signals that trigger it.

Improves Your Skin

The skin is the largest organ in the body, but it is prone to damage from various factors like air pollution, adverse weather, chemicals, sunshine, heat, and light, among other things. These make it grow old faster. When autophagy is activated, it helps in the replacement of the old cells with new ones while at the same time repairing the old cells. This is good, as the skin cells contribute to getting rid of bacteria that infiltrate the body; hence, you have to energize them for them to be active.

Helps to Improve Metabolism

Autophagy helps in boosting your body's metabolism. This is achieved through the regeneration and replacement of the important cells that are related to your metabolism, like mitochondria. This affects the performance of your muscles, effectively promoting the development of your muscle mass and the growth of your cells. This also prevents any stress that is linked to injuries to the muscles.

Protects from Neurodegenerative Disorders

Autophagy plays an important role in the prevention of the onset of some of the neurodegenerative diseases like Alzheimer's diseases, Parkinson's disease, and dementia, among others. These diseases are known to thrive with an accumulation of old and toxic neurons that pile in specific areas in the brain before they begin spreading to the surrounding areas. This means that autophagy has the capability of replacing parts of the useless neuron before they regenerate new ones.

Combats Infectious Diseases

Autophagy helps to swing your immune system into action. This process can help to eliminate some microbes like mycobacterium tuberculosis as well as other deadly viruses such as HIV from your body cells. Autophagy will take care of the toxins that come about because of the infections.

Helps to Strengthen the Immunity System

When activated, autophagy helps in keeping your body from possible infections through the removal of toxins from the cells. This process is also responsible for the destruction of harmful microbes through the promotion of inflammation on the cells and fighting diseases. Cellular inflammation will enhance the immune system of the cells when there is an impending attack from various diseases. Autophagy prompts inflammation by making the proteins to work actively by starving them of nutrients. This initiates a requisite immune response that fights diseases and infections.

Prevents the Onset of Cancer

One of the reasons why autophagy continues to draw the attention of the medical world is because of its ability to prevent the onset of cancer. Autophagy has been found to inhibit or prevent the development of early stages of cancer. This is linked to the fact that cancer is a disease that results from cellular disorders. Thus, the process of autophagy helps to prevent such disorders through the regulation of damage response that is caused by the promotion of cellular inflammation, DNA, and regulation of genome instability.

Helps the Body to Deal with Stress

The process of autophagy has been found to be helpful in the treatment as well as prevention of some psychiatric conditions such as depression and schizophrenia.

Despite all the benefits discussed above, you must keep in mind that autophagy also presents a number of negative side effects, for instance, it could provide a conducive atmosphere for certain bacteria such as Brucella, Coxiella, and Bartonella to not only divide but also multiply. When this happens, you'll end up with an overgrowth of bacteria. Moreover, recent studies have cast doubt on the ability of autophagy to hinder the multiplication of cancer cells. The studies suggest that autophagy could, in fact, promote the multiplication of cancer, causing cells. As such, autophagy is seen as a strong preventative measure as opposed to a treatment.

Chapter 6:

Intermittent Fasting for Women

The female body responds to calorie deprivation differently than the male body. As such, women who practice intermittent fasting experience a host of changes in their bodies. These changes are linked to hormonal imbalance, and they include missed menstrual periods, metabolic disturbances, and for some, menopause that kicks in early. In this chapter, we take a closer look at intermittent fasting in women and what women need to do to minimize the undesirable effects.

Effects of Intermittent Fasting in Women

Women must approach intermittent fasting with caution because failure to do so can result in adverse effects. A woman's body is extremely sensitive to the signals of starvation. This means whenever the body senses starvation, it'll raise the production of the two hunger hormones known as leptin and ghrelin. Consequently, when women experience hunger, it's actually because of the increased production of hunger hormones. This is a survival mechanism for the female body as it seeks to offer protection for a potential fetus. This will happen even when you're not pregnant.

On the other hand, restricting calories could also result in the inhibition of the production of female sex hormones. This can lead to infertility in some women, while others could experience irregular periods, halted ovulation, and hormonal imbalances. This could affect your menstruation and eventually cause the ovaries to shrink. Some women who practice intermittent fasting may also end up with disordered eating manifesting through eating disorders such as anorexia and binge eating.

Because of all these reasons, women who desire to practice intermittent fasting mist not focus on calorie restriction but the health and wellness angle. Otherwise, you will end up with a number of changes that you cannot bear and can hamper the normal optimal functioning of your body. Some of the common changes you can expect when you take on intermittent fasting include the following:

Hormonal Imbalance

It's not unusual for women who are practicing intermittent fasting for the first time to experience hormonal imbalances. After all, women are at one point or the other experiencing hormonal imbalances. Even then, you must keep in mind that when you introduce intermittent fasting, this could evolve to issues associated with genetics. Some of the concerns associated with hormonal imbalance during intermittent fasting include the irregular length of the menstrual period, irregular menstruation, irregular strength of your flow, and blemishes that are difficult to clear as well as changes in the color of your skin.

Emotional Instability

Hormonal imbalance comes along with emotional instability. You may experience periods of excitement, followed by periods of sadness. However, this doesn't go on for long and should ease up as you get used to your intermittent fasting schedule.

Excessive Fatigue

A reduction in the number of calories you consume on a given day comes with two most pronounced side effects that are fatigue and muscle weakness. These effects are compounded by the fact that the female body mostly depends on glucose from food than stored fat for energy. While these effects will be minimal as time goes by and even disappear, they make the adaptation as well as transition to intermittent fasting somewhat difficult.

How to Practice Intermittent Fasting Safely as a Woman

Despite the changes that you're bound to go through when practicing intermittent fasting, you can still come up with a safer way of doing intermittent fasting to minimize the negative effects and get the most out of practice. Here are some guidelines to help you practice intermittent fasting safely as a woman:

Start Slowly and Adjust Accordingly

Regardless of the intermittent fasting plan that you decide to start with, make sure that start slowly and gradually increases the hours of fasting as your body gets used to it. You can begin by limiting your consumption of carbs and instead focus on foods that are high in healthy fat and proteins.

Assess Your Levels of Stress

Fasting puts stress on your body with the potential of causing negative effects. Therefore, when you notice some adverse signs of hormonal imbalance at the beginning of intermittent fasting, make a point of stopping or modifying your intermittent fasting plan. Modifying your plan could mean increasing your feeding window as you shorten the fasting window.

Eat Fewer Calories

If you're embracing intermittent fasting in order to shed off some weight, you need to make sure that your overall calorie consumption is less than what you need to maintain your current weight. This will help you to shed off excessive weight.

Overall, women who follow a shorted fasting window of between 12 and 14 hours have reported better results.

Benefits of Intermittent Fasting for Women

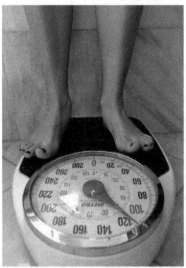

One of the most common benefits of intermittent fasting among women is weight loss. However, women who practice intermittent fasting enjoy numerous other benefits that include the following:

Improved Metabolic Health

Postmenopausal women have a high risk of experiencing cardiovascular diseases. This is attributed to the increase in LDL cholesterol, belly fats as well as high triglyceride levels. High levels of insulin and glucose are also considered to have an impact. Studies show that women who fast have a notable improvement in their metabolic health as these symptoms lessen, thereby removing the risk of cardiovascular diseases.

Reproductive Health Benefits

Various studies have associated intermittent fasting for women to reproductive health benefits. Several health conditions relating to endocrine dysfunction in women, such as Polycystic ovarian syndrome (PCOS), obesity, and metabolic syndrome, could be improved by practicing intermittent fasting. One study carried out among women who had polycystic ovarian syndrome established that there was a decrease in stress neurohormone levels, which had a positive effect on mental and physical health. Yet another study found that short term restriction of calories resulted in an increase in the luteinizing hormone, particularly in women who had PCOS. This hormone is produced in the pituitary glance and plays an important role in ensuring healthy patterns of ovulation. This is suitable, taking into account hormone balancing, as it's also a fertility marker.

Mental Health Benefits

Statistics from the World Health Organization (WHO) indicate that women have a higher percentage of mental health disorders, particularly depression and stress. One of the reasons for this trend is that the major stressor is food. The outer appearance and weight have been made to look like something that one needs to fix constantly. Unfortunately, this also affects how women feel about themselves, thus creating so many insecurities. Intermittent fasting will help you to tap into the inherent health and simplify the mental burden, so you don't have to think about what to eat. It will also help you to address hormonal instability during menopause that has been associated with emotional pressure tension, depression, and anxiety. Intermittent fasting will help to improve your self-esteem and mental status, reduce anxiety and depression, and promote social functioning.

Musculoskeletal Health Benefits

Chronic pain disorders tend to be on the rise in women who are in their 40s. They include osteoporosis, arthritis, chronic back pain, and fibromyalgia, among others. Intermittent fasting helps in supporting musculoskeletal conditions in women. One study showed the effect of the parathyroid hormone in improving bone health as well as cases of rheumatoid arthritis. Fasting will also improve the symptoms of intestinal permeability that effectively leads to decreased food intolerance. This also results in a reduction in the inflammatory markers as well as the prevention of the vicious circle of inflammation that includes rheumatoid arthritis. Weight loss from intermittent fasting will also support musculoskeletal health since fasting supports the normalization of hormones that determine your weight; thus, fasting is a great way of remedying musculoskeletal health.

The other benefits of intermittent fasting include more energy, sustainable weight loss, an increase in the lean muscle mass, reduced inflammation, reduced oxidative stress, an increase in cell stress response, an increase in the production of neurotrophic growth factors and improved insulin sensitivity. Intermittent fasting is an excellent way of making lifestyle changes to your eating pattern as well as taking charge of your health. This makes it ideal for women who have struggled with weight loss and other related issues for long.

Disadvantages of Intermittent Fasting for Women

In spite of all the benefits discussed above, intermittent fasting also presents a number of disadvantages in different categories of women. Some of the disadvantages of intermittent fasting include the following:

- Some women find it difficult to sleep because of the hormonal imbalance resulting from fasting.

- You may end up experiencing fertility issues. This is why it is important that you stop intermittent fasting whenever you experience something that is out of the ordinary.

- For some women, the ovaries could shrink, and this can be a huge disadvantage, especially in women of childbearing age.

- You could also experience metabolic stress, irregular periods, and anxiety—all of which are a cause for concern.

- Since hormones are mostly interconnected in the functionality, destabilizing one hormone is likely to have a negative effect on all the other hormones. This should not be a reason to give up intermittent fasting. Rather, you can use fasting to complement a healthy diet and lifestyle.

Intermittent Fasting in Post-Menopausal Women

Menopause is not often a great time for most women because of the host of changes that they experience that are out of their control. This includes hot flashes, mood swings, cravings, interrupted sleep, and low self-esteem, among others. For most women dealing with some of these symptoms can be extremely overwhelming. However, studies point to intermittent fasting to be a great solution that is producing great results. For instance, women who are post-menopausal have been shown to lose twice as much weight as women who are yet to attain menopause. This is linked to better diet adherence. According to these findings, intermittent fasting is seen as being beneficial for women who have already attained menopause.

Intermittent fasting is a great solution to losing belly fat and the prevention of weight gain both during and post-menopause. Fasting intermittently will also help to lower the risk of diabetes by reducing blood cholesterol and blood pressure while enhancing insulin resistance. Even then, you need also to understand that the fact that intermittent fasting may have worked for someone else doesn't mean that it will also work for you. The reason for this is simple. Different people will respond differently to different intermittent fasting methods. Therefore, it's up to you to identify the intermittent fasting method that suits you in terms of your needs and lifestyle. Remember, your body is highly sensitive to changes during menopause. Therefore, consider getting into intermittent fasting gradually so that you get used to your fasting window until you get comfortable as opposed to starting with fasting for long hours. You can also test to determine if taking fluids only during your fasting window will increase or ease your menopause symptoms. Should you notice that the symptoms are increasing, then you must stop right away, take a break before you consider trying another intermittent fasting method. Here are some tips for getting into intermittent fasting after menopause safely:

- Begin by fasting for 12 hours and a feeding period of 12 hours.

- Increase the fasting window gradually as you get comfortable until you get to fast for 16 hours with a feeding window of 4 hours.

- Avoid the temptation of extreme fasting beyond the 16-hour window.

  - Make sure you're well-hydrated by consuming a lot of fluids that are free of calories when fasting.

  - You can introduce gentle exercises as you pay attention to the way your body will respond.

How Intermittent Fasting Affects Fertility

Various studies done in worms and mice suggest that intermittent fasting is able to help in extending fertility in women. This is based on the understanding that when you restrict the consumption of food, the quality of eggs improves a great deal. This is because both the quantity and quality of eggs is linked to aging. A study conducted in adult female mice found that was under intermittent fasting found that the eggs from the mice that experienced calorie restriction were more likely to develop into fertilized embryos. Research also shows that as little as a 5 to 10 percent drop in weight has significant benefits in the improvement of psychological outcomes, reproductive features, and metabolic features.

Chapter 7:

Foods and Drinks Included in the Intermittent Fasting Plan

Unlike most diets that are specific about the types of food you should eat and in what proportion, intermittent fasting takes a different approach—that is, it's not strict on the foods you should eat; rather, you're free to eat whatever you want, but it emphasizes clean eating. The reason for this is simple; if you are battling weight, chances are it took time to get to where you are. Therefore, in the same manner, it'll take time before you shake off the excessive weight. This means that the fact that you're fasting doesn't mean that you can throw down some junk food when the feeding window comes and expect to get results.

Foods to Eat During Intermittent Fasting

Intermittent fasting eventually results in the form of calorie restriction because of the shortened feeding duration. I mean, you can only eat so much. As such, if you don't plan your meals well, chances are you'll end up being nutrient deficient. Therefore, it is imperative that you make the right food choices so that you get enough nutrients and keep your blood sugar stable. If you don't know what foods you can eat and drink, you can get some inspiration from the following:

Minimally Processed Grains

Most diets will omit carbohydrates because they are responsible for weight gain. Well, it's important to perceive the importance of carbohydrates as part of your nutrition and not an enemy for your ambition to lose weight. The fact that you spent most of the hours fasting, you must be strategic when it comes to getting your calories without being too full. You can consider including minimally processed grains as these are a quick source of fuel because they can be digested fast. Minimally processed grains are particularly great if you like to train because you get energy almost instantly.

Raspberries

The fact that you're fasting means that you need foods that are high in fiber to help in maintaining regular bowel movement as well as help you to feel fuller for longer. Interestingly, most dietary guidelines miss out on this. It has been observed that less than 10% of western populations consume sufficient amounts of whole fruits. Raspberries are a great choice when you're fasting because they're high in fiber. A single cup of raspberries will give you about 8 grams of fiber that is able to carry you through your fasting window.

Wild-Caught Salmon

This fish is mostly consumed across the blue zones of the five regions of Latin America, Asia, Europe, and the U.S. that are known for dietary and lifestyle choices that are linked to extreme longevity. Wild-caught salmon contains high levels of omega 3 fatty acids EPA and DHA that are also great in boosting cognitive abilities.

Seitan

It's a good idea that you incorporate plant-based proteins into your diet like seitan. This protein offers you amazing anti-aging properties in your diet to complement your intermittent fasting. This is a good alternative considering the recommendation by the EAT-Lancet commission that you should consume animal proteins in smaller quantities. In fact, red meat has been linked to an increase in mortality. Seitan offers the versatility of preparation as you can dip it, bake it, or even batter it in your favorite sauces.

Hummus

This is another great source of plant protein that will greatly boost your nutritional value of certain staples like sandwiches. Although you can take the adventurous path and make your own, the secret to the best recipe is ample garlic, as well as tahini.

Soybeans

Soybeans are not only a great choice because they help you stay fuller for longer but also have anti-aging properties. They contain an active compound known as isoflavones, which promote anti-aging, in addition to having the ability to hinder UVB induced cell damage. Including soybeans in your meals during intermittent fasting will certainly compliment the benefits you derive from the autophagy process.

Potatoes

Potatoes compare to bread by the mere fact that they are easy to digest with very little effort. Potatoes also make a perfect post work out snack when you pair them with a great source of protein because you can be sure to refuel the muscles better. One other factor that makes potatoes a great choice is because when cooled, potatoes go on to form a resistant starch that it plays a crucial role in fueling the good bacteria that is found in the gut.

Lentils

This is another excellent source of plant proteins that are also packed with fiber. Lentils can give you at least 32% of your daily recommended fiber intake. Additionally, lentils are also a great source of iron, taking up at about 15% of your daily needs. This is especially great for women who are active and are practicing intermittent fasting.

Milk-Fortified with Vitamin D

An average adult should take at least 1,000 milligrams of calcium per day. This translated to about 3 cups of milk daily. When you practice intermittent fasting, the short feeding window means a reduced opportunity to take as much milk as you should. This means that you must make a point of prioritizing your consumption of foods that are rich in calcium. Milk fortified with vitamin D is an excellent choice because it will enhance the consumption of calcium, thereby helping to keep your bones strong. You can add milk to smoothies and cereal or simply take it along with your meals.

Multivitamins

The fact that your nutrition during intermittent fasting is based on the amount of time you have to eat means you must make extremely good choices and opt for healthy meal considerations. This will help to avoid vitamin deficiencies that may be a result of shorter feeding hours. Therefore, make sure you include plenty of fruits and vegetables so that you have a sufficient intake of vitamins.

Other Food Options

There are many other food options that you can include in your diet during intermittent fasting. They include olives, blueberries, papaya, nuts, ghee, avocado, cruciferous vegetables, eggs, probiotics, and whole grains, among others. Most importantly, before making any changes to your diet significantly, it's important that you speak with a nutritionist or a health professional to make sure you're making the right strides.

Drinks to Take During Intermittent Fasting

One of the fears of most people who want to adopt the intermittent fasting lifestyle having to go for long hours without food and drink. Even then, intermittent fasting is quite flexible because you can be able to drink up fluids that do not contain any calories throughout the fasting window. Here are some of the drinks that you are allowed to take throughout your intermittent fasting period:

Black Coffee

There's a common misconception that taking coffee during intermittent fasting will break your fast. This is not true. In fact, studies have shown that consuming caffeine when you're fasting will actually increase your metabolism that will promote the loss of weight. Black coffee is also known to help in suppressing appetite, making it a great choice because it will help you to get through your fast and make it more manageable. However, you must not add any syrups, candied flavorings, or even cream, as all these have the potential of breaking your fast because they contain calories. Most importantly, you should also not go overboard with the coffee because taking too much coffee will make you feel weak, jittery, and anxious, especially when you're sensitive to caffeine. Moreover, too much coffee may also interrupt your sleep patterns and the quality of your sleep. Remember, taking coffee on an empty stomach will result in fast assimilation into the bloodstream compared to taking coffee alongside meals. Thus, you can limit your intake to about two cups that is equivalent to 400mg of caffeine.

Water

Staying well-hydrated is important when you need to maintain a healthy system. Drinking water does in no way break your fast. In fact, water is one of the best drinks you can take when fasting because it is full of minerals that are important in the restoration of electrolyte and mineral balance. When you abstain from food for 12-16 hours, your body will turn to the glycogen that is stored in the liver. Moreover, you'll also lose a lot of fluid and electrolytes as the stored energy is being broken down into glucose. This means that drinking 8 glasses of water shall promote the smooth flow of blood and cognition while preventing dehydration. Taking water also goes a long way in promoting your joint and muscle support. Ideally, you should drink at least half of your body weight but in terms of ounces. This is in addition to the other beverages that you'll be consuming. Taking water also helps you to deal with hunger as it helps you feel full, making it a lot easier to follow your intermittent fasting protocol to the latter with little or no struggle. Taking water will also help in lubricating joints, promote proper bowel movement, and regulate your body temperature. Water also plays a crucial role in transporting oxygen and other nutrients to your cells while at the same time flushing out waste. You can take flavored, plain or carbonated water as long as it's not sweetened. Taking plain water is not usually easy, so you can consider carbonated or flavored water. However, pay attention to the labels on the water just to be sure that it has not been sweetened. Remember, even non-calorie sweeteners like stevia will kick-start your craving for sugar, which will make it difficult for you to stick to your intermittent fasting plan.

Apple Cider Vinegar

Diluting a small portion of apple cider vinegar in the water will certainly not break your fast. A study that was published in the Journal of Medicinal Food established that apple cider vinegar is able to promote positive metabolic change that helps in promoting weight loss. Taking apple cider vinegar every day will also contribute to a reduction in your total cholesterol, triglycerides, and LDL levels. This is in addition to lowering your blood sugar levels and improving the digestion process. Even then, avoid the temptation of taking undiluted apple cider vinegar because the acetic acid in it is potent and could damage your teeth's caramel.

Tea

Just like coffee, taking tea when you're on an intermittent fast won't break your fast. In fact, tea is a great choice of beverage to take when fasting as long as you don't sweeten with sugar or other sweeteners. You should also not add cream. You can try different variations of tea, such as green tea that is packed with powerful antioxidants that will help in burning calories. Other alternatives to tea include chamomile tea, purple tea, and herbal tea, among others. While taking unsweetened tea may be difficult in the beginning, it will get better over time. You will be surprised that this can eventually become a part of your lifestyle.

There are certain drinks that you should avoid taking during intermittent fasting because even though they may seem to be calorie-free, they will break your fast. A good example is diet soda because it doesn't have any carbohydrates, sugar, or calories. Diet soda may appeal to you as a perfect alternative to taking water, but it's packed with artificial sweeteners that can increase your craving for sugar as well as insulin resistance. This will eventually increase your risk of developing diabetes, making it even more difficult to achieve weight loss. You should also avoid taking all kinds of juices during intermittent fasting because they contain sugar, vitamins, and minerals that will break your fast. However, you may take juices during your feeding window. Alcohol is also a no go zone when you're fasting because it will be absorbed in your bloodstream quickly, given that you will have abstained from food for several hours. As a result, you could end up with dehydration and increased intoxication.

Chapter 8:
Potential Risk of Intermittent Fasting

Many people, including celebrities, swear by intermittent fasting obviously because of the many benefits that it offers. However, this eating pattern can pose certain risks when not followed properly or when followed by individuals who shouldn't like expectant women, nursing mothers, people below the age of 18, and those who have previously battled eating disorders. Besides, it has also been argued that most of the studies on intermittent fasting have been done on animals, hence the need for more studies in human beings to validate those studies.

If you're going to practice intermittent fasting and are taking medications, you must begin by consulting the doctor. You need to be certain that fasting will in no way interfere with the effectiveness of your medication. Moreover, if you're the kind of person who has a tight schedule, you must give yourself time to get used to intermittent fasting by beginning with a few hours of fasting while you extend your fasting window gradually. Most importantly, make sure you stick to a nutritious diet and while staying well-hydrated.

The impact of intermittent fasting on your lifestyle cannot be underestimated. However, most people don't stop to think about the potential risks of intermittent fasting before getting into it, yet these risks have a huge impact on whether you will succeed with intermittent fasting or not. Although it is argued that you can easily make intermittent fasting a part of your lifestyle, this can apply to certain intermittent fasting methods. In fact, one of the issues that keep on coming up about intermittent fasting is sustainability.

While most people feel good following an intermittent fasting lifestyle, it becomes a struggle when you have to stick with it in the long term. This is particularly tricky when you have to fit the eating and fasting cycles in your social and work life. This is especially difficult if you have to work for long hours, go to bed late and wake up early. It's equally difficult if your schedule lacks consistency because you will end up being frustrated for not being able to keep up. For some people, it may be that you just jumped into the intermittent fasting bandwagon without proper preparation, so you end up with a mind-body disconnect making it difficult to establish an overall healthy diet in the long term.

That is why it is important that you begin by talking to your physician before you can begin following any of the intermittent fasting patterns. People who have health complications, an existing medical condition, or are over 65 are more susceptible to the risks of intermittent fasting. If you're taking any medication, you also need to choose an intermittent fasting pattern that is built around the time when you eat. Some of the potential risks of intermittent fasting include the following:

You Might Overeat

Most people fall for the temptation of overeating on their non-fasting days. This is dangerous because you will most likely end up with a net calorie surplus that will result in weight gain. The challenge could be that fasting will trigger binge eating. A study carried out in 2015 found that intermittent fasting increased the levels of the stress hormone known as cortisol. This eventually results in an increase in cravings. If you're used to eating three meals practicing intermittent fasting can cause stress. This is bad for a stress eater, make sure you engage in activities that lower your cortisol levels like listening to music or meditating. You also must make sure you fill up nutritious and satiating foods.

You Might Feel Lethargic

Don't be surprised when you start feeling groggy when you start intermittent fasting for the first time. The reason for this is simple. When you fast and have lesser hours of feeding, your body will be running on less energy, making you feel tired. Additionally, since fasting can boost stress levels, it is also likely to disrupt your sleep patterns. To counter this, avoid doing too many activities or even try meditating. If you follow a regular fitness routine, you need to schedule your workouts to the times when you get to eat. This makes it possible to have a pre and post work out meal. Besides, working out when fasting may result in low blood sugar levels with symptoms like confusion and dizziness in addition to putting you at risk of injuries.

You Might Be Dehydrated

The thing about intermittent fasting is that when you stop eating during the fasting window, you might also be unable to remember about drinking up. When you forget to drink water, you will end up being dehydrated. This may be interpreted as hunger so much so that you end up giving in to the cravings.

You Might Feel Hungry

When you set out to do intermittent fasting, you will notice that your stomach will start grumbling after the first few hours of fasting because your body is used to being fed after a few hours. However, you can take action to keep hunger in check so that you don't interfere with your intermittent fasting plan. Among the things you can do is avoid the thought or even smell of food that is likely to trigger the production of gastric acid in the stomach, making you feel hungry. You can consider finding various distractions, such as reading a book or getting involved in an activity that is mentally engaging. Taking water and beverages that do not contain calories will also fill your stomach, making you pull through the fasting window.

The other way to deal with hunger pangs is making sure that you take advantage of your eating periods by opting for a diet that is nutritionally balanced. This includes food laden with fiber to keep you feeling full for longer, as well as protein and healthy fats. Above all, start slow. You can begin intermittent fasting for a week and see how well it blends into your schedule as well as how your body responds as well as how well your fasting schedule fits into your lifestyle. Ultimately, you need to find what works for you.

You Might Feel Irritable

The hormones that regulate your appetite are also responsible for regulating your mood. Your nutrient consumption affects the activity levels of your neurotransmitters like serotonin and dopamine that play a role in both depression and anxiety. This means that dysregulating your appetite could turn your mood around. You will do well to stick to a diet that is not only nutritionally balanced but also satiating during your feasting window. You should also ensure you're getting enough sleep because it is also linked to your mood.

You Might Feel Cold

When you fast, the flow of blood to your fat stores will tend to increase. Consequently, your blood sugar levels will begin to decrease so that you're more sensitive to feeling cold, especially your hands and toes. This is a common feeling; however, you need to make sure you dress properly.

Your Might Have Constipation, Heartburn, and Bloating

The stomach produces acid that is very important to the digestion process. This means that you could experience heartburn when this acid is released, and you're not eating. As a result, you could experience some discomfort and burping. To avoid this, make sure you take adequate water while avoiding foods that are greasy and spicy.

You Might Have Headaches

Failing to sufficiently hydrated when you're doing intermittent fasting may result in headaches. Therefore, always make sure that you're drinking up enough water as other non-caloric fluids, whether you're within your fasting or feasting window.

You Might Have Cravings

When you go for extended periods without food, you could begin to have cravings for processed carbohydrates and sweet foods because your body needs glucose to keep you going.

You Might Have Poor Weight Management

When you practice intermittent fasting, it's unlikely that you will be able to manage your weight properly. This is because you could have cravings for certain calories that you may end up overindulging when it's time to eat. This will eventually be counterproductive to your intermittent fasting efforts.

Long-Term Downsides

When you fast for extended durations, your immune system may be compromised, eventually affecting your vital organs like the kidneys and liver. When you stay for long before eating, you may end up with malnourishment that can end up in untimely death when not checked. Overall, you should expect your body to react to withdrawal or abstaining from eating. While you will get used to the short term effects such as outbursts, weakness, dizziness, and low blood pressure, make sure you don't overlook serious intermittent fasting risks.

Chapter 9:

What Is Keto Diet?

The ketogenic diet refers to a diet that emphasizes on taking low carbs and high fats ostensibly to gain many health benefits. Several studies have shown that this diet is able to help you to lose weight, thus improving your health. The ketogenic diet is based on the fact that when you withhold carbohydrates, your body will be forced to turn to an alternative source of energy by burning fuel that is stored in the form of fat, thus promoting weight loss. When you eat foods that are high in carbohydrates, your body will convert the carbs into blood sugar or glucose that is then used as energy. Since glucose is the simplest form of energy that the body uses, it is always used even before your body can turn to the stored fats for fuel.

Therefore, when you go on a ketogenic diet, the idea is to restrict the consumption of carbohydrates so that the body has no choice but to break down the stored fat to obtain energy. When this happens, the fat is usually broken down within the liver, thus producing ketones that are by-products of metabolic processes. These ketones will then be used where there is no glucose as a source of energy. This process is known as ketosis. When ketosis takes place, your body will become efficient in burning fat as a source of energy that is supplied to the brain; Ketogenic diets are capable of causing massive reductions in insulin and blood sugar levels thus bringing along numerous health benefits.

How Does the Ketogenic Diet Work?

To understand how the ketogenic diet works, it is important to begin by understanding the fat-burning mechanism behind this diet. Generally speaking, the ketogenic diet pegged on the idea of getting your body into ketosis so as to maximize fat loss. Ketosis is a normal metabolic process that takes place whenever the body does not have enough glucose stores for energy. Whenever these stores are depleted, your body will tune to burning fat as a source of energy. It is during this process that acids referred to as ketones are produced that then build up in the body for use as energy. How then can you tell if you're in ketosis? One of the ways of determining whether you are in a state of ketosis is by looking at your urine to see if there are any ketones. You can do a quick test using ketone strips that are available at retail stores. If a ketone strip does test positive for ketones, then it means that you are in a state of ketosis.

However, most people try to link the high presence of ketones to a diabetic medical emergency that is referred to as ketoacidosis. It is important to keep in mind that the nutritional ketosis that is linked to a ketogenic diet is quite different from ketoacidosis. Why is this a major concern? A rapid increase in the ketone levels in people who have diabetes may signal a health crisis that must be attended to immediately. When the insulin hormone is not sufficient, the body is unable to use the glucose that is available for fuel. Thus, the body will turn to burn stored fat for energy through the ketosis process. This leads to the building up of ketones in the body. When these ketones accumulate in the bloodstream of a person living with diabetes, the blood becomes more acidic, hence ketoacidosis. This condition can be potentially fatal and thus should be treated immediately.

How Can Keto Help People with Type 2 Diabetes

Diabetes is a medical condition that is characterized by high blood pressure, impaired insulin function, and changes in metabolism. The ketogenic diet has been found to help in losing excess fat that is closely correlated to type 2 diabetes, metabolic syndrome, and diabetes. A study conducted on the effects of the keto diet on diabetes showed this diet contributed to improved insulin sensitivity by up to 75%. Another study with 21 participants with type 2 diabetes followed the ketogenic diet, and 7 were able to stop using medications for diabetes. In yet another research, those who followed the keto diet lost 24.4 pounds compared to 15.2 pounds lost by those who were on a high-carb diet. Furthermore, 95.2% of these participants stopped or reduced the use of diabetes medication.

The fact that the ketogenic diet is based on cutting consumptions of carbs, it's commonly used in controlling blood sugar. In fact, this diet has become quite popular among people who have type 2 diabetes and are looking to lower their A1C. That is the average measurement of their blood sugar levels over a period of two to three months. According to research, the ketogenic diet could lead to fast weight loss as well as potentially low blood sugar for people who have the disease. However, dieticians also warn that the ketogenic diet also presents a number of risks, particularly among those people who are living with and managing diabetes. These include potential low blood sugar as well as possible drug interactions if you're on medication. In some cases, it could also result in kidney damage, especially in those people who have dysfunctional kidneys because of an elevated amount of ketones in the bloodstream. If you want to try the ketogenic diet while managing diabetes, it is important that you do so after consulting your healthcare provider, so make sure that it's safe and effective.

Types of Ketogenic Diet

The ketogenic diet can be practiced in different variations even though only two of these have been studied extensively. The four different kinds of intermittent fasting are:

The Standard Ketogenic Diet (SKD)

This type of ketogenic diet is targeted for weight loss, healing disease, as well as therapeutic purposes. When following this plan, you will plan all your snacks and meals around fat, such as olive oil, olives, meats, fatty fish, ghee, butter, and avocados. Overall, you must get at least 150 grams of fat per day to be able to shift your metabolism so that your body can get to burn fat as fuel. You will also need to cut on your carbs from 300 grams daily to not more than 50 grams. This essentially means you will have to stick to non-starchy veggies, leafy vegetables/greens, as well as low-carb fruits like melon and berries. You will also have to eat moderate proteins that are about 90 grams daily or portion it to 30 grams per meal.

The Targeted Ketogenic Diet (TKD)

This type of ketogenic diet is designed for those who want increased work outperformance because it is holistic. As such, this form of the ketogenic diet is quite popular among athletes as well as individuals who are active and live on a keto lifestyle but with more carbs. This diet allocates an additional 20-30 grams of carbs immediately before and after workouts. This allows for you to be able to sustain higher intensity exercise as well as enhanced recovery. Thus, the total amount of carbs consumed per day is between 70 and 80 grams. The best food options for this diet include dairy, fruit, or grain-based foods, as well as sports nutrition products. Since any additional carbs are quickly burned off, there is no room for storage in the body as fat.

The High-Protein Keto Diet (HPKD)

This diet is perfect if you have high-protein needs. This diet plan entails eating about 120 grams for protein daily as well as 130 grams of fat daily. Even then, carbs are still restricted to less than 10% of your daily calorie consumption. Most people find this modified keto easy to follow since it allows you to eat more protein and less fat compared to the standard ketogenic diet. However, you need to take caution with this approach because it might not result in ketosis. The reason for this that the proteins are converted to glucose for fuel, just like carbs. Following this diet will, however, result in weight loss.

The Cyclical Ketogenic Diet (CKT)

The cyclical ketogenic diet is recommended for professional athletes and bodybuilders. It involves following the standard ketogenic diet for at least 5 or 6 days a week before following up with higher carbohydrate consumption for the next 1 to 2 days. The days when you get to consume a higher amount of carbs are referred to as refeeding days because they are meant for replenishing the depleted glucose reserves. When you follow this ketogenic diet approach, you will switch from ketosis during the refeeding days so as to tap into the benefits of temporary carb consumption. Those who want to improve their exercise performance and attain muscle growth mostly practice this type of ketogenic diet.

Although the cyclical ketogenic diet is usually compared to carb cycling, it's not the same thing. Carb cycling is different in that it involves cutting carbs on specific days of the week while increasing your intake on other days. Each week is often divided in 4 to 6 days of lower carbs and another 1 to 3 days of a higher intake. Although this method is the same, the difference is that carb cycling does not reduce the overall intake of carbohydrates drastically for the body to attain ketosis. To get the best results with the cyclical ketogenic diet, you need to eat wholesome carbohydrate-rich foods on the days when you're off. This includes dairy products, starchy veggies, fruits, whole grains, and dairy products.

Ketogenic Diets and Weight Loss

The ketogenic diet is an effective way of losing weight as well as lowering risk factors for various diseases. According to research, the ketogenic diet is quite superior and is often recommended compared to the low-fat diet. This diet is more filling so that you are able to lose weight even without having to keep track of the calories you consume. According to one study, people who followed the ketogenic diet lost 2.2 times more weight compared to those who followed a calorie-restricted low-fat diet. Moreover, the HDL and triglyceride levels of those who followed the keto diet also improved. In another study, people who followed the ketogenic diet lost 3 times more weight compared to those on a diet that was recommended by Diabetes. Some of the reasons that make the ketogenic diet superior include the increase in protein intake that has several benefits. The increase in ketones, improved insulin sensitivity, and low blood sugar levels also play an important role.

Getting Started on the Ketogenic Diet

There are a number of things you need to know before you get started with the ketogenic diet. First, following the diet requires a drastic restriction of carbohydrates from your diet as you carefully monitor your food choices to ensure that you're meeting your nutritional needs. You will do well to work closely with a registered dietician as they will help you to make sure that you implement this plan well while minimizing the risk for potential complications or side effects. It's also important to keep in mind the goal of making this dietary change is promoting a healthy lifestyle; therefore, make sure you select a meal plan that you can stick to in the long term. If you will be unable to follow the plan in the long term, then this diet is probably not meant for you.

Chapter 10:

Intermittent Fasting and Ketogenic Diet

Intermittent fasting and the ketogenic have both grown in popularity in health enthusiasts, as well as people who want to lose weight over the years. There are just as many people who are attracted to intermittent fasting as there are in ketogenic diets, obviously because of the promising health benefits the two offer. Over time, those who want to tap into both intermittent fasting and keto have come up with a combination of the two. Thus, it's possible to tap into the benefits of both because they go hand in hand. Intermittent fasting and the ketogenic diet complement each other very well.

The Difference Between Intermittent Fasting and the Ketogenic Diet

Before getting to know how intermittent fasting and ketogenic diet work together, it's important first to understand the key differences between the two. While intermittent fasting is more about when you should eat your food, the ketogenic diet limits the consumption of carbs while emphasizing the consumption of high-fat foods and moderate proteins. When you take part in intermittent fasting, you will prolong the periods you will go without food to between 16 and 24 hours, depending on the intermittent fasting method you will select. However, you can take plenty of water as well as plain coffee and tea during this time.

During intermittent fasting, you will have a feeding window and a fasting window. You can begin by fasting for fewer hours and expanding your fasting window gradually. Focusing on the keto-friendly foods during your feeding window will help in prolonging helpful metabolic pathways that are invoked during fasting. Ultimately, both methods of dieting work towards the goal of getting the body to use fat stores for their energy and getting the body in the state of ketosis. Both intermittent fasting and keto diet deplete body glucose so that your body gets into ketosis faster than it would when you depend on fasting alone.

Why Should You Combine Intermittent Fasting and Keto?

Doing intermittent fasting and keto can help with weight loss in the short term. However, since both diets are restrictive, they are certainly not for everyone. So does combining them post better results than following eat plan separately?

Some experts hold the view that it is better to combine intermittent fasting and keto. While the keto diet will increase the levels of ketones in your body, intermittent fasting also sees an increase in ketones. The brain will not overly rely on glucose for energy when it is in a state of nutritional ketosis. Thus, the transition into ketosis will become seamless when you're on a low-carb ketogenic diet. Adding intermittent fasting will definitely take things a notch higher. This may include overcoming the weight loss plateau because you may eat fewer calories when doing intermittent fasting. Intermittent fasting keto may also be a form of a natural progression from the keto diet, especially if you feel satiated eating so much fat and are not bothered reducing the eating window.

Who Can Follow Intermittent Fasting Keto?

Intermittent fasting keto is ideal for anyone who has been following the keto diet for more than two weeks and have the approval of your health care professional. However, intermittent fasting keto will most certainly be a no go zone for you if you have a history of an eating disorder, have chronic kidney diseases, or are undergoing active treatment for cancer. Pregnant and nursing mothers may also not practice intermittent fasting. In fact, you may not practice either of these diets at all. Additionally, if you are following a keto diet and are happy with the results or you feel good about the way you're progressing, then you might not need intermittent fasting.

Benefits of Fasting on the Ketogenic Diet

There's a significant overlap between intermittent fasting and the ketogenic diet. Here are some of the health benefits of intermittent fasting and why you should consider fasting when on a low-carb diet.

Intermittent Fasting Enables Your Body to Enter Ketosis Faster

Intermittent fasting works this way; when your body is in the fasted state, it will begin to burn the fat stores in order to access energy. This is similar to the process that takes place before your body enters into ketosis. When the glucose in your body is depleted, your body begins to burn the fat stores or ketone to obtain energy. However, when given a choice, your body will tap energy from glucose as its primary source at any given time. This means that by restricting your intake of carbohydrates significantly, your body will switch to burning ketones through a metabolic process referred to as ketosis. Sometimes, following a low-carb and high-fat diet is not usually enough; therefore, intermittent fasting can help to hasten the process of entering into ketosis. Fasting also helps to deplete your glycogen stores faster so that you enter the ketogenic state.

Intermittent Fasting on Keto Will Help You to Lose Weight Faster

One of the reasons why most people opt to complement intermittent fasting with the ketogenic diet is because it helps to lose weight much faster. Intermittent fasting alone has gained prominence for the mere reason that it's an excellent way to lose fat and weight. Combining intermittent fasting and the ketogenic diet will help you to break free from the weight loss plateaus in a number of ways. Having a shorter eating window will help in eliminating unnecessary snacking, particularly late into the night. Moreover, your body is able to comfortably accommodate a certain amount of calories at any given time; therefore, by limiting your feeding window, you also limit your daily intake of calories. Finally, when you are on a high-fat keto diet, the process of ketosis will reduce your appetite while increasing your satiety levels. This makes it much easier to practice intermittent fasting compared to when you're on a diet full of carbs that are likely to increase your need for snacking and cravings.

Intermittent Fasting on Keto Will Help You to Avoid Keto Flu

If you have never been on the ketogenic diet before, intermittent fasting will come in handy to help you in avoiding or managing some of the uncomfortable side effects of keto that include the keto flu. These side effects often occur when your body is transitioning to the fat-burning state. How then does intermittent fasting help in negating the keto flu? Well, since the keto flu will most certainly occur when you get into ketosis and tends to go away as soon as your metabolic switch is activated, you're less likely to experience the negative effects of ketosis if you can get into ketosis faster. The fact that a short fast is able to help you to get into ketosis, it can also help to reduce the likelihood of suffering from the keto flu.

Intermittent Fasting on Keto Helps the Body to Heal Itself

Intermittent fasting activates a process that is referred to as autophagy, which is a phenomenon that helps in healing the body. This process essentially promotes a cleansing process that eliminates and recycles all the dead and broken proteins, among other unwanted cells. The process of autophagy may be triggered during the windows of starvation when carbohydrates are restricted and could help the body to heal itself of chronic diseases like cancer.

Intermittent Fasting on Keto Helps in Stabilizing Your Blood Sugar

One of the benefits of intermittent fasting is that it helps in striking a balance in your insulin levels. When you get rid of sugar and carbs from your diet, you are effectively eliminating the possibility of blood sugar spikes that will often come with eating these foods. If you're looking to control your blood sugar levels, fasting on keto will go a long way in helping find a balance. Fasting also helps to improve insulin sensitivity as well as prevent insulin resistance that can reduce your chances of developing type 2 diabetes or heart disease.

Tips to Help You Manage Intermittent Fasting Keto

The truth is that it can be quite tricky at the beginning when you start experimenting on combining intermittent fasting and keto. Here are some tips to help you if you want to start on intermittent fasting keto and succeed:

Measure Your Ketone Levels

Although fasting will help you to stay in ketosis, you still need to make sure that you are not eating too many carbs or doing anything that might get you out of ketosis. When you track your ketone levels, you will be able to ensure that you are actually in ketosis.

Make Sure You're Eating Enough

When you go for extended durations without food, you may naturally eat fewer calories throughout the day. This could easily result in deficiencies in vitamins or even the development of metabolic issues; therefore, make sure your calorie intake is at a level that is considered healthy. Severe restriction of calories could lead to the loss of muscle mass, along with depleted levels of energy and other side effects that are unhealthy. Even then, you shouldn't take advantage of short fasts to eat sugary or carbohydrate-laden foods or go through phases of overeating. Rather your focus should be on nutrient-dense foods. You will do well to consider following a keto meal plan so that you eat plenty of healthy foods such as coconut oil, avocado, and MCT oil, plenty of leafy green vegetables and high-quality proteins from both plant and animal-based sources.

Begin with a Moderate Approach

If you are new to intermittent fasting, you will do well to consider beginning with by skipping a meal and slowly extending your fasting window. During this time, you will be observing how your body responds and if there are any negative side effects before you can finally transition to a full fast.

How to Start on Intermittent Fasting Keto

It's advisable that you don't begin intermittent fasting and keto at the same time. The reason for this is that you will shock your system because it will be switching from glucose as the primary source of fuel to ketone. Moreover, implementing intermittent fasting in itself is a significant change. For this reason, it is common for most people to begin with keto and only consider combining it with intermittent fasting after a couple of weeks or even months.

The most important thing you need to consider is choosing the right timing. A 12- to 16-hour fast is recommended in most cases because, for most people, it's almost natural not to eat for 12 hours because most hours are covered at night when you're sleeping. Moreover, this will not require any meal skipping. To start off, you need to consider delaying your breakfast by an hour and extend gradually. This will help in getting your body accustomed to going for longer durations without eating.

Once you've settled into your new pattern of eating, you can reintroduce breakfast earlier in the day and extend your fasting time because eating breakfast will not only lead to better cognition but also helps to improve insulin sensitivity and metabolism. How long it will while you follow intermittent fasting keto should not be more than six months after which you transition back to a standard low-carb diet.

In general, intermittent fasting is a practice that involves going without food for a designated period. Since intermittent fasting depletes your glycogen stores, it's great for complementing a keto diet. However, you must begin with a moderate approach because both keto and intermittent fasting can be too harsh on your body. Intermittent fasts offer benefits that are similar to keto, such as weight and fat loss, balanced sugar levels, and accelerating the process of ketosis. You need to make sure you give your body adequate time to adjust while eating the foods that are outlined in the keto plan. Intermittent fasting and keto diet both have risks associated with them; therefore, you need to make sure that you're doing it right to minimize the risks key among them being nutritional deficiencies.

Chapter 11:

Benefits of the Ketogenic Diet and Getting into the State of Ketosis

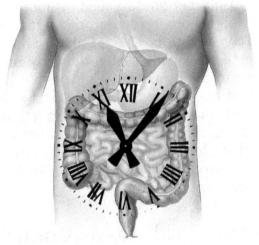

What makes the ketogenic diet a good consideration for you? Low-carb diets have attracted a fair share of controversy over the years. However, numerous scientific studies have been done to prove the worth of these diets and found them to be both beneficial and healthy.

Benefits of the Ketogenic Diet

Here are some of the benefits of following the ketogenic diet:

Low-Carb Diets Will Reduce Your Appetite

One of the worst side effects of dieting is hunger. In fact, this is one of the reasons why most people tend to give up on diets because they end up being miserable. On the contrary, low-carb eating will result in an automatic reduction in your appetite. Studies have shown that when people reduce their intake of carbs and instead eat more protein and fat, they end up eating fewer calories altogether.

Low-Carb Diets Will Enhance More Weight Loss Initially

Reducing your intake carbs is one of the easiest yet most effective ways of losing weight. Studies have demonstrated that people who followed a low-carb and high-fat diet tend to shed off more weight a lot faster than those who follow other low-fat diets that mostly focus on restricting calorie consumption. This is linked to the fact that low-carb diets act to eliminate excess water from the body and lower your level of insulin resulting in rapid loss of weight within the first or second week. In studies that have compared low-fat and low-carb diets, those who restrict carbs will, in some instances, lose 2-3 times as much weight even without having to feel hungry. A study carried out in adults who were obese found that a low-carb diet is effective up to about six months compared to the conventional weight loss diet, after which the difference is inconsequential.

Low-Carb Diets Lead to a Drastic Decline in Triglycerides

Triglycerides refer to the fat molecules that are found in the bloodstream. When these triglycerides are high in the blood, they are a strong risk factor for heart disease. One of the factors that could lead to an increase in the levels of triglyceride in the blood in people who lead a sedentary lifestyle is the consumption of carbohydrates. When people reduce the intake of carbs, they tend to experience a dramatic reduction in the level of triglycerides in their blood. Consequently, low-fat diets also have the potential of increasing triglyceride levels.

Ketogenic Diets Promote the Loss of Abdominal Fat

All the fat in your body is not the same. The place where fat is stored will not only determine your risk of disease but health as well. There are two main types of fat—namely, visceral fat that accumulates within the abdominal cavity and subcutaneous fat that is found under the skin. Visceral fat often lodges around organs, with the excess being associated with insulin resistance and inflammation. In addition, it may also result in metabolic dysfunction. Low-carb diets have been found to be quite effective in reducing the amount of harmful visceral fat, as a great proportion of fat and weight loss for those on low-carb diets seems to come from the abdominal cavity. Eventually, this also results in a reduced risk of type 2 diabetes and heart disease.

Keto Supports Reduced Blood Sugar and Insulin Levels

Low-carb diets are usually helpful for people who have insulin resistance and diabetes that affect millions of people across the world. Studies have shown that cutting carbs will lower both the insulin and blood sugar levels significantly. Some of the people who have diabetes and have started on a low-carb diet may need to reduce their dosage of insulin by up to 50% almost immediately. In a study conducted in people with type 2 diabetes, 95% had reduced or eliminated medications lowering glucose within six months. Even then, make a point of talking to your doctor if you take blood sure mediation before you can begin on the keto diet.

Keto Diet Will Increase Your Levels of Good HDL Cholesterol

The good cholesterol is referred to as High-Density Lipoprotein (HDL). When your levels of HDL are higher compared to the levels of the bad cholesterol LDL, you have a lower risk of suffering from heart disease. Eating a low-carb diet with a lot of fat will help to increase your good HDL levels. It's not surprising that the HDL levels will dramatically increase when you follow a healthy low-carb diet and only increase when moderately or even decline when you are on low-carb diets.

A Ketogenic Diet Is Effective Against Metabolic Syndrome

Metabolic syndrome refers to the condition that is associated with your risk of heart disease and diabetes. It's a collection of various symptoms, among them low levels of good HDL cholesterol, high triglycerides, elevated fasting blood sugar levels, abdominal obesity, and elevated blood pressure. A low-carb diet will help in treating all these symptoms resulting in the elimination of the metabolic syndrome altogether.

A Ketogenic Diet May Lower Blood Pressure

Hypertension or elevated blood pressure is another significant risk factor for various diseases that include stroke, kidney failure, and heart disease. Low-carb diets are effective in lowering blood pressure that should effectively reduce the risk of these diseases, thus increasing your lifespan.

A Ketogenic Diet Will Improve the Levels of Your Bad LDL Cholesterol, Thus Boosting Your Heart Health

People who have a high level of bad cholesterol have a higher risk of heart attacks. Generally, the size of the particles is significant because the smaller particles translate to a higher risk, while bigger particles translate to a lower risk. Lower carb diets will increase the size of the bad LDL cholesterol particles, thus reducing the overall number of LDL particles within your bloodstream. This will boost your heart health.

It's Therapeutic for Several Brain Disorders

Your brains require glucose, and its only certain parts of that are able to burn the kind of sugar. This is why the liver has to produce glucose from protein if you don't consume any carbs. Interestingly another part of your brain is capable of burning ketones that form when you're starved, and your carb intake is low. This is how the ketogenic diet works, a mechanism that has been used for decades in the treatment of epilepsy in children who don't show improvement with drug treatment. In most cases, this diet is able to cure children of epilepsy as one study found out that children who were put on the ketogenic diet had a 50% reduction in the frequency of seizures, with 16% becoming seizure-free.

A Ketogenic Diet Can Help to Reduce the Risk of Cancer

Studies have shown that the ketogenic diet is a great way of preventing or even treating certain kinds of cancers. In one study, findings show that the ketogenic diet may be suitable as a complementary form of treatment to chemotherapy as well as radiation in people who have cancer. This is linked to the fact that going on a ketogenic diet will result in oxidative stress in the cancer cells than in the ordinary cells. Other theories suggest that since the ketogenic diet will reduce your blood sugar levels, it can help in reducing insulin complications that are associated with certain cancers.

A Ketogenic Diet Helps to Reduce Acne

There are various causes of acne, and one may be related to blood sugar or diet. Eating a diet that is high in refined and highly processed carbohydrates may alter gut bacteria and result in more dramatic fluctuations in your blood sugar. These can have an impact on your skin health. Thus, when you decrease your intake of carbs, you could as well end up with a reduction in acne.

Ketogenic Diet Improves Health in Women Who Suffer from Polycystic Ovarian Syndrome (PCOS)

The polycystic ovarian syndrome (PCOS) refers to an endocrine disorder that causes the ovaries to enlarge with cysts. Women who suffer from this disorder are likely to experience negative effects from consuming a high-carbohydrate diet. Although there are few clinical studies on the ketogenic diet and PCOS, one study involving 5 women over 24 weeks found that the ketogenic diet aided hormone balance, increased weight loss, improved the amount of fasting insulin, and improved the ratio of the follicle-stimulating hormone and the luteinizing hormone.

How to Get in Ketosis Fast

Achieving ketosis not always easy. Although most people who desire to attain ketosis will adhere to the ketogenic diet, there are different other ways through which you can get into ketosis fast. Here are some tips to help you get into ketosis:

Elevating Your Physical Activity Level

If you use more energy during the day, you will need to eat more food in order to be energetic. Exercise will help you to deplete your glycogen stores in their bodies. In most instances, the glycogen stores become replenished whenever you eat carbohydrates. This means that when you're on a low-carb diet, these stores will not be replenished. It may take time before the body learns how to use fat stores instead of glycogen; hence, you may experience fatigue during the period when the body will be going through an adjustment.

Reducing Your Carbs Intake Significantly

Ketosis will take place when the absence of carbohydrates forces the body to use fat as the primary source of energy in the place of glucose. Whether you're looking to attain ketosis for weight loss or you simply want to reduce the risk of heart disease or even control and maintain blood sugar levels, you should aim at reducing your consumption of carbohydrates to a maximum of 20 grams daily. Even then, this number is not cast in stone; thus, you may need to do a little more carbs yet still manage to enter ketosis, while others may need less.

Practicing Short Fasts

Fasting or going for a couple of hours without consuming any calories may actually lead to ketosis. In controlled cases, a doctor could recommend longer fasting durations of between 24 and 48 hours. It is important to first talk to your doctor before making the decision to fast for longer durations. Fat fasting is a kind of fasting that involves reducing your calorie intake significantly and only eating a diet that consists of fat for not more than 2 or 3 days. According to research, this will have a significant effect on your weight loss efforts. The challenge is that it's difficult to sustain fat fasting making it less favorable for most people.

Testing Ketone Levels

One of the ways of getting to attain ketosis is by monitoring the levels of ketones in your body. You can do this by performing a number of tests that include breath, urine, and blood test. Using one or more of these tests will help you to keep track of your progress, thus allowing you to make educated adjustments in your diet.

Increasing Your Intake of Healthy Fat

As your intake of carbs decreases, you need to increase your intake of fats. Some of the fats you can consider increasing include olive oil, coconut oil, flaxseed, avocadoes, and avocado oil, among others. Even then, if your overall goal is to lose weight, then you must also keep the overall consumption in mind.

Maintain High Protein Consumption

It is important that you eat sufficient amounts of protein all through the day when you want to achieve ketosis. Protein provides two essential health benefits when you want to lose weight. That is, it helps in maintaining your muscle mass or provide amino acids to the liver to ensure proper functioning. You may experience loss of muscle mass if your intake of protein is not sufficient.

Consuming More Coconut Oil

Increasing your intake of coconut oil could help you to attain the state of ketosis. A study conducted with the focus on Alzheimer's diseases showed that adding coconut oil in your diet can help to increase the ketone levels. Coconut oil is rich in fats known as medium-chain triglycerides (MCTs). The body is able to absorb MCTs easily and quickly. It then sends these fats to your liver, where they are turned into energy or ketones.

Ketosis is a natural state that the body needs to be in occasionally. When ketosis occurs, the body will but all the fat reserves to be used as energy. Maintaining ketosis over a short period comes with minimal risk even though people who have type 1 diabetes need to avoid ketosis, as it will only increase the risk of complications.

Chapter 12:

Foods You Can Eat on Keto Diet

By now, you know that the ketogenic diet is high-fat and very low-carbohydrate with moderate protein. Carbohydrates are a preferred source of energy for the body, yet when you're on a strict keto diet, less than 5 % of the food you eat will account for carbohydrates. Although it may seem straight forward on what you need to eat while following this diet, the choice of foods can be confusing. Here's a guide to the foods you eat, as well as the foods you need to avoid when you're on the keto diet.

Foods to Eat on the Ketogenic Diet

Low-Carb Vegetables

There are various options of non-starchy vegetables that are low in carbs and calories that you can include in your keto diet. These vegetables are also great sources of various nutrients that include minerals and vitamin c. In addition, they also have antioxidants that help in protecting you against several cell-damaging free radicals. In the best-case scenario, you need to opt for non-starchy vegetables that contain less than 8g of net carbs for each cup. This means the total carbs minus fiber. Some of the low-carb vegetable choices that fit the bill include spinach, zucchini, bell peppers, green beans, cauliflower, and broccoli.

Seafood and Fish

Fish is a rich source of selenium, potassium, and B vitamins. This is in addition to being carb-free and protein-rich. Sardines, mackerel, salmon, albacore tuna as well as other fatty fish have high levels of omega 3 fats. These have been found to lower blood sugar levels while increasing insulin sensitivity. Frequent consumption of fish has been associated with improved mental health and a decrease in the risk of chronic diseases. You should aim to eat at least 3-ounce servings of fatty fish twice a week.

Cheese

Cheese is high in fats, yet it has no carbs. This makes it an excellent choice for the ketogenic diet. Cheese is also rich in calcium and protein with a single slice of cheese, delivering 30 percent of your daily recommended amount of saturated fats. If you have concerns about heart disease, you'll do well taking your cheese in small portions.

Avocados

Avocado is an excellent source of heart-friendly fats that are monosaturated. This fruit also contains potassium, a mineral that most Americans lack. Eating half of a medium avocado will give you about 9 grams of total carbohydrates and 7 grams of fiber. Plant fats like avocado do help to improve your triglyceride and cholesterol levels.

Plain Greek Yogurt and Cottage Cheese

Cottage cheese and yogurt are calcium and protein-rich. Taking 5 ounces of plain Greek yogurt will provide you about 12 grams of proteins and 5 grams of carbohydrates. An equivalent amount of cottage cheese contains 18 grams of proteins and 5 grams of carbohydrates. Studies have found that both protein and calcium have the ability to promote fullness and reduce appetite. Hence, taking cottage cheese and higher-fat yogurts while on the keto diet will help you to stay full for longer.

Poultry and Meat

Meat is a great source of lean proteins and a staple on the ketogenic diet. Poultry and fresh means do not contain any carbohydrates and are excellent sources of B vitamins and various minerals that include zinc, selenium, and potassium. Although you can take processed meats like sausage and bacon while on the keto diet, they are not the best for your heart and are likely to increase the risk of certain types of cancer when consumed in large quantities—thus, always choose beef, chicken, and fish while limiting processed meats.

Nuts, Seeds, and Healthy Oils

Seeds and nuts are packed with healthy monosaturated and polyunsaturated fats, protein, and fiber. They are also low in net carbs. Coconut oil and olive oil are the two oils that are recommended when you're on the keto diet. Coconut oil is high in saturated fat nut has medium-chain triglycerides (MCTs) that promote ketone production. MCTs have the ability to increase metabolic rate and promoting weight loss as well as belly fat too. On the other hand, olive oil has a high amount of oleic acid, which is associated with a reduced risk of heart disease. It's important that you measure the portion sizes of any of these healthy fats when consuming them.

Eggs

Eggs have a high proportion of minerals, antioxidants, and B vitamins. Two eggs have no carbohydrates but have 12 grams of protein. Eggs have shown to trigger hormones that are known to increase fullness while keeping blood sugar levels stable. They also contain antioxidants like zeaxanthin and lutein that help in protecting eye health.

Unsweetened Tea and Coffee

Plain tea and coffee contain no carbohydrates, protein, or fat—making them a good pick when doing your keto diet. According to studies, coffee has been found to lower the risk of cardiovascular diseases as well as type 2 diabetes. On the other hand, tea contains antioxidants and less caffeine compared to coffee. Thus, drinking tea could actually reduce the risk of suffering from a stroke or heart attack while helping you to lose weight and boost your immune system.

Berries

Berries are rich in antioxidants that are able to reduce inflammation and protect you against disease. They are also low in carbs and high in fiber.

Cocoa Powder and Dark Chocolate

If you have to take this, make sure you check the label because the number of carbs will depend on the type, as well as how much you will consume. Cocoa is referred to as a superfruit since it's rich in antioxidants. Dark chocolate contains flavonols, which have the ability to reduce the risk of heart disease by lowering blood pressure and keeping arteries.

Butter and Cream

These are good fats to include in your ketogenic diet because they both contain trace amounts of carbs for each serving. Butter and cream were previously believed to contribute to heart disease because of their levels of saturates fat. Even then, a number of studies have shown that there is no link between saturated fat and heart disease. Other studies suggest moderate consumption of high-fat dairy could possibly reduce the risk of heart attack or stroke.

Shirataki Noodles

These are a great addition to the ketogenic diet. They have less than one gram of carbs along with 5 calories per serving because they have water. In fact, these noodles are made from viscous fiber referred to as glucomannan, which can absorb at least 50 times the weight. The viscous fiber forms a gel that slows down food movement through the digestive tract. This can help in decreasing hunger and blood sugar spikes, thus making it quite beneficial for the weight loss process and management of diabetes.

Foods to Avoid on a Keto Diet

Foods That Contain Added Sugar

You must avoid any foods that contain sweeteners, as these are likely to raise your blood sugar effectively, causing your insulin levels to spike. When this happens, your appetite will also be stimulated, thus getting you out of ketosis.

Cereals

You must avoid all grains, including whole grains like rye, wheat, oats, corn, millet, barley, sorghum, bulgur, amaranth, sprouted grains, and buckwheat. This also includes any products that are made from grains like bread, pasta, pizza, crackers, and cookies, as well as sugar and sweets, taking into account ice creams, agave syrup, sugary soft drinks, and sweet puddings.

Vegetables That Grow Beneath the Ground

Most of the vegetables that grow beneath the ground are usually high at the start because they contain mostly carbs. It is better if you aim at consuming 12-15 net carbs from vegetables per day. Some of the vegetables you need to avoid include sweet potatoes, potatoes, baked potatoes, peas, yams, corn, parsnips, cassava, and artichoke.

Processed Foods

You should avoid all processed foods that contain carrageenan, MSG, sulfites, wheat gluten, and BPAs.

Artificial Sweeteners

Stay away from sweeteners that contain aspartame, sucralose, acesulfame, and saccharin because these are likely to cause cravings and have been linked to other health issues like migraines.

Legumes

Most leguminous plants like peas and beans are high in protein as well as other vital nutrients. But they are also high in carbs. They include lima beans, chickpeas, baked beans, black beans, pinto beans, black eye peas, lentils, green peas, kidney beans, navy beans, cannellini beans, and great northern beans.

Milk

Milk is not recommended on a keto diet for a number of reasons. It is difficult to digest, lacks the good bacteria, and may even contain hormones. Moreover, milk is also high in carbs; therefore, a small amount of milk could actually give you extra carbs.

Tropical Fruits

These include papaya, mangoes, banana, and pineapple, among others. These tend to be very sugary and hence are high in carbs and will most likely get your body out of ketosis. You should also avoid fruit juices and even smoothies.

Sweetened Yogurts

If you must take yogurt, make sure you stick to the plain one without any added sugars. Greek yogurt is preferred because it is higher in proteins but lower in carbohydrates compared to the regular yogurt.

Gluten-Free Baked Goods

Gluten-free foods don't necessarily translate to carb-free. In fact, most of the gluten-free bread and even muffins usually have a higher proportion of carbohydrates, just like the traditional baked goods. Even worse, they lack fiber.

Chips and Crackers

You also must avoid chips and crackers as well as other processed grain-based snack foods.
The difference between the foods that you can take while on the keto diet and those that you can't take is mainly in the net carb content. This refers to the number of carbs that your body can fully absorb from grams of dietary fiber that you consume in a particular food. Because fiber is not absorbed or even used in the same manner as the net carbs, it's important to subtract the total amount of fiber from the total carbs in order to determine the number of carbs there are in the food that could limit the production of ketones. This means that keto-friendly food is low in the number of net carbs. Even then, there are some exceptions. For instance, not all vegetables are keto-friendly. More specifically, you cannot compare leafy vegetables to sweet potatoes. This is because one will definitely have a high amount of net carbs. Thus, the difference between foods that are keto-friendly and those that

are not going down to the different amounts of net carbs that each contains.

Chapter 13:

Risks and Complications of the Keto Lifestyle

The benefits of following the ketogenic diet are quite impressive. However, there are a few risks involved. It's normal for people who start on this diet to experience various symptoms that can pass for flu, such as headaches and fatigue. So common is this side effect that it's referred to as keto flu. Yet, this diet has no signs of slowing, as it's still popular even among celebrities. It could be because this diet does not only promise quick results while letting you enjoy foods such as cheese and burgers. However, it's important to realize that this diet has its own risks that include the following:

Keto Diet Could Affect Your Athletic Performance

While the number of athletes who have jumped on the keto bandwagon is undisputable, researchers have a concern that following this diet can sabotage the fitness and strength levels of athletes. According to researchers, participants who followed the keto diet for four days posted a poor performance on running tasks and high-intensity cycling in comparison to those who were on a high-carb diet. This is probably because, during ketosis, the body is mostly in an acidic state that is capable of limiting its ability to perform at peak levels. While keto can help athletes to lose weight that is crucial for improving speed and endurance, however, these benefits may be canceled out by a decline in the performance.

A Ketogenic Diet May Lead to Deficiencies in Minerals and Vitamins

When you limit carbs to at least 50 grams or less per day, it means you're doing away with all unhealthy foods like refined sugar and bread. This also means that you're putting on your consumption of vegetables and fruits that are a source of carbohydrates. This raises a concern, particularly if you will be doing the keto diet for a long duration because vegetables and fruits are often very high in antioxidants as well as minerals and vitamins. This means that by eliminating them, you will end up with deficiencies in those minerals over time. In addition, it may also be difficult to get sufficient fiber as you're cutting back on the carbs because grains are a good source of fiber. As a result, you may end up with serious digestion problems from weight gain, bloating, and high blood pressure and cholesterol levels.

You're Likely to Regain the Weight When You Relax the Rules

Let's face it. The keto diet is extremely strict, with many variations of the diet recommending that you incorporate a number of stages. The first stage is often the most intense as it involves an extremely low-carb diet, although it gives room for very few cheat days. Furthermore, it also requires that you keep track of your fat and carbohydrate performance to make sure your body enters into ketosis. Later, you can transition to the relaxed form of keto that lets you have more carbs with less monitoring. This stage is referred to as maintenance mode or keto cycling. The only problem with this approach is that you will certainly regain the weight. Although keto can be considered a great jumpstart to weight loss, the truth that it's difficult to adhere to in the long term— this can be frustrating, even though the weight you will gain back is important. Although you may have mostly lost some muscle mass initially, you will probably regain more fat and less lean muscle that not only looks and feels different on the body but will also burn calories at a slower pace. This may have an impact on your metabolism, making it difficult to lose weight in the future.

Taking Too Much Fat Could Increase the Risk of Chronic Diseases

There is a concern about the long term effect of the keto lifestyle can affect the arteries and heart. According to a study by the American College of Cardiology, people who follow low-carb diets have a high chance of developing atrial fibrillation (AF) in comparison to those who consume carbohydrates moderately. This is the most common form of heart rhythm disorder that also raises the risk of heart failure and stroke. Another research also found that people following the low-carb and high-fat diet have a high risk of dying from cancer as well as all other causes. Even then, it's important to keep in mind that most of this research is observational such that it has only found associations with certain health outcomes and not the cause and effect relationships. More long-term research needs to be done to know just what the impact of the ketogenic diet is to the body over an extended period.

You May Suffer Fatigue and Other Symptoms Due to Keto Flu

Keto flu is one of the most common side effects of starting on the keto diet. This is generally a combination of unpleasant symptoms that are fatigue-inducing symptoms that you may feel as the body adjusts to the reduced levels of carbohydrates. When you have keto flu, the glucose in your body begins running, forcing the body to adapt by producing and using ketones as a source of energy. Some of the common symptoms of keto flu include dizziness, fatigue, sleep problems, cramps, and palpitations. Even then, these tend to reduce and even clear as the body adjusts accordingly, usually within two weeks.

Keto May Cause Damage to Blood Vessels

Enjoying a cheat day in the short term while following the ketogenic diet can have long term consequences. A recent study found that indulging in high sugar treats such as a bottle of soda when following a high-fat, low-carb eating place can damage your blood vessels. People who follow the keto diet for weight loss or even management of type 2 diabetes and are posting positive results could end up undoing the gains by blasting them with glucose.

You May Experience Constipation

When you have a diet that eliminates fruits and most grains while emphasizing on fats, you may end up with gastrointestinal related side effects like constipation. This is inevitable, especially where the keto diet is not done properly.

You May Get Diarrhea

You could find yourself running to the bathroom more often when following the ketogenic diet. This may be attributed to a number of reasons like the gallbladder being overwhelmed or lack of fiber in your diet that is common when you cut on carbs. Diarrhea may also be a result of being intolerant to dairy or sometimes the use of artificial sweeteners.

You May Experience Unhealthy Low Blood Sugar

If you have diabetes, you must discuss any dietary changes with your healthcare provider before you jump into intermittent fasting. This is because carbs are usually broken down into glucose in the blood; hence, cutting your intake of carbohydrates could result in low levels of blood sugar. This kind of change requires proper adjustments to your insulin as well as medication so as to prevent unwanted side effects like low blood sugar, among others.

Well, while so many people can attest to the benefits of the ketogenic diet, it's important to take into account the effects and health risks that this diet possesses because if the risks outweigh the potential benefits, then you might as well consider abandoning this diet completely.

Chapter 14:

Common Intermittent Fasting Myths and Mistakes

Intermittent fasting has attracted a huge following for a good reason. However, there are equally numerous myths and misconceptions surrounding this pattern of eating that only provide wrong information that can be misleading, especially for those people who want to try intermittent fasting for the first time.

Intermittent Fasting Myths

Here are some of the common intermittent fasting myths:

Intermittent Fasting Is Only Applicable to a Select Population

Intermittent fasting is one of the diets that can be practiced by the majority of people because it is modeled around your lifestyle. It can be tiring when you have to eat around the clock. Thus, following the intermittent fasting pattern of eating comes as a big relief because you don't have to think about what you will eat after about two to three hours. If anything, most people have schedules that favor intermittent fasting because you will not have all the time to prepare meals and sit down to eat them. Besides, it makes more sense to have three large or moderate meals than have six meals in a day.

Intermittent Fasting Promotes Loss of Muscle

There's a widely held belief that the body needs to have a constant supply of amino acids in order to be able to repair, maintain, and even build the muscle tissue. Thus, by following the intermittent fasting diet, there will be a breakdown of your muscle tissues to obtain energy. This is not true because fasting doesn't set off your body into a catabolic mode. What those who hold this belief don't pay attention to overlook is that you can have a huge bolus of proteins that digest slowly from the last meal you had that keep on releasing amino acids enough to last the entire time of fasting.

Intermittent Fasting Results in Binge Eating

Intermittent fasting has for long been associated with binge eating. However, it is not true that intermittent fasting will result in binge eating or any other eating disorder. When you're fasting, you need to be careful to ensure that you meet your daily macronutrient requirements. This may sometimes require you to eat a large meal, but it is in no way equivalent to binge eating, keeping in mind that this may come after working out. You need to pack up more nutrients to ensure that your daily calorie intake is met. It's impractical to imagine that you can survive on just a few raisins or nuts after following through an entire day of fasting.

Intermittent Fasting Is Equivalent to Starvation

Fasting and starvation are not the same. Intermittent fasting is only about changing the times when you will be eating. On the other hand, starvation is extreme because the body enters starvation mode when all the stored body fat has been used up as energy. As a result, the muscles are cannibalized along with the other vital organs for survival. This can obviously not happen just because you have skipped a meal or two. If anything, your body has an immense capacity to withstand long periods of going without food during fasting bearing in mind that the body stores energy in the form of fat while the muscles serve as functional tissues.

Frequently Eating Boosts Metabolism

Although you may eventually end up consuming fewer calories than you would normally eat, intermittent fasting is not about calorie restriction. If anything, you can plan your meals well enough to ensure that you're eating at maintenance if your goal is not weight loss. The belief that having fewer meal times slows down your metabolism is not true because you are simply postponing when you will eat. On the contrary, practicing short-time fasts can increase your resting metabolic rate.

Intermittent Fasting Decreases Your Training Performance

Most people who are into training shy away from intermittent fasting because they believe that fasting will hamper their performance. However, a number of studies have been conducted on a number of athletes who trained during the time when they were fasting in the month of Ramadhan found that fasting doesn't stop anaerobic and aerobic performance. Remember, intermittent fasting doesn't prohibit you from taking non-caloric drinks or water. So you can stay well-hydrated for most of the day, whether you're fasting or not.

When You Fast, You Will Feel Hungry Throughout the Entire Period of Fasting

You will not feel hungry throughout the fasting window, as it is largely assumed. The thought that you will feel hungry the entire time is mostly psychological. Remember, you still need to go about your daily chores and activities as usual. You must make sure that you're drinking up enough fluids because both hunger and thirst are processed by the same part of the brain. You might feel hungry in the initial hours of your fast, but you will get used to it over time.

You Can Eat Everything You Want During the Feeding Window

This is a big misconception for people who have unsuccessfully tried intermittent fasting. The fact that you have not eaten for a couple of hours doesn't mean that you can throw down pizzas and other calorie-packed meals when it is time to eat, especially if your goal is to lose weight. You must pay attention to healthy food choices because it takes time to shed off weight just like it took time to gain. Generally, eating more calories than you are supposed to will result in weight gain, thus jeopardizing your weight loss efforts.

Women Cannot Follow the Intermittent Fasting Plan

It's assumed that just because the female body is sensitive to the starvation signals than the male body, then women can't fast. When your body senses starvation, it increases the production of leptin and ghrelin, the hormones that are responsible for controlling hunger. This will result in a feeling of insatiable hunger because this is a result of these hormones. Besides, this is the body's way of protecting a potential life even in women who are not pregnant. Women may also experience negative energy because of other reasons that include excessive stress, poor nutrition, and too little recovery, inflammation, or illnesses.

You Should Not Take Anything During Intermittent Fasting

Some people assume that fasting is equivalent to abstaining from both food and water. In reality, you need to make sure you're well-hydrated and are free to take as much water and unsweetened tea and coffee. These are great because they contain no calories and cannot cause your insulin levels to spike. Keep in mind that the whole point of intermittent fasting is to make sure that you keep your insulin levels low.

You Can Lose Weight with Intermittent Fasting No Matter What You Do

Many people practice intermittent fasting because they want to lose weight. But this is not always the case unless you do it the right way. Therefore, you can expect to indulge in burgers, candy, and pizza during your feasting window and lose weight. Intermittent fasting will have to work hand in hand with a healthy diet. Therefore, don't expect to lose weight if you are not focusing on healthy food choices.

Skipping Breakfast Will Make You Lose Fat

It's widely believed that breakfast is the most important meal of the day. However, intermittent fasting allows you to skip breakfast and still be able to lead a healthy lifestyle. You'll be surprised how you can be able to have a great day despite having skipped breakfast.

You Need to Eat Smaller Meals to Lose Weight

It's not true that eating small meals will boost your metabolism or speed up the burning of calories. In fact, taking small meals every so often will not help to reduce hunger or even the number of calories you will burn.

Intermittent Fasting Mistakes to Avoid

Getting into intermittent fasting as a fast timer can be overwhelming because you don't really know how your body will handle it. You might end up making some mistakes that could hamper your intermittent fasting efforts. Here are some of the intermittent fasting mistakes you should avoid:

Overeating When the Feeding Time Comes

It's easy to find yourself eating too much after hours of successful fasting just to make up for the hours you went without food. The reason for this is usually because of being emotionally starved so that you feel hungry more than you are in reality. To avoid this, you need to ensure that you carry on with your daily routine as usual, despite not eating. This is great as it will stop you from being preoccupied with your next meal when you're fasting. In addition, aim at preparing a healthy meal that is nutrient-dense as this is more satiating.

A Fast Transition

If you have been eating after every 3-4 hours, you cannot transition to a 16-hour window suddenly as this will shock your system. As a result, you will end up with a feeling of general weakness, hunger, and discouragement to the point of giving up. Therefore, begin by fasting for fewer hours and gradually extend the fasting window until you're able to get to the 16-hour mark. This allows your body to adjust to the fasting schedule smoothly without affecting your lifestyle.

Choosing a Wrong Intermittent Fasting Method

There are different intermittent fasting methods that you can choose to follow. However, you must make sure that you choose a method that fits into your lifestyle. Refrain from the temptation of going for an intense intermittent fasting method in the beginning. Most importantly, choose a plan that compliments your lifestyle. For instance, if you work at night, you need to go for an intermittent fasting method that allows you to eat at night so that you're fasting during the hours when you're less active.

Failing to Take Sufficient Fluids

Intermittent fasting allows you to drink up as much fluid as possible so that you're well-hydrated. You can take water or plain tea and coffee. Avoid those fluids that contain calories and are likely to cause your insulin levels to spike because then your body will not be able to burn fat that promotes weight loss.

Undereating During the Feeding Window

The ambition to lose weight is likely to result in eating little food when the time to eat comes. The truth is that eating too little will not facilitate more weight loss. If anything, it just might contribute to gaining weight. When you eat too little food during your feeding window, your muscle mass will be cannibalized, thus slowing the metabolism process. The absence of metabolic muscle will interfere with your ability to process the remaining fat.

Taking the Wrong Fluids

You must make sure that you stick to non-caloric fluids. You should avoid drinks containing sweeteners as most of these can cause a spike in insulin as well as trigger the release of the hunger hormones. You also must avoid fruit juices and alcohol since they too are packed with nutrients and sugar and are akin to eating.

Inactivity

If you prefer having a pre-workout snack before going to the gym, you might be tempted not to engage in any activity during fasting leading to a sedentary lifestyle. What proponents of this idea forget is that the body has the ability to generate energy even after going for a few hours without food. Therefore, consider taking up an activity even if it means walking if you don't want to maintain your usual high-intensity plan. Most importantly, focus on eating foods that can help to build muscle.

Eating Unhealthy Foods

The fact that intermittent fasting promises weight loss doesn't mean that you can indulge in all manner of calorie-packed foods. Don't use intermittent fasting as a scapegoat to eat unhealthy food. Instead, focus on eating food that is packed with nutrients. Paying attention to the nutritional value of the food you eat will help you reach your goal without having to struggle too much.

Taking on So Many Things at the Same Time

When you resort to begin intermittent fasting, make sure you're not attempting to do many other things alongside it. This is not the time to begin following a new work out plan, taking on a new diet, or even making changes to other areas of your life. You need to focus on one thing in order to be able to track your progress and meet your goal, whatever it is. Trying to do so many things at the same time could just result in problems.

Engaging in Intense Work Out During the Fasting Window

Although you need to make sure that you are not sedentary as you follow the intermittent fasting lifestyle, you should also avoid intense work out during the fasting window. Instead, schedule your work out during the feeding window when you are able to have a pre or post-workout meal. Don't engage in working out during the fasting window.

Giving Up

Some people get on to the intermittent fasting bandwagon expecting quick results, and when this doesn't happen immediately, they quit. When you begin intermittent fasting, you must realize that it will take time before you get used to the new lifestyle. Moreover, while some people may begin to see the results immediately, not everyone will do because of the differences in physiology.

Obsessing Over the Timings

In some instances, you may find yourself obsessing over the timings of your intermittent fasting plan so that all that is on your mind is when you will eat and when you will be fasting. This can get the best of you, disrupting so many aspects of your lifestyle. Instead, you need to carry on with your life as usual because the major thing that will be happening is a simple shift in your eating pattern.

Transitioning into Intermittent Fasting

It's not everyone who starts intermittent fasting that makes it to the end with a happily ever after story. So many people start intermittent fasting only to give up along the way. Sometimes, this is a result of not making the right move when transitioning into this new way of life. Here are tips to help you make a smooth transition into intermittent fasting:

Consult Your Doctor

This is the best place to start because your doctor needs to tell you whether you can follow this pattern of eating or not. Moreover, they will also help you to identify the right intermittent fasting method for your lifestyle. Talking to your doctor also helps to clear any doubt you may be having as they will answer all the questions you have.

Begin with Short Fasts

You cannot make a switch from your normal routine of eating 6 times a day to fasting for 16 hours. You must ease yourself into intermittent fasting before you can begin fasting for extended hours. You can start off with an 8- to 12-hour fast and increase the fasting window over time to the point where you can fast for 16 hours comfortably.

Eat Normally in the Initial Stages

It's impractical to make too many changes at the same time. Now that you have decided to begin on intermittent fasting, make sure there is nothing else that you are doing out of the ordinary. While you may want to overhaul your diet, you will do well to do this over time as you get used to the intermittent fasting routine. Only then can you make other changes as desired.

Drink Plenty of Fluids

Hydration is as important to the success of your intermittent fasting as the hours you get to fast. Therefore, ensure you're taking as many fluids. This helps to give you a feeling of satiety, making it possible to cope through the hours of fasting. Besides, drinking up also helps in fighting hunger so that the hunger hormone will not send a hunger signal when you're just thirsty.

Eat Foods That Are High in Fats and Carbs at Night

Although this may appear to counter your efforts to shed off excess weight, the truth is that it's not possible to eliminate carbs completely. Having carbs at night helps in increasing your blood sugar levels. This means that it will take time before this falls, as you will be adding it on to protein and fat. By the time your blood sugar levels dip, you will have fallen asleep. Having carbs also helps to increase the production of serotonin that leaves you feeling great after meals.

Adhere to Your Fasting and Feeding Windows

When you start intermittent fasting, make sure you pay attention to your fasting and feasting window so that it doesn't keep in shifting. When you don't have a fixed time when you begin and end your fasting and feasting window, you confuse the body because all you will be doing is reprogramming your hunger cues each time you come up with different timing.

Adjust Your Fasting and Feasting Times to Fit into Your Lifestyle

Whatever you do, you need to make sure that the intermittent fasting method you will select will work for you as opposed to you working for it. Therefore, you need to adjust the timings to fit into your lifestyle in terms of when you will be eating or fasting while still being able to work out and reap the benefits of intermittent fasting.

Come Up with a Mantra That Will Serve as a Motivation

Intermittent fasting can be lonely, especially when you're doing it alone. Thus, you need to come up with creative ways to cheer yourself up so that you're able to attain your goal. One of the ways of doing this is by having a mantra that you live by. This will go a long way in improving your will power and summoning it into action. Words of affirmation and encouragement serve as a motivation to carry on even then the times seem to be toughest.

Don't Stay Idle

You need to make sure that that you have something you're doing to keep you occupied during the day, especially if you are not working. This is a perfect way of distracting yourself from thinking about fasting and feasting or even obsess about how hungry you are. This may involve anything from attending meetings to running errands, among other things.

Avoid Social Media Before Going to Bed

Today, social media platforms are a great way of sharing with our friends and family what we've been up to. As such, some of your friends may use their social media accounts to share their favorite recipes or even pictures of the delicious meals they have had, and this can tempt you to follow suit. You might end up being preoccupied with those images that you are unable to think about anything else other than obsessing over the feasting window.

Manage Your Expectations

If you're getting into the intermittent fasting way of life just to lose weight, you need to approach it with realistic expectations. Being able to manage your expectations includes having the understanding that it took months of eating pizza, chocolate, and even ice cream before you put on excessive weight. Therefore, you should not expect to see the weight melt away within a short time. Being too ambitious can make you fail; instead, keep in mind that it will take time before you can start noticing the change.

Have a Meal Plan

Although intermittent fasting doesn't have a stick meal plan to follow, and you can eat whatever healthy food you desire, you need to consider coming up with a meal plan. This will help you to stay grounded, especially with regard to your meal choices. It will also help you to ensure that you don't end up with any nutritional deficiencies that can come up because of not consuming sufficient amounts of certain foods.

Know Your Caloric Needs

You need to make sure that you have a proper understanding of just how many calories you need to maintain your current weight or lose weight. This will inform your calorie intake so that you are certain of making progress towards the weight loss goal that you're seeking to achieve. One of the ways of establishing your calorie needs is by using the free calorie calculators that are available online. All you have to do is anonymously provide your age weight and height and let it calculate and return the results with a single click.

Focus on Purpose

By the time you're getting into intermittent fasting, it's most likely that you have a purpose. This should serve as your driving force or an indicator that you can hold on to through the journey.

Resist the Temptation to Overeat

When you're new to intermittent fasting, you may have the temptation to eat too much when the feasting window comes. You need to be careful so that you don't fall for this as it can result in serious complications like weight gain, bloating, and sickness.

Track Your Progress

You need to keep a journal that helps you to keep track of the strides you're making with intermittent fasting. Journaling helps you to determine where you started and how much progress you have made. It also serves as motivation so that you stay on track and not give up.

Conclusion

Intermittent fasting and the ketogenic diet have so many similarities that make them a great combination for weight loss. Scientific studies have backed both diets by producing incredible findings that go a long way in validating these two methods of weight loss. However, you also must make sure that you're practicing intermittent fasting keto from the right environment in order to get the most out of it.

Intermittent fasting and keto diet will allow you to go for a couple of days without eating and still be able not to feel tired, lose muscle mass, or even get hungry. The keto way of life lets you shift your body into a primal state functioning, making it efficient at bioenergetics while you perform at peak. Similarly, intermittent fasting is an easy-to-implement pattern of eating that is capable of improving your life and health at the cellular level.

If you're still looking for a weight loss solution that produces results, then you need to think about combining intermittent fasting with the ketogenic diet. You only need to work a schedule that will allow you to the most out of this program. The fact that intermittent fasting can perfectly fit into your lifestyle is a reason for you to take the bold step and begin on this diet now.

What are you waiting for with all this information? The next step is to take action and implement intermittent fasting keto today. I guarantee you that when you begin this plan, your lifestyle will positively change with more motivation and you will enjoy your well-being.

Over to you now!